T3-BPX-771

DISCARDED

UNIVERSITY OF WINNIPEG, 515 Portage Ave., Winnipeg, MB. R3B 2E9 Canada

When Government Goes Private

HD
3888
F43
1988

When Government Goes Private

Successful Alternatives to Public Services

Randall Fitzgerald

A Pacific Research Institute
for Public Policy Book

UNIVERSE BOOKS   NEW YORK

Published in the United States of America in 1988
by Universe Books
381 Park Avenue South
New York, NY 10016

© 1988 Pacific Research Institute for Public Policy

All rights reserved. No part of this publication may be reproduced,
stored in a retrieval system, or transmitted, in any form or by any means,
electronic, mechanical, photocopying, recording, or otherwise, without
prior permission of the publishers.

88 89 90 91 92 / 10 9 8 7 6 5 4 3 2 1

Printed in the United States of America

Library of Congress Cataloging-in-Publication Data

Fitzgerald, Randall.
    When government goes private.

    Bibliography: p. 300
    Includes index.
    1. Privatization—United States. 2. Waste in govern-
ment spending—United States. I. Title.
HD3888.F43   1988   338.973   88-1160
ISBN 0-87663-679-2

Contents

Preface

Every revolution of ideas produces certain key players whose thoughts or actions accelerate, if not initiate, changes in the attitudes and perceptions of opinion-makers and the public. From the quiet revolution of privatization can be singled out a sequence of events and a handful of catalysts that helped create an environment conducive to change, and in the process transformed the agenda of public policy debate for this country and much of the rest of the world.

During John Lindsay's term as mayor of New York, that city's sanitation department took more than a week to clean the streets after a heavy snowstorm in 1969, a delay that produced political problems for the Lindsay administration. One of the mayor's aides, E. S. Savas, an economist, was assigned to investigate why the city department failed to perform efficiently. He began a cost comparison between the city sanitation department and private refuse collectors in the suburbs, finding that it cost the city $49 per ton to remove solid waste compared to only $19 per ton for private firms. As he examined other city services, such as street repair, he found a continuing ratio of about 2.6 to one in city costs over private costs. Later, in a 1971 article for *Harper's,* Savas described how consumers of municipal services are victimized by unresponsive, monopolistic agencies in need of private-sector competition. "The inefficiency of municipal services is not due to bad commissioners, mayors, managers, workers, unions, or labor leaders," Savas wrote; " it is a natural consequence of a monopoly system."

A management professor, Peter Drucker, had written a book in 1968, *The Age of Discontinuity,* in which he argued that "government should spend more time governing and less time providing, should either purchase services from the private sector or, simply, stop producing." He called for the design of "new nongovernmental, autonomous institutions as agents of social performance," using the term "reprivatization" to describe the central job for tomorrow's political architects. Drucker further clarified this idea in a 1973 article for *Saturday Review,* calling privatization a process to employ private enterprise rather than government, to satisfy the country's social and economic needs. Privatizing or contracting-out postal services, garbage collections, and even firefighting, would produce an infusion of choice and competition resulting in cost savings and greater efficiency. Other visionaries like Norman Macrae, an editor of *The Economist* in London, wrote about privatizing an entire city using a board of directors, with all voters acting as stockholders entitled to annual dividends.

These ideas attracted the attention of a young MIT-trained engineer and systems analyst, Robert W. Poole, Jr., who in 1971 became publisher of *Reason* magazine, a journal of libertarian philosophy, which began to devote articles to the practical applications of privatization. With a recent Harvard graduate, Mark Frazier, Poole in 1976 established the Local Government Center in Santa Barbara, California, to advise municipalities on how to cut budgets. Poole wrote a pamphlet, "How to Cut Local Taxes Without Reducing Essential Services," financed by the National Taxpayer's Union, and later expanded into the book, *Cutting Back City Hall.* Based on a *Reason* article by Poole, CBS's *60 Minutes* aired a program in 1978 on the efficiency and cost-effectiveness of a private fire department serving Scottsdale, Arizona. That segment inspired the formation of at least three new private firefighting companies in other states and brought nationwide attention for the first time to privatization's quiet revolution.

Over in Britain Poole's book influenced three young men who would rapidly move to the forefront of the privatization debate— Stuart Butler, his brother Eamonn, and Madsen Pirie. They established the Adam Smith Institute in London, dedicated to advancing privatization and free-market ideas. All three had worked for the Heritage Foundation in Washington, D.C., and Stuart Butler became its director of domestic policy studies and a principal proponent of enterprise zones to revitalize inner cities. After Margaret Thatcher's election as Britain's prime minister in 1979, privatization proposals promoted by the Adam Smith Institute became national policy, altering Britain's traditional political debate from whether spending should be cut to the question of whether certain government services and nationalized industries should be moved entirely into the private sector.

Simultaneous with developments in the political realm, a cross-fertilization of ideas had been occurring with emergence of the "public choice" school of economic analysis—pioneered by two George Mason University economists, Gordon Tullock and James Buchanan, recipient of the 1986 Nobel Prize for Economics—which seeks to explain political and bureaucratic decision-making according to economic principles. Expansion of government in its institutional size and spending levels, from this view, can be accounted for by examining the incentive structures that affect behavior—one within the bureaucracies of government which encourage public employees to constantly advance their powers, budgets, and agency staffing levels; another set of incentives within the political system itself, where interest groups compete in the voting marketplace to redistribute for themselves income plundered through taxation of others.

Conducting interviews and accumulating information for this book took me on a quest that crisscrossed the nation, from visiting a contracted-out Air Force base in northern Oklahoma, to a for-profit community hospital in rural Texas, a successful private school for minorities in lower Manhattan, an enterprising but poor neighborhood in St. Louis, underutilized federal properties in Los Angeles and San Francisco, and out to the welfare-laden Pacific island chains of Micronesia.

Some of the resulting articles appeared under my byline in *The Wall Street Journal* and *Reader's Digest,* whose Washington editor, William Schulz, initiated numerous assignments that brought the term privatization into more common usage. Other people assisted in many ways to bring this book into print, among them Willard Garvey, Joan Kennedy Taylor, the National Center for Privatization, and the people at the Pacific Research Institute for Public Policy, where the idea for this book originated.

When Government Goes Private

Introduction

*"Those which we call necessary institutions
are simply no more than institutions to
which we have become accustomed."*
—Alexis de Tocqueville

America confronts a deepening crisis, like many other nations of the world, between the need to provide basic services and a shortage of money to fund them. Everywhere service quality seems in decline, as costs continue to escalate. Public officials grope for solutions, warning that we face the prospect of either ever higher taxes or meat-ax reductions in the community life-support systems on which we all depend.

Our nation's government-operated mass-transit monopolies already shoulder deficits exceeding $6 billion annually; our public hospitals groan under deficits requiring new infusions of tax money; and more than 30 states are under federal court orders to relieve prison inmate overcrowding, creating demands for new prison construction. Our infrastructure-repair needs already far exceed our willingness or ability to pay. Bridges and highways are deteriorating faster than we can replace or rehabilitate them—the cost of just maintaining highway conditions to the year 2000 will be $324 billion, a figure the U.S. Department of Transportation concedes does not include bridge maintenance or necessary new highway construction. We have legislated ourselves another layer of unfunded liability under the Clean Water Act, which the Environmental Protection Agency estimates will require $120 billion just to provide immediate sewage treatment mandated by the law. Altogether, across the entire spectrum of infrastructure needs, the Joint Economic Committee of Congress has calculated the shortage of funds at $1.1 trillion by the year 2000. For taxpayers this translates into roughly $12,000 worth of new, immediate charges each of us has been assessed and which we will eventually be obliged to pay.

Are we truly facing a new, unavoidable era of austerity, demanding that we lower expectations about the quality of our lives? Can we reasonably expect to extricate ourselves from this conflict between service needs and taxing limits without further mortgaging the future of our children? Have we vested public officials and public institutions with entirely too much discretion and responsibility for managing our lives, delegating roles that we ourselves should more closely monitor, if not exercise? Are there really only two sides to this story, just two options to choose between — slashing services, raising taxes — or can we do more with less, erecting structures of incentives for the private sector to relieve the burdens imposed on government?

What we often take most for granted in our everyday experience are those very human services over which we have abdicated direct control, and yet for which we continue to shoulder, much as if we were sleepwalkers, a mounting burden of debt and financial responsibility. Government at all levels envelops us in a deceptively fragile cocoon of protections and promises. For most of us it manifests on an average day the first few moments we are awake in the morning. We pad into the bathroom to make use of the municipal digestive tract, relying on government to dispose of each flush properly. We sometimes wash with government-supplied water and shave using government-produced electricity. We stick first-class letters in the mailbox for collection by the government post office and take garbage to the curb for removal by a government sanitation truck. Along our neighborhood's government-owned street, just that morning cleaned by a government sweeper, a government police car chases the siren of a government fire engine or ambulance. To get to work we find ourselves dependent on a government infrastructure of highways, bridges, and mass transit. Our children catch a government bus to the government public school, as we board a government subway train or bus for the trip through suburbia into the city center and government's inner sanctum. Along the way we might pass the underutilized grounds of a government military base, now obsolete but kept open by the local congressman; next door might sprawl a dingy government public-housing project, and further on we might see the debt-ridden public hospital, the public library, a series of public parks; then finally a cluster of public buildings housing our congested public courts, an overcrowded public jail, and the legions of public employees that make all of these systems either function or fail.

Ordinarily we keep track of every personal expenditure, knowing what was spent each month on the mortgage, on telephone service, on food, gas, and other bills. If someone tries to cheat or overcharge us, provide shoddy goods or inefficient service, we usually know when we have been taken advantage of, and most of us will respond like avenging angels to protect our rights and pocketbook. Yet the single most onerous financial burden we face also happens to be the one most of us know the least about. It has hidden costs, escalating liabilities, and over it we all too often exercise little control or assurance of quality: it is the vast array of public-service functions performed by government.

Each American on average pays about $6,000 a year in total taxes of all kinds to government at all levels. This includes state and federal income taxes, sales taxes, property taxes, and dozens of other direct and hidden assessments such as corporate income taxes passed on to consumers in the form of higher prices for goods and services. U.S. Census Bureau figures provide a revealing breakdown of expenditures for each citizen supporting the various combined activities of local, state, and federal government.

For a typical family of four, maintaining that obsolete military base the local congressman keeps open comes out of $4,500 annually that represents their share of expenditures toward national defense and foreign aid. Next highest category of spending is the $4,160 or so a year for a family of four that goes to finance old-age security and medical-benefit programs. When our typical family deposits the kids at public school they might well be advised to ponder how the $3,380 donated in their name to education is actually being spent. Their portion of the government's interest payment on the national debt — our legacy of deficit spending — amounts to $2,516 annually and promises to be the fastest-growing line item of all the hidden costs for which government will bill them. For public welfare, that entire range of income-transfer programs, their share of support amounts to about $1,500. Another $968 goes to government utilities, including a subsidy we all pay to keep electric rates for users of government power in the western states lower than in the rest of the country. Just to help defray the cost of retirement benefits for government employees, our typical family will donate about $800 during the year; about $730 will go in support of government hospitals, at least $720 to build and maintain highways, $500 to the government postal service, $400 for police protection, $320 for housing programs, $260 to offset the financial-administration costs of government, $220 to keep the prison system functioning; and the list of obligations flow on like a river of reddening ink.

Americans delegated all of these roles to government and now, if only to rescue ourselves, government needs our help and expertise, our wise counsel and understanding. We no longer have the luxury of complacency. We must rethink these delegations of responsibility, question accepted methods and strategies, and search for a range of options and solutions that transcend divisions of party and ideology. The central question should not any longer be confined to whether taxes need to be raised or essential services cut—it is whether government should even be in the business of providing many of the services it monopolizes.

Over the past few years a recognition of systemic failure to control debt at the federal level accelerated changes already underway nationally from the bottom up, an undercurrent away from reliance on traditional government approaches and toward increasingly novel applications of voluntarism, self-help, and private-sector strategies to deliver services and satisfy social needs. Until recently the trend had been more predicted than evident, so subtle are the changes, so quiet is the revolution.

In 1982 the International City Management Association predicted that within a decade communities would be forced to devise survival strategies to reduce public expenditures, dilute demand for government services, and further decentralize regional government. Communities will be forced to rely on "increased involvement of the private sector in traditionally public sector concerns," concluded political scientist Laurence Rutter. "Contracting out will be much more popular—and voluntarism will become necessary if not fashionable," as local governments begin to buy back their independence from the federal government. Two of the ten new directions "transforming our lives" identified in futurist John Naisbitt's bestseller *Megatrends* were the decentralization of our society—rebuilding America from the bottom up—and the trend away from reliance on political institutions in favor of individual self-help initiatives. "Reclaiming America's traditional sense of self-reliance after four decades of trusting in institutional help," wrote Naisbitt, translates into community activism to prevent crime, revitalize the neighborhoods, and provide alternatives to traditional schooling, all with little or no government involvement. Naisbitt and a management authority, Peter F. Drucker, have both concluded that this emerging social self-help movement may force us to undertake a reevaluation of, in Naisbitt's words, "the very purpose for which government was created and the relationship of citizens to it."

Questions raised by that reevaluation involve redefining the proper role and performance limitations of government at all levels of society. Should we assume more direct responsibility for our own neighborhoods, or must we remain dependent on decisions made by government planners insulated from the realities of our separate needs and aspirations? Must we tolerate costly, inefficient bureaucracies unresponsive to our wishes, or can we better address social priorities by harnessing the power of the marketplace to deliver a wider range of options and solutions? Are the bureaucratic structures of government constituted to tax us arbitrarily to finance whichever interest groups happen to exercise the most political influence, providing unlimited services on demand, or is the role of government more properly to insure that only essential services are provided, with government acting as the facilitator of delivery rather than as the provider?

If we compare public-service performance against private-sector alternatives, glaring differences emerge. Studies by groups as diverse as the National Science Foundation and the International City Management Association found that the private sector performs the entire range of community life-support services at costs significantly lower than government and at levels of quality and performance as high or higher. What enables many private firms to collect residential garbage at costs half that of city sanitation departments? How are private companies able to build prisons at costs 25% less than public facilities, and complete the design and construction in less than a year when it takes government up to five years? Why is the same true for wastewater-treatment plants, with privately built facilities taking less than three years versus up to eight years for government, and at private costs half that of public costs? When repair work of the federally subsidized Amtrak railroad is compared to repairs by private railroads, why are the private ones able to remove 344 miles of track with a crew of 77, while it takes Amtrak a crew of 129 to remove only 71.8 miles of track over the same period and under comparable conditions? Why are our government-monopoly city mass-transit systems able to cover an average of only 40% of operating costs with revenues?

Answers to such questions in no way reflect on the relative competence or commitment of public employees. Their limitations spring from straitjackets imposed by their institutional surroundings. Those structures of incentives that separate the private sector from government force human beings to behave differently when they are in government as opposed to private employment. Management policy in government exhibits few of the pressures produced by competition or the profit motive, with decision-making constrained by political choices and influenced by considerations of career advancement based on seniority and the size of budgets and departments. Competition and profit incentives are far stronger efficiency tools than any bureaucratic management ploy, except perhaps the threat of death, that government has ever devised.

For this reason, no matter how noble the intentions of public employees, no matter how skilled or energetic their efforts, they usually find themselves unable to transcend their bureaucratic restraints to achieve policy goals in a timely, cost-effective manner. As Peter Drucker, considered the dean of the nation's management analysts, argues in his book *Innovation and Entrepreneurship,* "The most entrepreneurial, the most innovative people behave like the worst time serving bureaucrats or power hungry politicians six months after they have taken over the management of a public service institution, particularly if it is a government agency. Forces which impede innovation in a public service institution are inherent in it, integral to it, and inseparable from it."

The revolution quietly and subtly reshaping America, and much of the world, has come to be known generically as privatization. Although the word made its debut in *Webster's Dictionary* in 1983 — defined as the process of changing from public to private control or ownership—it has been in use among free-market advocates for several decades. One of the fathers of the privatization movement, E. S. Savas, describes it as more reliance on private-sector institutions and less on government to satisfy societal needs, which means that urban dwellers practice it when they form neighborhood security patrols and suburbanites when they join volunteer fire departments. A libertarian economist, Murray Rothbard, calls the entire privatization process simply "desocialization." Some definitions from a different ideological perspective have mostly succeeded in spawning confusion. For instance, James Sundquist, a senior fellow at the Brookings Institution, writes: "In true privatization, the government's role is only reduced; it does not disappear." But Ted Kolderie, senior fellow at the Hubert Humphrey Institute, applies the term only to the loadshedding of responsibility: "It is not privatization when a county board contracts the management of its public hospital to a private firm. It is not privatization when a county board sells the hospital to be run by the private firm. It is privatization when the county board says it will no longer pay for the care of the medically indigent."

For the purposes of this book privatization will be used to encompass a range of alternatives to the traditional, or recent, roles of government at the center of our economic life. Under this umbrella will be stationed the denationalizing of state-owned enterprises, the transfer in part or whole of government assets, infrastructure, and service functions to the private sector, and those instances of neighborhood self-help and community voluntarism that wean people from dependence on government methods and solutions. Contracting-out public services to the private sector will be treated as a limited, or partial, form of privatization, while in its purest state the term will refer to the creation of structures of incentives and a climate of self-interest that will encourage private providers to fill the service vacuum left by the departure of government.

Until a few years ago "selling or giving away public property was just a gleam in the eye of a few freemarket zealots," editorialized *The New York Times* in early 1986, but today "the idea of privatization is generating enthusiasm from the Potomac to the Ganges." Within just a three-year period, global denationalization reached more than 40 countries, both developed and developing, capitalist and socialist, and in the case of China and Hungary, the communist world as well. Britain pioneered the trend by selling one million public housing units to tenants, and by auctioning off to its citizenry dozens of state-owned companies. Japan sold off Nippon Telegraph and Telephone, Socialist-led Spain sold its national car manufacturer, Turkey sold a major bridge and hydroelectric dam to private investors, Bangladash privatized 100 state-owned enterprises, Brazil did the same with 20 companies, and Chile privatized its entire social-security system.

In the United States, with one of the least nationalized economies of any highly industrialized country, privatization has been largely a widespread local phenomenon involving the service functions of government. Between 1973 and 1982 the number of cities and counties shedding their service-production roles and contracting with private firms escalated rapidly. Street repair went from 63 contracts to 444 a decade later, data-processing contracts from 9 to 337, parks-maintenance contracts from only 5 to 142. Numerous communities have been almost totally privatized, farming-out all service activities except the policy-making and contract-oversight functions of government.

Never before has the private sector been involved so intimately in the full range of life-support needs of our communities. Four-lane highways and freeway interchanges have been privately financed and built by local businesses and landowners unwilling to wait for government construction. One city placed all its streets except major thoroughfares up for sale to private buyers to pay for the surfacing and upkeep of streets remaining in the city inventory; another sold its city hall and leases the building back; still another abolished its municipal garbage department and turned the whole service area over to private suppliers. A northeastern state hired a management-consultant firm to privatize the state's Department of Motor Vehicles, while several southwestern states approved legislation to turn the construction and operation of new prisons over to private firms.

Philosophy borne of suspicion for big government may underlie this revolution in America, but necessity is the mother of privatization. At least four pressures converged to account for privatization's rapid spread and acceptance. First is the specter of budget cutbacks, particularly those emanating from the federal level, with President Reagan threatening to veto tax increases, which produced pragmatism if not panic among local officals. A second pressure originates with the series of tax-limitation measures passed in states like California with Proposition 13 and in Massachusetts with Proposition 2½ that have hampered the search for new revenues. Another pressure emerged in 1981 in the form of incentives contained in the Reagan administration tax bill offering investment-tax credits, accelerated depreciation, and industrial-development bond features that for several years persuaded the private sector to play a more active role in financing, building, and managing capital public-works projects like wastewater-treatment plants. Still another pressure came from court decisions. In 1982 the Supreme Court ruled that local governments are subject to antitrust review for all service-provision activities unless their states provided specific authorizing legislation. Although that ruling was modified by the Court four years later, this initial decision resulted in the filing of at least 250 antitrust lawsuits against municipalities, mostly by private firms, charging these governments with restricting competition in providing waste collection, utility services, water and sewage systems. The explosion of interest in prison privatization can be attributed to federal court decisions ordering most states to relieve prison overcrowding at a time when public funds for new prison construction are scarce and often nonexistent.

Even though *Newsweek* magazine calls privatization "the perfect symbol of the libertarian belief that small is beautiful when applied to domestic government," the concept has transcended its origins among free-market disciples to generate interest and enthusiasm across the political spectrum. New York Governor Mario Cuomo may occasionally be an evangelist for the liberal theology of government intervention, yet he nevertheless has conceded: "It is not government's obligation to provide services, but to see that they're provided." At the Hubert Humphrey Institute of Public Affairs in Minnesota, which has been associated with the progressive wing of the Democratic Party, a Public Services Redesign Project was endowed in 1980, and its theorists have formulated a redefinition of government's social role—divesting it as a producer of services to become instead a skillful buyer, shopping around in the private sector for producers that will accomplish the policy goals set by government at the least possible cost. The strategy is to do more with less, rejecting the notion that the only choices available to public officials are to reduce services or to increase taxes.

At the activist level one will find privatization embraced by people like Larry Silverman, Ralph Nader's chief anti-pollution lobbyist before he formed an organization to promote the privatization of wastewater-treatment and water-purification plants. Silverman reasoned from personal experience that the private sector can be held more accountable to the public for clean water than can government. Lupe Anguiano was a labor organizer for Cesar Chavez before she created a private-sector group to rescue mothers from welfare, seeing in a nongovernment approach the most effective and least costly method of training welfare recipients for employment. Frustrated public employees seeking more flexible service systems have turned to privatization as a release for entrepreneurial activism. A woman court judge in Arizona started a private court system for dispute resolution as an alternative to overcrowded public courts; a former federal prison warden in Pennsylvania began a private prison company to escape the bureaucracy that stifled innovation under government operation; in Minnesota three public-school teachers formed a company to become vendors of education, selling fifth-grade teaching services. The dramatic shift in attitude of *The New York Times* provides another barometer of broadening ideological acceptance. In 1980 the newspaper published an editorial calling privatization the dangerous fantasy of the "patrician elite" that should ring alarm bells because "what is being nurtured by privatization is not the consent of the governed but the convenience of the rich." Five years later the news-paper respectfully editorialized that privatization was a healthy trend that would reduce incentives for waste and temper political pressures to continue inefficient government services. "Privatization is not a cure for every economic ailment," the paper admitted, "but the spreading skepticism about public enterprises offers opportunities to re-examine them with an eye to raising productivity and paring unjustifiable government subsidies."

A realization has dawned that, irrespective of political party or ideology, privatization may afford public officials a less painful, more palatable budget remedy than raising taxes or cutting services. Fiscal reality demands that we use our understanding of human nature to restructure public-service institutions to utilize the strengths of the private sector. We cannot afford to be any less distrustful of the monopoly privileges of government than we already are of corporate monopolies that periodically evolve in the marketplace. Each kind of monopoly can thwart cost efficiency, stifle innovation, and suffocate the spirit of human enterprise.

By carving out a new role for itself, that of a service facilitator rather than sole provider, government might lend flexibility and creativity to service delivery mechanisms while simultaneously en-couraging the formation of attitudes and values that enhance neigh-borhood and individual self-sufficiency. The challenge remains to ad-vance these goals without sacrificing the sense of community that binds us as a nation. That, in large measure, is what this book is all about. When people actually begin to see the benefits of privatization in practice, they may glimpse not only strategies and tools with which to harness the private sector for public good; they may recognize as well, within themselves and in others, an entire spectrum of possibilities for the release of their own human potential.

1
Giving Power Back to the People

Saving Neighborhoods That Refuse to Die

An entire neighborhood received a death sentence in 1966 when a white St. Louis city official told a crowd of blacks from the city's north side that the slum area where they lived "wasn't worth saving." No one disputed that the community had immense problems: Hundreds of abandoned and condemned buildings littered the 700-block landscape. Unemployment was chronic and crime the highest in the city. Banks refused to make loans in the neighborhood, and insurance companies were reluctant to provide coverage. Many poor homeowners who tried to sell could find no one who would buy. Residents feared that the urban renewal being proposed as a salvation by city officials would result only in eviction from their homes.

"Urban renewal means our removal," Macler Shepard, an upholstery shop owner, told residents who met to discuss the situation. "We don't have anywhere left to go but the Mississippi River. We don't even have no towel to throw in. All we can do is build!"

Shepard and a handful of other residents formed a nonprofit organization, Jeff-Vander-Lou, Inc. (JVL), named after three of the streets bordering the neighborhood, and drew up a plan for restoring the spiritual and economic health of the community. They applied for funding from the federal government's Office of Economic Opportunity (OEO), then engaged in its war on poverty. Weeks became months, and nothing happened. Twenty years later they still await a reply. It turned out to be the most fortunate form of rejection they could have imagined. With nowhere else to turn, with the city indifferent and the federal government deaf, they began to look within their own community for answers.

They knew that no neighborhood could long survive without decent habitable housing. Nor could neighborhood decay be reversed without jobs and a stable, flourishing business environment. So Jeff-Vander-Lou took the original OEO grant proposal and turned it into a creative, ambitious blueprint for self-help. Shepard visited churches in the area, telling the congregations to mobilize as if a disaster had been declared. "If a tornado had struck right here, we could have gotten fixed up," he told them. "But we have to look at it like a slow tornado that's been happening over the last 30 years."

Gradually the message attracted support. A local Mennonite church group gave JVL an interest-free loan of $30,000 for housing rehabilitation and sent in volunteer skilled craftsmen to help with the work. Other contributions came from a collection of churches called the Northside Ministry. JVL members contributed their own money and volunteered their labor—"sweat equity"—to buy and renovate 15 of the estimated 500 abandoned buildings scattered throughout the community. They stripped the buildings to the foundations, added new floors, walls, and plumbing, substituting whatever they found discarded in the neighborhood—bricks and railroad ties, for example —for materials they could not afford to buy. In 1968 the 15 rehabilitated houses were opened for sale and rental to local families, with the proceeds being pumped back into the JVL building fund.

St. Louis businessman Thomas DePew, whose boyhood home could be found in the JVL neighborhood, marveled at the group's enterprise and determination. In 1968 he formed the nonprofit Arrowhead Foundation to lend support to JVL's revitalization effort. Over the next six years, Arrowhead gave JVL about $1 million in grants and interest-free loans, providing the first big turning point in the JVL success story.

Shepard set in motion the next stage of JVL's blueprint for self-help by luring job-creating businesses back into the community. He approached the Brown Shoe Company of St. Louis, owner of 30 manufacturing plants nationwide, and offered JVL's services as a real-estate agent to buy up, under the JVL name, a two-acre section of the neighborhood at bargain rates and turn it over to Brown for construction of a manufacturing plant. In return JVL wanted Brown to train and hire local unemployed residents to staff the new facility. The company's board of directors accepted JVL's offer. Some businesspeople warned that Brown would regret this decision, predicting that the company would be victimized by vandalism and theft, and that residents of the area would prove to be poor, uncooperative workers. None of the accusations came true. "I don't think we lost a single screwdriver or foot of copper piping in the construction of that factory," says Hadley Griffin, chairman of the board of Brown Group, Inc. "It became a very rewarding and satisfying experience for us." As construction on the shoe factory proceeded, 40 of the JVL residents underwent training. When the two-story, air-conditioned plant opened in January 1970, it went into production with a skilled work force, and within a year Brown had expanded employment to 150 neighborhood residents.

Nearly two decades after its creation, Jeff-Vander-Lou not only came of age; with more than 70 full-time employees, it blossomed into one of the most remarkable inner-city success stories in America. More than 800 units of housing were rehabilitated for rental and another 80 houses were renovated and then sold. It is no exaggeration to say that these wide, modern brick rowhouses resemble the fashionable Georgetown neighborhood of Washington, D.C., just as JVL builders intended. Three day-care centers provide service for 300 children. A three-story red-brick senior-citizens' complex was built with 100 units of housing for the elderly and handicapped. A meal program feeds about 200 daily, while another kitchen was designed to enable JVL to feed 1,500 of the neighborhood's sick, elderly, and disabled. A communications resource center in a spacious two-story building offers neighborhood children and students from four area high schools training in motion pictures, still photography, and radio and television journalism.

In recognition of these achievements, the Missouri House of Representatives passed a resolution declaring, "Despite such impediments as the lack of money, staff, power, influence, or support from the city government, Macler Shepard had the courage, motivation, determination and unique ability to incredibly transform his neighborhood from inner-city rubble to an oasis." The humble, mild-mannered Shepard shrugs off such accolades. He says JVL's job has only just begun. He won't rest until every structure in need of repair has been renovated, until every family has found suitable housing. He expresses dissatisfaction with the quality of public-school education, vowing to build a school for grades one through twelve to compete with the public-school system.

The story of JVL is not unique. "There are substantial strengths and resources in poor communities waiting to be tapped, if only people are given a chance," contends Harvard Professor of Government Glen Loury. These strengths, resources, and problem-solving abilities in communities like Jef-Vander-Lou have been virtually ignored by all layers of government, which is more inclined to "parachute in" programs and experts without regarding real community needs or the innate potential of residents to organize themselves.

Sorely neglected have been the institutions known as "mediating structures" that can be found between the individual and the mechanisms of government. Such structures include the family, the neighborhood, the church, and voluntary organizations, each of which generates and maintains social-value systems integral to self-sufficiency. These are the institutions people instinctively turn to in times of community crisis, personal need, or collective self-doubt.

America is the most voluntaristic society on earth, supporting hundreds of thousands, if not millions, of voluntary groups, clubs, and organizations, ranging from the service orientation of Kiwanis and Lions clubs to hobbyists, sports, professional, and church groups. Contrast that with a nation like Hungary, considered one of the more liberal communist societies, where the only two voluntary organizations permitted independent of government are a nudist club and a small association of homeowners at an exclusive vacation spa.

Helping oneself and assisting others to help themselves through volunteering are traits endemic to the American spirit and one of our fundamental strengths as a nation. Within every diseased and seemingly hopeless community can be found a social entrepreneur, someone that Robert Woodson, president of the National Center for Neighborhood Enterprise, calls an "anti-body." They are anti-bodies because neighborhoods, like the human body, have the capacity to heal themselves after sickness or injury. Anti-bodies are people who precipitate or advance that healing process by magnetizing the creative strengths and productive energies of those around them.

Today, in all parts of the country, we are witnessing the revival of self-help strategies and voluntarism as expressions of independence from government. Such sentiments have welled up from within some of our most depressed neighborhoods as social entrepreneurs organize the productive talents of their neighbors, and from within public-housing projects where residents have begun to reassert control over their own lives by assuming control over their surroundings.

By making the mediating structures of society the centerpiece of human-service programs, these communities establish a "user-friendly" environment that is conducive to self-help because it privatizes responsibility. Organizations like the National Center for Neighborhood Enterprise are trying to make it happen in hundreds of other communities. "Our challenge is to remove old-line policies that inhibit self-help efforts and instead appeal creatively to that positive spirit in every human that craves self-sufficiency and independence," declares Robert Woodson.

In Woodson's view, social-service professionals share much of the blame for having encouraged government to legislate strict standards and certifications that severely hamper voluntary associations from being effective. As is true of all occupational licensing, though the stated motivation is to protect public health and safety, in the words of economist Walter Williams, "virtually always the real effect is to create monopolies for some people at the expense of the consuming public." Professional monopoly privileges over social services evolve in tandem with government monopoly controls. The result is that social-service delivery has become what Woodson describes as "the exclusive purview of a vast professional bureaucracy whose unique function is to keep its citizens dependent."

In Washington, D.C., nearly 60 written forms are required for day-care licensing and monitoring. A person capable of caring for children may be incapable of dealing with an impenetrable bureaucracy, much less conforming to a maze of regulations dictating how each child must have 60 square feet of playground space, how one toilet must be provided for every ten children, how reserved parking spaces must be provided for staff, and how the staff cannot be hired unless they have a master's degree in childhood education. Requirements like these add $100 and more to costs each month for every child, making it almost impossible to keep tuition at a level that the poor can afford. Instead of erecting barriers to the private solution of social problems, a creative approach would be to encourage self-sufficiency. Syndicated columnist William Raspberry has described a possible model in the efforts of a Chicago neighborhood organization that asked its low-income residents what skills they could perform, rather than what services they needed. After interviewing occupants of 80 apartments the group found that health care, whether in a nursing home or a hospital, was the most common work experience. So the group advertised the services of these "health-care workers" in a nearby middle-class neighborhood, and succeeded at placing 50 of the unemployed in jobs that were within a dozen blocks of their homes. Raspberry calls this a "capacity" approach, focusing on the ability of the poor to become producers, instead of a "deficiency" approach, which treats them as nothing more than clients in need of services.

The deficiency approach historically has sowed its sourest results in places like the mountains of Appalachia, where over $15 billion in special federal programs during the past two decades has done little to erase the abject poverty and sense of despair that haunts the region; in fact, some think the programs have helped to create the problem. "The federal government has turned this section of the country into a tremendous welfare reservation," laments Harry Caudill, a former Kentucky legislator and a regional historian. "We have a medical condition down here—the Appalachian syndrome—the chronic, passive dependency syndrome, in which our people just give up. Will and brains, give us those two things and we'd be rich. Without them, all the rest is superfluous."

Our nation's 283 Indian tribes together own 58 million acres of land on which about 750,000 tribal members live. By one estimate, they own up to one-third of America's remaining developable resources, including half the nation's uranium supply, $8-billion worth of coal, and huge reserves of oil, gas, and timber. Yet these resource-rich people continue to be dependent on about $2.6 billion a year from the federal government, nearly all of it for social-welfare programs.

Why is the single most resource-rich group of people in America also the poorest? Why do Indian reservations remain the single most regulated part of our entire economy? Economist Walter Williams has put the question into focus another way: "Can it just be coincidence that Indians have the greatest dependency on government [of any ethnic group] in the nation and the lowest median income, while the Japanese, who have the least dependency, have the highest median income?"

In New Mexico, on the largest and most populated reservation in America—the 25,000-square-mile Navajo community—unemployment hovers at 75%. The wealth of this resource-rich land is untapped, its pastures overgrazed, its human occupants bitter and filled with despair. "People are really depressed," Faith Abeita, an employee of the tribal health service, confessed to *The Washington Post*. "They have left behind the traditional life and now they have nothing else. You start to wonder if the federal aid just made the people more dependent, if it killed their spirit."

A little-noticed presidential panel, the Commission on Indian Reservation Economies, released a report in 1984 that provided some evidence to support this assumption. After field hearings throughout the nation, the nine-member body, six of whom were Native Americans from four tribes, identified 40 separate major obstacles to economic development on reservations. Practically every obstacle was rooted in federal government policies. "Economic development, without subsidy, can be successfully put together only within a new social and economic setting which entails a radical break with the past dependency on the federal government," concluded the commission. That new setting and radical break means privatization: restraining government while encouraging self-determination.

On the Warm Springs Reservation of the Confederated Tribes in Oregon, a young Indian hands a tourist family the key to their suite in the tribe's 160-room mountain resort, a $5-million mineral-hot-springs recreational complex that offers golfing, swimming, and horseback riding. Elsewhere on the reservation, about 150 Indians operate the tribal sawmill that boasts timber sales of $26 million annually. A short distance away Indian engineers run the tribe's hydroelectric dam on the Deshutes River, built with $10 million of the tribe's own money. Profits from all these ventures yield nearly $2,000 in yearly dividends to each tribe member. At Warm Springs the Indians succeeded because they had leaders who were catalysts and anti-bodies, who understood the enterprising strengths of their people and how to harness those qualities despite a tradition of dependence.

It is not just the poorest and most dependent Americans who are starting to solve their own problems. In numerous small towns and cities, individuals and neighborhood associations are taking over the responsibility for providing municipal services, building a better urban life for themselves, and in the process, solving fiscal problems.

Across middle America the phrase "Power to the people" has taken on more than symbolic meaning. Outside the coastal city of Savannah in the town of Garden City, Georgia (population 6,895), voluntarism is regarded as a way of life. Residents pay no property taxes, the fire and recreation departments are staffed by volunteers, and the mayor and city council—all serving without pay—often can be found with tools in hand helping other citizens to dig city sewers and pave city streets. "If something needs to be done and there's not enough money in the budget," town mayor Ralph Kessler told a reporter, "we don't raise taxes, cut services, or go into debt. We just get people together and go out and do it ourselves."

Encouraging Self-Help Housing

Social worker James P. Butler established the nonprofit Housing Opportunities, Inc., in 1975 after concluding that government bureaucracies had "done more harm than good" to the cause of low-cost housing and neighborhood revitalization. Despite over $50 billion in federal subsidies spent on housing construction and rehabilitation over the previous decade, he could see little evidence that the programs had succeeded at anything other than making poor people more dependent on government.

In McKeesport, Pennsylvania, 14 miles southeast of Pittsburgh, the then 28-year-old Butler took over a program called Earned Home Ownership, begun several years earlier by an interfaith human-services agency. It financially assisted low-income home buyers by adjusting the interest, amount, and terms of mortgages to make payments conform to individual circumstances. To supplement this approach Butler added counseling services in finance and budgeting, and a profit-making subsidiary to perform the residential construction work.

The U.S. Department of Housing and Urban Development (HUD) already served the community with its Scattered Site Program, which also renovated vacant, deteriorated single-family homes. Here the similarity between these two approaches ends. Under Butler's private-sector program families actually owned their homes, whereas HUD relegated families to the status of renters from the federal government. Expansion of public housing under the HUD program tends to depress the value of surrounding property, but the private approach moved property owners to a level, in Butler's words, "that supports a healthy and active private-sector involvement and raises property values in the area." Costs of the respective programs differ considerably. A remodeled house in McKeesport cost HUD, and through it the American taxpayers, an average of $153,949, and brought in only $125 a month in rent, while the private program remodeled the same-sized house for $57,715, which brought in an average of $285 a month in rent even though the average income of families in both programs was about the same. At this rate, three families can be housed using the Earned Home Ownership Program model for every one family housed by HUD's public-sector approach.

What accounted for the huge disparity in costs? Butler singled out two contributing factors. The federal program involved HUD area offices, regional offices, and central offices, which resulted in significant administrative expense and delay, compared to the private, community-based alternative which had minimum administrative needs. Excessive HUD construction costs were mandated in part by federal adherence to Davis-Bacon wage rates that Butler's group was exempt from paying. "As absurd as it may sound," Butler complained, "the Davis-Bacon Act is a federal law that requires craftsmen building houses for the poor to be paid significantly more than when they are building houses for middle-income Americans."

Northeast of McKeesport, in the grim desolation of East New York (a neighborhood in Brooklyn), another private-sector approach to housing the working poor is yielding similarly impressive results. The project is sponsored by 48 congregations of area churches organized behind the Nehemiah Plan—which refers to Nehemiah, the biblical prophet sent to rebuild Jerusalem—and provides decent affordable housing to mostly black and Hispanic buyers who otherwise could not afford homes of their own.

A community that was once considered a graveyard, one of the poorest neighborhoods in America, emerged from its own rubble like the proverbial phoenix from its ashes. The Nehemiah Plan involved the construction of 5,000 two- and three-bedroom homes, each with 1,150 square feet of space and a basement, sold for $41,000 each, half the price such a home might normally bring. An initial revolving construction fund of $5 million was raised by the churches, supplemented by tax-default land donated by the city of New York— which also deferred property taxes for ten years—and special 9.9% mortgage financing that reduced monthly homeowner payments to about $350.

This project grew entirely as a brainchild of the community, owing nothing to government planners. It puts into practice the belief that only through home ownership can a blighted area be transformed into a stable community. Forty percent of Nehemiah's new owner families came from public housing projects. Elevating them into homes of their own freed up units for the over 150,000 families still on the area's public housing waiting list. Those visitors from elsewhere who have seen the Nehemiah project in practice call it a housing miracle. "The question is whether our city's residents can be mobilized to take their housing fate into their own hands and force our politicians and bureaucrats to move in new directions," wrote a *Washington Post* columnist, Dorothy Gilliam.

"America is changing the way it is housing its poor, its large families on small incomes and its low-income workers," is how *The Post* in 1987 described the expanding housing role of nonprofit groups that provide loans with little or no interest. "Public housing is out; home ownership is in... nonprofit organizations are becoming almost as important in providing low-cost housing as is the U.S. Department of Housing and Urban Development." Creative solutions emphasizing smaller, varied approaches are replacing massive-scale centralized methods and strategies. Habitat for Humanity, for example, operates in 170 cities with an $11-million budget raised from churches, businesses, and foundations, helping low-income workers with financing when they cannot afford homes of their own.

Investment in community development has traditionally been viewed by banking officials as a form of charity, or a method of avoiding accusations of redlining—the refusal to lend money within the boundaries of rundown, high-risk neighborhoods. With city and state governments beginning to demand that out-of-state banks prove their commitment to local communities as a condition for approval of mergers by financial institutions, and with federal regulatory agencies now taking into consideration a bank's record of community service when considering applications for branch offices or mergers, financial organizations have been forced to revise their perceptions of charity. In Chicago the First National Bank lends money for, and invests in, community-development projects, primarily because of federal, state, and local requirements. Property-improvement loans have become a staple for the Security Pacific National Bank in California, directed at low- and moderate-income residents. Altogether, 40 major banks across the nation have set up community-development subsidiaries over the past decade, and more are expected to follow their lead in providing low-interest loans to finance housing for the disadvantaged.

More efficient use of existing buildings, especially abandoned or dilapidated schools, factories, and other commercial space, an area of housing potential called the "shadow market" by William C. Baer, a University of Southern California urban planning professor, could provide still another alternative to traditional government housing programs. Single-family zoning restrictions make accessory apartments illegal in many parts of the country. Simply by lowering zoning barriers to allow subdivision of existing housing units, a new, large housing market could be stimulated without government subsidies.

Most major cities have unused or abandoned buildings in the city inventory that could be rapidly turned over to profit or nonprofit groups for conversion into housing. Habitat for Humanity, operating on New York's Lower East Side, bought a six-story building that had been abandoned for five years, paying $19,000 to the city, and transformed the structure into 19 apartments for sale at no profit to low-income persons under long-term, no-interest mortgages.

Transforming the Public Housing Environment

On a cold night in December 1974, 29-year-old Kimi Gray answered a knock at her door in the Kenilworth public housing project in Washington, D.C. Standing on her doorstep were three young residents of the project. "Miss Kimi," began Veronica Pollard, who had graduated from high school earlier that year, "we have something serious to talk about."

"Okay," said Mrs. Gray, ushering them in, "shoot."

Veronica and her two high-school friends wanted to attend college, but they had no idea how to go about it. They wanted Mrs. Gray, youth coordinator of the community, to help them find a way. "Okay, you all come back tomorrow and let me see what I can do about this."

It seemed like an impossible dream. Kenilworth Courts was a depressed community of 464 housing units, sheltering 3,000 low-income persons. To Mrs. Gray's knowledge only two youngsters from the project had ever escaped that environment and gone on to college. She collected information about scholarships and college programs anyway, anticipating that when she met with the kids again their interest might well have faded. To her surprise the three returned with friends and kept returning until 25 young people began meeting every week in her living room, calling their group "College Here We Come."

Their first hurdle was to overcome the reluctance of parents to participate. For too long both parents and children had been told that public-housing residents were not college material. She had to explode that myth and demonstrate that enterprise and determination could overcome the steepest hurdle of all: the financial cost of higher education.

Through the winter months College Here We Come met religiously, members drilling each other in school work, practicing exams, writing essays, and together dreaming their impossible dream. Gradually the parents were infused with their enthusiasm as they saw the children improve in school. A Parents Booster Club was formed. This became the organizational tool Kimi Gray needed to begin the arduous task of fundraising. They held sales and raffles, auctions and yard sales, sold chicken dinners, cakes and cookies, and organized public-housing bazaars to sell knitwear and ceramics the parents made. Slowly the money accumulated. When acceptance letters from colleges actually began to arrive in the spring, excitement seized the entire community. Now everyone seemed eager to help because it had become a matter of civic pride.

Mrs. Gray purchased used trunks from Goodwill and the Salvation Army, which she and the parents fixed and painted, then packed them with jeans from thrift shops and cosmetics donated by local merchants. No child was going off to college without at least one trunk of possessions. Next, with the money they raised, the parents bought one-way bus or plane tickets for the students who had been accepted. Mrs. Gray had encouraged each student to pick a college far from Washington. Most had never left their Anacostia neighborhood, and she knew that to break the dreary cycle of poverty they needed exposure to a new way of life. During that week in August 1975, as 17 youngsters prepared to leave for college, Kenilworth Courts rejoiced as if it were Christmas. A large crowd of parents and friends escorted the students to airports and bus stations, hugging, kissing, and crying. Just as Kimi Gray wanted, their destinations were small colleges and junior colleges in places like Tyler, Texas, and Monterey, California.

Over the years, Gray expanded College Here We Come by soliciting support from local service organizations like the Kiwanis Club and Deltas Sorority, each of which sponsored students through college. The Parents Booster Club continued with the bake sales and yard sales until that fundraising mechanism became a community institution. Students who go away to college now must promise to return during summer breaks and work to enhance the quality of life at Kenilworth Courts.

More than 600 young people have been sent to college and given a chance to better their lives and their community because of College Here We Come. Similar programs emulating their approach have sprung up at other public-housing projects, and Mrs. Gray sees no reason why it can't be a role model for poor communities across the nation. "What we are doing is simple," she explains. "If they come to us with a dream, we'll help them reach it. If they come to us without a dream, we'll give them a dream to reach."

Buoyed by the success of this program, Kenilworth residents formed their own management corporation in 1982, elected a board of directors headed by Kimi Gray, and convinced the city of Washington to let them take over running their public-housing project. Within a year the results were dramatic. The per-unit monthly rental receipts increased by 60% and administrative costs associated with the housing project declined by over 60% under tenant management. Within three years positive reverberations were being felt in other areas. Before Kimi Gray took over as resident manager, 30% of the residents were totally dependent on welfare and 85% of the households relied on some government assistance. Under tenant management both welfare dependency and teenage pregnancies were reduced by half, and crime dropped by nearly 75%.

"You can put all the money that you want to into rehabbing buildings," Kimi Gray describes her management philosophy, "but if you don't rehab the residents, you are wasting the government's money." To "rehab" the residents, she helped create small businesses within the housing project, including a co-op market, a laundry facility, a barbershop and beauty salon, thrift store, boutique, trash company, and roofing company, together employing over 100 community residents.

The ultimate goal of Kimi Gray and the Kenilworth tenant management is to own their housing project and give every resident a vested interest in its future. They do not want to see the public-housing trap perpetuated for their children and grandchildren. "I am speaking on behalf of public-housing residents," Kimi Gray declares. "We do not want any more public-housing plantations built. And that is what is created by the system."

More than one million public-housing units have been built in the United States, costing the federal government up to $4 billion a year. Most of the projects are in the nation's worst slums corroded by crime, vandalism, and indifference. Housing authorities set up by cities to operate the projects have become dumping grounds for political-patronage jobs. When State Judge Paul Garrity placed the Boston Housing Authority—landlord to nearly one-tenth of Boston's residents—into receivership several years ago because he found the housing conditions to be worse than deplorable, he raged: "If the Boston Housing Authority were a private landlord, it surely would have been driven out of business long ago or its board jailed or most likely both."

At least 70,000 boarded-up public-housing units can be found across America, with another 1,000 a year abandoned or demolished because the cost of repairs often exceeds the value of the units. Local public-housing authorities clamor for more federal spending, but they share responsibility for the worsening conditions. In 1984, for instance, more than $1 billion in federal funds reverted to the federal treasury because mismanaged housing authorities had failed to use the money within the required three years from appropriation.

City planner Oscar Newman headed a nationwide team that studied the Chicago Housing Authority (CHA), where he discovered that it costs American taxpayers exactly three times as much to house the poor in Chicago's public housing than the private sector would charge for comparable but decent and well-maintained housing. Chicago's projects were found to be huge ghettos of ten thousand families and more, living in squalid, rat- and roach-infested buildings that were literally falling apart around them. Newman learned that no one, not the housing authority staff or Chicago city administrators, seemed too interested in seeing the situation improve. "The CHA exists to provide the mayor with patronage jobs, favored suppliers and contractors with financial opportunities, political hacks with millions of dollars to transfer into favored banks, trade unions with high-paying, low-performance jobs, and incidentally housing for the poor."

Over a two-year period ending in 1985, two of the Chicago Housing Authority's scattered-site housing projects were placed under private management in an experimental program to determine if costs could be lowered. Results exceeded federal expectations. The nonprofit Housing Resources Corporation saved 7% of its authorized budget at one housing project, while a for-profit management participant spent 25% less than what had previously been budgeted for its project. A study by the Business and Professional People for the Public Interest later found that housing units had been better maintained under private operators, and a majority of tenants questioned in a survey preferred private management to what they had experienced under government care.

"When residents acquire an equity stake in the future of their building, and hence their neighborhood," declares Stuart Butler of the Heritage Foundation, "they gain incentives to change their behavior from destructive to constructive and to urge their neighbors to do likewise."

Developing resident management associations like the Kenilworth project can be a transition to forms of privatization that result in tenant homeownership, with public-housing units and buildings sold at substantial discount to those associations of tenants already occupying the projects. Such a demonstration program was initiated in 1985 by the U.S. Department of Housing and Urban Development at 16 of its public housing authorities. Ironically, the first purchasers of their public housing home were a couple in McKeesport, Pennsylvania, where the local HUD Scattered Site Program had been embarrassed by the ability of James Butler's competing Earned Home Ownership to build three houses for low-income people for the price of every one unit of public housing. The second purchasers under the program were Jesse Corbin, 64, and his wife, Fay, 49, who had lived for five years in a Newport News, Virginia, project. They purchased their public-housing home for $18,397 by obtaining a mortgage through a private savings and loan institution, in contrast with the McKeesport couple who relied on a government loan. The Corbins put no money down, and the purchase price of their home was calculated according to how much they could afford rather than how much the house was worth. A similar right-to-buy program in Britain under the Thatcher government resulted in the sale of more than one million public dwellings to their occupants, creating a massive infusion of money into the public treasury while substantially reducing operational costs for maintaining the inventory of public housing.

A political odd couple, conservative New York Rep. Jack Kemp and liberal District of Columbia Rep. Walter Fauntroy, co-sponsored two bills in 1986 to expedite the sale process in this country. One bill provided management-training programs for public-housing residents, enabling them to manage their projects after training, and permitting tenant-management groups to use any resulting operational savings toward self-help programs designed to alleviate dependence on public-welfare spending. The second bill authorized the sale of public-housing units for a maximum of 25% of their market value, providing loans with interest at 70% of market rates. A study by the Congressional Research Service, shortly after the legislation was introduced, reported that 25% of public-housing occupants could afford to purchase their residences under the conditions of this bill, affecting property worth roughly $14 billion.

In June 1987, by a vote of 258 to 161, the House of Representatives killed Rep. Kemp's plan, called "urban homesteading," to allow public-housing tenants to buy their housing units. Democrats led by Rep. Henry Gonzalez of Texas assailed the plan as a "cruel hoax and a raid on the Treasury," because of their fear that new public housing would not be constructed as other units were sold.

The Reagan administration proposed substituting vouchers for all of the nearly $8 billion spent annually on housing assistance, arguing that vouchers can shelter more of the needy with fewer inequities than public-housing construction projects. Public-housing tenants receive only 34 cents of benefit from every tax dollar spent, with the sponge of government bureaucracy absorbing the rest. Under a voucher system at least 84 cents of every tax dollar spent would go directly to those in need, freeing-up more money for the poor at less cost to taxpayers, since vouchers would cost only half as much as new housing construction. A voucher-demonstration program began in May 1985, when the first of 12,000 families received federal vouchers for use in signing apartment leases. A 1987 investigation by *The Wall Street Journal* of how the program was faring found that it had been stymied by "bureaucratic logjams in Washington" and by opposition from local housing authorities.

Public-housing sales and vouchers are ideas with potential to benefit both taxpayers and the poor. Transforming public-housing tenants into owners could help revive many of our neighborhoods and encourage self-improvement among individuals who may never have had the opportunity to exert meaningful control over their environment. It would enable many of the poor to finally realize the American dream of home ownership, endowing them with an investment stake in the nation's future economic health.

Lowering Barriers to Affordable Housing

Until a few years ago the residents of cheap single-room-occupancy (SRO) hotels in New York City could be safely categorized as the down-and-out poor, the elderly, and the mentally ill. By 1986 hundreds of such people had been replaced in these small, dingy rooms of communal kitchens and baths, by young working professionals unable to find other housing. "Many homeless people in city shelters used to live in SROs," tenant organizer Henry Perlin told *The New York Times*. "Now, the SROs that haven't been converted to co-ops or luxury apartments are renting to a higher class of people, and the poor are once again being displaced."

UNIVERSITY OF WINNIPEG, 515 Portage Ave., Winnipeg, MB. R3B 2E9 Canada

What were once hotels of last resort for the city's poorest people have become a last resort for the college-educated. The conditions they must tolerate in return for affordable rents boggle the senses. As the *Times* reporter wrote, describing the rat- and roach-infested SRO life of a young professional named Susan Ross, she "walks down dark, often smelly hallways, contends with an ancient mattress and drafty windows and shares a bathroom with twenty other people. She said the bathroom is usually so dirty she showers with shoes on."

New York City has among the most pervasive and stringent rent-control laws in the nation, and, simultaneously one of the worst housing shortages and the most serious problem of any city with the homeless, who overflow its streets and shelters at night. That there is a connection between rent control and a decline in the quality of life may escape the notice of politicians who, after all, must respond to the wishes of renters who benefit from controls, but it has not escaped the scrutiny of economists. If there is one universal recognized truth in economics, it is that rent controls—suppressing prices below market values—create housing shortages.

American economist Thomas Hazlett describes rent controls as "a legal jamming device placed to intercept the messages sent by consumers of housing to the providers of housing." Swedish economist Assar Lindbeck writes of the effects such jamming have on the economic health of cities: "Next to bombing, rent control seems in many cases to be the most efficient technique so far known for destroying cities."

Rental units in America decreased by more than 500,000 a year in the decade after rent control became a nationwide phenomenon. After eight years of control in Washington, D.C., for instance, rental-housing stock dipped from nearly 200,000 units to 175,000. In New York City, residents have been known to scour the obituary pages looking for possible apartment vacancies. Because rent controls create black-market premiums for renters to keep controlled apartments, Manhattan residents who move out of apartments that cost $800 a month might typically sublease them for up to $1,500 and keep the profit rather than pass any benefits on to the landlord or actually give up the apartment.

Actress Mia Farrow's rent-controlled apartment in New York City, a ten-room suite on exclusive Central Park West, costs her only $1,870 a month when the going rate, according to real-estate agents, should be $12,000 per month. Even Mayor Ed Koch maintains a rent-controlled apartment in Greenwich Village, paying $351.60 a month for an apartment worth five times that amount. As a form of investment, well-off renters hold on to rent-controlled dwellings for decades, sometimes for their entire lives, whether or not they continue to occupy the unit.

In a 1987 editorial strikingly titled "End Rent Control," *The New York Times* made the following points: Nothing distorts a city worse than rent control, as it accelerates the abandonment of marginal buildings and deters improvement of others; rent regulation does little or nothing for the poor, and instead shields the middle-class and wealthier tenants from rent increases; rent control "favors the lucky, not the needy"; because occupying a rent-controlled dwelling is "a little like winning the lottery, its benefits are distributed without regard to need." Just to administer rent-control regulations, New York City must employ a bureaucracy of more than 1,100 persons, at a cost of millions of dollars. *Times* editorial writers recommended a "return to free-market incentives" in housing through vacancy decontrol. A similar plea was made in May 1987 by *The Washington Post,* which urged the District of Columbia government to relax controls, pointing to neighboring Montgomery County (Maryland), where rent controls were abolished and 8,000 new apartments were constructed as a result.

Advocates for the homeless often blame cutbacks in federal public-housing assistance for dramatic increases in the nation's homeless population over the past decade. Yet the number of new public-housing units actually rose significantly during that period, from 10,000 new units annually between 1977 and 1980 to more than 28,000 annually in the years 1981 to 1986. Struck by this statistic, journalist William Tucker began examining the per-capita homeless populations of 50 cities, comparing each by factoring in poverty and unemployment rates, public-housing availability, annual mean temperature, rental vacancy rates, and the absence or presence of rent controls. No correlation was found between rates of homelessness and the extent of unemployment, poverty, or public-housing units.

Of the 50 cities selected for the study, only nine were rent controlled: San Francisco, Los Angeles, Santa Monica, Washington, D.C., Boston, Hartford, Newark, Yonkers, and New York City. But, as Tucker related in a 1987 article for *The New York Times,* "all nine ranked among the top 17 cities for per capita homelessness. Cities with rent controls had, on average, two and a half times as many homeless people as cities without them...the nine rent-controlled cities have the nine lowest vacancy rates in the country—all under 3%." Since 1970, about 200 cities large and small, have joined New York—the first rent-control city—and enacted controls. Before controls their housing vacancy rates averaged 7%; after controls it was below 3%. Rent controls effectively expand the ranks of the homeless by about 250%, as moderate and upper-income people cling to low-income housing and developers refuse to develop.

Developers often try to avoid the confiscatory repercussions of rent control by immediately raising rents before controls go into effect, or they convert their units to cooperative and condominium apartments. If they remain landlords many will stop investing in their properties, since there are no incentives to make improvements. This harms building maintenance and leads to deterioration and neighborhood blight. Rent control also discourages prospective landlords from investing in or creating any new rental housing.

Early in 1986, an Oakland, California, group involved in housing aid to low-income tenants, the Center for Community Change, found in a study that the middle class who are able to afford market rents have become the primary beneficiaries of controls. In its report, "Who Benefits from Rent Contol?", the group concluded that controls already in place, especially in Berkeley and Santa Monica, had decimated the landlord population and stifled new construction that would benefit low-income groups. Since 1978 Berkeley has been losing nearly 500 units of housing a year because of controls, and this comes in a community that has only about 20,000 units of rental housing but tremendous demand since renters make up 60% of the population. To further complicate housing prospects and diminish property rights, the Berkeley City Council passed a law in 1986 to force landlords to pay their tenants "relocation expenses" of $4,500 for each apartment before it can be recaptured if they intend to go out of the rental business. Few developers or prospective landlords can be expected to establish new rental units under such circumstances.

In the long run, rent controls most directly benefit middle-income tenants at the expense of both owners and the poor, destroying our housing stock and local tax base in the process, and undermining the ability of young renters to obtain the housing they need. As Wisconsin Senator William Proxmire has commented, "The problem of our cities is a housing problem," with too many Americans living in decaying, constricted, and unsafe housing, and "the major reason for all of this is rent control."

With continued rent controls have come the waves of the homeless, compounded by inept attempts by government to treat the symptoms rather than the cause. New York City's biggest landlord, and by virtue of that, its biggest slumlord, happens to be city government itself, owner of more than 40,000 apartments and 6,000 vacant buildings. An entire housing stock accumulated in city hands when property owners, many of them squeezed out by rent controls, went broke and failed to pay city taxes. It costs New York $37,000 and more a year to keep a homeless family sheltered in a welfare hotel, when the city could keep those families in private housing—much of it already in city hands—at a cost of $4,000 per family. When told that New York City was spending $37,000 a year to house each homeless family of six, President Reagan asked the obvious question: "I wonder why somebody doesn't build them a house for $37,000?" In 1986 the city had spent $72 million to house 3,300 familes in welfare hotels, and half of the funding came from the U.S. Department of Health and Human Services, through its Emergency Assistance Payments program.

In Washington, D.C., the city Department of Human Services was found to be subsidizing homeless families in two-bedroom apartments costing $3,078 a month while just a few blocks away near Robert F. Kennedy Stadium, the nonprofit Community of Hope Inc. was housing poor families for $848 a month, a fee that included job counseling, health-care services, and child care.

Renters used to rent because they preferred the experience of renting. Now a majority of those who rent are trapped, simply priced out of the housing market. From 1972 to 1981, the median price of homes nationwide went from $31,900 to $80,700, a 153% increase—far above the 115% increase in the consumer price index over the same period. In California, which has been called "the vanguard of the nation's hopes and problems," the median home price exploded from $32,400 to nearly $130,000 in the same time frame, a 300% increase. California, not coincidentally, has the strictest zoning and growth-control standards of any state in the nation.

"The official position taken by state and local authorities does not quite come to grips with the causes of the shortage of buildable land," says Dr. M. Bruce Johnson, past president of the Western Economic Association. "Instead of looking to their state and local growth control ordinances. . .local authorities continue to endorse the same system of regulations and controls that led to the current housing crisis."

A presidential Commission on Housing concluded in 1982 that controls had added as much as 25% to the final sales price of houses in numerous communities. "Unnecessary regulation of land use and buildings has increased so much over the past two decades," read the Commission report, "that Americans have begun to feel the undesirable consequences: fewer housing choices, limited production, high costs, and lower productivity in residential construction."

The supply of available land and housing in the United States, and especially in states like California, has been reduced by a range of growth-retardant measures: rent controls, restrictive zoning, water and sewer hook-up moratoriums, building codes, condominium-conversion controls—with the ultimate result of all these actions together being substantial increases in the price of buying a home. Already established homeowners directly benefit from such controls with inflated, windfall appreciations in the value of their residences, and by wielding the power of controls to exclude lower-income families, or those whose life-styles seem not to conform to local standards or prejudices.

Two University of California at Santa Barbara economists, studying the Santa Barbara housing market, discovered that during the period beginning in 1972—after a water hook-up moratorium had been imposed—through 1979, housing prices jumped by a 27% figure directly attributable to the restrictions. Development costs passed on to home buyers have been raised significantly by the processing time that results from growth controls. It took less than a year for most California subdivisions in 1970 to receive building-plan approval, but by 1975, with the addition of new layers of controls, approval took two years, and by 1980, it was three years. As indicated by Bernard J. Frieden, professor of urban studies and planning at the Massachusetts Institute of Technology, such delays increase overhead costs for developers because normal office expenses, staff salaries, and other fixed expenses have to be paid out over a longer period. The combined cost of these delays as passed on to home buyers can represent up to 21% of the total sale price of an average home.

Land has been frozen from development by requiring large minimum-lot sizes for new homes. This happened in western Marin County, California, outside San Francisco, part of which is zoned for 60-acre lots, effectively limiting home-building to the wealthy. At least a quarter of the cities across America now require new homes to be constructed on minimum-size lots of half an acre, forcing developers to build expensive single-family homes and pricing out of the market most first-home buyers, the lower middle class, and the poor. Another growth-control technique has been the setting of quotas on the number of new building permits, throwing the entire construction process further into the political arena.

Zoning, as opposed to deed-based restrictions, remains the primary tool used by residential neighborhoods in an attempt to protect their life-styles and investments by controlling real-estate decisions. The main gainers from zoning laws are relatively wealthy single-family homeowners, according to economist Carl Dahlman, and zoning losers are "poor people who have not been able to make their demands for cheaper housing effective in the marketplace, due to the artificial controls imposed on the price system as an allocator of land. In effect, zoning has become a tool for redistributing income from the poor to the rich."

Jane Jacobs, in her 1961 book *The Death and Life of Great American Cities,* demonstrated how zoning contributes to urban decay by imposing straitjackets of uniformity. In his seminal work *Land Use Without Zoning,* Professor Bernard H. Siegan of MIT studied land usage in Houston, where there is no zoning, comparing it to zoned cities of comparable size, and found economic forces to be a more efficient, equitable, and less costly control over land uses than restrictive zoning.

An absence of zoning does not mean Houston's growth and land use are uncontrolled. Private forms of controls such as deed restrictions or restrictive covenants affect most of the city and surrounding suburbs. These private restrictions usually last up to 30 years, at which point they can be renewed, and are enforceable in court. Without zoning ordinances to constrain its supply of housing, Houston has been able to more effectively satisfy the demand for new housing, while keeping down its prices relative to other parts of the country. Compare the housing situation in Houston to that of California. Observes Professor M. Bruce Johnson: "Demand for housing has soared in Houston. Unlike California, the consequence of soaring demand has been soaring supply—not soaring price." Again, the real difference appears to be land-use policy—California has layer upon layer while Houston has none.

But what, someone may ask, other than zoning can prevent a factory from moving into a residential neighborhood and polluting it with noise, odors, and ground seepage? The answer is already written into law in most areas of the country—simply by enforcing public-nuisance ordinances and encouraging citizens to file suit if the sanctity of their air, water or property is threatened or violated. In Houston this seems not to have been a problem for the additional reason that factories and industrial services choose to locate near ports, railroads, and other areas away from neighborhoods, if only because residences are as much a hindrance to factory operations as a factory would be to residential life. Numerous tools unburdened by the negative side effects of zoning are available to achieve and maintain stability in a community, whether through deed-based restrictions or through price discrimination in the property-tax structure to influence growth patterns.

In large cities the negative consequences of inflexible land-use standards, coupled with stringent rent controls, provide a barometer for measuring homelessness. A zoning ordinance mandated by New York City government in 1961 created manufacturing districts where no housing could be located, along with density restrictions that further limited new housing construction. The result was that housing renewal began a steady plummet, from 243,833 housing-unit completions during the period 1961–65, to 104,212 units during 1966–70, and down to just 42,754 units during 1981–85. With the stagnation of residential renewal came a housing-vacancy squeeze and, with it, more homelessness. In 1965 the vacancy rate for the city stood at 3.19%, but by 1970 it had been reduced to just 1.5%. Declining supply in turn raised the median gross rent from $265 a month in 1981 to $330 in 1984. Predictably these results began showing up in the numbers of homeless families seeking shelter provided by the city, from 633 shelter families in 1976 to more than 4,300 shelter families in 1986.

New York planners in 1961 believed that manufacturing employment would be preserved through zoning. But that has proved fallacious reasoning, given that in the areas zoned for manufacturing, employment declined precipitously anyway from 1 million jobs 25 years ago to 400,000 today. As Seymour Durst, head of a real estate group, noted in a letter to *The New York Times,* "A visit to the Avenue of the Americas manufacturing district below 32nd Street reveals block after block front of parking lots, which would provide excellent (now prohibited) sites for additions to the housing supply. Farther west, in the manufacturing zoned districts, tens of acres of additional parking lots and undeveloped land exist. No factories have been built for 50 years."

Gradually it is dawning on advocates of housing for the poor that zoning and rent controls constitute twin evils. Most communities in Nassau and Suffolk counties, outside New York City, restrict or forbid two unrelated families from residing in the same house. In a pastoral letter on affordable housing in 1987, Bishop John McGann of Long Island's Roman Catholic Diocese pleaded for two-family houses to be permitted in both counties by loosening up zoning ordinances. He predicted that such loosening "would make a profound contribution to the present and immediate needs of affordable housing on Long Island."

Squeezing the supply of moderate- and higher-income-level housing, such as that in Nassau and Suffolk counties, affects the lower-income housing market by disrupting the "musical chairs" effect of new housing construction. Families generally trade up in housing quality as vacancies at higher income levels occur, passing the housing stock to successively lower-income persons. In a free-market housing boom, unwanted housing will eventually accumulate in poorer neighborhoods, further lowering the price and raising the availability for all. Constipating the system at either end—through rent controls or restrictive zoning—will eventually disadvantage every income level except the exceedingly wealthy.

Increasing the availability of low-income housing means scuttling rent controls, zoning impediments, certain housing-code requirements that are insensitive to realities of the poor, and relinquishing city-owned supplies of housing and structures that could be transformed into housing. Our nationwide housing squeeze in supply and affordability, to whatever extent it has been induced or exacerbated by the actions of government, limits our individual options, our hopes for the future, and many of our basic freedoms, as it further expands the ranks of the homeless we find everywhere in our midst.

Forging Tools for Independence

Drug pushers, prostitutes, and crime ruled the streets of central west St. Louis in the early 1970s. As the middle class began fleeing to the suburbs, the blight accelerated, houses deteriorated, trash piled up, property values plummeted, and indifference spread its ugly spiritual decay. Isolated pockets of resistance sprang up among homeowners too settled or too stubborn to sell out and join the outward migration. Here and there, on streets like Waterman Avenue, a racially mixed neighborhood of single-family homes, residents grappled with a limited range of options. Either they had to fight for survival, banding together to try unconventional solutions, or they could succumb to panic and sell their homes for less than they were once worth. The choice they made was to literally buy back their neighborhood.

At the turn of the century wealthy communities on the periphery of St. Louis had built private streets to protect their elite enclaves, a concept they borrowed, like the continental design of their villas and palatial mansions, from Europe. Closing the streets to traffic assured privacy, but collective ownership also created a sense of community beyond just an elite camaraderie. The private-street associations that evolved functioned like miniature cities and vested directly in residents the ability to exercise power over their lives.

In 1974 the residents of racially integrated Waterman Avenue petitioned the city of St. Louis to transfer street ownership to their newly formed Waterman Place Association. The block's property owners established the self-assessing association, with deed covenants to extract maintenance dues, because they felt the city was no longer capable of assuring adequate crime prevention, stable property values, or the necessary sense of community for them to survive.

Once transfer was completed, residents spent $40,000 to erect a gate closing the street to through traffic. The money came from a bank loan made possible only because the deed covenants now in place guaranteed repayment. The city continued to provide police, fire, and utility services. The Waterman Place Association took care of all street maintenance, in return for which the city granted a small tax abatement. Standards were set and penalties specified in the deed covenant for property owners to maintain their homes, performing all necessary repairs, painting, and litter collection. "Overnight, we doubled our property values," claims William Bosse, a past president of the Waterman Place Association and employed as a city engineer. "We anchored that part of the city. The rest of the area was deteriorating, and we would have, too."

At least 1,000 streets have now been privatized in St. Louis and the adjoining community of University City by neighborhood associations. Researchers from the Institute for Community Design Analysis extensively studied the private-street phenomenon in St. Louis and found that, in contrast to nearby public streets and neighborhoods, residents of private streets experienced higher levels of security, stability, and comminity pride. Urban planner and architect Oscar Newman selected several predominantly black, blue-collar-populated streets for comparison and discovered that the private streets on average are up to 60% safer and 25% higher in property values than comparable public streets. Numerous positive repercussions from street privatization were evident. Neighborhood businesses on the verge of relocating elected to stay, the neighborhood property-tax base sharply rose in value, and private streets helped stem white flight to the suburbs.

Street privatization is fundamentally an economic rather than racially motivated phenomenon, if only because so many private streets are in predominantly black neighborhoods. "It's safe to say that no one on these streets cares what color the person is who moves in, so long as they agree to the principles set down in the street's charter and pay their dues," Missouri State Senator Steven Vossmeyer, a private-street resident, explained to *Reason* magazine.

Few cities other than Houston have followed the lead of St. Louis in using street privatization to help staunch the hemorrhage of urban decay. Houston has raised as much as $4.5 million a year by selling streets to their residents. Typical was the sale of Courtlandt Place, designated as a historic district, a broad, tree-lined street occupied by ten two-story houses of mostly Mediterranean and Tudor architecture. About 50 yards away is the tenderloin area of Westheimer, a busy and noisy thoroughfare of fast-food restaurants, night clubs, and massage parlors. After residents purchased their street from the city for $103,000, they closed off one end and erected several dozen large gaslight-style lamp posts to discourage loitering and intruders. Since Houston has no zoning laws, street privatization became a matter of self-preservation for the Courtlandt Place homeowners.

Private streets are an experiment in decentralization, giving power back to individual citizens to regulate their environment, endowing them with control over the quality of their lives. The newer an emerging city or suburb, the less likely it is to rely on traditional forms of government. Entire communities are forming associations to play the policy-making and service-providing roles normally associated with government. In effect they become, through a one-home/one-vote allotment of power, a hybrid species of mini-government with corporate structure and character.

In the ten-year period from 1975 through 1985, the number of community associations nationwide more than tripled from 25,000 to over 90,000. Of that number about 50,000 are condominium associations, and the rest homeowner associations. With deed covenants as mini-constitutions, these associations assess fees and regulate social order. While they rely on members to voluntarily pay their assessments on time and obey the rules, an ultimate enforcement mechanism exists in the deed-based private-contract agreements each member must sign. Members elect officers who in turn usually hire managers to handle the daily life-support needs of the community.

These shadow governments move into vacuums, evolving highly original, locally produced approaches to solving specific problems beyond the reach or resources of traditional government institutions. Says Jerry Frug, professor of local government law at Harvard University: "The privatization of government in America is the most important thing that's happening, but we're not focused on it. We haven't thought of it as government yet."

Government has been defined as having three primary attributes: It can assess fees to support itself; it legislates laws and rules, including modification of residents' behavior; and it retains the power to force compliance when it levies taxes and fees and legislates laws and rules. The primary practical difference between shadow governments and traditional local government relates to a resident's power of choice—by choosing to live under an association's guidelines and signing its contract, a person freely chooses a form of governance; traditional government rarely if ever affords such a direct consumer choice.

Critics of shadow governments worry that democracy—the process of selecting who will levy laws and taxes—diminishes under any principle that fails to adhere to a one-person, one-vote form of organization. Under the homeowner's-association form of shadow government, only property owners may vote according to how much each individual owns. Yet, it must be remembered that residing under a shadow government in no way gives residents immunity from protection from laws made by federal, state, and surrounding local governments, such as laws mandating fair and open housing.

A typical community association will directly provide or contract for garbage pickup, street sweeping and maintenance, recreation facilities, and, especially within elderly and resort communities, vanpool and other transit services. Many provide police and security patrols. In more rural areas developers often build sewage-treatment plants for operation by the association, and in New Jersey developers commonly dig wells and connect association homes to a private water-supply company.

In Montgomery County, Maryland, outside Washington, D.C., a retirement community known as Leisure World, with a population of 5,500, mostly federal government retirees, has a 28-person private police force and a private government with a $20-million-a-year budget. Protected by walls, fences, and police, and with every conceivable form of recreation from golf courses to swimming pools, Leisure World residents often repeat a saying: "If Heaven is any nicer than this, it must be one hell of a place."

Texas, Florida, and California have experienced the sharpest growth in the number of community associations, or shadow governments. The city of Houston alone has nearly 400 homeowners' groups. In the residential development of Clear Lake City, adjoining NASA's LBJ Space Center south of Houston, 30,000 residents belong to the Clear Lake Community Association, which describes itself as "a state chartered, non-profit, private corporation, formed primarily to provide municipal-type services." The association maintains three full-time firemen on its payroll, and contracts for ambulance services, trash pickup, median maintenance, and operation of its six parks and six swimming pools. Residents are assessed a maintenance fee of eight-tenths of a cent per square foot of property per year, a rate that remains unchanged from 1963, the year an Exxon subsidiary built the community and established the association. Houston rebates $6 a month per home in taxes to associations that provide for their own trash removal. This sytstem went into effect in 1977 when a homeowners' group petitioned the City Council complaining that it was unfair for association members to pay twice for sanitation services, once through association fees for private collection and a second time through taxes for undelivered city sanitation services. In 1980 Houston unveiled a formal program of tax rebates to any deed-based self-assessing association that provided its own trash collection. Within three years more than 150 associations had taken advantage of the rebate program.

Similar tax rebates have taken root in Kansas City, where 38 self-assessing associations signed up in 1983, and in Alexandria, Virginia, which provides a rebate on garbage pickup in areas considered inaccessible for city trucks. In Montgomery County, Maryland, the concept has been extended to private roadways, with a portion of county taxes intended for county roads rebated to associations that conduct their own road and street maintenance.

Some associations have mobilized in open revolt against encroachment by local government. Pennsbury Village, a 503-unit townhouse community south of Pittsburgh, became the nation's first condominium complex to declare itself an independent municipality after the nearby township of Robinson attempted to force the condos to hook into a municipal sewage system. Pennsbury already had its own sewage-treatment plant, but Robinson Township lobbied the state to withdraw the permit. Pennsbury residents discovered that it would cost them $9,000 a month in user fees and a tap-in charge of $56,000 to be hooked into an inferior sewage system compared to their own. They would be forced to pay significantly more for an inferior service they did not want or need. Residents banded together and raised $20,000 to fight and eventually win their independence in court.

What these examples signal is another trend in the privatization revolution: Neighborhood and community groups are beginning to exercise political clout to extract political concessions and to declare, by steps and degrees, independence from traditional forms of government.

As neighborhood self-sufficiency increases, consumption of public funds declines. If only 10% of the service responsibilities of local government were transferred to neighborhood organizations, a study prepared by the Sabre Foundation for the Joint Economic Committee of Congress estimated that savings to taxpayers could exceed $7 billion a year, with an additional $2.2 billion in new property-tax revenues available to local governments if federal incentives were to encourage the formation of these associations. Tax policies penalize association members by treating self-assessed fees for services as nondeductible for calculating federal and state income taxes, although local tax payments for identical municipal services are considered deductible.

While liberals and conservatives seem in agreement on the desirability of responsive, decentralized neighborhood institutions, what works in a middle- or upper-class environment may be doomed to failure in a disadvantaged community. But should we simply continue to pour tax dollars through the various sponges of government bureaucracy, hoping that enough handouts will seep into poor neighborhoods to reap, if nothing else, good will? Or can't we find some way to maximize self-help, perhaps using a homeowner-association model that develops rather than just preserves the neighborhood?

Sabre Foundation specialists, under the direction of a community-enterprise expert, Mark Frazier, conceived a development vehicle they call an enterprise association to link the deed-based advantages of homeowners' groups with the income-generating potential of neighborhood development organizations (NDOs). Typically NDOs, such as Jeff-Vander-Lou in St. Louis, operate like small corporations and provide job training, day-care services, and housing rehabilitation to low-income residents. Until a few years ago most NDOs were dependent on foundation and government funding. Now many have found a replacement source of revenue in the acquisition and development of real estate, much of it abandoned, in depressed communities.

The Union–Sarah Economic Development Corporation of St. Louis ranks as one of the pioneers of income-producing real estate projects. It purchased city-owned properties at discounted rates of $10 per square foot, now worth three times the purchase price. It has ownership interest ranging from 40% to 100% in 500 units of area housing. These holdings generate more than $400,000 a year in income, enabling Union-Sarah to be fully self-sufficient and pump its profits back into programs directly benefitting low-income residents.

Crime remains a central stumbling block to inner-city stability and development. For every 10% reduction in the crime rate, the value of an urban single-family house rises by about $3,300, and the prospects that a business will remain or relocate into an area consequently increase. Union-Sarah responded to crime by establishing a covenant-backed town-house association in one of its projects that had previously been the second-highest crime neighborhood in the area. The association mobilized its residents, chased away criminal elements, and lowered the crime rate significantly, because the deed covenants forced everyone to take an active interest in the collective condition of their properties.

As public funds dried up, neighborhood groups have reemerged in a stronger position to supplement or replace government in the provision of local services. "A lot of people see us in a time of problems while we see it really as a time of opportunity for community groups," says Stephen Glaude, executive director of the National Association of Neighborhoods, which encourages local government to contract-out to neighborhood organizations those services normally performed by government employees. By turning what were once handouts into services rendered, government contracts for local services—collecting garbage, repairing streets or managing property—give communities a sense of control over those institutions most directly affecting the quality of their lives. Service contracts to neighborhood groups provide employment within the community, narrow the gap between service provider and consumer, and allow for almost instantaneous feedback on service quality.

Since the Reagan administration depleted the outflow of direct federal aid, neighborhood groups have received contracts to maintain parks in Baltimore, carry out inspections for neighborhood health-and-safety-code violations in Kansas City, construct sidewalks in Louisville, and manage social-service centers in Florida. This explosion in entrepreneurial activity by neighborhood organizations prompted a *New York Times* reporter in 1983 to note, "Such delegations of authority, unheard of in the past, are writing the latest chapter in the fast evolving role of neighborhood groups and in the 'privatization' of local governments."

The potential for neighborhood groups to reduce the spending pressures on government could be almost without limit. At the federal level, successful neighborhood-development organizations and enterprise associations can lower expenditures for welfare, training, and employment programs, subsidized housing, and block grants for social services. Local governments in turn can benefit from reduced demand for police protection, sanitation, parks and recreation maintenance, urban renewal and transit services.

Local governments can take several relatively painless steps to accelerate the process of strengthening community groups and encouraging neighborhood self-sufficiency. Idle properties in the city inventory, especially those confiscated for nonpayment of taxes, could be transferred for development to those neighborhood groups in the inner cities that demonstrate active, self-assessing association memberships. For those associations that assume responsibility for providing municipal services, the problems of double payments could be eased by rebating taxes paid for those services based on the degree of self-sufficiency the groups achieve.

There are many extraordinary people leading ordinary lives, antibodies that could become the catalysts for fighting disease in our neighborhoods. Some of these anti-bodies are already bringing about profound changes using private-sector strategies at a time when everyone else around them seems paralyzed by despair. They are succeeding with little money or expertise, against tremendous odds, and in the process, making the American dream a bit more accessible for us all—not with reliance on government handouts from above, but with an act of will from within.

2
Making Local Government More Responsive

Living Without Federal Dependence

With the end of federal revenue sharing in 1987, hundreds of counties and small cities no longer receive any direct assistance from the federal government for the first time since enactment of the Great Society programs of the 1960s. Over the past two decades local governments had become increasingly dependent on the federal government for funding. Layers of dependence built up like sediment as Washington began to distribute revenue sharing, mass-transit operating subsidies, and a laundry list of other program funds that enabled states and municipalities to create and expand government departments and hire more full-time public employees. From 1940 to 1970, the fraction of local-government revenues derived from the federal government had escalated only gradually—from one-quarter of local funding to one-third—an increase of just 8% over 30 years. During the 1970s an explosion in dependence occurred as federal funding jumped by another 7%, leaving local government nationwide reliant on Washington for about 40% of its total revenue.

Passage of the Gramm–Rudman–Hollings budget-reduction law by Congress in 1985, mandating spending cuts to achieve a balanced federal budget, and the resulting end of more than $4 billion a year in revenue sharing, threatens this framework of intergovernmental dependence. State governors regard these developments as symptomatic of a breakdown of the federal power structure. "For decades, governors looked to the federal treasury and Congress to bail them out of their problems," wrote a reporter for *The Washington Post*. Without Washington to depend upon, state officials must themselves become innovators or else become, much as they see federal politicians, pass-the-buck artists dumping responsibility on county and city officials.

A survey by the National Association of State Budget Officers in 1987 found 19 states operating under spending ceilings of varying severity, forcing state officials to choose between voiding limits imposed by voters, or reducing state spending on programs like education and transportation. California's Gann amendment to the state constitution, limiting annual budget increases to a formula based on the rise in state population and the consumer price index, means that both state and local governments there must find alternative methods to provide public services without expanding overall revenues or expenditures. "The impending state and local revenue raising and spending limits, due to kick in in 1988, will force public employee organizations to give in to the call for privatization," predicts Tracy Morgan, a consultant to the Local Government Committee of the State Legislature.

At the municipal level officials screamed loudest that federal cutbacks will inevitably mean higher local taxes and reductions in essential services like fire and police protection. A report compiled in 1985 by the U.S. Conference of Mayors, after surveying 157 large cities, predicted that the end to federal revenue sharing will "trigger wide-ranging and disruptive cuts in the most basic public services, such as police and fire protection, and would force some local tax increases." A National League of Cities survey of 545 municipalities in 1987 produced more pessimistic if not catastrophic assumptions about the future of local finances. "We are worried about what lies ahead," said Alan Beals, executive director of the league. "Most of the quick solutions—capital cutbacks, new fees, hiring freezes and contracting out—have been wrung dry. The signals are pointing to tougher times and more stress on local government finances." San Antonio mayor Henry Cisneros, president of the League of Cities, predicted that finances in every American city will be "devastated" by federal cutbacks and result "in the end of the federal system as we know it."

We should take this doomsaying seriously only if we are convinced that local officials suffer from such rigid, doctrinaire myopia about the proper role of government as to be blind to the broad range of alternatives. What many local officials have learned to play is a version of the Washington Monument Game, long used by federal agencies to protect their budgets and levels of employment. In this game an agency like the National Park Service, faced with budget cutbacks, will threaten to close the Washington Monument on July 4th unless money is restored to its budget for employee overtime, forcing Congress to either relent on cutbacks or absorb the outrage of constituents denied access to Washington's most popular tourist attraction. Early in 1981, when the Reagan administration targeted NASA for its share of budget cuts, NASA officials warned the news media that reductions would rob NASA of the capability for detecting meteors that, once on a collision course with Earth, "would wipe out the human race."

By threatening to curtail community life-support systems, firing police and firemen rather than garbagemen and librarians, municipal officials exercise a form of extortion with the intent of terrorizing taxpayers into besieging Congress with demands for continued federal support. Their objective in provoking such pressure may not always be so much to protect essential services as to safeguard the economic interest of other "public servants." As Gordon Tullock, a Public Choice school economist, has observed, "Bureaucrats who actually administer cuts have put almost the whole of the burden on various beneficiaries of the programs rather than on civil servants. It is easier to cut off school lunches for 1,000 poor children than to fire good old Joe who sits in the next office and whom you have known for ten years."

If one examines the list of cities whose officials complain loudest about federal funding cutbacks, it becomes apparent that few of them utilize alternative-service delivery mechanisms to avoid raising taxes or cutting services. Those cities that have flirted with bankruptcy or consummated the act—such as New York, Boston, and Cleveland— allow the least privatization, while those that allow the most—such as Phoenix—are in the best financial shape.

Eighteen miles southeast of Los Angeles, on hilly terrain once dominated by olive trees, sprawls the city of La Mirada, which in Spanish means "the view." Looking from City Hall out over this suburban community of 41,000, the view held by its administrators of how a city should be organized differs dramatically from the bureaucratic vision clung to by most of City Hall U.S.A. It is a view that, as described by *Government Executive* magazine, "has elevated the idea of contract services to a municipal state of mind."

Since being incorporated in 1960, La Mirada has been a contract city relying on outside contractors to perform nearly every service normally provided elsewhere by city employees. Altogether, by 1986, the city maintained 89 contracts, including provision of police and fire services, trash collection, transit, street sweeping, public-works inspection, data processing, accounting, and operation of the local library.

The only function city administrators have not contracted or considered contracting-out is monitoring and oversight of the contracts themselves.

La Mirada employs 59 full-time employees on an annual city budget of $11 million; by contrast the neighboring city of La Habra, comparable to La Mirada in both population and budget, keeps nearly 300 permanent employees on its payroll. La Mirada spends its money on services for residents, while La Habra and other cities must spend much of their funds on employees. With about the same budget to work with, La Mirada provides a wealth of services and resources beyond the capability of its neighbors: medians throughout the city, more than 200 acres of park space, a $300,000 Dial-A-Ride transit system for the handicapped and elderly, a 1,300-seat civic theater worth $11 million, and maintenance of a general fund reserve that exceeds $5 million.

Savings from contracting come in a variety of ways. When La Mirada contracts for a service the price includes fringe benefits for contractor employees, which means that retirement does not represent an unfunded liability for the city as it would if city employees were performing the jobs. By contracting for police protection with the Los Angeles County Sheriff's Department, La Mirada avoided having to build its own police station or jail, buy its own police cars, or hire radio dispatchers. If it had to perform in-house the services it now contracts-out, La Mirada would be forced to hire additional supervisors, increasing overhead costs, creating more paperwork, and resulting in the city assuming performance liability coverage that is now the insurance reponsibility of contractors.

Nine of La Mirada's 59 employees monitor the service quality of contracts full time, but all city-employees play some monitoring role, such as reporting whether the contract for graffiti removal is being fulfilled. A parking-enforcement officer will routinely follow street sweepers to report on the quality of their work as part of his regular parking-enforcement duties. During the period 1981–86, with more than 80 contracts, only one contractor failed to perform adequately and had to be replaced.

Rather than being in the position of having to settle endless grievances, or handle in-fighting within a bureaucracy between divisions and departments over turf and responsibility, La Mirada administrators are free to plan for the future. "In most cities a lot of management time is spent in monitoring contracts with unions, in personnel matters like hiring and firing," says City Administrator Gary Sloan. "Since we are lean and paying for services directly, our time can be spent more productively."

While most cities nurture a fear verging on panic about the effect on their finances of the federal Gramm–Rudman–Hollings deficit-reduction law, La Mirada officials were unconcerned. If all federal funding to La Mirada were cut off at once—about $1 million of mostly revenue sharing, transit subsidies, and community block-grant money —city reserves are sufficient to cover the shortage for several years. Even without reserves, city administrator Sloan feels confident that a few user fees could be raised to make up the loss, and not a single city employee would have to be laid off. "Other cities are going to be killed, but we can withstand whatever will occur," Sloan declares. "A big ship takes a long time to turn, but a small ship like ours can move quickly."

La Mirada is one of 75 towns in California that call themselves contract cities, buying and selling services from each other, from the private sector, and from other government entities. The first officially designated contract city was Lakewood, California, incorporated in 1953, now with a population of about 60,000. Though Lakewood has only eight city employees, a full range of municipal services is provided using contracts monitored by the eight, who serve solely as contract officers.

Few other areas of the country have gone as far as California in perfecting the contract-city approach to administration. An exception may be Phoenix, Arizona, the ninth largest urban area in the nation, which makes use of an innovative program that produces efficiency and significant cost savings by forcing city agencies to compete with the private sector for city contracts.

For Phoenix, which has tended to treat fiscal crisis as an opportunity rather than a catastrophe, the pivotal moment came in 1978, in the wake of California's Proposition 13 and a nationwide tax revolt, when the city was faced with the dilemma of how to trim costs without curtailing services. The City Council had just approved a call for bids on contracting-out city refuse collection.

"Are you going to compare their bids with your own costs?" then-Mayor Margaret Hance asked Ron Jensen, director of the city's Department of Public Works.

"Yes, and we will bid too," Jensen replied offhandedly.

When the council meeting ended, Jensen realized that he had just committed his department to compete with private companies. Doubts immediately began to surface. Could a large municipal agency, one that might be overstaffed and overpaid, ever possibly hope to outbid efficient private companies? After conferring with his staff, Jensen decided: Why not try? Why not use the contracting-out of city services as a method of forcing city departments to be more efficient, while at the same time relieving the financial burden for taxpayers.

To keep political considerations out of the bidding process, an independent auditor examined the books of municipal departments, estimated equipment and labor costs, then prepared the city's sealed bids. The only difference between bids submitted by the city and by private contractors was that Phoenix had exempted itself from performance bonds since it would be doing business with itself.

Custodial services involving the cleaning of 63 city facilities became the first contract put out for bid after an internal city study found that department to be a resting ground for unproductive city employees. By Jensen's calculation the city would never be competitive with private custodial services, so the cleaning of municipal buildings was contracted-out without a city bid, and savings to the city are estimated at $800,000 annually. All city custodians were transferred to other positions once contracting began in July 1979. Few problems were experienced with the contractor, although affected city employees tried to manufacture grievances. As the International City Management Association would later report, in a study analyzing custodial performance: "It was found that city employees had filed fictitious complaints about thefts [by contractor employees] because they were displeased about the contract service and their loss of control over the custodial staff."

The Phoenix Public Works Department lost the bidding to private contractors on the first four contracts let for trash collections in various parts of the city. These setbacks only strengthened Jensen's resolve to make his department more productive. New management techniques drawn from the private sector along with new technology were added, and attrition and transfers reduced the number of sanitation employees by more than a third. A change in attitude came over those employees who were left. "Before contracting-out, there was little pressure on our department," Jensen reports. "We had nothing to compare our performance against. There were no real incentives. Now employees have been seized by a competitive spirit."

In 1984 Jensen's department handily outbid five contractors for garbage collection in one section of the city, beating the next lowest bidder by almost $1 million a year. During the seven-year period since contracting-out began, Phoenix placed 43 major contracts up for bid—for such services as water-meter repair, landfill operation, and bill processing—with city departments winning the bids on 15 contracts and private firms winning 28. Savings are estimated in excess of $3 million annually.

After the contracting-out program was introduced, Phoenix began measuring city-employee morale because fears were voiced that apprehension and resentment over contracting had surfaced. An employee-attitude survey, using 54 questions to gauge opinion in all city departments, instead found that the overall positive attitude about working conditions actually increased in every department, even in those that had been partially contracted-out. Concluded Leland Verheyen, Phoenix's employee-development administrator: "Contracting out has helped productivity and has had no detrimental effect on morale in this organization, and may have been a plus."

Contracting-out can improve both morale and city-agency efficiency because public employees are forced, often for the first time, to compete for the respect of taxpayers and elected officials. Such pressure forced public employees to summon more pride in their work, concedes Charles Fanniel, a ten-year Phoenix employee and secretary-treasurer of the local public employees union. "When you know the contractor is beating down City Hall's door to get your job, you know you have to become more responsive, and it improves work habits and productivity."

Phoenix's mayor, Terry Goddard, a 38-year-old Democrat elected with strong union backing, opposed contracting city services when he took office in 1984, before he had an opportunity to see the benefits. "My feelings about the process have changed since I've been in office because I saw it was creating some significant cost savings, and because it gives you a whole realm of options. Contracting-out provides a yardstick by which the city can measure itself."

Phoenix's experience clearly has implications for other cities around the nation that are under pressure to reduce costs or curtail services. In 1984 a study conducted for the U.S. Department of Housing and Urban Development examined the provision of eight public services in depth, in each case comparing 20 different municipalities in Southern California—ten that used public employees for the service and ten that contracted-out. Researchers found no real differences in service quality between the public and private systems, but the disparities in cost were staggering. Of the eight services studied, seven — asphalt paving, janitorial duties, traffic-signal maintenance, street cleaning, refuse collection, and lawn and street-tree maintenance — were at least 37% more expensive when supplied in-house by local governments. Asphalt paving, for example, cost 95% more when provided by municipal crews, while janitorial services cost 73% more. The only exception among the eight services studied was payroll preparation, where municipal and private costs were found to be about even.

This study also demolished the notion that lower private-sector salaries account for the cost differences. Of the eight services analyzed, contractors actually gave their workers an average of $106 a month more in salary and benefits than municipal agencies paid their employees. For instance, private firms in ten of the cities pay asphalt-overlay workers an average of $2,421 monthly, compared to only $1,532 monthly by the ten municipal governments. Yet it costs private firms only $42.85 per ton of asphalt laid compared to $83.99 per ton for municipal departments. What accounts for this huge disparity? Contractors achieve lower costs, the study concluded, because they make more frequent use of employee incentive programs, take responsibility for their own equipment maintenance (a role that most city departments farm out to other departments), operate with leaner organizations and fewer managers, while adopting more quickly and using more extensively advanced technology in the workplace.

Other exhaustive studies examining a range of municipal services have come to similar conclusions about the private-sector advantages. One study funded by the National Science Foundation in the 1970s compiled data on solid-waste collection in 2,200 U.S. cities, and found that municipal provisions of this service cost from 29% to 37% more than private delivery. If one factored in the amount of taxes the private delivery firms pay in the communities they service, along with pension-fund and other costs cities typically exclude from departmental operating budgets, private delivery becomes more than 60% cheaper for taxpayers than garbage collection by municipal sanitation departments.

Groups like the Urban Institute and the International City Management Association list dozens of potential benefits from the contracting of municipal services. For management officials, they gain guaranteed service-contract costs, the flexibility to shop around for the best service performers, relief from bureaucratic personnel problems, and a method to circumvent departments paralyzed by political-patronage appointments. For municipal taxpayers, savings accumulate because private providers are not restricted by political boundaries, enabling them to achieve economies of scale by serving two or more neighboring cities or counties, thus drawing upon wider resources for service delivery. Private firms cut costs by employing only those persons needed and those with specific skills; using part-time and temporary help to handle peak service periods, and paying market rather than civil-service wages; rewarding employees based on performance, and structuring performance incentives by use of profit-sharing and stock ownership; spreading equipment costs over many jobs, and renting other equipment quickly as needed; and finally, private firms are willing to take risks for innovation that municipal governments have neither the incentive nor the flexibility to pursue.

Voters tend to recognize the cost advantages inherent in contracting. In a 1978 referendum, Los Angeles County voters favored by 65% to 35% an amendment to the county charter permitting competitive bidding for county contracts. Following the referendum, union and bureaucratic opponents continued to stall and thwart implementation. Not until two years after the voters had spoken, when former State Assemblyman Michael Antonovich and two others sympathetic to contracting were elected to the County Board of Supervisors, could the referendum results be translated into policy. Even to accomplish a partial contracting-out, Antonovich and his allies had to soften bureaucratic resistance and loosen the public-employee monopoly over services. Utilizing recommendations made by the UCLA Graduate School of Management, a bureaucratic consolidation was made reducing from 58 to 48 the number of county departments, which helped eliminate one entire layer of bureaucracy that opposed contracting. In 1981 over 100 contracts were put out for bid, more than twice the number in the previous year. In the five years since Antonovich's election, 434 competitive contracts were awarded in such areas as flood and forest-fire control, insect extermination, and health care. Total estimated savings reached $21 million annually, with another $40 million saved through the consolidation maneuver itself.

Contracting-out has demonstrated its worth widely and persuasively in the Sunbelt's rapid-growth areas which are accustomed to change. But can it help revitalize the older big cities of America where a declining tax base, ingrained attitudes, and a firmly entrenched bureaucracy often combined to smother innovation? The answer could be yes, precisely because these areas struggle in fiscal and institutional straightjackets.

Southwest of New York is the graying, industrial city of Newark, New Jersey, a mostly blue-collar working population of about 300,000. Under leadership of its mayor through the late 1970s and early 1980s, Kenneth Gibson, Newark moved by steps into the ranks of contract cities to an extent unequaled by any other major northeastern metropolitan area. Between 1975 and 1985, Newark reduced its Department of Engineering from 1,052 to 600 employees as the city began to contract-out across a range of services: solid-waste collection in one-third of the city, street sweeping in two-thirds of the city, snow plowing, sewer reconstruction and cleaning, water-line connections, street resurfacing, street-sign installation.

After the first year of a contract for residential refuse collection, Newark officials compared contractor performance to that of the city sanitation service and found glaring differences. The cost of municipal collection was $47.77 per ton, about 21% higher than the private contractor, and the municipal figure did not include complete overhead expenses. Projected savings to the city over the three-year life of the contract came to $5 million. The contractor, Pet-Am, collected 5.7 tons per man-day, compared to only 3.2 tons per man-day for the city department. Higher productivity was due to Pet-Am's more efficient routes, better-conditioned, newer, larger trucks, and a younger, more energetic work force. Particularly galling to the predominantly black city officials of this predominantly black city was the discovery that the contractor employed considerably more black workers than the city sanitation department. Trained observers conducted an analysis of how clean city and contract crews left the streets and sidewalks, and found "the Pet-Am area was significantly cleaner." Into the second year of the contract, city collection costs increased by 10% while contract costs rose only 2%, a figure which includes the city's expense for monitoring the work of the contractor.

"Our public-sector employees worked harder, and equipment broke down less, when private-sector competition was presented," observed Mayor Gibson, former president of the U.S. Conference of Mayors. "Competition introduced in our city helped to keep the lid on costs, and the net result of contracting was an 18% spending reduction in our city."

The range of municipal services that can be and, in many cases, already have been successfully placed on contract is limited only by the imagination. Self-described "free-lance bureaucrat" Caleb Christian's company, Administration, Inc., which functions as private-enterprise competition to government bureaucracy, maintains contracts with two Florida municipalities — the Jupiter Inlet Commission and the Loxahatchee Council of Governments — for their total management and administrative services. Another Florida firm, Regional Research Associates, has a similar contract handling government administration for Golf View, Florida. The potential advantages of administrative contracting include lower cost, greater accountability, and higher-quality performance, observes Dr. Philip Fixler, director of the Local Government Center. "Professional management firms probably tend to give more independent recommendations to municipal policy-makers than a city manager whose job depends entirely on having to satisfy, at least some of the time, the political needs of elected officials."

Harvey M. Rose worked for the city/county of San Francisco as a budget analyst, then resigned to form his own accounting corporation. He took his old job as San Francisco budget analyst back under contract, and won several dozen other contracts with surrounding jurisdictions for budget analysis, financial accounting, audits, and other management services. Elsewhere, other city employees, sometimes prompted by the prospect of losing their jobs to contracting, have resigned as public employees to resume their positions, as contractors. In West Covina, California, the former parks and recreation supervisor contracts with the city to coordinate recreation services. And in the county of Ventura, California, a park-maintenance contract was awarded to a group of county employees who submitted a sealed bid.

A private engineering and management consulting firm operates and staffs the entire public-works department of Lafayette and Rancho Palos Verdes, two southern California communities. Roy Jorgensen Associates, Inc., the contractor, uses subcontractors to handle much of the street and other maintenance duties, reducing costs by about 25% from when the cities maintained public-works staffs. A study of the Rancho Palos Verdes contract experience, conducted for the International City Management Association, found that "productivity had increased significantly" and that "the contractor has reduced significantly the response time to citizen complaints." Only one problem seemed evident — personnel in other city agencies, particularly in the planning department, became concerned that "salaries are higher for the private firm's employees and fear that the use of contractors might be broadened to take over other activities."

Since 1983, ARA Services, Inc. has replaced the Des Moines, Iowa, city public-works department in repairing and maintaining city vehicles and the city garage. Even by retaining on its staff most city public-works employees, ARA realized a first-year saving of $388,092 from what costs would have been under the public-works department. In South Carolina the town of Conway became the first in that state to contract-out its sanitation department, signing a five-year contract in 1985 with Chambers Development Company for garbage pickup, street sweeping, commercial-waste pickup, and related services. Chambers kept most of Conway's city sanitation employees on its payroll and still saves the community more than $100,000 a year. Westchester County, New York, began contracting-out management of its 698-acre county airport to Pan American World Services in 1982, turning what had been a deficit-plagued operation into profits exceeding $1 million a year. Both Orange County, California, and Prince Georges County, Maryland, contracted-out all county data-processing activities to private for-profit firms at savings reaching into the millions of dollars annually.

Half of all U.S. municipalities will exhaust available landfill space for garbage by 1997, according to Environmental Protection Agency estimates. One solution would be the installation of huge incinerators which can reduce trash volume by 90% and indefinitely extend the life of some landfills, but they cost up to $250 million to construct in order to meet EPA and various state air-pollution guidelines, a prohibitive expense for most localities. Two northeastern states have communities that found an answer to the disposal payment problem using privatization models. Twenty towns north of Boston, with a combined population of 600,000, rely on an incinerator built and operated by Signal Environmental Systems, the first commercial garbage-to-energy plant of its kind in the nation. These towns pay Signal $22 a ton to take their garbage, compared to $100 a ton charged at the area's remaining landfills. Signal burns the trash to boil water and make steam for electricity, producing 37 megawatts of power, of which 3 megawatts power the plant and the rest is sold to a Massachusetts electric company. This resource recovery process filters out 99% of particulates flowing through the plant smokestacks before the exhaust reaches the outside air. "They took a technology and made it work," observes Bruce Maillet, director of the air quality control office of the Massachusetts Division of Environmental Quality Engineering. Ash must still be buried, but there is much less of it and, unlike raw garbage, it is less likely to contaminate underground water. In Westchester County, New York, Signal operates a similar refuse-to-energy disposal plant servicing a population of 863,000. Signal financed, designed, built, and now operates the plant, charging the county $18.72 per ton of trash under a 20-year contract signed in 1984, and sells the electricity generated to a Con Edison utility. Westchester County got an environmentally sound waste-to-energy facility for no capital outlays, and all the costs and risks associated with performance remain the responsibility of the private-sector provider.

Privatization may soon render even these incinerators obsolete. A newer technology based on an ancient Egyptian distillation process turns garbage into natural gas, resulting in power for producing electricity. A recyclable residue of carbon is all that remains of the garbage after processing. It is a far cheaper process to install than incinerators, with fewer potential environmental concerns. A company in Westchester County, New York, Waste Distillation Technology, Inc., licenses the process to private companies which then contract with municipal governments for trash disposal, splitting the revenues from the sale of electricity and recycled materials. Since Americans spend an estimated $100 billion annually on garbage disposal, such a process offers the prospect of transforming a big money loser into a revenue generator.

Once a decision has been made for government to continue providing or insuring the provision of a service, contracting-out can be utilized as a varied and flexible strategy. Government can encourage competition for the entire contract or for certain elements of it, can contract separately just for management of the service, or can break the service up into pieces among many contractors. Government can also introduce free choice of vendor arrangements in which individuals eligible for the program, such as those receiving housing or day-care subsidies, are given money or a voucher and allowed to make their own decisions about which producers of the services they will choose. Ted Kolderie of the Hubert Humphrey Institute calls these options an integral element of public-services redesign, relying "on the introduction of incentives, which are likely to work better than commands."

This myriad of examples illustrates the variety of applications in which contracting has demonstrated its worth. There are proven alternatives to the unpalatable yet all too typical choices offered voters between raising taxes and cutting services if public officials will exercise the political will. Fiscal austerity need not mean a decline in the level and quality of municipal services. Seeming disaster can be transformed into opportunity, and savings for taxpayers, if local officials will only summon the vision and resolve to break with habits of the past.

Maintaining Parks and Recreation

In a tree-shaded corner of Manhattan's Central Park, the Wollman Memorial skating rink had for 30 years been the largest outdoor rink in America, a celebrated feature of New York's wintertime recreation. In 1980 city officials closed the rink for repairs, estimating that the two-year job would cost $4.9 million. Six years and $12.9 million later, in what *The Washington Post* called "one of the most embarrassing fiascoes in municipal construction history," New York officials announced that two more years and $3 million more in tax money would be needed to finally complete the renovation.

From his office in the Trump Tower overlooking Central Park, Donald Trump, a 40-year-old billionaire developer, had observed the disaster in progress and offered Mayor Ed Koch a challenge. Renovation essentially involved nothing more than pouring a slab of concrete, said Trump, and "I can do the job myself in four months." Mayor Koch took up the challenge and offered Trump $2.9 million to rebuild the rink. The extent of shoddy workmanship and poor design shocked officials of the Trump organization. "I couldn't believe what we had here," marveled Anthony Glideman, New York's former housing commissioner who had become a Trump vice president. "The rink looked like a ransom note."

Two weeks under the four-month deadline and $750,000 under budget, Trump finished renovating the three-quarter-acre rink. He even added burnished teak railings, an exposed-brick changing room with padded benches, a 200-seat restaurant, and other amenities. How could Trump have finished in less than four months at $2.8 million what city government was unable to do in eight years at a cost exceeding $12 million? For some New Yorkers the answer was obvious. "I wasn't terribly surprised when the city bungled repairs," Joel Muhlstein, a local high-school teacher, told a reporter. "You see, I work for the city school system and they don't know what they're doing. But at least in this case they were big enough to admit they didn't know what they were doing."

While Mayor Koch admitted publicly, "There's much to be learned from the private sector," privately he was fuming. Koch called a meeting of his key advisers and told them to "find out what is in city laws that prevents us from having the freedom Trump has." Koch, as a lifetime public servant with no private-sector experience, apparently could not comprehend that changing a few city laws would not overcome the inherent inefficiency differences between public and private construction. Koch did understand that, unlike the city, Trump could tell his contractors, "Look you get this done on time and in budget or I'll never hire you again." Under New York State's Wicks Law, government must hire separate contractors for construction, plumbing, electrical and ventilation work. Only by declaring an emergency contract in the case of Wollman could the city circumvent the law and hire Trump.

Between the date of its reopening in November 1986 and closure for the season on 1 April 1987, Wollman's rink under Trump's management made an unexpected $500,000 profit, far exceeding the best years under city operation. Trump donated the profits to a collection of charities, including the Partnership for the Homeless.

Why does local government provide many of these specific recreational services that it does? Why, for instance, does the private sector provide miniature golf, while the public sector provides tennis courts? Or why does local government often provide baseball fields, while the private sector provides movie theaters? User fees in place of taxes to support recreation and park services are often resisted because it is feared they will further disadvantage the poor. But it is the middle and upper class, not the poor, who usually make use of city and county golf courses, tennis courts, and boat marinas. "Yet the poor are paying for them by means of sales taxes and property taxes paid as part of their rent," Robert Poole, founder of the Local Government Center, points out. "So by providing recreation facilities as public good, we are carrying out a large-scale transfer of income from the poor to the middle and upper middle classes. A user-pays system would be a lot more equitable."

Municipal golf courses, often big money losers, can show handsome profits once privatized. At least 150 public golf courses nationwide are privately managed: Miami Beach saved $600,000 by privatizing its courses, which had run huge deficits; Los Angeles County placed 11 of its 20 courses under private-contractor management, turning a $300,000 yearly deficit into a $2-million surplus. By offering more flexible part-time and full-time schedules for employees, and managing more than one course at a time using maintenance equipment geared to scale, private operators seem able to perform the service at less cost than government in nearly every circumstance. Additional big revenue generators are concessionaires, like the Trump restaurant at Wollman's, which function more efficiently under private ownership and management, yielding rent or tax revenues to the local government. At the municipal level, cities have also begun privatizing grounds keeping, playground maintenance, and recreational activity programs, some under contract with volunteer, civic, and neighborhood groups.

Should municipalities be in the business of providing such monumentally expensive public facilities as sports stadiums? Given the results of a study by the Chicago-based Heartland Institute, provision of sports facilities strains the public purse in a surprising variety of ways. The study compared 96 stadiums and arenas that have hosted professional football, baseball, basketball, and hockey teams, examining construction costs per seat, parking spaces, and other amenities. Construction of a private hockey or basketball arena was found to be $613 a seat cheaper than in government facilities, and private baseball and football stadiums on average $601 a seat cheaper than public ones. Parking proved to be three times more plentiful and acceptable at private stadiums. Even more revealing, of 22 franchise moves in the major leagues only two involved teams that left privately owned facilities, apparently making the point that private incentives are a far stronger mechanism for insuring a stable sports-franchise environment.

Miami Dolphins football team owner Joe Robbie raised $100 million privately and built a new football stadium in 1987 after local city and county governments refused taxpayer funding and voters had three times voted down bond issues for improvements to the Orange Bowl, a decaying structure where the Dolphins had played for nearly two decades. Robbie now seems happy he proceeded without taxpayer funding. "What I have done has caused the politicians to look to the private sector to build what are essentially public facilities," he told reporters. "We have the opportunity to show government anything they can do we can do better." Similarly in Miami, Decoma Venture, a Houston-based development group, received a contract from the Miami Sports and Exhibition Authority to design, help finance, then build and operate a $53-million multipurpose sports arena in downtown Miami on city land. The privatized facility helped convince the National Basketball Association to award the city an expansion franchise, the Miami Heat, beginning in 1988.

Preserving Public Safety Privately

Throughout the nation of Denmark the name Falck, a private company owned by a single family, appears on fire trucks, ambulances, auto wreckers, and emergency vehicles. Red-and-white Falck trucks constitute the fire brigades of over 60% of Danish municipalities, 98% of the country is served by Falck ambulance services, and roughly one out of five Danes subscribes to one or more of 21 other Falck services from animal transport to burglary security. Nearly half of all Danish drivers subscribe to Falck's emergency road service for autos, coverage which includes towing charges and transportation for stranded passengers back to their homes from anywhere in Denmark.

Falck's first rescue station opened in Copenhagen in 1906, and the company introduced the first motorized ambulance into Scandinavia in 1908. Over the next two decades private fire brigades were created, road-repair service by subscription, and municipal ambulance service by contract. As government provision of public services and the welfare state expanded rapidly during the 1950s and 1960s, Falck remained so highly regarded that few municipalities dared challenge its public-safety role. "We were there, we were doing the job, and we were doing it better and cheaper than the municipalities could do it," explains a Falck company official.

Surveys have indicated that the vast majority of Danes oppose a state takeover of services provided by Falck, the world's largest private fire-protection company, making it a private monopoly both tolerated and admired. Every Falck employee receives training and experience in a variety of skills — ambulance service, first aid, rescue, firefighting. The result is a versatile work force with a high level of job satisfaction combined with a public-spiritedness exceeding what one might normally expect of private-sector employees. Falck regularly turns a profit, and does so without sacrificing the quality or responsiveness of its services.

More than any other of the community life-support systems, public-safety issues generate citizen concerns borne directly of dependence. People need the reassurance that comes from believing that police will diligently thwart crime and apprehend criminals, firemen will quickly smother flames, and ambulances will materialize when medical emergencies do. Such concerns and needs are so obsessive, so endemic to human nature, that cost considerations in the provision of these services have largely been rendered immune to challenge. There exists as well a perception, fostered largely by public-employee unions, that it is somehow unseemly and exploitative for people to profit from the crime, fire, and health emergencies of society. That arms contractors profit from defense, smoke-detector manufacturers from fire prevention, or physicians from illness, generally gets overlooked when such an argument is made. Much of the fervor for protecting the status quo of government's public-safety institutions is nothing more than reflexive habit, comforting tradition, and the jealousies of vested self-interest.

For the small northern Ohio town of Reminderville, population less than 2,500, an announced price increase for the police services offered by the county sheriff's department would have severely strained town finances. The county wanted to charge $180,000 a year for the use of a single patrol car, yet could only guarantee a response time of 45 minutes. So in 1981 the town signed a contract for police services with a local firm, Corporate Security, Inc., which provided two patrol cars, seven officers, and a six-minute response time for only $90,000 annually. The contract lasted nearly two years until town council members decided, even though they were pleased with the service, to set up their own police department, apparently for the sake of prestige.

In Elk Grove, Illinois, officials calculated that it would cost taxpayers $2 million to establish a city fire department and another $1 million a year to operate it. At that point in 1979 a 38-year-old entrepreneur, Gary S. Jensen, using money raised from bank loans and private investors, founded American Emergency Services Corporation, bought four fire trucks, and signed a fire-protection contract with the city for $549,000 annually.

When the city of Santa Barbara, California, studied the cost of providing its own emergency medical services, it discovered that taxpayers would save $730,000 a year if a private firm was hired. Paramedic services were contracted-out and now the firm is entirely self-supporting, requiring no city taxpayer subsidies. Similarly, when Newton, Massachusetts, switched from public operation of its ambulance service to a private firm, savings accumulated at the rate of $500,000 annually.

Almost imperceptibly over the past decade a dramatic realignment has been occurring in the public-safety field, as the private sector responds to public needs by supplementing and even partially replacing roles traditionally played, at least in this century, by government. During this most recent decade the number of private security guards doubled to 1.1 million, twice the number of police maintained by all levels of government, indicating the public desire for more responsive and less costly forms of security protection. For some people privately run police forces may smack of vigilante justice. Yet for those who have need of such services, private security can mean the difference between affordable protection or no protection, between a prosperous life or simply surviving.

The concept of private police protection at the neighborhood-patrol level has found successful applications both in this country and abroad. In Switzerland the private police firm of Securitas maintains contracts with more than 30 Swiss townships and villages, patrolling and performing crime-prevention duties like any other city police force, but at a level the Swiss Association of Towns describes as more affordable and efficient. The American city of San Francisco pioneered private police patrols in residential neighborhoods, for nearly 90 years keeping a system of private law enforcement in place to augment its city police force.

San Francisco's 1899 city charter created a network of Patrol Special officers vested with all the authority of city police. Each section of the city was divided into beats which were then sold to the highest bidders. Over the years these patrol beats have been sold like taxi licenses to new owners, regulated by the city Police Commission, which also oversees the training of private police. A beat sells for up to $100,000 depending on whether it is primarily a residential or commercial location, and according to how many accounts the Patrol Special, who acts as his own salesman, is able to secure. By 1985, San Francisco had 135 Patrol Specials walking 65 clearly defined beats. They have the power to arrest lawbreakers, write traffic and parking tickets, and, like their city police counterparts, they are trained and authorized to carry and use firearms. They wear uniforms almost indistinguishable from those of regular San Francisco police officers, except that their private badges have six points instead of seven, and their buttons are silver, not gold.

"We are employed by the public, just like municipal police officers, and we perform the same kinds of jobs for the public that municipal police officers do. The only difference is that the public pays us directly—not through their taxes," says John Candido, who has walked a commercial district beat between Polk Street and Van Ness Avenue for more than 20 years. It is a system that offers numerous distinct advantages. Clients are able to choose specific police-protection services tailored to their needs, without further burdening the public system, which must provide an inflexible, uniform level of service. And, as the *San Francisco Examiner* has observed, "Patrol Specials also have the advantage of being able to devote more time investigating a customer's complaint than the city's regular officers."

A study funded by the National Institute of Justice concluded that 80% of work undertaken by municipal police departments is unrelated to crime. At least half of an officer's time is spent waiting for something to happen, providing some evidence that police manpower is inefficiently allocated, argues economist Bruce L. Benson, a professor at Florida State University and expert on criminal justice. "Police officials claim that this time is spent in preventative patrolling, but systematic observation of actual police has discovered that such time is largely occupied by activities like conversation with other officers, personal errands, and sitting in parked cars on side streets."

Much police time is wasted responding to burglar alarms, about 94% of which are false. At a cost of about $25 per response, cities spend untold thousands of dollars on false alarms because it is a service generally provided free. "If this service were handled by private alarm firms, individual property owners could be billed for each false alarm," speculated Theodore Gage in *Reason* magazine. "This would encourage people to be more responsible about setting and maintaining their systems, and would put the burden of payment squarely on those who benefit from the service, and would free up police departments from the response and administrative hassle."

Burglar-alarm response is one of several dozen police-support functions that could be contracted-out to the private sector, if not privatized entirely. Certain jurisdictions have already taken such steps. San Diego contracts-out park-patrol services in the Balboa Park area. Wallace Security of Portland, Oregon, acts as contractor for police, fire, and ambulance dispatching services in Woodland, Maine. Two huge private security firms, Wackenhut and Pinkerton's, provide security for some federal courts, and parking-lot enforcement services for municipal and state governments. Firms in Maryland and California contract with state and local prisons for prisoner-transport services.

The Institute for Local Self Government in California, in an extensive study of alternatives to traditional public-safety delivery systems, found a wide range of police functions conducive to contracting. "The use of private security firm personnel to perform selected police functions can offer significant cost savings over the use of sworn personnel...by contracting, the city would be relieved of interviewing, selecting, training and supervising civilian employees." The study made a cost comparison of using private security personnel in place of sworn police officers in selected patrol and investigative functions, finding the savings to be well in excess of 50%.

One of the keys to such cost savings is the willingness of private firms to use more cost-effective equipment, vehicles, and staffing. For instance, a 1977 report by the Police Foundation concluded that it is usually "more efficient, safer, and at least as effective for the police to staff patrol cars with one officer" instead of the standard two, a proposal police unions resist. Municipal police continue using large cars for patrol duties when studies have demonstrated 33%-a-year savings in operating costs if compact cars were driven. *Motor Trend* magazine conducted an experiment for the Los Angeles Sheriff's Department, applying seven evaluations of car performance including patrol performance needs, and found that compact cars rated the most cost-effective, followed by two intermediate-sized cars, with the standard large police vehicles last.

Perhaps the greatest waste of police resources comes in the enforcement of laws against victimless crimes. Robert W. Poole of the Local Government Center analyzed the expenses of a California county and discovered that 33% of its $19-million annual criminal-justice budget was spent arresting and prosecuting prostitutes, drug users, bingo players, and dirty book and movie sellers — limited funds which could have been used for apprehending the perpetrators of crimes against people and property. Victimless crimes are the easiest cases to process, points out Professor Bruce Benson, and they provide benefits to government police institutions by producing "the desired statistical data that indicates production in order to justify large budgets."

Fire-service privatization emerged in America directly through private-sector fire departments, and indirectly but no less importantly with the shifting of emphasis from fire suppression to fire prevention. Standards imposed by insurance companies and government accelerated a trend already underway to use fire-detection and alarm systems, sprinkler and other suppression devices, and building inspections, to reduce the need for fire-smothering services. Reduced demand means less need for manpower and, in theory, a decline in budgets for government fire departments. Here institutional self-interest rears its predictable head.

"For the firefighters there are few rewards for reducing fire runs and thus, department costs," writes Ted Kolderie, senior fellow at the Hubert Humphrey Institute in charge of its Public Services Redesign Project. "In this age of intense competition for public dollars, unused budgeted amounts are seen as allocation mistakes and are quickly dispersed elsewhere. Organizations that seek to prolong their lives will not work to undermine their usefulness."

Kolderie argues convincingly that the prospects for any change within public fire departments that would lead to efficiency and cost-effectiveness are inherently limited. Fire departments don't receive rewards for reducing costs. "In fact, at times departments have received more resources when they did *not* accomplish their mission: a high incidence of fires is traditionally thought to reflect the need for additional money." With government as a monopoly provider determining the level of service to be available, few incentives exist for altering institutional behavior in a way that would benefit consumers and taxpayers.

In 1979 the five commissioners of Hall County, Georgia, about 50 miles north of Atlanta, decided to abolish the county fire department because they had concluded that its 86 firemen were slothful, wasteful, and beyond hope of changing. The fire chief, said one county commissioner, "delighted in wasting tax dollars on fancy equipment that he saw on the 'Emergency' television program," and other fire officials used county money to buy $300 dress uniforms that they never wore to fires. The commissioners voted to hire a private firefighting company, Rural-Metro of Scottsdale, Arizona, which promised to save the county in excess of $100,000 a year.

County firefighters organized a petition drive and recalled the five commissioners from office. But when the five new commissioners came to power, they too, concluded that the county fire department had outlived its usefulness, and voted to continue contracting-out. Wackenhut Services, Inc., of Florida eventually won the contract for fire and emergency ambulance services, hired most of the county fire-fighters, and began saving local taxpayers nearly $200,000 annually. Since the contractor took over, the national Insurance Service Office rating for commercial and residential properties in the county has improved from a nine, before contracting, to a quite respectable six rating.

Grants Pass, Oregon, population 15,080, has had its unincorporated surrounding area served since 1979 by the private Valley Fire company, a partly employee-owned firm. Valley Fire built a fire station for the area and supplies equipment and 48 firefighters to cover the more than 6,000 subscribers to its service. Grants Pass city manager J. Michael Casey estimates it would cost the city $125,000 a year to provide similar coverage and $250,000 to build a fire station.

Firefighters in Fort Walton Beach, Florida, placed a referendum on the November 1986 city election ballot to require that police and fire departments be manned by city employees, a tactic to deny city officials the chance of ever considering privatization. The private firefighting service, Rural-Metro, based in Arizona, which had offered to provide the city with services comparable to city firefighters for $300,000 a year less, countered with a radio, television, and newspaper advertising blitz pointing out the advantages of private service. On election day voters rejected the public-employee attempt to sabotage consideration of private-sector remedies, 3,634 to 2,547, leaving the city council free to decide the issue on its own merits.

Specialized fire-protection services at U.S. airports are already being provided for cities in at least five states, the largest being Kansas City International Airport, Sioux City Airport, Iowa, and Reno, Nevada. Kansas City cut costs by about 55% when it contracted with Wackenhut Corp. for firefighting and rescue services.

Scottsdale, Arizona, has been served since 1948 by Rural-Metro, an employee-owned company founded by Lou Witzeman. The company builds many of its own fire trucks, redesigns other pieces of equipment, and has introduced numerous innovations to the fire-suppression field, including a firefighting robot and a radio-controlled device to open or close fire hydrants. Cost savings for Scottsdale have been significant. By National Fire Protection Association calculations, the average annual per-capita firefighting cost for cities between 50,000 and 100,000 in population amounts to $50, versus only $25.68 in Scottsdale. Another study conducted by the Institute for Local Self Government compared the dollar loss from fires, the response times, and firefighter salary range for Scottsdale and the nearby towns of Tempe, Mesa, and Glendale, all of which have public fire departments and similar residential patterns. Scottsdale had the fastest fire-response times and the lowest dollar loss per capita from fires—$5.74

compared to $7.60 on average for the others—but higher salaries, paying on average $1,500 more for a starting firefighter and $1,100 more for a captain. "Although no problems have occurred in the direct act of fighting fires," concluded an analysis of Rural-Metro by the International City Management Association, public fire departments near areas served by Rural-Metro have engaged in negative media campaigns in an attempt "to undermine the credibility of the private contractor in the eyes of the public."

Over the years Rural-Metro has expanded into a $25-million business, with 400 vehicles, 1,600 employees, and contracts with 16 communities in five states providing ambulance, forestry-fire suppression, and fire-code enforcement, as well as the standard fire-protection services. It became the founding member of the Private Sector Fire Association, headquartered in Boulder, Colorado, representing most of the nation's 17 private fire companies that were serving, as of 1985, at least 36 locations.

Private fire companies have proven as efficient, yet more cost effective, than their public-sector counterparts for many reasons. Municipal departments tend to staff, and firefighter unions tend to insist on staffing, based on full-time peak levels of service, while private firms use a less costly but just as effective mix of paid reservists and full-time firemen. Public-sector firemen generally resist cross-training for other jobs, while private firms utilize their employees in diverse and creative ways, whether it is rebuilding equipment or engaging in fire-prevention programs. Private firms have cost incentives to innovate by designing or adding new equipment, or experimenting with novel organization structures.

Most Americans pay twice for fire-protection and emergency medical services. For fire protection, they contribute through taxes for local fire departments to protect their property, and again through fire and property insurance. For emergency services, they pay through private medical insurance, which covers two-thirds of the population and reimburses for paramedical service, and through taxes used for municipal paramedical functions. Los Angeles Fire Commissioner Jerry Field admitted to the Local Government Center: "We're saving insurance companies money at the expense of the city," by providing a municipal ambulance and paramedical service financed by taxes. Two forms of privatization can help alleviate these inequities. The first is a voluntary, pre-paid subscription service such as that provided by Acadian Ambulance, serving the rural area around Lafayette,

Louisiana. Like the payment structure of health maintenance organizations, protection could be provided by lumping the service and the insurance into one payment to one provider. Ted Kolderie has proposed a similar insurance program for homeowners, linking fire insurance and fire-suppression services. A second approach is to provide, within either a system of user fees or a free-market entry for providers, a voucher program for the poor, insuring that those below the poverty level will not be denied fire or paramedical attention in an environment where services are priced at their proper value.

To answer the charge made by public-employee unions that strikes would cripple private fire services, one has only to examine the record. No contracted-out fire department has ever experienced a strike, while unionized municipal fire departments record an average of 12 debilitating strikes a year. Some have been violent and ugly, as when firefighters in Dayton, Ohio, ignored a state law banning public-employee strikes and walked off the job, then stood by and watched as 22 fires were fought by city residents. They finally ended the strike on receiving both amnesty and hefty pay increases.

When Philip Fixler attempted to explain the advantages of contracting ambulance services to members of the Santa Ana (California) City Council, dozens of city firefighters in the audience jeered and heckled him. Dr. Fixler, director of the Local Government Center, then based in Santa Barbara, testified that turning over emergency medical services to a contractor would result in an upgrading of service and $1 million a year in savings. But the firefighters performing that service—who were then earning $48,300 a year in salary and benefits, yet had a low productivity rate—did not want to hear the facts. Threats of physical abuse forced city police to escort Dr. Fixler out of the council chambers and to his car. Even though no layoffs had been proposed or anticipated under contracting, these firefighters saw private-sector competition as symbolic of government officials making public employees scapegoats for local budgetary problems. They felt as if they were being punished without reason and their job performance were being condemned without trial.

Steps can be taken to insure that municipal employees are spared the entire burden of change from contracting. Phoenix maintains a policy of requiring contractors to offer jobs to any city employees displaced by contracting, and in other communities public employees have actually formed their own companies to win bids for their old jobs as contractors. Whatever alternative is chosen, public officials must not lose sight of the reasons for contracting. The purpose of local government is not to provide jobs; it is to deliver services to people. Making municipal services more efficient with contracting is not anti-labor, it is pro-consumer and pro-taxpayer.

Protecting the Public from Abuses

For the city of Poughkeepsie in New York State's Hudson Valley, population about 40,000, contracting-out its parking authority for the central business district promised savings of $311,453 a year. Operational problems under public-employee administration had worsened until the parking facilities were an embarrassment and an object of public ridicule. Beginning in January 1980, Poughkeepsie contracted for parking administration with a New York City firm, one of four that made contract offers. Shortly thereafter, the local Civil Service Employees Union, part of the American Federation of State, County, and Municipal Employees (AFSCME), filed suit to force the return of the parking facilities to municipal management. The case eventually reached the State Appellate Division, New York's highest court, which ruled that the city had circumvented the "Taylor Law," a union-inspired state provision requiring municipalities to negotiate for all city services through the local public-employee union. In January 1985, the city was forced to fire its private contractor and reinstate all city parking employees with full retroactive pay and benefits for the almost five years of contracting, effectively erasing hundreds of thousands of dollars in savings for local taxpayers.

In Philadelphia a public watchdog group, the Committee of 70, released an investigative report in June 1986, contending that the city's ability to deliver public services had been sabotaged over the years by a succession of mayors who gave away too much administrative control to the public-employee unions. A few weeks after issuance of the report, two of the city's municipal unions called a strike of 13,000 city workers to protest the city's right to hire private contractors to perform some city services, a right which Mayor Wilson Goode insisted was necessary, especially in sanitation work, because contracting was cheaper and more efficient. Over the next two weeks a mountain of uncollected, rotting, stinking garbage accumulated on city streets, as city workers stayed off the job until a local judge issued a back-to-work order and found one of the unions in contempt of court.

To preserve union jobs and the stranglehold public-employee unions exercise over many states and municipalities, particularly in the northeastern United States, the one-million-member AFSCME has resorted to every conceivable tactic, legal and not, to "protect" the public from all manifestations of privatization. On television AFSCME airs commercials showing diligent, smiling public employees working government jobs, a portrayal ending with the AFSCME brand name and leaving the impression that it is the union, not government, which is responsible for whatever good deeds are performed in service to society. About 5,000 government officials around the nation received a book in the mail, *Passing the Bucks,* which AFSCME bankrolled to make the strongest possible case against contracting-out of government services.

As an example of contractor unreliability, the book cites a 1980 case when the District of Columbia city government suffered financial loss from its five-year, $20-million contract with a private firm to haul sludge. "The firm had never performed such work before and had no plant, trucks or barges for hauling and treating sludge," AFSCME declared. "The firm was even unable to get the necessary permits. When the contractor defaulted, the city was forced to spend an additional $6 million to hire a new contractor." The obvious question from this example is why did the District of Columbia contract in the first place with a company having no track record, no facilities, and no prospect of performing the job? The answer has less to do with the drawbacks of contracting-out than with the competence of District of Columbia public employees.

Another case cited of poor contractor performance occurred in New York City, where a street-light repair monopoly had been granted one firm without true competition and in a process that actively discouraged other firms from bidding. The city failed to enforce provisions of the contract and, predictably, the result was a decline of service. AFSCME draws the obvious logical conclusion from this case study: "Companies which are awarded noncompetitive contracts or which attain a monopoly over a municipal service have little incentive to be accountable." That the same can be said of government monopolies the book conveniently chooses to ignore.

Elsewhere the book proclaims that noncompetitive trash-collection contracts are a way of life in many jurisdictions. From this revelation the books author draws a strange connection—this serves as "a sharp rebuttal to contracting advocates who contend the impersonal forces of free marketplace will enable private firms to provide services at a lower cost than work done by public employees." Again, when government steps in and awards noncompetitive contracts for a service, it is restraint of trade, perhaps even monopoly coercion, that is being exercised, not the competitive forces of a free market. Of several dozen examples of alleged contractor problems used in the book, nearly every one concerns contracts awarded without competition. The entire AFSCME book amounts to an attack on government's failure to insure competitive bidding, a sentiment the advocates of privatization would undoubtedly share.

As with any system subject to the vagaries of human nature, the contracting-out of public services harbors its share of potential pitfalls and problems. It goes without saying that proper steps must be taken and care exercised to protect the public from possible abuses of a contractor system, as well as to insure that terms of the contract are fulfilled. Questions relating to the theory, practice, and promise of privatization can now be posed with reasonable certainty that the track record of performance is sufficiently developed to supply us with credible if not persuasive answers.

Does privatization automatically produce corruption?

Some critics fear that to expand profits, contracting companies will routinely resort to bribery, kickbacks, payoffs, bid-rigging, and other questionable practices. In this context the real question should be whether the solution to ending corruption is the elimination of contracting. To make that leap in faith is to assume that public employees do not engage in bribery, kickbacks, and questionable practices. Obviously, corruption among public servants has been with us since even before the introduction of contracting. In certain states public employees must still pay a percentage of their salaries to the political party in power, amounting to extortion for their jobs. Corruption in contracting is possible only if public officials and public employees are themselves unscrupulous. "It is important to remember," concluded a study by the International City Management Association, "that thousands of service contracts are written every year about which no question of fraud and corruption is raised." As Robert Poole of the Local Government Center notes, his data base contains 28,000 specific instances of local-government contracting in the United States, yet of that number AFSCME has been able to publicize only a few dozen cases of alleged corruption.

A widely publicized case of corruption occurred in New York City during 1986, when it was revealed that bribery and extortion were epidemic in the awarding of contracts for the processing of parking tickets. Such corruption occurred because the most basic tenet of contracting-out — a competitive-bid process — was flagrantly violated. New York's Parking Violations Bureau granted its contracts without competitive bidding, which facilitated the use of payoffs to gain city business. "Probably the best insurance against fraud and corruption is simply open, competitive bidding and tightly written, closely monitored contracts," reported the International City Management Association.

It is the role of public employees to insure that taxpayers receive fair value for their tax dollars. "The private sector could not waste money on useless contracts if the contracts were not given by bureaucrats in the first place," wrote two economists, James T. Bennett and Manuel H. Johnson, in their book *Better Government at Half the Price.* "It's the job of the public sector to enforce standards; when these standards are not enforced and corruption occurs, the public sector has not been doing its job of monitoring properly."

Other relatively easy-to-implement steps can be taken to help prevent corruption in contracting. Local governments should have conflict-of-interest and campaign-finance laws, so the public can be made aware of whether public officials have connections to contractors. Post-employment prohibitions, closing the "revolving door" between government and industry, might help to insure a higher degree of integrity in the process. Whatever steps are deemed necessary and taken, as Harrison J. Goldin, New York City comptroller, has observed, "The price of effective privatization is eternal vigilence — on reflection, the price is not high."

Will contracting reduce government accountability?

Under contracting, government cannot make a private firm responsive to public needs, it is sometimes alleged, making the services less accountable and flexible. To that contention La Mirada city manager Gary Sloan, who oversees 89 contracts, argues instead that contracting has given him considerably wider administrative latitude than he would expect from a public work force. "If a citizen complains about trash removal, can I fire that public employee responsible for poor service? No. Can I discipline him? Well, possibly if I have enough evidence. How long does that take? Well, he has due process, appeal rights, and grievance procedures and you're talking months. With our current contractors I can call up and say get this employee out of the city tomorrow, and he's gone. That's pretty responsive to the public. But in other cities it won't happen because unions like AFSCME guarantee employee rights at the expense of the public and taxpayers." Government contracts can be written to assess contractors monetary penalties for citizen complaints, or award bonuses if no complaints are recorded. Using a public-employee work force offers far fewer incentives to make the service accountable to consumers. As the International City Management Association reports in its publication *Rethinking Local Services*: "The responsiveness of most contractors will depend on the contract and the interest of the government in enforcing its terms. In addition, a contractor that wants to continue to do business with the local government will have a very strong incentive to be responsive to the government and its citizens."

Can private firms really provide services at less cost?

Public-employee groups often claim that a contractor's expenses for providing services should be greater than in-house public provision because companies must make a profit and pay taxes, while government must bear the cost of contract administration. The sentiment seems to echo what one southern official self-assuredly told Dr. E. S. Savas: "Government can always do a service cheaper than the private sector because it doesn't have to make a profit!" Economic ignorance about the inherent structural differences between public and private provision of services seems widespread. The clearest yardstick by which to judge which system is more cost effective comes when city agencies are forced to reveal every cost, both direct and indirect, for providing service. Private firms must factor into their bids *all* costs, including insurance, overhead, fringe benefits, and local, state, and federal taxes, if they are to remain financially viable. In computing government cost, public agencies routinely exclude expenses, usually found on the books of sister agencies in the same municipality, for equipment maintenance, capital expenditures, fuel, utilities, debt retirement, and fringe-benefit costs, especially retirement. This form of misleading accounting thrives on stating service prices as if they were costs. Finally, the cost of contract administration and oversight would

be more than outweighed by the expense of having to hire administrators to manage public employees were the service to remain
in-house.

"One of the things I liked about contracting-out was that it forced
me to look at what it really cost to do a service," Bill Donaldson, the
former city manager of Cincinnati and now director of the Philadelphia Zoo, explained to a *New York Times* reporter. "In theory,
government ought to be more efficient than the private sector because
it doesn't pay taxes or pay for the use of capital. Unfortunately, because there is no competition, most governments don't have the
faintest idea what it costs to do anything. Also, if a private contractor
falls down on the job, the contract eventually runs out. But civil service never runs out."

Must government maintain certain services as monopolies?

College and high-school economics texts sometimes describe the free
market as superior to government at supplying consumer goods, but
then elsewhere will assert that only government can efficiently provide
roads, justice, education, and an array of other "public" or "collective"
goods. Public goods have been defined as services that benefit everyone, whether or not everyone pays—an example being the bug-
spraying programs government initiates to fight disease. These activities, it is argued, must be performed and financed by government
monopolies to overcome the "free rider" problem, a situation in which
some beneficiaries would not otherwise pay, or would not pay enough
for the service.

On closer scrutiny this public-goods argument breaks down. As
Steven Hanke, an economist formerly with the President's Council of
Economic Advisers, has written, "We must realize that goods can be
either supplied by public or private enterprises, and that this supply
can either be financed by public user fees and taxes or private charges.
Once the distinction between private versus public supply and finance
is made, it should be clear that...the supply of the products with
either of these characteristics can be private, while their finance is
public. For example, schools could be private and insect abatement
could be supplied by private firms by using public finances to compensate the private suppliers."

What distinguishes public from private assets is that since public
ones are not "owned," they cannot be effectively transferred. Only by

moving to another political jurisdiction can taxpayers change their portfolio of public assets, unless they have the power to change the way in which local public enterprises are managed and operated. But the public dare not directly challenge a government monopoly, for it has, so Walter Bainbridge discovered, the power of law behind it. After a series of snowstorms paralyzed Fairfax County, Virginia, a suburb of Washington, D.C., in early 1987, Bainbridge wanted to make three streets near his home passable so he and his neighbors could get to work. He attached a snowplow to his pickup truck and did what the county was unable to do. Police soon appeared at his door and charged him with "unauthorized work on a public highway without a valid permit," carrying a fine but, fortunately, no lengthy jail term. "If I hadn't plowed the street out," Bainbridge observed philosophically, "the police wouldn't have been able to get to my house."

"Natural monopoly" conditions are said to exist in many service areas, such as the municipal provision of electricity or water. Government usually assumes the role of provider in these areas, ostensibly, to protect the public from price gouging and to prevent wasteful duplication of effort. Even if one accepts this as necessary, benefits of competition can still be achieved if government will establish franchises — exclusive service provisions — and require bid competitions by private firms to operate them. In this way some of the benefits of competitive enterprise could be obtained by placing government in the role of bargaining agent for customers in the franchise area.

Electric utilities constitute one of these alleged natural-monopoly situations because, as many people reason, you cannot have two power providers in the same area with separate lines, poles, and meters, competing for customers. Yet, even that has been proven false. In 23 American cities, unknown to most Americans and even many economists, separate utilities already compete for the same customers, utilizing separate meters, lines, and generating facilities. Studies by economist W. J. Primeaux, Jr. found average electric rates to be 33% lower in those cities with competing utilities — such as Lubbock, Texas — compared to other cities served by a monopoly.

It is taxpayers and consumers who are victimized by the dead hand of monopolies, yet it is elected officials and "public servants," who, in theory, should be protecting their constituents from exploitation, that all too often become the staunchest of monopoly protectors. "What's fascinated me is the attitude in the public sector that if you contract for something it must mean you somehow failed," marvels

Verne Johnson, developer of social-responsibility programs for General Mills and other corporations. "The political parties are in no disagreement about the need to force private monopolies into real competition. What some of us are arguing for is just to apply the same strategy to public monopolies."

Generally a direct effect of monopolies, be they public or private, is that they raise costs to the consumer. George Watson, writing in the British publication *The Journal of Economic Affairs,* makes the case that the monopoly status of government should logically be opposed most strenuously by the poorest of its constituents. "Monopoly favors the rich (on the whole)—just as competition (on the whole) favors the poor. And a nationalized industry or service, or a public corporation, is a state monopoly. In other words, you would expect the rich to want it and the poor to be opposed." Monopolies favor the rich by keeping prices high, which only they can afford, and by creating impenetrable bureaucracies, which only they have the legal means to navigate.

"The inefficiency of municipal services is not due to bad commissioners, mayors, managers, workers, unions, or labor leaders," wrote E. S. Savas, a former New York City official. "It is a natural consequence of a monopoly system."

Can we defuse the public pension timebomb?

More than 6,000 state and local retirement programs cover about 12 million public employees. Most contributions to these plans are paid by taxpayers rather than by the employees themselves, thus creating huge unfunded pension liabilities for states, counties, and cities. Just the unfunded liability of state pension debt has been estimated at more than $1,000 for every American adult. New York City has a liability exceeding $3 billion, and Boston has a pension liability in excess of $1.2 billion, representing nearly $2,000 in pension debt for every citizen of that city. The fastest-growing pension liability of all public-employee job categories has to do with public-school teachers, whose unfunded pension costs exceed $400 billion.

Since most of these public pension systems are funded pay-as-you-go, taxpayers of today are paying the retirement of public employees who served previous generations of taxpayers, while today's public employees are being promised that future generations of taxpayers will finance their retirement. A huge and growing public liability has been created by the chasm between pension promises and pension assets.

We are simply deferring the true, current costs of government.

While government may continue to push its pension costs into the future for our sons and daughters to pay, a few bills are already coming due, with disastrous consequences. In the small city of Hamtramck, Michigan, outside Detroit, population less than 30,000, about 99% of city-property-tax income had to be channeled into police and fire pension funds to keep them solvent. One Hamtramck city employee was reported by *Time* magazine to have contributed only $35 to his retirement plan during the years he worked, yet was able to collect $250,000 in benefits after retiring.

During wage negotiations public officials have traditionally agreed to settlements with public-employee unions that keep current wage increases relatively low in return for generous increases in pension benefits, thus passing costs down from current taxpayers and voters to future taxpayers. Politicians acting as agents on behalf of taxpayers have struck deals with the employees of taxpayers to obscure the real costs of public services by deferring payments to support those services. It is as if a family had in its employ an accountant and a housekeeper, and left the terms of employment to be handled between them; the accountant promises the housekeeper that she can keep her job without threat of dismissal for as long as she wants, and she can retire at near full salary, indexed to the cost of living, with the entire future cost to be shouldered by the unborn children of her employer. As one can see, somewhere along the way accountability is lost or sacrificed.

Deferring pension costs cannot go on indefinitely. The size of our nation's public work force is already staggering. As of October 1985, employment by federal, state, and local governments had grown by 254,000 over the previous year, to a total of 16,690,000. Of that number, 4.4 million were employed by school districts, 3.9 million by state governments, 5.2 million by local governments, and 3 million in federal civilian jobs. Adding in military personnel, 5.2 million were federal employees. On top of the pension liabilities of state and local governments, our federal pension debt exceeds $5,000 in liability for every American adult. Unlike most private-sector pension plans, the two main federal pension systems fully index their retirement benefits to the cost of living. Since federal employees can retire after 20 years of service under the military system to receive a pension of half their base pay, and after 30 years under the civilian system with benefits of over half their final-year salary, the sum total of retirement benefits for the remainder of a federal employee's life often exceeds the sum total of salary made during his or her entire working career. Given the sheer numbers of current public employees—most of them future retirees—the future funding problems associated with keeping the pension systems solvent combine to boggle the imagination.

A serious question of generational equity is raised by these forms of public borrowing that constitute our public pension systems. "The financial integrity of pension funds depends crucially on the tolerance of taxpayers who are at present largely unaware of the magnitude of the pension burdens they face," writes Professor Herman B. Leonard, a Harvard University political scientist and author of *Checks Unbalanced: The Quiet Side of Public Spending.* "Current taxpayers are borrowing a part of the services of current public servants, promising to pay them later in the form of pensions. The large and, of late, rapidly increasing liability for retirement payments in recognition of current services is cheerfully handed on to future taxpayers, only some of whom were also the beneficiaries of the services when they were rendered."

Unlike governments, which defer pension obligations like a chain letter that will eventually overwhelm future generations, private contractors must factor employee-pension costs into their bids for contracts, which enable taxpayers to realize immediately the full costs of public services. Defusing the public-pension time bomb means we must quickly embrace one of two options: either we begin paying the true current costs of government now, which means each and every living American, man, woman, and child, must pay at least $10,000 in new taxes almost immediately, or we begin to whittle down through attrition the size of our public-sector work force by privatizing and contracting-out many of the functions now performed by public employees. For any society with a conscience about the legacy it intends to leave its children, the reasonable choice between the two would seem self-evident.

Should contracting-out be the last or first stage?

A cautionary note that contracting-out may not take the privatization process far enough, or insure continued benefits for consumers, is added by John Blundell, vice president of the Institute for Humane Studies at George Mason University. Along with other free-market purists, Blundell draws sharp distinctions between competitive-bid processes in contracting and the ongoing competitive or market process. To win bid competitions firms must "serve primarily the wants of elected officials and bureaucrats," whereas to win the competitive process in open markets a firm must directly serve the wants and needs of consumers. "The company that can win in a political process is not necessarily the one that would win in a market process," Blundell cautions. Monopoly contracts, whether performed by government agencies or private firms, fail to generate market information about the applicability of appropriate technology and management to perform the contract with the best possible results.

While Blundell concedes that contracting-out usually produces appreciably better service and at lower cost than what government agencies provide, he argues that this is no guarantee of creating either smaller government or lower taxes. Savings resulting from contracting-out could go back into other new or expanded government services, rather than reduce the burden of taxpayers. As contracts proliferate, so do the number of contractors and the range of "needs" they will identify for additional contracting, advancing persuasive arguments to government bodies to create new services or additional delivery mechanisms for already existing ones.

As contractors increase in number, they may form associations and lobby to restrict competition for contracts, couching their arguments in terms of protecting the public from the repercussions of "unsafe or unfair" competition. There is equally the prospect that contractors will mobilize to lobby for increased government spending in program areas served by contracts. As more business occurs with government agencies, relationships develop in which corporations "see their interests joined to those of the political bureaucracy," in the words of economists Allan Meltzer and Scott Richard. The result might be a growing number of businessmen who would find reason "to support the expansion of agencies and programs relevant to their interests."

Ted Kolderie of the Hubert Humphrey Institute thinks that opponents of government spending and program expansion should want to resist the widespread use of contracting-out. "But if you favor larger public programs, you may find it highly strategic to expand the use of this form of privatization." The reason is that commercial firms have already proven their skill at persuading the public to acquiesce in the spending of tax dollars. Companies like the Bath Iron Works, and the various aerospace firms, generate an enormous advertising volume in campaigns encouraged by the Defense Department to convince us we need a larger Navy, or new, more sophisticated aircraft built by these companies.

By using defense contractors as a political-coalition model, advocates of increased social-welfare spending might see the contracting-out of social-service provision to be tactically advantageous. "Advocates of expanding social welfare services in the United States need to rethink their stance toward privatization," wrote Marc Bendick, an economist and welfare-state proponent, in a paper for the National Conference on Social Welfare. "They should become fervent and creative advocates for its implementation throughout the social service delivery system." He reasons that by mobilizing social-service providers into political coalitions similar to those in the defense industry, the political momentum for privatization could be co-opted and "a flourishing and politically secure social welfare system" could emerge in this country that "would constitute a distinctly American welfare state."

Spending opponents can frustrate this clever strategy for program expansion in several ways. Tax limits and program-spending ceilings could be imposed on federal, state, or municipal governments, perhaps modeled after the State of Delaware's constitutional amendments that restrict appropriations to 98% of projected revenues and require that any new tax or tax increases be passed by a three-fifths vote of each house in the legislature. Still more important, simply by the act of "loadshedding," removing government entirely from the service area, a vital link in the symbiotic relationship between private firms and the government bureaucracy can be severed. And if government retains a role as facilitator rather than provider, vouchers targeted to program recipients—such as in mass transit and housing—can be used to dilute potential lobbying coalitions of private providers, spreading the tax dollars so diffusely that no one provider or group of firms can benefit inordinately from political activity to increase spending on the program.

Under service shedding, or "loadshedding," the government turns over its service functions to a profit or nonprofit firm and no longer provides continuing financing support through taxes, although it might continue its regulatory role. Local government has at its disposal numerous incentives with which to lure the private sector to assume delivery of services previously provided by government. These incentives include tax rebates, tax credits, tax reductions,deregulation, and the turnover or use of government equipment or assets used in providing the service.

John Blundell complains that too many privatization proponents are concerned with making government efficient at what it does than with questioning whether the government should even continue the broad range of services it provides and pays for out of our taxes. He cites the case of Pima County, Tucson, Arizona, where for many years two contractors held exclusive rights to the collection of refuse. When this policy was abandoned in favor of an open, free market, 15 private firms went into competition and prices to consumers were cut in half from what the monopoly holders had charged. His point is that making the monopoly situation there more efficient was not the answer— getting government out of the business of maintaining the monopoly was, and consumers benefited.

On 1 January 1979 the city of Wichita, Kansas, phased out its trash-collection department to allow the free market to meet public needs. More than 70 companies began competing for residential trash-hauling, resulting in lower costs and higher efficiency. In most cities private firms perform commercial collection within city limits and at least some residential collection outside city boundaries, meaning an entire array of potential suppliers is available should a city decide to shed its provider role and withdraw.

Though it is certainly possible that any economies produced by higher efficiency and lowered costs of provision under contracting-out may be canceled by the pressures created for increased public spending, other reasons can be found to support contracting-out as a transition from government monopolies. Greater freedom of choice, argues Princeton University sociologist Paul Starr, leading to a more just distribution of benefits, "is unquestionably the single strongest point in the case for privatization." Uniformity in pricing, service quality, and range of services available ranks as one of the greatest inherent weaknesses in public-service programs. Privatization as a concept, says Starr, can help us to "rediscover the rationale of the public services we need and to remind us, if we had forgotten, that the public-private mix ought not to be considered settled for all time."

3
Streamlining Our Justice System

Buying Judges Honestly

As the community caseworker listened in horror, the Japanese man described how he intended to settle a long-festering dispute with his next-door neighbors, a Canadian family. "I intend to kill them," the man, a mechanic for a major airline, calmly explained. "I will shoot them one by one." For months, each day when he would come home to sleep just before noon after working the night shift, the young children next door would be up playing in their backyard, making unbearable noise, and throwing toys over onto his property. He was constantly being disturbed, and the lack of sleep threatened to drive him mad. He repeatedly called the police to complain, brandishing the toys as evidence, yet no one had been willing or able to stop the distractions. Now he wanted to take justice into his own hands. It was just the sort of initially petty dispute flirting with tragedy that the American court system was ill-prepared to handle.

After coaxing by the caseworker both the Japanese man and his neighbors agreed to try an innovative approach to neighborhood dispute resolution in San Francisco called Community Boards. In a stormy, emotional appearance before a trained three-member volunteer panel, both sides aired their grievances. "The reason I hate you is that you don't respect me," the Japanese man exclaimed at one point. The Canadian couple stared at him, flabbergasted and uncomprehending. He had never even approached them directly about the problem before, always calling the police first, and now he was accusing them of disrespect. As the session continued the man's position became clearer. "I have children and they don't behave this way toward you, because mine are disciplined. But your kids by the way they behave show me disrespect, which means you know what they're doing and you show me disrespect." It quickly became apparent to the community panel that the root cause of the problem was simply a cultural misunderstanding about how each culture raised its children. A Vietnamese man on the panel, in America for only eight years, told the Canadian family how important the concept of "face" was to the Asian culture. He then asked the Japanese man how his neighbors could demonstrate respect for him. From that point on, a resolution to the dispute rapidly emerged from the dialogue. The session had gone from "I'm going to do something really violent" to "I'm prepared to be your friend." For the first time the Japanese man was introduced to his former tormentors, the small children. He returned their toys, and in a further gesture of goodwill and newfound understanding, he took the children on a tour of the airport where he worked. This approach to dispute resolution, excluding lawyers and public courts from the process, draws the accolades of law-enforcement officials like San Francisco's sheriff, Michael Hennessey: "Community Boards handle important neighborhood problems better than the courts or the traditional justice system could ever hope to do!"

After the American Can Company filed a $61-million breach-of-contract suit against Wisconsin Electric Power, litigation dragged on and the trial was expected to last 75 days. Rather than proceed with the costly and time-consuming public court process, both companies agreed to retain the Washington, D.C., for-profit firm of EnDispute, an alternative dispute-resolution service, to hold a private mini-trial. It lasted three days in 1983 and resulted in a mutually satisfactory settlement. Similarly when Telecredit sued TRW Inc., charging patent infringement, both sides agreed to a two-day private hearing that produced a compromise and jointly saved the companies $1 million in legal fees. Avoiding the public court system afforded these companies the advantages of speedy resolution, confidentiality, and simpler, more flexible procedures. Additionally, as TRW's vice president for law James McKee explained: "Lots of times the outside lawyers are the obstacle to quick settlement, because it's in their self-interest to keep the litigation going so they get higher fees. With a mini-trial or the other private hearings we've tried, you can get control back into the hands of the businessmen, who will bring some common sense to bear."

A quiet revolution against our government court system is underway within the commercial law field no less than among average citizens frustrated by the costs and delays of obtaining justice. Because America has become the most litigious society on earth, justice is literally being rationed by court congestion. It takes four years to get to trial in Los Angeles Superior Court, up to five years in New York City. At any one time the number of civil cases pending in federal district courts totals nearly 250,000, more than double the caseload of a decade earlier.

To relieve these time and cost pressures on government and the public, an entire new industry has evolved over the past decade known as alternative dispute resolution. The array of approaches to privately dispensed justice encompasses profit and nonprofit private court systems, arbitration and mediation services, a "rent-a-judge" system in California, and neighborhood-based Community Boards. Each approach, in its own way and on its own terms, serves to advance a movement whose expanding influence and acceptance erodes the government monopoly over the dispensing of justice.

A resource directory published by the National Institute for Dispute Resolution, a clearinghouse in Washington, D.C., lists 100 organizations involved in the arbitration or mediation of problems, such as consumer complaints, land-use disputes, and inter-family squabbles, that might otherwise end up in public courts. The oldest of these groups, the American Arbitration Association, nearly doubled its caseload in a decade to 40,000 in 1984, arbitrating everything from commercial disputes to labor-management disagreements. A nonprofit group, The Center for Public Resources based in New York City, has assembled a judicial panel of prominent legal figures, including former U.S. Attorney General Griffin Bell, to hold private mini-trials for clients. In 1975 only one dozen community dispute programs existed nationwide; by 1985 at least 182 had sprung up to resolve landlord-tenant, merchant-consumer, and other categories of neighborhood disputes. And in one two-year period, four major for-profit private court systems were established using current and retired public court judges to try cases, creating what amounts to a nationwide private judicial system.

A Phoenix municipal court judge, Alice Wright founded Civicourt, Inc., as a private for-profit court in 1983, after reaching her limits of frustration with the delays and expense of public court justice in Arizona. She offers clients a choice of 24 former Superior Court judges to handle civil lawsuits ranging from contractual disputes to insurance claims and disputed issues in divorces. All parties must agree on a presiding judge and to abide by the judge's decision, although they retain the right to appeal. Hearings are held at the convenience of both parties, at night or on weekends. Three hours of time before a judge costs each party $250, and $75 an hour after that, but most trials are speedily concluded. Former Superior Court Judge Gerald Strick describes the first Civicourt case he presided over: "I remember the witnesses. They got on, they told their story and got off. There was no rancor. There was no jury. So nobody had to perform wonderful tricks. No Perry Mason bull. Everybody knew why they were there." Alice Wright predicts that within a decade most civil cases in America will be heard in this manner. "It is the answer to the problems currently faced in our courts—overcrowding, delays, skyrocketing expense, inconvenience. It is especially exciting to me to use the free enterprise system, the backbone of this country, to solve problems that would otherwise be handled by expanding government and raising taxes."

Since two economists joined with an attorney to establish the private trial service Judicate in Philadelphia in 1983, offering its stock over the counter as a publicly held corporation, several hundred cases have been heard and settled. Most of the suits involved personal-injury disputes or corporate contracts, but one concerned a student raped on her college campus who successfully used Judicate to obtain compensatory damages from the college and a security firm. The entire menu provided by government court systems, with pretrial conferences, discovery process, settlement conferences, and so forth, is maintained by Judicate using rules of procedure streamlined from versions of existing state and federal rules. Awards made under Judicate proceedings are enforceable under the Uniform Arbitration Act. "This will be a court without a backlog and without juries," says attorney Alan Epstein, one of the founders. "Since we're a profit-making venture, we have to deliver fair and prompt justice or we won't survive." Judges doing substandard work won't be selected for other cases, while those suspected of unethical behavior will be brought before a disciplinary board in the judge's home state. An attorney with experience handling cases before Judicate's judges offered this assessment to *The Pennsylvania Lawyer*: "It's easier, it's quicker and it's an efficient way to dispose of a case. I'd like to see a public courtroom run as well as this. If you go with private enterprise, they treat you better."

Judicial privatization in this country got a boost from the emergence of California's "rent-a-judge" system in 1976, the year two attorneys resurrected an obscure section of state law that had lain dormant for 100 years allowing the use of privately retained judges. California then became the only state to institutionalize a private judiciary, perhaps because it was and remains the largest and most overburdened civil court system in America. In Los Angeles, where 40,000 civil cases were awaiting disposition in 1986, litigants can bypass the congested public system by choosing among 58 retired judges available for day, night, or weekend trials. Satisfaction among those who use the system is widespread. A San Francisco man suing his insurance company avoided a two-year trial delay in the public system by hiring a retired judge who decided the case within two weeks, saving both sides considerable money, time, and heartache. Car-maker John Z. DeLorean used the private judiciary for his celebrated divorce from wife Christina, and comedian Johnny Carson used the system in his contract dispute with NBC television and in his own divorce case. One of the rent-a-judges is Joseph Wapner, star of the "People's Court" television program, who handles over the airways small claims with damages of less than $1,500.

Critics of judicial privatization fear it will create an "apartheid legal system" with two classes of justice, one for the rich who can afford private judgments, and another for the rest of society condemned to remain within the sluggish public system. Attorneys for Public Advocates, a San Francisco public-interest law firm, once sought unsuccessfully to outlaw the private courts, contending that a private judiciary would "ease the pressure to reform a legal system that clearly needs reforming." They attacked the secrecy of private proceedings, but leveled the brunt of their argument on the need to force everyone to endure the costs and delays of government justice. "So long as there are two systems of justice one of which is readily accessible, relatively inexpensive, and efficient, the major defects in our legal system as a whole will remain uncorrected, thereby making permanent exclusion of the majority of middle class and poor persons from effective use of our legal system."

The logic used in these arguments appears flawed in several respects. If the private system is "relatively inexpensive," why do they describe it as justice for the rich, rather than a justice of easy access that is of potential benefit to everyone? And if we continue to force everyone into the already congested public court system, are we not even more effectively excluding others in our society who can't afford the longer delays that a higher caseload will bring? *The New York Times* weighed in with an editorial denouncing private courts as a corrosive that will loosen the ties that bind a democratic society. According to the *Times* in its 1980 denunciation, judicial privatization is designed only for the convenience of "a growing patrician elite." Yet the same argument can be made against public courts. Congestion and delay cost money, both for litigants who must pay attorney fees and suffer from the withholding of justice, and for taxpayers who must extend expanding levels of support to the public court system. Only the rich can afford the unending legal fees and inconveniences produced by overcrowded public-court dockets. The real threat to ties binding democracy comes from a lack of access to justice, from interminable delays in addressing grievances, and from the expense and inequities of finding and keeping adequate legal representation. For those reasons one can expect much of the opposition to judicial privatization to spring from elements of the law profession whose livelihoods depend on stretching out the legal process and rendering it as complex as possible.

In most public-court cases one side wants speedy resolution and the other side does not. This phenomenon alone, contends Gary Pruitt in a paper for the *Journal of Contemporary Studies*, "will leave numerous affluent litigants in the public court system. So there is no reason to assume that the rent-a-judge procedure will eliminate political pressures for civil court reform." The legal cost-saving resulting from the speed and flexibility of private courts ultimately benefits all of society. Points out Philip Fixler, Jr., of the Local Government Center, "Savings can be channeled into more productive uses—such as company expansion, job creation, or additional disposable income."

Alternative dispute resolution offers the poor and the middle class an affordable and accessible range of legal options. Law Professor Ray Shonholtz founded the Community Boards as a non-profit corporation in 1977, intending to democratize the law by giving neighborhoods the tools to resolve their own disputes without resort to the public courts. His San Francisco group handles nearly 1,000 disputes a year citywide, drawing on a pool of 1,700 specially trained volunteers who act as mediators, and relying entirely upon private foundations and corporations for funding. About 10% of cases involve landlord-tenant disputes, with the remainder spanning the spectrum of neighborhood problems from ordinary noise complaints to juvenile-gang problems and ethnic conflicts. Similar Community Boards have been formed in other cities—Rochester, New York, for example. Legal activist Jake Warner, whose Nolo Press publishes self-help legal guides, predicts that Community Boards and the community dispute-resolution movement will continue their rapid spread because people are "just being fed up with the notion that we pay lots of judges lots of salaries and maintain lots of courthouses, and have almost no access to them. And when we do, our chance of getting a good result within a reasonable time and a reasonable price is poor."

As of 1986 nearly 200 cities and towns in America had established community dispute-resolution centers to handle minor civil and criminal cases, according to a report by the National Institute of Justice, a research agency of the U.S. Justice Department. "Unresolved family violence, landlord-tenant disputes or contract problems can create enormous emotional conflict and destroy a person's sense of living in a just world," said James Stewart, director of the institute. "The greatest benefit these centers have afforded us are not in easing system stress but in ameliorating sources of potentially damaging conflicts and personal retribution." These private mediation centers receive referrals from local criminal and civil courts, and typical disputes range from consumer complaints to petty crime and assault.

"It's private justice," admits Edith Primm, director of Atlanta's nonprofit organization, the Neighborhood Justice Center, which has 120 trained mediators to hear cases. "But is society better served by a judge and a trial, or by having two parties resolve their differences?" For her the answer is an obvious yes to the first alternative, since the cost and overcrowding of local courts, with attendent delays and uncertainties of trial, make flexible private alternatives all the more attractive. With more time to probe the root causes of problems, mediators can extract agreements in the form of "consent decrees" which more readily satisfy all parties involved in the dispute.

After Superior Court in Orange County, California, became one of the nation's first to adopt a courtwide mediation program in the late 1970s, court officials were quickly able to reduce their civil-suit backlog from 13,000 cases pending trial to less than 5,900 cases. "My prediction," adds Larry Ray, director of the American Bar Association's Standing Committee on Dispute Resolution, "is that most big city courthouses during the next couple of years will integrate these alternatives into their court processes so that for almost any dispute you will be able to come to the courthouse and there will be some options to going to trial."

Surveys indicate that public courts are held in low esteem by most Americans because of chronic problems with delays in case processing, high costs, assembly-line procedures that are too complex, and general dissatisfaction with the quality of justice. Most public courts are located in inconvenient areas with inflexible operating hours. Community dispute programs offer accessibility—hearings can be scheduled on evenings and weekends—and simplicity, with filing procedures kept simple to avoid confusion and intimidation. Because representation by attorneys is unnecessary, costs are greatly reduced.

Community-level, private justice can empower individuals with a sense of internal control over their lives, and in the process can systematically reduce the level of tension within a community by uncovering any underlying problems or misunderstandings based on ethnic, racial, or cultural differences. Mediation also improves compliance over traditional public-court approaches. A study of private mediation of minor civil cases in Maine found that 70% of defendants in mediated cases paid their settlements in full, while only 34% of defendants in comparable public court cases complied fully with the judgments. A study by the National Institute of Justice discovered that only 47% of persons involved in public-court proceedings expressed satisfaction with the verdicts rendered, compared to an 87% satisfaction level in cases handled by neighborhood resolution centers.

"If we want to reduce violence and have a more cohesive society, and we want to communicate the sense of fairness and justice that binds us together as a people, we must make justice available," says Stewart, an Oakland police offical before he became director of the National Institute of Justice. "Justice delayed is justice denied. We've asked too much out of our justice system. Alternative dispute resolution programs are a market response to the government's monopoly on courts. This is part of the end of the era that government can solve all of our problems."

Advocates for the poor in Washington, D.C., have embraced local dispute-resolution programs because they often help poor clients whose wealthier adversaries, once in the court system, might seek indefinite delays to force the poorer party to end the litigation. But equal access to justice for the poor may ultimately require a generous dose of that aspect of privatization known as voluntarism. With federal funding of legal services for the poor being scaled back, perhaps the goal of the federal Legal Services Corporation could be, in the words of Ripon Society theorist Frederic R. Kellogg, "to induce the legal profession, not the government, to institute an acceptable standard of equal access to justice, and to make that standard a reality." Kellogg notes that, with an annual income of $32.5 billion in 1983, the American legal profession is the wealthiest profession in the world. "If the profession can meet this public need principally through decentralized, private-sector and voluntaristic means, the justice which is dispensed will be more effective justice, and it will not require the increased amounts of federal disbursement which fully adequate delivery of services would inevitably demand." He recommends federally enacted incentives for law firms and attorneys to provide more free legal work for the disadvantaged. More programs can be developed following the Florida Bar Association model, in which funds held in trust by lawyers are invested in common NOW accounts, with the $1 million and more a year in interest donated toward legal services for the poor.

Perhaps the greatest barriers to providing low-cost legal services to the poor are laws protecting the legal profession, argues W. Clark Durant III, chairman of the federal Legal Services Corporation. He proposed that statutes making it a crime for lay people to practice law be repealed to encourage entrepreneurs who are not attorneys, but who have some legal training or background, to offer legal help for the poor. All 50 states prohibit the unauthorized practice of law, restrictions which Durant believes "are really barriers to competition, not guardians of competence. The legal cartel's heaviest burden falls on the poor. They are denied choices and access. They are denied advocates and opportunities."

In rebuttal to critics and skeptics of privatized justice, Robert W. Poole, Jr., offers this perspective: "Privatization is nothing more than the application of businesslike ideas to the process of dispensing justice—ideas like specialization, division of labor, and payment for services rendered. Those ideas may threaten a society based on egalitarianism—where everyone is forced to be treated the same, regardless of differing needs and wants. But they do not threaten a society of diversity, a society of choice—in short, a free society."

Building Prisons for Profit

Faced wth a court-ordered ceiling on the city's jail population, Washington, D.C., officials in early 1986 bused 55 inmates to a privately owned prison in Cowansville, Pennsylvania, north of Pittsburgh. The misdemeanants spent less than a week in the minimum-security facility before a Pennsylvania state judge ruled that they must be returned because the District of Columbia had failed to consult with Pennsylvania state government authorities about using that state's private jail. As the inmates were rounded up for their trip back to the nation's capital, a *Washington Post* reporter on hand for the occasion detected their considerable resentment at leaving the Center's simple brick and concrete facility. They bombarded the reporter with praise for the center's roomy cells, relaxed atmosphere, catered food, and friendly guards. "It's like the difference between night and day," said a 51-year-old inmate, Luther McGee, comparing the private prison with the D.C. Jail. "It doesn't feel like a prison. They give you a feeling of being a human being." By contrast, the D.C. Jail was "built for chimpanzees," remarked an inmate serving time for driving with a suspended license. "The guards (at D.C. Jail) ignore everything you say; the place is filthy. It was a nightmare for me."

Pennsylvania officials apparently could not summon the inmates' enthusiasm for privately owned and operated prisons. The private facility, known as the 268 Center, had been conceived when nearby Pittsburgh fell under a court-ordered population ceiling at its jail and a facility was desperately needed to handle those inmates and the overflow from neighboring county prisons. Other private prisons were being developed by the firm of Buckingham Security, founded by a former state prison warden. These developments galvanized opposition from the union representing state and local prison guards, which feared the competition of private prisons, and from the American Civil Liberties Union, which said it had to protect inmates from mistreatment by "profit-hungry" private operators. Pennsylvania Governor Richard Thornburgh responded to this political pressure by asking for the court order to return the D.C. inmates, as members of the state legislature improvised legislation placing a moratorium on the operation of private prisons.

The dilemma confronting our nation's capital city underscores the severity of the crisis that grips penal systems nationwide. Prisons in 33 states and the District of Columbia have been under federal court orders to reduce overcrowding that resulted when the state and federal inmate population increased by 66% between 1980 and 1986 to 546,000 prisoners. In Pennsylvania 14,000 prisoners were squeezed into facilities designed for only 9,500. A frustrated Tennessee county sheriff with an overcrowded jail handcuffed inmates to a state prison fence all day in 1985 to protest a federal court order barring their entry into the already burgeoning state system. Too little space in Texas state prisons produced the highest prison homicide rate in the nation. (It was three times safer to drive on Texas highways than to spend time in a Texas jail.) Violent prison uprisings caused by cramped conditions struck prison systems in nearly every state. A maximum-security prison in Pittsburgh erupted, and 24 inmates, three prison guards, and two firefighters lay injured. Four buildings burned to the ground and 32 persons were injured at the District of Columbia's Lorton Reformatory, and three died and several dozen were injured at a West Virginia penitentiary.

An obvious remedy would have been the construction of more prisons and larger jails. But most states require public referendums to authorize the issuance of bonds to finance prison and jail construction, and during the 1980s an average of 60% of jail-bond proposals were being defeated at the polls in local elections. These defeats combined with constitutional and statutory debt limitations on general obligation bonds forced governments to attempt new approaches. Some responded to overcrowding by prematurely releasing convicts. The result was more crime in the streets. Of 613 prisoners given early release from New York City jails in 1983, two thirds either were arrested for new offenses or skipped bail. Public outrage rapidly eliminated early releases as a safety valve to relieve overcrowding.

The corrections field suffers from outmoded facilities, rising staff costs, a failure to innovate, increasing judicial demands for improved services, and public clamorings to incarcerate even more prisoners less expensively. From these pressures sprang both budgetary and credibility gaps, as prison officials scrambled to quell inmate revolts that erupt each time overcrowding reaches unbearable limits. To relieve these pressures, the private sector, beginning in earnest about 1983, began its rush into the prison construction and operation business, with at least ten companies forming or expanding to meet the demand.

Our nation's first prison built in 1814 turned out to be the most expensive building constructed in this country through the early 19th century. Little innovation has occurred in prison construction since that time. "Because of the character of the way that these buildings are built, there is little or no incentive to introduce new technologies or new ideas, because there is no profit motive on either the part of the user or the builders to consider an alternative," testified Paul Silver, a New York architect and prison designer, in a 1984 appearance before the Joint Economic Committee of Congress. Privatization of prison construction, according to Commissioner Thomas Coughlin of the

New York State Department of Correctional Services, is "the quickest, most inexpensive way to go."

In 1983 the Immigration and Naturalization Service desperately needed a new detention facility in the Houston area to hold illegal aliens before their deportation. Lacking the funding for either construction or the staffing for a new facility, INS solicited bids from the private sector. Corrections Corporation of America (CCA), based in Nashville and backed by some of the same investors involved in the Hospital Corporation of America, won the contract. In April 1984, at a cost of $8.2 million for land and construction, the first wholly designed, built, owned, and operated private detention facility in the world opened — just six months after construction started. Had INS undertaken the construction project, it could have taken two years and cost in excess of $12 million.

Private prison builders lower their costs by 15% and more below government costs by using more innovative design and building techniques, taking advantage of flexibility, and avoiding the time-consuming multi-agency contract-negotiation processes that characterize government construction. If during construction a government agency needs to make a design alteration, approval must be sought in the form of a change order that must drift back through various layers of bureaucracy, a procedure that could take months. Private firms can make such changes immediately. During construction of the Houston detention facility, CCA discovered the need for a significant modification in door design. A decision was made and the new doors were ordered within six hours, whereas it could have taken six weeks or more in government. Private firms avoid overdesigning buildings, while government prison designs often suffer from too much complicated detail and not enough attention to functional needs (meaning more guards than necessary must be retained). Private builders also select only the most appropriate materials to meet goals of economy, construction speed, and security.

"The checks and balances within government have become too paralytic and self-defeating," contends Gay E. Vick, CCA vice-president for design and construction, who formerly designed prison facilities for the State of Virginia. "Government tends to lose sight of the goals. There are so many regulations the goal becomes how to get around the regulation rather than solving the problem. Industry lets the process be flexible in pursuit of the goals, while government is overly concerned with the process."

A creative form of prison financing and construction has been pioneered by the National Corrections Corporation, based in Denver, a firm involved in jail construction since 1972. If a county needs a new jail, this company builds it, then leases it back to the county. Such a maneuver enables local governments to circumvent voters who otherwise would have to vote on bonds or taxes for new jail construction. In 1985 the company expanded into prison operations, signing a contract to build, staff, and operate a jail for three New Mexico counties.

Prison privatization began as an evolutionary process when support services like medical care and food provision were contracted-out several decades ago, followed later by contracting for pre-release, work release, and halfway-house facility operation. Residential supervision of juvenile offenders became the next phase of contracting, followed by federal contracting for the construction and operation of illegal-alien detention centers.

Privatization of health-care services within jails was pioneered by Prison Health Services, which brings nurses, physicians, dentists, and psychiatrists into prisons for a monthly fee of $90 to $120 per inmate. Only 160 of the nation's 4,000 jails are accredited by the National Commission on Correctional Healthcare, and of that number 31 have health services provided by Prison Health Services, which guarantees its clients accreditation within one year. In 1979 the Federal Bureau of Prisons began contracting-out all of its 300 halfway houses to nonprofit agencies and private for-profit companies; today at least 1,500 privately operated facilities for juveniles can be found nationwide; and since 1983, the Immigration and Naturalization Service has turned over a dozen illegal-alien detention centers to private operators. Concludes a study by the National Institute of Justice, "Private sector participation in correctional programs is thus a relatively old idea which is being expanded and reconsidered in the face of modern needs and pressures."

California in 1986 became the first state to allow its corrections department to contract-out for care of state prisoners, utilizing two firms—Eclectic Communications, Inc., and Management and Training Corporation of Ogden, Utah—to operate return-to-custody facilities for parole violators. Eclectic, of Ventura, California, operates 13 corrections facilities under contract with state and federal agencies, including work-furlough, alien-detention, halfway-house, and parole-violator centers. In 1983 it opened the first privatized federal juvenile detention facility in America at Hidden Valley Ranch in La Honda, California.

RCA Service Company operates a state youth facility, the Weaversville Intensive Care Unit near Allentown, Pennsylvania, that is regarded as an unqualified success story. Twenty-two youths ranging in age from 14 to 18 who have committed serious crimes are housed there, supervised by a nonunion staff of 28. The youths receive instruction from public-school teachers and counseling from an RCA Service psychologist. Robert H. Sobolevitch, director of the Pennsylvania Welfare Department's Bureau of Group Residential Services, estimates that costs at Weaversville run significantly less than spending at comparable state-run institutions, and he is lavish in his praise of how RCA handles serious offenders. "It's the best example of a private operation. This is going to be the national model. It's the hottest thing in corrections."

Behavioral Systems Southwest of Pomona, California, founded by a former San Quentin prison guard, Ted Nissen, after he became disenchanted with traditional approaches to corrections, operates 12 halfway houses and detention facilities which brought in revenues to the company approaching $5 million in 1985. Six of the minimum-security prisons are designed to prepare inmates for their reentry into society. States and the federal government are charged from $14 to $33.50 a day per detainee, about 15% less than what the State of California spends on similar programs. Nissen believes that a perverse set of bureaucratic incentives have helped overfill our prisons and raise the costs to society. "Status in the corrections system goes to those who run the highest-security prisons, so the whole system promotes classifying people as more of a security risk than they are. We have built a prison industry based on concrete walls, guard towers, and the overclassification of inmates." Nissen and other reformers among the private prison entrepreneurs see this bureaucratic inertia as an opportunity to build better, cheaper prisons, while developing programs behind bars that prepare inmates for survival outside prison.

Under private ownership and operation of adult facilities, operating costs can be reduced with no decline in the quality of life for inmates. Private firms say they generally can obtain a better price on supplies using bulk-purchasing arrangements, require fewer employees because of innovative building designs, and function with greater flexibility than can government.

CCA operates its Houston detention facility for nearly $3 per detainee a day cheaper than the Immigration Service can run its own facilities, a gap which is probably much higher because CCA includes construction costs in its per diem while the INS uses only operating costs in figuring its rates. Lowering costs need not come at the expense of corrections employees. The starting salaries of guards at the Houston center are higher than those of personnel performing comparable jobs in other government detention centers in the region. When CCA took over operations of the Panama City, Florida, jail in late 1985, each jail employee received an immediate 7% pay raise plus a $500 bonus. As additional motivation, CCA provides its employees with stock-ownership and profit-sharing plans, something government can never duplicate. Private companies also lower costs by reducing dependence on bureaucracy. "Government is so easy to beat because it is so inherently inefficient," argues Tom Beasley, president of CCA, which has seven former state commissioners of corrections on its payroll. "So much of prison budgets is allocated to bureaucratic overhead that has nothing to do with the institution. We don't have that layer."

Private operators endow their managers with the authority to actually manage. Before becoming administrator of the Houston center, John S. Robinson spent 12 years working for the Virginia Department of Corrections, where he never found the freedom to be a true manager. "I had always been frustrated in state government by budgets and purchasing procedures. To be a good manager in government is to spend every penny you get so you can get the same if not more the next year. If I can run an efficient operation and save money without sacrificing quality, it helps the company and the facility. At the end of the year we can divide up some of the savings among staff and that's an incentive reward for being efficient. In a state system you don't have to worry about your facility being closed down, and that spawns indifference and lethargy. Privatization gives you more of a motivation to do an exceptional job, because if you don't you could lose your contract."

A comprehensive study of private prisons released in 1985 by the National Institute of Justice, compiled a list of possible benefits from private ownership. Funding for new jail construction would be easier to obtain with private providers, taking the capital-appropriation burdens off government. Much bureaucratic red tape would be eliminated along with the political considerations and patronage connected with the public system. Using private companies would allow government more flexibility to experiment with new models of corrections facilities and programs. Private companies would be more cost-effective and efficient, and would pay taxes on their profits, thus providing additional returns to taxpayers. Eliminating civil-service restrictions allows private providers to control employee performance more closely and to tailor staff to changing program needs. "Independence from the bureaucracy also gives the private provider greater freedom to innovate and to deal more rapidly with problems in the management or delivery of services. Finally, unlike government providers, the private sector is under competitive pressure to perform—pressure that can provide significant incentive to delivery high-quality services."

Critics of privatization initially worried that when the Houston detention facility opened, detainees would be mistreated and conditions would deteriorate under the private contractor. Those concerns evaporated as INS administrators, lawyers with clients in the facility, and the detainees themselves, many of whom had been held in other INS facilities, praised the 350-bed center as clean and its guards, none of whom are allowed to carry weapons, as humane professionals.

"They are absolutely fantastic," insists INS District Director Paul O'Neill. "We've had no major difficulties of any kind. We have a very concerned contractor with people that are experienced, who know how to handle both criminals and illegal alien detainees." The former director of INS in Washington, D.C., Lionel Castillo, calls it "by INS standards by far one of the best facilities," and an immigration lawyer with clients in the facility describes it as "the Holiday Inn of prisons." With its eight dormitories, color televisions, three basketball courts, pool and ping-pong tables, detainees are kept active. One Haitian detainee told *The Houston Chronicle* that he had been in the Miami detention center, run by the government, where "they treat you like a dog." In the private center, said 27-year-old Baudelaire Audate, "they give you respect." A Hispanic reporter for *The Texas Catholic Herald* went to verify these glowing reports independently and ended up writing, "Everything we observed or heard concerning the new detention center indicates that compassion and dedication are not merely a glossy surface image."

Although the center was intended to accommodate only illegal aliens who would be deported within two weeks, about 30 Mariel Boatlift Cubans convicted of crimes in the United States and released from Texas prisons spent six months and more on the premises, creating a maximum-security situation within a minimum-security environment. Their presence tested whether the contractor could handle hardened criminals, and the results went far beyond INS expectations. The stage was set for the private sector to begin moving into the provision of medium- and maximum-security prison operations.

In October 1984, Hamilton County, Tennessee, encompassing the city of Chattanooga, became the nation's first county to turn its jail over to a private operator when CCA was hired to manage its 300-inmate medium-security penal farm. As in Houston, CCA bought pool and ping-pong tables and color televisions for inmates, and took away guns and nightsticks from the guards. Relations between inmates and guards improved almost immediately. "I think most of us would back up a guard if there was trouble," 38-year-old Jim Martin, serving three years for bad checks, told a local newspaper. "When you're treated like a human, you act like it." Seeing its role as providing detainment rather than punishment, CCA first eliminated the "hole," an airless cell where inmates could be thrown on the whim of the guard. "Things used to be real prejudiced around here," 23-year-old Kevin Richards, serving three years for rape, explained to the *Winston-Salem Journal.* "You've got some old dogs who refuse to change, but most of that's gone." Taking weapons from the guards meant that "suddenly they had to earn your respect. You got to see how big a man was without his stick."

The lingo of commercial prisons also replaced the terminology of government. A warden became a "facility administrator," guards became "resident supervisors," and prisoners became "clients." CCA began a $3.5-million construction and renovation of the prison's aging 1910 dining and kitchen facility and housing stock. Medical staff services were introduced 24 hours a day, whereas under county management there had been no nursing services on site. CCA appointed a full-time recreation director and trainer, introduced psychological and psychiatric services, and installed a computer system, which for the first time enabled the county to know the daily inmate population, what crimes they committed, and their work and eating assignments. Security was upgraded and the number of guards was increased. Since Hamilton County can renegotiate the contract every year, should it ever become displeased with CCA's service and costs—$21 a day a prisoner versus $24 a day under county operation—it could resume control over the facility, or shop around among other private providers for a better deal.

Buckingham Security took over operation of a 96-bed medium-security prison for Butler County, Pennsylvania, in October 1985. Buckingham's president, Charles Fenton, had been warden of the Marion, Illinois, and Lewisburg, Pennsylvania, prisons, two of the toughest institutions in the federal system, before he and his brother Joseph formed their own private-prison company. Like CCA, Buckingham adopted a policy of banning firearms from the prison grounds. Although Buckingham inherited the entire county correctional staff, savings under private management were calculated at $100,000 and more a year.

An innovative approach to corrections is being pioneered by Buckingham in Gooding, Idaho, where a 650-bed maximum-security prison is being planned to serve the western United States as the first protective-custody facility for special-needs prisoners. These inmates are seriously ill, geriatric, handicapped, or in need of special protection because they have been informers or prosecution witnesses. The Criminal Justice Institute estimates that special-needs prisoners cost government up to 185% more than ordinary inmates, or about $34,200 to $57,000 per year per inmate compared to about $20,000 a year for others. The 35,000 people in protective custody nationwide live in constant fear for their lives, necessitating a form of solitary confinement that is a costly, cruel, and unusual punishment. Buckingham claims it can save prisons tens of thousands of dollars by putting all special-needs prisoners in one place, while saving the government $10 million in construction costs for the new facility.

State inspection reports of the overcrowded Bay County jail in Panama City, Florida, 100 miles west of Tallahassee, became so critical of conditions that the Department of Corrections filed suit against the jail and its operator, the county sheriff. Other lawsuits had already been filed by inmates complaining of unsafe and inhumane conditions and treatment. Rather than vote new funding the sheriff requested, county commissioners voted 3–2 to privatize the jail and a new work-camp facility, accepting a bid from the Corrections Corporation of America to operate both.

CCA took over effective 1 October 1985. For just the operation of the main jail, excluding the work camp, CCA negotiated a rate of $24 a day per prisoner, compared to $37 a day per prisoner offered by the sheriff in his bid for continued operation of the jail. CCA then designed and built an expandable 175-bed work-camp facility for $4.3 million and remodeled the 196-bed downtown jail at a cost of

$700,000. A provision of the contract required CCA to secure $15 million of insurance for liability resulting from inmate lawsuits or personal injury.

One of CCA's first acts was to raise the salaries of existing jail guards from $8,100 to start, up to $13,500 upon certification, plus profit-sharing and other benefits. Every one of 75 county employees at the jail was offered a position with CCA. In the belief that better treatment of prisoners would minimize security problems, CCA improved conditions quickly by air conditioning the work camp and providing all prisoners with access to ping-pong tables, color televisions, softball diamonds, basketball courts, and other recreational opportunities. Inmates were issued pillows for the first time, and medical care was upgraded.

Despite CCA saving the county $700,000 in 1986 from what its corrections budget would have been under continued county operation, Sheriff LaVelle Pitts found reason to gripe—conditions at the two jails had been made too comfortable. "Why, they're running a Holiday Inn," Sheriff Pitts complained. "Jail is supposed to be a place you'd a whole lot rather not come back to. That work camp is so nice, they're using it as a model. People are coming in from all over the world to look at it." Soon after Bay County had privatized its jail, State Rep. Dick Locke, a former sheriff's deputy himself, responded to appeals from national and state sheriffs' associations and introduced a bill in the state legislature to outlaw all private prisons and jails in Florida. But when Rep. Locke visited Bay County's new private facility, he declared it to be "the cleanest jail I've ever been in" and one of the best operated. He quietly withdrew the bill to prohibit private correctional facilities.

A former Texas prison official, David Myers, oversaw the jail for CCA during the initial 17 months under private operation. He compares public and private jail operations from the vantage point of a seasoned administrator: "The corrections officer was always at the bottom of the criminal justice system in government. Positions in jails and prisons were too often staffed with people who couldn't cut it in law-enforcement jobs, friends of the sheriff or superintendent. But with us, the corrections officers are it. They're the top." CCA has passed every state inspection since 1985, prompting one inspector for the Florida Department of Corrections, Garland Keeman, to marvel at the difference between public and private operation of the jail: "You can tell they've brought the tension down. But the most important thing is staffing. All the posts are manned now. Things there improved so much our litigation was dropped. That says it all."

For the city of Wichita, Kansas, prison privatization became the issue in an April 1986 vote to authorize $23.6 million in bonds for a new jail. Wichita's county jail was under court order to relieve conditions under which over 200 prisoners were kept in a building designed for only 90 inmates. Once interest was factored in, the new jail could have cost taxpayers up to $50 million, about $100,000 a bed. The National Center for Privatization, a free-market institute based in Wichita, guided and funded by an industrialist, Willard Garvey, launched a campaign to convince local voters to reject the bonds in favor of a privately financed and operated facility. Garvey and his assistant, Craig Miner, presented architectural plans for an alternative $12-million privately financed jail, and through the media made the case for a private operator. Residents responded by voting down the government jail proposal by 58% to 42%, forcing the county to begin serious consideration of the privatization option.

By avoiding the tax-exempt general-obligation-bonds form of financing that requires voter approval, jail privatization becomes "an end run around the taxpayers" and eliminates the public from decisions about prison construction, contends Ira P. Robbins, a professor of law at American University. Yet, that may be a blessing without disguise. Taxpayers want more criminals incarcerated, and with longer sentences, but are increasingly reluctant to appropriate their own money for government to perform the service. Through privatization more lawbreakers can be incarcerated without resort to tax money for construction, and probably at less cost for operations, without forcing voters to register their disapproval of government and its taxing authority. Questions relating to the sites of new prisons, the issue usually generating the most voter interest, would still be subject to political pressures through the issuance of building permits by local authorities, and through details of the contracting process as negotiated by public officials.

Texas state government confronted voter disapproval of a different sort in 1987, as it grappled with a nearly $6-billion state budget shortfall and an intractable prison problem. For much of the year the prison system was closed to new convicts more than it was open; a "No Vacancy" sign hung out in front with the regularity of a popular motel. Not even the early release of inmates, which generated state-wide public outrage, had relieved the overcrowding pressure, and the state was facing $840,000 per day in contempt of court fines for failing to meet deadlines set by a federal judge to ease overcrowding. Hanging out the "No Vacancy" sign to new inmates had simply exacerbated problems in county jails, most of which had crowding worse than the 27 units of the state system. In Houston, where the Harris County jail was under a separate court order to reduce the inmate population, it could no longer send its usual quota of 150 inmates a week to the state system and began sleeping many of its 4,000 prisoners shoulder-to-shoulder on concrete floors.

State officials knew they could not raise taxes sufficiently in this traditionally low-tax state to simultaneously build new prisons and cover the $6-billion deficit in their general fund, so Democrats in the House and Senate introduced a bill to privatize new prison construction and operation. It passed the legislature with little dissent and was signed into law by the Republican governor, William Clements. It directed the Texas Department of Corrections to house up to 2,000 inmates during fiscal 1987 in minimum- and medium-security prisons built and operated by the private sector, and it allowed counties for the first time to contract independently with private operators to build and run county jails. The private prisons have to meet all recognized standards and court orders and must house prisoners at a cost at least 10% less than the rate it costs the government. This new law requires private prisons to adhere to American Correctional Association standards governing pay scales, sanitary conditions, medical care, food services, and rehabilitation programs—standards which the Texas system under state operation had failed to meet. Releases and release policies remain the sole discretion of the state; contractors must insure themselves and the state against all claims resulting from private operation; and the private facilities are subject to state purchase and takeover if the contractors go bankrupt or fail to perform adequately.

Several dozen contractors made proposals to the state to build and operate the initial four 500-bed prison units. The Corrections Corporation of America proposed two prisons outside Houston, a third in San Antonio, and a fourth near Dallas. Emerson Private Prisons, owned by Carl Emerson, an ex-con-turned-criminal psychologist and entrepreneur, offered a plan to build a prison and three related businesses in an economically depressed area of Texas under a philosophy of corrections emphasizing meaningful work for inmates with fair pay, to turn prisoners "into taxpayers and give them a chance to save money for family support and victim restitution." Other plans were submitted by Concepts Inc. based in Louisville, Detention Centers of America Inc., and the American Correctional Systems Inc., an arm of Bechtel, the world's largest construction company. It proposed a factory within its prison to employ and train inmates while producing goods for export.

"Many of the vendors render quality service," conceded Dr. George Beto, former head of the Texas prison system, speaking of private operators. "An inspection of facilities operated by Corrections Corporation of America will reveal well-run institutions. Several of the key employees in that corporation at one time worked with me. They were exceptional correctional workers then, and continue to be." *The Lubbock Avalanche* newspaper hailed privatization for placing the Texas Department of Corrections one step removed from the new prison operations, putting it "in a better position to look for cost-effective results rather than defend its own costly practices." And a statewide survey of public opinion just as the bill was signed into law found Texans in favor of the privatization concept by 48% to 35%.

Kentucky had become the first state to house prisoners in a private facility in 1986, using the 200-bed Marion Adjustment Center in Marion, Kentucky, operated by the U.S. Corrections Corporation. In 1987 legislatures in other states—Oklahoma, Arkansas, Arizona— followed the lead of Texas and Kentucky and passed laws authorizing the construction and operation of private prisons.

Prisons could be organized around various industrial activities— creating real factories with fences instead of just warehouses with walls —to be managed by the major corporations already involved in prison construction and operation. Under our current system, instead of prisoners paying their "debt" to society, they increase the debt of American taxpayers by consuming public resources without offsetting the expense of their incarceration, which averages more than $20,000 a year per inmate.

Wages earned by working prisoners could be divided three ways: to contribute toward the cost of their confinement; to make restitution to the victims of their crimes; and to help support their own families during imprisonment, or accumulate funds for use on their release to lessen any temptation for a return to a life of crime. Productive work behind bars would also reduce prisoner idleness, which is a major cause of gang warfare and other violence in our prisons.

At the turn of the century 80% of inmates in this country were engaged in some form of labor, mostly without pay, which created a system of slave labor with attendent scandals involving brutal conditions and exploitation. During the Depression, labor unions succeeded in having Congress outlaw inmate-produced products from interstate commerce, and soon thereafter most states passed laws forbidding the sale of inmate products, reducing prisoners to manufacturing license plates. Union pressure even prevents inmates from maintaining their own facilities—in Pittsburgh a union interceded to prohibit prisoners from painting their cells unless they were union members.

Congress in 1984 reopened interstate markets to prison-made goods, and some states have lifted the prohibition on inmate labor for pay. A Justice Department study in 1986 found only 1,000 prisoners at work for 19 private companies in 17 state correctional facilities nationwide, generating annual sales of $21 million. Inmate wages were found to run up to $7.75 an hour. With nearly 600,000 people incarcerated in this country, the wasted manpower could translate into billions of dollars.

One unique arrangement involves the Kansas State Penitentiary and a company called Zephyr Products of Leavenworth, a sheet-metal firm established in 1979 by Fred Braun, a Harvard MBA. Several dozen inmates are transported each day on a Zephyr-owned bus by prison guards to the company's facility a few miles outside the prison walls. They earn a minimum wage for sheet-metal work, but they often receive bonuses. From their earnings the inmates pay taxes and Social Security, save for the future, make restitution payments, and help repay the state for the cost of their incarceration. Braun started the company to employ inmates because he had been appalled by the extent of prisoner idleness he observed while a member of a governor's task force. He selected a business in which he had prior experience but which was not yet operating in Kansas, in part to allay the fears of job losses by local unions. Many of the inmates once paroled have found jobs in the private sector because of skills learned at Zephyr.

"The small programs now in place suggest possibilities, but they aren't likely to be realized without a sustained effort to persuade business and the public," editorialized *The New York Times*. "For a presidential candidate seeking a new idea, here's an opportunity."

Opponents of prison privatization include the National Sheriffs' Association, whose members exercise jurisdiction over most of the nation's county jails, and public employee unions like the American Federation of State, County and Municipal Employees (AFSCME), which represents 50,000 persons employed in the nation's prisons and jails. Gerald McEntee, president of AFSCME, claims private companies will produce incompetence and corruption in the corrections field. "An unfortunately high percentage of this country's corporations discover that crime pays—their own crimes. Now they've gone one step farther. They want to make money on the crimes of others." One could extend his reasoning and say that hospitals profit at the expense of the sick, or that private schools profit from the ignorance of the young. Such emotional arguments ignore the benefits to society from these forms of "profit."

A somewhat more challenging quibble with prison privatization is advanced by J. Michael Keating, executive vice-president of the Institute for Conflict Management and a frequent contributor to AFSCME publications. He contends that the "application of modern business methods and technology offers no better promise of creating humane and effective prisons than any of the other nostrums pushed by earlier generations of prison reformers." From his rather suffocatingly pessimistic perspective, "the fact is we do not know how to create and maintain efficient, fair, and humane correctional institutions." He believes that an emphasis on cost-effectiveness in corrections will inevitably lead to "brutality and inhumanity." Furthermore, he ridicules the idea that private management can produce cost savings in the corrections field. "One can only wonder where the wizards of correctional management, now transplanted from the public to the private sector, have been hiding the expertise and knowledge they are now prepared to apply so efficiently for their corporate bosses."

The "wizards" of correctional management Keating refers to, corrections officials who defected from the public to the private sector, did so in part precisely because the dead hand of government bureaucracy stifled any innovative applications of their knowledge and expertise. Fundamental differences in the structures and incentives of public and private management, as Peter Drucker and others have demonstrated, more than explain the cost and efficiency advantages of private operation. The National Institute of Justice makes a similar point: "It is entirely possible that there are simply greater natural incentives to satisfy the customer built into the work ethic of private enterprise—in contrast to government service where pleasing the customer can be a highly political exercise." The Institute goes on to predict: "The relevant question may not be whether the private sector can do it more efficiently, but whether the public sector can do it at all, given the pressure for immediate action."

Creating and maintaining efficient, fair, and humane correctional facilities will never be possible unless innovation from beyond traditional prison models is allowed to play a role. "Only true innovation will address the larger problem of why our system of incarceration is such a mess," concludes Peter Greenwood, the Rand Corporation's chief criminal-justice researcher. "And when you're looking for innovators you don't look to government; you look to business." Bringing about experimental models of institutional corrections practice, new ideas with concrete improvements, should be the goal of privatization innovators, rather than simply attempting to jumpstart an outmoded and decaying system into a momentary flicker of efficiency.

Private prison operators can be financially penalized by government for jail violence and escapes, and rewarded for programs behind bars that succeed at reducing recidivism rates. Neither approach can be duplicated within government. Using private operators may also give the public sector a new ability to enforce correctional standards, since the contractor can be held accountable for any deterioration in prison operations or conditions. Government can afford to operate unconstitutional facilities, and continue to do so despite court orders. The private sector will not have that luxury since the threat of fines and contract severance would hit where it hurts most — in the pocketbook. Government confronts the real costs of incarceration, and the impact of stiffer sentencing laws, only when a private contractor bills it on the basis of the number of inmates housed.

"Prisons and jails have been operated as public monopolies for so long that there is no alternative to which they can be compared," argues Charles R. Ring, author of a report on private prisons for the American Correctional Association. He answers critics who believe that in cutting costs, private prison operators would ignore the welfare of the inmates, and that since profit might depend on expanding inmate populations, private operators would lobby for harsher laws, longer sentences, and more prison beds. Ring is not convinced they could manipulate public opinion and lawmakers that easily, especially since "given current levels of overcrowding and public sentiment already in favor of stricter sentencing, there will be no shortage of inmates to fill new facilities." Efficiency is not synonymous with exploitation, he argues, and the primary advantage of private correctional services is their ability to adjust the level of services more quickly to meet changing needs. "By establishing and enforcing population limits and operating standards, the government can, in fact, require much better conditions at private prisons than currently exist at many public institutions."

Some civil-rights advocates question the propriety of government delegating any of its police powers over what they perceive is a quasi-judicial function of criminal justice. Answers CCA's president Tom Beasley: 'We're not policymakers; we implement. Ours is a care and custody function. We provide better facilities, better inmate care, better working conditions and higher pay for employees — all at less cost to the taxpayer. Now give me a moral impropriety in that!"

If anything, the focus of civil rights concern over moral propriety seems misplaced. Other policy questions deserve greater attention. Does it truly serve the cause of justice, for instance, to incarcerate in detention centers mostly hard-working, honest people who happen to be in this country illegally in search of a job? It is humane to imprison victimless crime offenders with hardened criminals convicted of offenses against people and property? Can we call any system fair that refuses to allow the perpetrators of crimes to labor behind bars to compensate their victims?

With privatization, government does not relinquish its authority and responsibility to punish lawbreakers, it only delegates those roles to subcontractors. This power resides with government only because the citizenry has transferred to government the authority to punish, a grant dependent upon and wholly derived from the consent of the governed. In that sense government itself is a contractor in the employ of the public. "The state does not own the right to punish," argues Professor Charles H. Logan, a fellow of the National Institute of Justice. "It merely administers it in trust, for the people and under the rule of law. There is no reason why subsidiary trustees cannot be designated, as long as they, too, are ultimately accountable to the people and subject to the same provisions of law that direct the state."

Critics of the profit motive condemn any process that enables one group of human beings — private prison companies — to benefit from taking away the freedom of other human beings. Yet the more one examines this argument, analyzing as well the motives of public employees, their unions, and government prison agencies, the more economic motivations that begin to surface. Government employees have a financial stake through salaries and benefits in the jailing of other human beings, no less than public-employee unions that profit from compulsory dues paid by prison employees, or state prison bureaucracies that grow in personnel, power, and budgets in concert with the growth in prison populations. Observes Professor Logan, "The notion that any activity carried out for profit, as compared to salary and other benefits, is thereby tainted, is simply an expression of prejudice." What should concern us in our criminal-justice practices and policies is not motivations, but results that are simultaneously fair and effective.

A Russian novelist, Fyodor Dostoevsky, wrote that "the degree of civilization in a society can be judged by entering its prisons." Government at all levels has simply failed to confront the problems of our prisons in a cost-effective and humane way. "It is hard to imagine that the private sector could do any worse a job than government has done," Claudia Wright, an American Civil Liberties Union lawyer, admitted in a *Dun's Business Month* interview. As the *Chattanooga Times* newspaper has put it, endorsing the prison privatization trend, "Private enterprise should be given a chance to find the corrections solutions that have eluded the public sector."

4
Harnessing the Private Sector for Public Good

Philanthropy overlaid with a nauseatingly sweet coating of public relations used to pass for "social responsibility" within the business world. As the recognition spread that business cannot remain healthy in a sick society, nor for that matter in a sick neighborhood or urban center, connections were forged between self-interest and our unmet social needs. When the profit motive is linked to social good in the marketplace, with incentives creatively structured, and government, if it is involved at all, acting as a facilitator, everyone in the equation—business, government, taxpayers, and the needy—stands to benefit.

An attitude that self-interest be manipulated to serve social goals now embraces a wide swath of corporate thinking. Deputy U.S. Secretary of State John C. Whitehead, a former corporate executive, devoted his remarks at the 1983 graduation ceremonies of the New York University Graduate School of Business to the untapped profit opportunities for American business in solving social problems. "I believe that it should be possible for the management skills and the administrative structures of corporate America to be effectively harnessed, singly and in groups, to solve our social problems. I am convinced that a quiet Sunday afternoon meeting of the heads of the dozen leading private-sector employers in Newark would develop more practical ideas for solving the problem of black youth unemployment than could another billion dollars of federal handouts."

Peter Drucker argues that government is so overextended that our social needs will be financed only if the solutions begin to generate capital, which means profits. "Only if business, and especially American business, learns that to do well it has to do good, can we hope to tackle the major social challenges facing developed societies today," says Drucker, a leading corporate-mangement guru. One of the earliest exponents of such a view within corporate boardrooms was William C. Norris, chairman of Control Data Corporation, the Minneapolis-based computer company, who formulated an entire corporate philosophy built around the idea that the solutions to urban problems can be transformed into profitable business opportunities. The spectrum of needs he talks about includes reductions in unemployment through job training and job creation, more responsive education, revitalization of poverty-stricken urban and rural areas, and lower-cost, more efficient public services.

Beginning in 1967, the visionary—some would say eccentric— Norris and Control Data began establishing manufacturing plants in blighted communities. Seven plants employing 2,000 were eventually created, putting into practice a form of urban enterprise zone some 14 years before legislation with that name—offering tax incentives to influence business locations—was introduced in the U.S. Congress. Two consortiums, Rural Ventures Inc. and City Venture Corp., became vehicles Norris used to experiment with creating agricultural and inner-city jobs, although both ventures lost considerable money and raised questions about misuse of stockholder funds. Norris proposed that corporations, not government, should be running prisons and public schools some years before the business community actually began making a commitment in those areas.

Philanthropy differs from its cousin, charity, in that the latter is aid to the needy or poor, whereas the former is intended to improve the quality of life or promote the culture of humanity as a whole. Direct philanthropic gestures continue to dominate corporate involvement in social problems, more so now than in the heyday of Andrew Carnegie, who almost single-handedly endowed us with free public libraries. A survey of 315 large corporations found that their philanthropic contributions leaped 26% to $1.2 billion from 1984 to 1985. Similarly, Americans gave a record $2.3 billion to United Way charities in 1985, a nearly 10% jump over the previous year and a 130% increase over a decade. Such giving affords corporations priceless image-polishing, especially when private charity is harnessed on a massive, well-publicized scale, as with the Live Aid production to alleviate famine in Africa. Four corporate sponsors of the Live Aid concert—AT&T, Chevrolet, Eastman Kodak, and Pepsi—donated $750,000 each to the event, proving that good will can command a high price.

Across the spectrum of social needs, innovative applications of voluntarism, self-help financing, and public-private cooperation have become commonplace. When Hallmark Cards, Inc. experienced a slack period at its Kansas City manufacturing plant, rather than lay off several dozen employees, Hallmark donated their labor and all necessary materials to weatherize 75 homes in a distressed neighborhood near the plant. In this case Hallmark responded to more than just neighborly good will—Missouri maintains a tax law allowing businesss and corporations to receive 50% credit against state taxes for all contributions of money, services, and materials to neighborhood-assistance projects. In the Dallas area, customers of Texas Utilities, the parent company of Dallas Power & Light Co., Texas Power & Light Co., and Texas Electric Service Co., have been encouraged to check an Energy Aid box on their bills to add $1 or more to their monthly payments for a fund to help pay electric and natural gas bills for the poor. About 14,000 families in the Texas Utilities service area receive benefits which average about $100 per family. "I thought they were just a huge, heartless corporation," remarked Dorothy Roberts, director of social-service programs for the Red Cross, which administers the money. "That's really not true. They're very compassionate people and the corporation really has a heart." In San Diego, businessmen concerned that their conservative city would be judged by how it treats the least desirable portion of their population raised $7 million for a privately funded, 350-bed shelter for the homeless.

Most Americans have been conditioned to regard aid to the poor as the role of government, so as to relieve themselves of compassion or responsibility for the fate of strangers in need. But if each of the tens of thousands of churches in America adopted just one welfare family, public-assistance rolls would diminish and recipient resourcefulness would revive. Incentives for the haves to help the have-nots need to be reintroduced. "Government ought to be considering ways by which it can relinquish primary responsibility for the poor and return it as a privilege, not a burden, to churches, charities, civic groups, and individuals in local communities," wrote Cal Thomas, a syndicated columnist and former official of the Moral Majority. Why are religious institutions receiving tax exemptions, asks Thomas, "if not, in part, because they are expected to perform services beneficial to the nation, such as caring for poor people?" He advocates the forfeiture of tax exemptions for religious and civic organizations failing to help welfare recipients in their communities.

Charitable action needs a new marketplace of ideas, tools, and innovations to address the entire range of community problems and unmet or inadequately met needs—homelessness, hunger, recreation, even fine-arts deficits. Writes Neal R. Peirce, a *National Journal* columnist: "There's not an American metropolis that doesn't have within it sufficient resources from private wealth to corporate coffers to untapped skills of its talented citizens, to address every problem on its doorstep."

More than $1 billion in charitable donations is given annually by the private sector in New York City, and about 2,500 nongovernment agencies in that city provide health and human-resource services, enlisting hundreds of thousands of volunteers. "Suspicion toward programmatic remedies remains healthy and formidable," concluded Pete Hamill, in an essay for *New York* magazine. "The government's insistence that charity be returned to the private sector has helped awaken a sense of individual responsibility, something that in part evaporated during the height of the welfare state . . . What starts out as a splendid idea in Washington oftens ends up in the Bronx wearing the cement face of the state; money for the poor is eaten by poverty racketeers, the poor once again defrauded by con men and hustlers."

One need not accept the dictum of John D. Rockefeller III, the philanthropist, that "throughout our history, virtually every significant step in social progress sprang from volunteerism," to understand the vital symbiotic link between entrepreneurial behavior and the greater public good. Every dynamic society finds innovative ways to meld public interest with self-interest. An alternative to tax-financed support of art evolved in Japan, for instance, because the distinction between public art museums and private art collections has always been blurred by the entrepreneurial activities of art patrons. Showing art for profit is a part of customer service for numerous Japanese corporations. Yasuda Fire and Marine Insurance Co., Japan's second largest, owns 450 paintings, including Renoirs and van Goghs, displayed in its own museum named for painter Seiji Togo, whom the company supported while he studied art in Paris in the 1920s.

Despite positive trends in the level of charitable giving, unless a shrewd alignment of corporate and social needs continues to evolve, government will be faced with divisive and intensifying pressures to meet demands for social spending with the usual panoply of dependence-inducing, coercive financing approaches. Much of this nation's early philanthropic giving was predicated on rational self-interest, not altruism, as ultimately the best servant of the public interest. For example, railroad barons financed construction of YMCA hostels in the late 19th century to provide cheap accommodations for their train crews, with the wider social benefits of public lodging merely an afterthought. Business must begin treating urban and civic problems as corporate challenges to wring profit and public-relations dividends from satisfying social and human needs.

Unfortunately, during the Reagan administration's first term, exhortations on behalf of vague corporate do-gooding often substituted for actual privatization initiatives that might have yielded measureable results. Corporations set up to produce computers or assemble automobiles offer no comparative advantages in solving social problems, nor will philanthropy alone have an enduring impact on the pervasive and seemingly inexhaustible needs of the poor. But flexible relationships between government and the private sector can still be forged to take advantage of the relative strengths of volunteers, philanthropy, charity, and the profit motive.

In public-policy jargon these new, more collaborative relationships between government and business are known as public-private partnerships, a term that may chill some privatization proponents because it brings to mind the economic structures embodied in fascism or socialism. Such partnerships could degenerate into a national industrial policy granting government the power to "steer" the private sector, bringing our economy that much closer to confinement in a bureaucratic straitjacket. That is a major reason why, in the context of privatization, government must assume the role of facilitator and not that of manager in responding to the service demands of the electorate.

By rethinking their traditional roles, government officials can develop flexible policy tools to erect incentives or dissolve obstacles to private-sector involvement in social problem-solving. These incentives take many forms, depending on the circumstances, business climate, and the range of unmet needs. A study for the International City Management Association identified a series of possible partnership approaches. "Policy tools can provide incentives for private initiative—as when housing developers are given zoning bonuses to exceed normal density levels if they agree to build low-income housing units in their development . . . . policy tools may eliminate barriers to private-sector initiative—as when overly rigid day-care regulations are revised so as to make corporate on-site day care more affordable." Singled out as the leading example of corporate initiative in recent years was Detroit's Renaissance Center, a project of the Ford Motor Company and 50 corporate partners, which privately financed and planned the development. Detroit's city government simply used its zoning powers to help expedite the process.

Broad national, corporate coalitions have formed around the privatization and public-private cooperative concepts. The Privatization Council based in New York, composed of several dozen corporate and business enterprises ranging from Big Eight accounting firms like Arthur Andersen and Touche Ross, to construction giants such as The Parsons Corporation and Research-Cottrell, seeks to advance private-sector participation in public works and public services by expanding public-private partnerships. "Through the use of creative financing, participation in the ownership and implementation of capital projects, and the operation and maintenance of public functions, corporate America can be added to the public's arsenal," wrote David Seader, editor of the Council's quarterly *Privatization Review.*

Since 1982 enterprise zones have been the growth industry of public-private partnership arrangements. Modeled after federal legislation that had languished in Congress, enterprise zones at the state and local level offer varied menus of tax and regulatory relief to businesses as incentives for them to locate in depressed areas suffering high unemployment and chronic poverty. Between 1982 and 1985, at least 19 states established 450 zones encompassing areas from as small as a few blocks to the size of small towns. These zones created or saved 50,000 jobs and stimulated $2 billion of investment, according to the U.S. Department of Housing and Urban Development. Research by Dick Cowden, executive director of the American Association of Enterprise Zones, found that manufacturers accounted for one-third of new business creation in the zones, taking advantage of readily available labor pools. Less then 3% of new zone companies had relocated from nearby, deflating the argument that zones would simply redistribute the job-creating wealth of a city.

Incentives have often been tailored to the unique circumstances of each zone or business. Some states emphasize industrial development, others commercial development; some focus on job retention, others on job creation. Several states provide for the transfer of unused public property to resident associations within the zones. Others offer tax credits to businesses for new employees hired, or allow property-tax abatements and exemptions from sales taxes on materials used for zone construction. In Norwalk, Connecticut, for instance, companies that locate or expand in Norwalk's one-square-mile zone receive a 50% break on state business taxes for ten years, and an 80% reduction in local property taxes over a five-year period. The State of Maryland induced Citicorp to locate several job-creating facilities in state enterprise zones in return for allowing out-of-state banking.

Within a few states the enterprise-zone idea quickly became another rope for political tug-of-war. In New York, Republican State Senator Roy Goodman, chairman of a legislative commission on public-private cooperation, advanced the concept by linking a wide variety of tax incentives—exemptions, abatements, credits—to the promise of low-interest loans for zone businesses. Democratic Governor Mario Cuomo responded with a program he called "Opportunity Zones," offering Senator Goodman's full-course menu but adding an entire new dessert tray of public funding —taxpayer subsidization of low-cost power and the wages of public-assistance recipients hired in the zones.

At the federal level enterprise-zone legislation passed the U.S. Senate twice, yet died each time in the House of Representatives largely because of Illinois Rep. Dan Rostenkowski, chairman of the tax-writing Ways and Means Committee. He opposed stimulating development through a tax policy based on geography, arguing that the tax code should be used only to raise revenue, not provide incentives for social-policy goals. Other opponents of the idea imagined it to be nothing more than a scheme to undermine our nation's regulatory system.

Once again inaction by the federal government had forced localities to act independently, and in so doing take the pressure off Washington to provide more social-welfare spending. Each measure of success for the zones means fewer persons to utilize federal relief programs, and that many more productive people paying taxes into the federal treasury. By playing the role of facilitator, structuring incentives to respond to business needs, local government provides itself with a new tool to unleash entrepreneurial impulses toward the revitalization of urban and rural America.

Privatizing Social-Service Provision

Maria Rosa's life as a welfare mother in San Antonio, Texas, resembled that of thousands of other welfare recipients. She collected her check every few weeks to support her three children, and she waited, like so many others, for opportunities that never materialized. The demeaning cycle of welfare poverty and dependence seemed unbreakable. But she was rescued, thrown a lifeline, by a unique program originated in her city called "Let's Get Off Welfare." She found a job as a flagger on a construction site, and with training, counseling, and encouragement through the program, she eventually started her own business and achieved self-sufficiency.

The program evolved in 1973 as the brainchild of Lupe Anguiano, former nun, migrant worker, and union organizer for Cesar Chavez, after she spent three years of frustration working for the Department of Health, Education and Welfare in Washington. She concluded that the welfare system trapped, dehumanized, and destroyed young, healthy, intelligent women, and that reforming the system at the federal level would be virtually impossible. So she moved into a San Antonio housing project and began her odyssey of working directly with welfare mothers. She organized a group of 100 women who converged on a local welfare office, handed over their welfare checks and demanded jobs instead. The resulting media attention prompted the local business community to rally its support, lifting 500 women out of welfare and into jobs within six months.

Anguiano's program recruited, then screened and trained, welfare mothers in basic job skills, using local colleges as training centers and volunteers from participating businesses as teachers. Then she jawboned local companies and national corporations into hiring her trainees. The San Antonio Chamber of Commerce estimated that her program, named National Women's Employment and Education, Inc., could train a participant for $671 in private funds, compared to $3,000 to $15,000 in costs per trainee for the local public-sector programs.

Counselors in Anguiano's program meet with clients once a week for a year to monitor their progress; federal job-placement programs allow for only three-month follow-up contacts. Once women are matched with jobs in the private sector and their child-care and transportation needs are arranged, they go through three weeks of employment-readiness classes before actually meeting the employer. It is this extensive, sensitive support system that helps explain why the Anguiano method has achieved 90% job placement, and an 88% job-retention rate for clients after one year. Her program model is so successful that she routinely turns down government funding, such as a $200,000 grant offered by the New York City Department of Human Resources, because that would mean following government rules, which she finds a stifling, confusing influence. Even in the worst economic times she has been able to secure jobs for clients. "We started the Tacoma, Washington, program and there was 23% unemployment, and yet we never had problems finding jobs for the women." In 1978 the model program was field tested in eight communities in five states, using a combination of federal, state, and private funds. At the end of the trial period Anguiano discovered that those groups that took state and federal money had performed more poorly than the privately funded groups, even though all used the same program formula. She attributed this phenomenon to the strings attached to government funds in the form of regulations that diverted too much management and program time to compliance, diluting the program mission.

With corporate sponsors like Atlantic Richfield, Texas Instruments, Manufacturers Hanover, and dozens of others, Lupe Anguiano can be said to have perfected a technique for tapping the social-responsibility conscience of business. She sees her success in more practical terms. "My program appeals to corporate America because it's realistic. It takes into account how the employment process really works." After having freed thousands of single mothers from the welfare-dependency syndrome, she is confident that within five years, if her program were spread nationwide, she could liberate 85% of the poor from welfare. Her biggest obstacle remains the human-service bureaucracy, those in government, in welfare "rights" organizations, and those still wedded to the mystique of Great Society programs, who "are locked into social-delivery systems they don't want to give up even though they patronize and degrade the poor."

Increasingly some of those who most directly represent the poor and disadvantaged in our society have begun questioning, if not resisting, government activities in such areas as housing, health care, and human services, because they see centralized programs enlarging the power and income of the service-producer industry. "Most social-service professionals are earnest and well-meaning people, hoping to do good; but the plain fact is that the elimination of poverty by itself would cost most of them their jobs, and the proliferation of the consciousness and mechanisms needed for emotional self-care and mutual aid would drive the first nail into the profession's coffin," writes Steven Wineman, a radical leftist social worker and critic of the centralized welfare state. Wineman and other decentralists want urban neighborhoods to be the primary social units, with the poorest neighborhoods, those having the highest concentration of welfare recipients and the unemployed, becoming the focal point for the development of networks of nonprofit, job-producing businesses. Small, low-cost housing corporations could evolve to provide decent, low-cost housing, reducing reliance on government housing programs, even as public funding of medical care could be "virtually eliminated" if there were "cooperatively organized, nonprofit health-insurance plans among workers," says Wineman.

Privatization has been assailed as an abandonment of the concepts of public needs, the general welfare, and society's responsibility to the poor. Ted Kolderie of the Hubert Humphrey Institute turns that argument around by pointing out that it is the human-service bureaucracy that propagates laws and regulations that deprive nongovernmental and nonprofessional institutions of the right to care for themselves and each other, which translates into a fundamental restraint on the ability of society to adequately carry out most if not all of its obligations to the less fortunate. Kolderie calls it a mistake to think of the debate over privatization, especially in the human-service field, as one between the idea of community and the idea of individualism. Privatization proponents recognize inherent dangers in a society "more than half of whose members have their incomes determined politically."

Economist Marc Bendick, Jr. advocates expanded social-welfare services but has concluded that "the American social welfare system can best be advanced by making pervasive appropriate forms of privatized delivery." He believes that private delivery of publicly financed social-welfare services might help restore public trust and faith in government. In a paper for the Project on the Federal Social Role, established under auspices of The National Conference on Social Welfare, Dr. Bendick argues for nonprofit privatization of human services over the for-profit approach because of, he claims, "the inability to specify precisely program goals and performance standards" inherent in social services; for-profits need clear goals to help identify a return on their service investment. Privatization through the neighborhood nonprofit sector would produce gains in service targeting and quality, lowering costs yet raising the level of compassion for clients. Even modest gains in efficiency producing a 5% or 10% saving in production costs "would represent billions of dollars, given the vast scale of the American social-welfare system," claims Bendick. Compounding the savings would be "various improvements from the clients' point of view in terms of greater choice, enhanced personal dignity, greater cultural accessibility, and reduced complexity."

Profit need not mean efficiency at the cost of quality in the provision of human services. In Minneapolis, the Alpha Center for Public/Private Initiatives, Inc., a nonprofit group, seeks to accelerate the privatization of human services by fostering the expansion or creation of for-profit businesses in roles traditionally played by government or nonprofit organizations. Alpha provides seed money for the formation of profit-making service providers, then creates marriages between these entrepreneurs and public-sector officials. Its corporate backers, each committing $50,000 per year for a minimum of four years, include Chemical Bank, the Hospital Corporation of America, Illinois Bell, and the Ginn Corporation.

Alpha views profit as essential to the process of transforming resource users into resource contributors. "We need to create capital at the same time we're delivering human services — that's the only way we can plug the drain on taxes or ease the strain on philanthropy," argues J. Arthur Boschee, Alpha's vice-president and a former Peace Corps volunteer who became a senior public-relations executive for the Control Data Corporation. "Profit will enable us to expand solutions as quickly as we can to as many Americans as possible. If you go back to the idea of creating capital rather than consuming it, profit is really a misnomer. It's all just cost. Costs of today and of the future, and our present revenues have to cover both."

Status-quo elements charge that privatization will make its profit off the backs of the poor, replacing compassion with concern for the bottom line of business. Boschee counters that market disciplines will mitigate this prospect because compassion becomes a part of what must be delivered with the service or the company will fail. Government will not renew the contract for the next year, or the business will be sued for non-care. "It comes back to proper monitoring on the part of the public sector. Government has to set the standards — it has to address the equity issues, the quality issues, the quantity issues. Government has to monitor performance and, where appropriate, allocate funds. If government does so, then most of the objections to privatizing human services can be met," says Boschee. The best means to help people reach self-sufficiency is to give them a service-provider role model that is itself self-sufficient — something that for-profit organizations can best accomplish.

Profit-making success stories in the human-services field have begun to emerge. In Hastings, Minnesota, day treatment for emotionally disturbed teenagers is provided by a private firm called Human Resource Associates, Inc. Children are treated at home, keeping the entire family involved in the rehabilitation process, rather than shipping the kids off to residential centers. Home-treatment costs are half those of publicly operated residential centers, and the percentage of teenagers ending up in trouble again is less than half the rate of public programs. Hospice Care, Inc., of Miami was a nonprofit organization until 1982, providing home care of the terminally ill, when company founders decided that in order to expand their care quickly and effectively they would need investment capital, and that meant going for profit. Using Medicare reimbursements, Hospice Care tripled its admissions in 1985, expanding into Dallas and New York, and continued providing care to the indigent without reimbursement.

Rhode Island's Opportunities Industrialization Center (OIC) had been dependent on federal money since its founding in 1967 as a vehicle to train minority and disadvantaged people for jobs. As government funding in the 1980s evaporated, executive director Michael Van Leesten began to see that dependence on federal grants was like any other form of welfare—you may need it, but it's deadly if you become addicted. To achieve self-sufficiency for OIC, Van Leesten hit upon the idea of training low-income clients for jobs in their own workplaces rather than as employees for somebody else. OIC entered a consortium to purchase a $2-million machined-metals company, of which it owns half, and undertook another joint project to form a profit-making company to produce high-protein fish products. Both ventures are being used to provide jobs, training, and income to replace the government tax money. "I'm not saying that we don't need help from society," Van Leesten told syndicated columnist William Raspberry. "But the major part of that help must come from our own efforts. That's the only way we'll ever attain real economic power."

At least 90% of America's shelters for the homeless are operated by religious and private voluntary organizations, and most emergency food distribution is similarly performed by the private sector. A network of groups called Second Harvest operates nearly 100 food banks around the nation to distribute food donated by private individuals, groups, and the food industry. Using these outlets as a model, John C. Goodman, president of the National Center for

Policy Analysis in Dallas, proposes that government social services be totally privatized, or in his words "denationalized," by allowing taxpayers to decide how their contribution of tax dollars to the human-services budget will be spent.

Any qualified private charity could be designated as a recipient, placing it on equal competitive footing for that part of the federal budget allocated to the various poverty programs. Taxpayers could either deduct their percentage contribution to welfare from their income taxes based on the minimum amount by law they must give private charity providers, or alternatively they could check off one of several boxes on their tax forms, much as they do with the $1 contribution to political parties, indicating which human-service providers they wished to support. By replacing public-welfare monopolies with competitive providers, allowing freedom of entry into the taxpayer-subsidized human-service marketplace for all enterprises meeting government standards, Goodman hopes to squeeze inefficiency and waste from federal poverty programs while denying special-interest groups much of the political control they now exercise over the distribution of welfare. Even more important, in Goodman's view, forcing charitable organizations to appeal directly to taxpayers would create a new layer of public accountability.

Because government is not out to make a buck, government provision of human services has been wrapped in a perception of safety and honorable intentions. But ultimately it is performance, not assertions of superiority, that will claim the moral high ground. Doing well by doing good, effectively and profitably, yet humanely, delivering educational, health, and social services, can be an achievable and a desirable goal.

Insuring Hospital Survival

Navarro County Memorial Hospital in Corsicana, Texas, 55 miles south of Dallas, faced a gauntlet of insurmountable problems. Because more than 100 of its 177 beds were in violation of life-safety codes, the hospital was threatened with a loss of accreditation. Space was lacking for expansion, serious budgetary problems loomed, and the county had squandered its capital fund for hospital maintenance and equipment on other unrelated county projects. New physicians were proving difficult to recruit or retain because of antiquated 30-year-old facilities and equipment that increasingly drove paying patients away to other hospitals.

In an attempt to avoid decertification, hospital administrators created a series of task forces comprised of 150 community residents to study the problems and issue detailed recommendations. After a year, a committee of these residents concluded that the county could not raise the over $20 million needed to build a new hospital or rehabilitate the old one. Outside help was needed, so the committee invited two nationwide for-profit hospital chains and two nonprofit hospitals to propose solutions.

Hospital Corporation of America (HCA), based in Nashville, the largest and fastest-growing investor-owned hospital chain — from 11 hospitals in 1969 to more than 360 in 1985 — proposed to finance, construct, and operate a new 200-bed hospital on land adjacent to the old facility that it would buy for $300,000 from the county. The firm agreed to purchase transferable equipment from the county for $800,000, guarantee that its patient charges would not exceed those of comparable hospitals in the area, keep on its payroll all existing county-hospital employees with their retirement program, pay, and benefits, and provide care for indigent patients without county tax assistance. Unlike the nonprofits, HCA could promise that all county residents would have access to the hospital and that major policy decisions affecting its operation would remain locally controlled. If for any reason the county became displeased with the hospital's management, a repurchase agreement would take effect.

In March 1981, the county commissioner's court voted to accept HCA's proposal; within three years the chain had built its new five-story, $27-million hospital and supplied it with modern eqiupment. A medical foundation was established with the $5-million purchase price HCA paid for operating rights, to be used solely for the care of county residents too poor to pay. Today the new private hospital provides this rural county more than $300,000 a year in tax revenue, a significant turnaround from the $50,000 a year the old public hospital was costing county taxpayers.

Since the late 1970s, fiscal strains on public hospitals characterized by large operating deficits, obsolete equipment, deteriorated buildings, declining patient loads, and local resistance to raising improvement taxes, have forced nearly 200 of the government facilities to seek purchase, lease, or management arrangements with for-profit hospital chains. Between 1979 and 1985 the number of investor-owned hospitals in America grew from 952 to 1,300, while the total of not-for-profits placed under for-profit company management increased from 237 to 330 hospitals. Abroad, ten American companies owned and operated 83 hospitals and managed another 18 hospitals in 19 countries during 1986. In a larger context these developments should be seen as elements of the overall privatization of health care that has produced hospices, the midwifery or birthing movement, and Health Maintenance Organizations as private-sector responses to the spiraling cost of medical care.

At the turn of the century about 56% of all hospitals in America were for-profit. By 1938 that number had fallen to 36%, and it fell even further to a mere 11% of all hospitals in 1968, before the large for-profit hospital chains emerged, primarily to feed off Medicare payments. The decline is attributable to competitive disadvantages imposed by government policy. State laws often hampered or even prohibited the emergence or expansion of for-profit facilities. In 1976, the mayor of New York actually attempted to force the closure of all nine for-profit hospitals then operating in that city. Economist John C. Goodman, of the National Center for Policy Analysis in Dallas, identifies the most important disadvantage to the for-profits as the Hill-Burton Construction Act of 1946, which provided federal funding for the construction and equipping of government and nonprofit hospitals and resulted in the creation of 1,680 new facilities and additions to 2,998 old ones. Government and nonprofit hospitals also enjoy the government-conferred advantages of property-tax and income-tax exemptions, favored treatment under antitrust laws, access to tax-exempt debt financing, the ability to finance much capital equipment with government tax money, and a freedom to utilize charitable contributions generally unavailable to for-profit firms because of federal tax law.

Despite these competitive disadvantages the for-profit hospital industry has reemerged and begun to thrive, partly because of its ability to raise large amounts of equity capital through stock sales. Communities also now realize that if they sell a facility to one of the profit-making firms it will generate immediate revenue for the locality, save taxpayers money by avoiding renovation or new-facility construction costs, and place a valuable asset on the local tax rolls. Private investment then frees up government funds for use in other critical service areas.

Officials of the Federation of American Hospitals, representing the for-profit hospital industry, recommend that a community consider selling its hospital or placing it under private hospital management if the public hospital is an aging facility, understaffed, with poor, outdated equipment, and if it lacks sufficient operating funds or access to new funds because of a small tax base. On the positive side for communities that choose to sell, reports the *Los Angeles Times,* "profit-making companies pump money into quality medical technology and research, pay for new teaching facilities, set up regional networks of hospitals to reduce duplication of services and turn money-losing community hospitals into tax-paying, private successes."

During 1982 the community hospital managed by the University of Louisville was losing $10,000 a day, a hemorrhage that threatened to get worse. The university had just built a $73-million, 404-bed hospital to replace the community facility, but it lacked the funds to cover first-year operating losses, estimated at $10 million, and the state, county, and city governments refused to escalate financial support. To bail itself out, the university reached an agreement with Humana Inc., a Louisville-based for-profit hospital chain, for the company to lease and operate the new hospital, renamed the Humana Hospital University. In a vote of the university medical faculty, three-quarters opted for the Humana takeover, an unprecedented arrangement in which a private, investor-owned corporation would operate a debt-ridden publicly owned teaching hospital that had become a refuge for patients unable to pay for their care.

Within the first year of operation in 1984, Humana pumped $5.7 million into new equipment for the hospital. Some departments were reduced; others had personnel levels raised. The installation of computers helped decrease the hospital supply department's staff from 90 positions to 50, while the nursing staff was expanded from 480 to more than 600. A big turn-around occurred in room-occupancy rates, from 55% before privatization to 78% a year afterward. This infusion of patients, most carrying private insurance, came about because the hospital now offered a wider range of medical services in a physical plant with extensive amenities. Since private insurance generally pays more for the same treatments and services than Medicaid and other public-health systems, private patients help support hospital programs benefitting the poor.

In the first year of operation indigent care jumped nearly 12% to $27 million, of which $6.4 million of uncompensated cost came from

Humana's pockets and the rest from a combined state and local fund for the indigent. Humana agreed to assume all risk for growth in the cost of indigent care beyond a fixed fee based on past levels of funding. It assumed all financial risks for operating the hospital despite paying 20% of the hospital's pre-tax profits to the university, on top of support for its medical-teaching programs.

Altogether, Humana returned another $16 million to the community during 1985 in the form of taxes, rental payments to the state for the hospital, and support for the teaching programs at the university. Humana still enjoyed $7.7 million in profits in 1985, accountable to the increase in paying patients, gains in staff productivity, a 5% decrease in operating costs, and the use of a computerized billing system. Humana later opened a new burn center, a diabetes unit, an outpatient surgery service, a skin bank, and a medical library. An *Orlando Sun-Sentinel* reporter, after visiting the facility, wrote glowingly: "At the end of the first 16 months, the indigent were getting care, the patient complaints had dwindled to almost nothing at City Hall, the university had a state-of-the-art teaching hospital and $1 million in profits from Humana."

For-profit firms generally manage public hospitals more efficiently than local governments, if only because they can insulate themselves from most political pressures and patronage interference. When Sonoma County, California, contracted with National Medical Enterprises in 1975 to manage its public hospital, the county tax subsidy was $1.7 million annually. National Medical undertook a management reform and cost-containment program that by 1981 had transformed a tax-drainer into a money-maker, with revenues exceeding costs by nearly $1 million a year.

Critics of the hospital privatization trend, primarily public-employee unions and the *New England Journal of Medicine,* believe that profit considerations will tempt the hospital chains to keep patients longer than their condition warrants. But the evidence seems to indicate that better-managed hospitals release patients more quickly. Several studies have shown that average patient stay in for-profit hospitals is 6.5 days compared to 7.8 days in nonprofit community hospitals. At Humana's Louisville hospital, patients average 7.3 days per stay versus 8.2 days per stay under the previous public management. "Many health economists believe that length of stay is the most important indicator of a hospital's efficiency," says Dr. John C. Goodman, an authority on health-care regulation. What matters is not the cost per day of hospital care, an area in which for-profit hospitals are often higher than public, but the total cost of a stay in the hospital. A patient who pays $100 for a day in the hospital is better off financially than patients receiving the same treatment paying $50 per day but staying for three days or more.

Will privatization mean the wholesale deprivation of care for those unable to pay? A Vanderbilt University economics professor, Frank A. Sloan, cites studies of bad-debt and charity-care cases in U.S. hospitals between 1978 and 1983 to show that for-profit hospitals located outside of cities actually rendered more charity care in relation to charges than their nonprofit counterparts, "and almost as much as state and local government hospitals." Endowments like that created in Texas by the Hospital Corporation of America can help insure the long-term provision of indigent care. Governments could also use sale or lease contracts with for-profit firms to require certain levels of indigent support, or even direct that a fixed percentage of hospital profits be set aside for the health care needs of the poor. If government wants to encourage more than a minimum of good acts by the for-profit industry, tax breaks or a tax-free status linked to charity care could stimulate the desired level of commitment.

Hospitals in all three categories—public, nonprofit, and profit— have not had in the past those necessary and meaningful incentives to always be efficient because of Medicare, Medicaid, and other costs passed through third-party payments. "Money has been made in this industry by manipulating reimbursement rules rather than by cutting costs," contends Professor Sloan. However, under new hospital-payment systems in which Medicare reimbursement rules reward hospitals that keep their costs low, "only the fittest will survive, irrespective of ownership form."

Until relatively recently, hospitals had simply been administered; now they will have to be managed. Within this emerging competitive market the most efficient will thrive, adding an inexorable, perhaps irreversible momentum to the privatization of American health care.

Profit motives can be merged with moral imperatives to produce quality services for the disadvantaged. With government agencies continuing to assess needs, set contract standards, and monitor performance, human-service entrepreneurs can relieve government of many of its provider burdens.

Breaking the Public Education Monopoly

Boston's quandary reflected a microcosm of the nation's public education problems. In 1981 the city was spending $4,000 per pupil, an increase of nearly $3,000 per pupil from 1971, yet the number of teachers and administrators remained about the same even though student enrollment during that decade had declined by 31%. Boston's mayor had actually threatened to close down the schools because city finances fell short of the $240 million needed to operate the system. At this point Dr. John R. Silber, president of Boston University, a private institution, boldly offered to take over and run the public schools for whatever amount the city could afford.

"It is ridiculous to believe that one cannot educate primary and secondary students in Boston for less than is spent nationally on the education of young people in four-year liberal arts colleges," Silber declared. He vowed to reduce overstaffing and patronage hiring in the public system. *The New York Times* editorialized its prediction that teachers' unions "would oppose and sabotage the Boston University contract" Silber proposed. Resistance from local school teachers, administrators, and status-quo politicians proved that prediction prophetic, and Silber's idea was ignored.

By 1985 Boston's public schools had deteriorated even further. Of the 120 largest school districts in the nation, Boston's ranked as the second most expensive, but its high-school seniors were scoring more than 200 points below the national average on the scholastic-aptitude test. With state and federal costs added, Boston was spending $300 million on its school system—about $5,400 per student. Enrollment had dropped more since 1981, and Silber estimated that the teaching ranks were overstaffed by at least 30%, creating the highest teacher-to-student ratio in the United States. Once again Silber renewed his offer on behalf of Boston University to administer the local public schools. "Any child who is forced by the circumstances of his parents to attend the Boston schools has already been denied equal opportunity for an education," President Silber told reporters. "I would stop the nonsense about the school system needing more money."

This time Silber received support from an unexpected quarter. Former U.S. Senator Paul E. Tsongas, a widely respected liberal Democrat, endorsed Silber's proposal and suggested that it be extended to the public schools in Lowell, Massachusetts, where Tsongas had taken up residence after retiring from Congress. "The kind of change you need to create excellence in a public school is not incremental change. It's radical change and you're not going to get it any other way," Tsongas insisted.

School administrators and teachers closed ranks and denounced the proposals as leading to the destruction of public education in Massachusetts. "It's an insult to every teacher, student, and parent of the city of Lowell," bristled the Lowell school superintendent. Legal research soon uncovered the finding that the concept of a private university taking over a public school system violated both state law and city charters, ultimately leaving the entire idea at the mercy of the state legislature, where teachers' unions exerted their greatest influence. Silber's proposal died of political neglect.

For the revolutionary founders of this country, government-run education symbolized an instrument of social control and domination, a vehicle by which government would impose a dulling uniformity on its citizens. To them pluralism in education represented the natural extension of their limited government and individualist philosophy. Our public-education establishment often tends to view its role less in terms of educating than as a molder of the social and political attitudes of the young. "Each child belongs to the state," insisted University of Virginia Professor William H. Seawell in writing about the role of government schools. Public education's purpose, according to this professional educator's view, is the "training of citizens for the state so the state may be perpetuated..."

To this end parental control over school and teacher behavior has been weakened with each corresponding increase in the monopoly power of public education. From 1960 to 1970 the number of school districts in the United States dropped from 40,520 to 17,995. Such consolidations diluted parental influence by adding insulating layers of bureaucracy and red tape, while expanding the bargaining power of teachers' unions over school policy. As the size of districts expand, salaries for teachers, supervisors, and administrators consequently increase. For administrators in particular, salaries are directly tied to the number of teachers and students under their control. "It follows then that as school districts' size increases through consolidation, the individual parent or voter has less influence on educational outcomes. Given this impotency, the rational citizen will choose in favor of ignorance and apathy," concluded economist Robert J. Staaf, in a series of studies of the education bureaucracy and parental choice.

Although education accounts for 40% of all state and local government expenditures, public-school administrators have no incentives to make their systems cost-effective. Cost-saving ideas are generally not rewarded, much less implemented. Decades of guaranteed tax funding erected accounting procedures and attitudes that discourage saving money. Since most states reclaim unspent appropriations at the end of each year, or base future budgets on most recent expenditures, few administrators are willing to acknowledge any ability to provide more education for less money, nor must they be automatically responsive to cost pressures given the absence of real competition for their student-customers.

Teacher salaries, which nationally averaged $23,546 in 1985, are higher than those of state and local government employees, the Carnegie Foundation has found. Yet only 36.6% of public-school budgets went for teachers' pay. Public schools have become top heavy with administrators, counselors, and support personnel, which helps explain why alternative parochial and private schools are so much more cost-effective. A typical Catholic school spends only $1,000 per student, and usually far less, compared to $3,000 and more per pupil expended in the public systems. For one-third of the cost, parochial schools achieve significantly higher academic scores that their public counterparts in every testing area. The same pattern of lower costs and higher achievement levels holds true for the nation's 300 independent private minority schools which must compete, like parochial systems, for the patronage of student-customers.

A 1983 report by the National Commission on Excellence in Education revealed that in 19 academic achievement tests given in 21 nations, students from the United States were last seven times and never finished first or second. Between 1963 and 1980, scholastic-aptitude-test scores in this country fell continuously. Ironically, this decline in quality occurred as spending for public education more than doubled from $41 billion in 1970 to more than $90 billion in 1981. That student achievement declined as funding soared directly contradicts the contention of public educators and teachers' unions that only by spending more on education will we improve its quality.

Why do parochial schools elicit greater achievement from students than public schools, even from students with family and socio-economic backgrounds comparable to public systems? It may be precisely because parochial systems have fewer resources, report James Coleman and Thomas Hoffer in their book *Public and Private High*

Schools. Since Catholic schools spend considerably less per student than public schools, available resources, or the lack thereof, may in fact be the secret weapon in parochial education's achievement advantages because with less money and tighter finances than public schools, it must by necessity be less flexible and retain more of a traditional curriculum and a stronger academic structure. Money consciousness also brings parents closer to other parents and school administrators and instructors, creating a common purpose, a bond and shared values in the face of fiscal adversity.

American public education's failure has less to do with inadequate financing, or incompetent teachers, or ambivalent parents, than with a delivery system that itself is in need of structural reforms to introduce the innovation-producing incentives of choice and competition. Quality might be improved and costs cut dramatically if support and educational services were contracted-out, more private-school competition was encouraged, and vouchers and tax credits were used, either widely or selectively, to further broaden the range of parental choices.

"It is ironic that in this land of choice there is so little choice in the public school system," concluded a 1986 report on public education by a task force of the National Governors' Association, chaired by Richard Lamm, then governor of Colorado. "We propose something in the great American tradition: that you increase excellence by increasing the choices."

In Chicago, 46% of public-school teachers send their children to private and parochial schools, in Memphis 36% of public-school teachers do, 29% in Los Angeles, 30% in Albuquerque. "Clearly," the governors' report concluded, "choice is being exercised by people who are a part of the public education enterprise, people who are most knowledgeable about the system's quality. This is something like an IBM engineer purchasing an Apple computer for the home."

A 1987 study by the Brookings Institution surveyed almost 500 public and private schools nationwide to determine why previous studies had found that private high schools were so much more successful at imparting knowledge than government-run high schools. The conclusion was that environment played the greatest role — public schools are governed by the politics of democracy, whereas private schools are governed by the marketplace and must please the consumers of educational services or see parents and students take their business elsewhere. Private schools "have much clearer standards" and generate more parental involvement, while public schools "have a semi-captive clientele with little choice but to patronize the local monopoly."

Why should public school boards even operate public schools? asks Myron Lieberman, professor of education at the University of Pennsylvania. He provides at least two good reasons why they should not. First, school-board agendas are too often dominated by noneducational matters like vehicle maintenance, food service, and personnel recruiting. Contracting-out these noneducational services to a firm like Service-Master, an Illinois service company specializing in maintenance for school districts, would free board members to devote more time to educational policy and classroom quality. Second, a school board is involved in a conflict of interest when it hires teachers and administrators because then "it has seriously compromised its ability to evaluate them objectively. Because the board is a political body, it has a larger stake in appearing to have made the right decision than it has in correcting wrong ones."

Contracting-out the provision of educational services to competing vendors, transforming teachers into independent contractors who serve clients rather than a government monopoly, may emerge as a high growth area for privatization. In the Chicago suburbs, about 40 school districts contract with Ombudsman Educational Services, Ltd., for instructional services to students in danger of failing their course work. In the South St. Paul, Minnesota, school district a four-person teaching partnership won a contract to provide area elementary schools with art and theater instruction. A similar program will be tried in Indiana, where teachers were permitted to organize as private professionals in 1988 to offer public-school instructional services in a competitive environment.

Failure within public schools, that "rising tide of mediocrity" identified in a 1983 presidential commission report, has driven large numbers of parents, especially in our poor inner-city neighborhoods, to take their child's future into their own hands. At least 300 independent neighborhood schools serving minority students operate nationwide, most of them started since 1975. A survey by the National Center for Neighborhood Enterprise found the average enrollment to be about 200 students, and waiting lists are long. Many school founders and instructors have formerly worked in the public-school system as teachers or administrators. Some tuition is free, while other schools charge about $855 a year, forcing numerous families to rely on welfare checks to help pay tuition costs—a phenomenon that underscores the depth of their concern for quality education. These schools are "often located in inadequate physical facilities in some of the poorest inner-city neighborhoods," concluded the surveyor, Joan Davis Ratteray. "Yet, teaching and learning in these schools are unparalleled."

An already well-publicized example is Westside Prep, a Chicago school started in 1975 by Marva Collins, whose tenure as a public-school teacher convinced her that the system was destructive to intellectual achievement. Using $5,000 from her pension as capital, and books salvaged from wherever she could find them, Westside Prep opened with half-a-dozen parents in her impoverished neighborhood paying $80 a month per child in tuition. She expanded the school to accommodate 30 students, many of them drawn from among underachievers so as to dispel the notion that she was "skimming the cream" from local public schools. Her program has been acclaimed for raising both the self-esteem and achievement levels of students whose potentials were starved in the public system.

In New York City, a few blocks from a public school with reading levels two years behind the national average, the Lower East Side Community School offers further testimony for the rewards to black parents who undertake self-help initiatives. A former public-school teacher, Mrs. Wallie Simpson, established the school in 1976 when her two children reached school age because she knew from first-hand observation that the local public schools would quash any desire for them to succeed academically. After discovering an empty building once used as a schoolhouse, she and a few other parents persuaded the city to rent them the first two floors. More than 300 students applied for the initial 175 openings, and 75 teachers applied for seven teaching positions at a starting salary of only $7,100 a year, far less than what they would have earned in the public schools. Most told Mrs. Simpson they preferred the prospect of working in an environment where scholastic standards would be high. Simpson is understandably proud that over the years she managed to keep tuition down to about $600 a year per student. Anything higher would have been beyond the reach of most neighborhood families, virtually all of which are low-income black and Hispanic.

Only the financially able members of society are currently free to painlessly choose whether their children will attend public or private schools. These upper classes already possess the power to pay twice for schooling—once in private tuition, again in taxes. To empower the poor with similar educational choices, the Reagan administration in late 1985 proposed turning the federal $3.2-billion "Chapter I" remedial-education aid program into vouchers, which would be distributed to the parents of the 5 million eligible American children in amounts averaging about $600 each. Parents could use the vouchers toward tuition at any private school they chose, or send their child to another public school if they were dissatisfied with the one to which they were assigned. This system would improve educational quality by forcing public schools to be more responsive, said Education Secretary William J. Bennett, and "serve the cause of social justice by providing disadvantaged families some of the educational choices already available to more affluent families."

In response, the National Education Association (NEA) argued that the voucher proposal would provide little choice at $600 a student, but would destroy public schools and promote racial segregation. "Vouchers would open the gates to white flight and educational inequality in our country. Only more wealthy Americans—the majority of whom are white—would have enough money to send their children to private schools. Lower-income families—a great percentage of whom are minorities—would be left to attend our public schools," the NEA claimed in a written position paper. That vouchers for the poor would somehow result in more wealthy Americans being able to send their children to private schools ranks as an argument worthy of logic gleaned from a back issue of *Beyond Reality* magazine. Syndicated columnist William Raspberry dismissed the NEA in two sentences: "Voucherizing a program for children from disadvantaged families would send wealthy white families scurrying into private schools? Surely the NEA knows better." Contrary to NEA's contention about the worthlessness of the vouchers, most of the 300 independent minority schools around the nation could accommodate students in the $600-tuition range, while 67% of parochial schools had average tuitions below $600 during the 1985 school year.

Clearly the spectre of allowing parents to vote with their dollars for the quality of education they desire threatens the educational establishment, which naturally prefers to have our tax dollars forced down through the absorbent layers of its self-perpetuating, self-serving bureaucracy. Vouchers, even in limited form, would help break the cohesive monopoly of the present education system. As Peter L. Berger and Richard John Neuhaus have argued in their classic study of mediating structures, "Monopolies endowed with cohesive powers do not change easily. The best way to induce change is to start breaking up the monopoly—to empower people to shop elsewhere. We trust the ability of low-income parents to make educational decisions more wisely than do the professionals who now control their children's education. To deny this ability is the worst class bias of all, and in many instances it is racism as well."

· Vermont education officials deny that their school system, which allows students to "tuition out" of public education, in any way constitutes a "voucher" plan. For public educators and teachers' unions, giving parents the power of choice over their child's school assignment using the economic tool of vouchers ultimately means the destruction of their public-education monopoly. For them it is jobs, status, and authority that are at stake, all cloaked under the egalitarian rhetoric of preserving the monopoly to engender a national community of values.

Since the early 19th century many Vermont towns have financed the education of children at private academies, a practice that lingers in some rural towns of at least two other New England states—Maine and Connecticut. Today almost 100 Vermont towns still receive high-school education payments or, dare we say it, vouchers, from their local school districts. Such payments are made for use only in nonsectarian private schools that have been approved by the state's education department. In the town of Kirby, population 285, one of the 25 Vermont towns with a voucher system for all grades, not just high school, can be found John McClaughry, president of the Institute for Liberty and Community. McClaughry sends his daughter Anna to a prestigious private school in Washington, D.C., with nearly $2,000 of her annual tuition paid for by the town school district of Kirby. "Now Vermonters have never used the word voucher to describe what happens there," McClaughry reported in an article for *Reason* magazine. "Nevertheless, long before the rest of the country had ever heard of the idea, many Vermonters were benefiting from a system whereby the local government uses tax monies to pay for education rather than to provide it."

· Vermont's deputy commissioner of education, Jim Lengel, bristles at the insinuation that "tuitioning out" resembles vouchers. Out of all the state's high-school students, he points out, 92% attend their local public or union-district high school. "I think it's a pretty strong argument that private education is just not popular in the state of Vermont," he says. If anything, Lengel's statistics, and Vermont's experience with vouchers, no matter how limited, contradict the assertion of teachers' unions that a voucher system will undermine support for public education.

Other states have begun responding to pressures from parents for more flexibility in determining educational choices. Local school districts in New Hampshire are authorized to pay the tuition of students who attend private academies in that state. Minnesota law now allows tuition tax deductions of up to $700 for both private and public education at the elementary and secondary school levels, a law upheld by the U.S. Supreme Court in 1983. Louisiana has a somewhat more limited tuition tax-credit law permitting payments of up to $200 per child in direct credits and related assistance for private-school students. Washington State provides vouchers to public-school dropouts who may finish their schooling at either public or private institutions.

Widespread dissatisfaction with public education, its escalating costs and declining student achievement scores, spawned an entire new industry in the 1980s to dramatically expand the scope of acceptance of private-sector alternatives. American business responded to parental frustration over the pace of learning in public schools by franchising for-profit learning centers nationwide, teaching the basics in reading and math. Student-to-teacher ratios are generally three-to-one—and most instructors are former public-school teachers. Charges average $18–$25 an hour per student, and prizes are often used as learning incentives. Three nationwide learning center chains emerged —The Reading Game, Sylvan Learning Center, and the Huntington Learning Centers—and growth for each has been phenomenal. Oldest of the group is The Reading Game, operated by Encyclopaedia Britannica, with 300 franchises, more than double the number from 1983. In 1983 Sylvan had just nine franchises; by 1985 it had 159 across the country. Several studies have found evidence that these centers can raise some students' academic performance by two grade-levels after just 36 hours of instruction. Educators are beginning to concede that the success of these centers "is a prime example of what can happen when free enterprise is applied to a field often stultified by bureaucracy and red tape," commented *The Wall Street Journal.*

The quiet revolution in education is fueled by parental frustration. An absence of competition and choice in public education to assure user responsiveness and fiscal accountability will only enable the system to spread its contagion of mediocrity, while continuing to nurture the myth that only fresh infusions of tax money can cure the system's many self-induced maladies. Teachers and administrators must share in the profits of better schools if they are to have sufficient incentives to elevate pupil achievement. Educational-service contracting, vouchers and tax credits, and profit-making schools could provide just such an incentive structure for educational innovation and the salvation of the future of learning.

5
Rebuilding Our Infrastructure

We depend on infrastructure to support the entire range of human activities essential to survival. Without these basic public-service systems—mass transit, highways, bridges, sewers, water-supply utilities—it is hard to imagine a life resembling what we have come to expect of civilization. Infrastructure usually shapes if not dictates how we will organize and conduct ourselves, affecting the quality of our lives, where and how we choose to live, no less than the strengths we enjoy as a nation. Infrastructure constitutes the basic investment underpinning of the national economy. It is necessary for productivity growth and the creation of an expanding job market. When a company seeks to locate or expand a plant, or when persons decide to start a small business of their own, they must ask questions relating to the adequacy of infrastructure. Can we rely on local transit to transport our employees? Can we expect a new freeway interchange or a widened road to relieve traffic congestion? When will sewer repairs be completed, and do we have sufficient access to clean drinking water?

Life as we have come to know it in this country, reliant on a stable, expanding infrastructure, appears perilously close to disruption. We simply have too many unmet needs competing for too few public funds to address them. Various congressional estimates project the shortage of infrastructure funding at from $1.1 trillion up to $3 trillion through the end of this century, which translates into between $11,000 and $30,000 in new taxes or debt for each American taxpayer.

Our nation's entire structure of mass-transit systems, owned and operated almost entirely by government monopolies, qualifies for wholesale bankruptcy, with a deficit exceeding $6 billion annually. Our highways and bridges continue to erode and collapse, as maintenance is deferred and new construction is foregone. Nearly half of the nation's 574,100 highway bridges surveyed by the U.S. Department of Transportation have been found to be deficient—many should be immediately closed. By the summer of 1988, every municipality in the nation must satisfy the sewage-treatment requirements of the Clean Water Act passed by Congress, mandating minimum discharge standards to protect streams and waterways. More than 6,000 wastewater-treatment plants remain to be built, and the financing burden will soon be falling almost entirely on local governments. Amendments to the Safe Drinking Water Act in 1986, setting ambitious requirements to remove contaminants from our drinking water, will force the nation's 60,000 water utilities to provide new treatment technologies or build more sophisticated treatment plants. Many of these supply systems already suffer from maintenance neglect and old age—some water mains in northeastern cities have been in service for more than a century.

An insight into the depth and gravity of the problem, as experienced at the state level, is provided by New Jersey Governor Thomas H. Kean: "In our 1983 state budget the $80 million we had allocated for infrastructure needs was cut back to $20 million, and the need is more on the order of $20 billion. About 4,500 of our 6,000 bridges are in need of repair. To meet Clean Water Act goals, New Jersey must construct 237 wastewater-treatment plants in the next decade. With funding currently planned, we can only build twenty-four. We've got infrastructure needs of staggering proportions and shrinking financial resources to meet them."

Before we even consider renewing any tax-supported investment in infrastructure, we must ask why our current systems are crumbling and how our financing mechanisms failed. The answer involves fiscal processes of government that, in the view of Herman Leonard, an associate professor of public policy at Harvard, systematically deprive public services of adequate preventive and supportive maintenance. Unlike the private sector, which treats maintenance as a form of investment, government agencies routinely ignore depreciation in public assets. Whereas a private company will compute the yearly depreciation of, let us say, a bus it owns as a cost in calculating annual company income, a government agency usually ignores this hidden accumulated cost side of the ledger until the vehicle wears out and money must be appropriated for a replacement.

—See complaints on pg 157, about the Transit System,

Such practices create a negative incentive structure for public officials. "Far from getting any budgetary credit or recognition for using scarce funds to improve the condition of the public's investment holdings," says Professor Leonard, "public officials who find room in their budgets for maintenance spending find themselves with fewer remaining operating resources to meet vocal demands for immediate public services." Nor do political rewards accrue to officials who assign funds for maintenance. Ribbon cuttings, laudatory plaques, and media attention typically attend new, highly visible spending projects like dams or cable cars, rather than applause for the repair of leaky sewer pipes or the trestle of a bridge. Maintenance remains the most politically attractive portion of the budget to be cut during periods of fiscal strain, yet it is arguably the most important spending done to insure the long-term quality of life.

Deferring maintenance costs allows one generation of taxpayers to levy a hidden spending burden on future generations. Unfortunately for the current generation of taxpayers, we are already exhausting the infrastructure assets conferred upon us, creating an ever-larger unfunded maintenance liability. Bills incurred only recently are already coming due.

If America intends to adequately rehabilitate its mass-transit systems, repave its roads, fix its bridges, clean its water, and treat its sewage, then ways must be found to introduce market incentives into the construction, operation and maintenance of infrastructure. No longer can we afford to allow political considerations to shape our perception of infrastructure needs or dictate our infrastructure priorities. Gut sint a Superman.

Injecting Competition into Mass Transit

Across America the problems of mass transit haunt policymakers and soak taxpayers. Two years after Miami's Metrorail system opened, daily ridership hovered at 24,000, about one-eighth of what had been predicted, with taxpayers contributing $3.40 for every $1 passenger ride. It is a subway that does not go where people want — there are no stations at the airport, the Orange Bowl, or the beach. The 20-mile system prompted a *Miami Herald* reporter to describe it as "like the town drunk hired by medieval villages to reel about the streets, demonstrating to the populace the evils of alcohol." Presumably the people are passing judgment on Miami's transit infrastructure by their refusal to use it, yet the warning signs of indifference should have been apparent to local officials even before the system was built. In 1976 Miami voters rejected by almost two-to-one a penny increase in the sales tax to help pay for Metrorail. Despite this repudiation local officials built the subway anyway using mostly federal funds. "Where was the local commitment?" Ralph Stanley, the administrator of the Urban Mass Transportation Administration (UMTA), demanded to know. If Miami residents really thought the system was important to their city, they should have been willing to help pay for it. Then Office of Management and Budget director David Stockman estimated that it would have been cheaper for the federal government "to buy everybody who uses Metrorail a new car every five years for the next fifty years" than to build and maintain the system.

When construction began in 1969 on a 63rd Street subway tunnel on Manhattan's East Side, costs were projected at $245 million for the three-mile link intended to relieve rush-hour congestion across the East River to Queens. By 1985, when UMTA finally suspended further federal financing for the project—still uncompleted after sixteen years—more than $1.2 billion in federal and state tax money had been spent and the project's usefulness had so eroded that less than a train full of passengers was expected to ride the line each day. Over the years red tape so entangled the project, with 17 federal, state, and city agencies overseeing construction, that the resulting costly delays and management bungling, combined with the ill-conceived nature of the project, created a public-works disaster. "No one ever bothered asking the simple question how many riders will benefit from the investment," fumed Ralph Stanley. "Instead the attitude was the federal money is there, why not spend it."

Back in 1973 transit officials in Detroit predicted that an automated "People Mover," a 2.9-mile downtown elevated rail loop, would cost $30 million to build. By 1979 that figure had reached $110 million. As costs mounted, the Reagan administration in 1981 attempted to withdraw federal participation, only to have Congress appropriate money for it anyway. By 1986 the system was budgeted at $210 million, with no end in sight to spending needs. UMTA calculates the system will attract no more than 15,000 daily riders, far short of the 37,000 a day Detroit needs for the system to break even. The People Mover has no money budgeted to operate the system at a time when the city already has a $50-million annual transit deficit. The Detroit News ridiculed the system in an editorial, calling it "one of the most absurd transportation projects in American history."

What each of these transit infrastructure projects—in Miami, New York, and Detroit—has in common is the attitude of local officials that the federal role in transit should be like a bank that does not ask what it is buying. Because the federal government was paying 75% of the capital expenses of each project, local officials had incentives to build the systems based only on political considerations, appeasing special interests and favored neighborhoods with extensions of lines that could not otherwise be justified. They kept building the projects when every other indicator would have told them to stop. Some local officials have developed such dependence on federal subsidies that they seem to regard future transit funding as an entitlement program like Social Security. When Ralph Stanley suggested that budget cutbacks might necessitate more reliance on local financing to finish the 130-mile Washington, D.C., subway system, a Virginia county supervisor threatened to sue UMTA if any federal funds were cut.

Wisconsin Democratic Senator William Proxmire awarded his December 1985 "Golden Fleece" for the most wasteful use of tax money to UMTA, the federal agency that has given local transit systems nearly $50 billion over 20 years. UMTA has been "playing Santa Claus to the nation's mass-transit systems," Senator Proxmire declared, and the result has been "a spectacular flop, the Edsel of federal programs. Taxpayers were taken for a ride." In the decade that Senator Proxmire has been awarding his Golden Fleece for waste, no recipient has been willing to accept it. "Usually the award is as popular as ants, or maybe a skunk, at a picnic," chortles the senator. But in this instance the administrator of UMTA not only accepted the Golden Fleece, he congratulated Proxmire for awarding it.

"Unlike most federal department heads who are embarrassed by this honor, I embrace Senator Proxmire's Golden Fleece award and totally agree with his criticism, " said 34-year-old Ralph Stanley, a lawyer who became administrator in 1983. "My agency has earned this award the old-fashioned way—we paid for it." Two years on the job had convinced Stanley that much of the federal money used for local transit construction was wasted, and that years of federal operating subsidies, used by local transit agencies to make up the difference between low-fare revenues and escalating costs, had instead encouraged inefficiency, high operating costs, and further insulated public-transit monopolies from the cost-effectiveness a healthy dose of private-sector competition would bring.

Nearly a century of entrenched attitudes will need exorcising before the nation's transit industry can ever regain its fiscal health. The origins of today's problems stretch back to the late 19th century, when the electric-streetcar systems were introduced. Typically a single street-railway company was granted a franchise to operate, creating a monopoly in virtually every American city. In 1914 the jitney bus—a modified Model T Ford carrying five to twelve passengers—emerged in Los Angeles to compete with streetcars by offering higher speeds and flexible routes for the price of a nickel, or a "jitney." As jitney use spread to other cities, municipal governments that had become depen-dent on streetcars for tax revenues began to outlaw jitneys. Within just a few years, in the words of UCLA transit scholar Dr. George Hilton, the result was "a nationwide prohibition of a competitive market in ur-ban transportation." Bus systems later began replacing streetcar lines utilizing the same area-wide monopoly status; by 1944 buses were carrying more passengers than streetcars. These bus companies gener-ally had their fares and levels of service strictly regulated by local governments.

As taxis became more common, cities began strict regulation, with laws limiting the number of taxis in service, the kinds of transpor-tation services that could be provided, the fares charged, and the number and types of passengers that could be served. Some taxi com-panies welcomed such regulation because it assured them of monopoly privileges where fares were stabilized and part-time drivers were ex-cluded. The consequence in New York City has been that the price of a taxi medallion—allowing an owner to operate—reached $100,000 in 1985, generating a new class of investors who buy and sell medallions. Setting taxi rates amounts to price fixing, and most taxi regulations now seem designed primarily to protect taxi operators rather than in-sure public safety, convenience, and benefit.

Mass transit began its steep decline in the 1950s as automobile use increased and suburban living expanded. Transit ridership fell from 17.2 billion passenger-rides per year in 1950 to fewer than 9 billion in 1961. To survive, bus companies needed to raise fares, adopt distance-based pricing, or drop routes with low ridership. But what they got in-stead was more regulation and price control from local governments.

Economist Steve Hanke describes how such processes typically evolve: "Private firms raise nominal prices, either because service im-provements are mandated or because of inflation; this brings forth demands for politicians to control prices. After price controls, the private firms find that the only way they can maintain profit margins is to reduce the quality of services; as service declines, the public becomes anxious and demands that the private firms be taken over by a public entity because the private firms are not capable of providing reliable service."

When local regulatory authorities across the nation refused to approve the service and fare adjustments bus companies needed to stay solvent, 194 companies were forced out of business between 1954 and 1963. For those that remained, strict government regulation, a lack of competition, and continuing declines in ridership made them easy prey for takeover by state and local government. Many owners even welcomed these takeovers.

Passage of the Urban Mass Transportation Act of 1964 provided federal grants for cities to buy their local transit companies. Private monopolies were rapidly transformed into public monopolies until, within 15 years, 92% of all bus and rail service in the nation was government owned and operated. Mass-transit use declined further, commuter ridership continued to fall, and the nationwide transit deficit, which had been only $880,000 in 1963 before wholesale nationalization, passed $500 million in 1972. Again the federal government organized a rescue effort. In 1974 the U.S. Congress initiated a federal subsidy of local transit operating expenses, distributed through UMTA. These subsidies rather than dousing the fiscal fires, reacted more like gasoline — commuter ridership tumbled another 10%; the nationwide transit deficit hit $2 billion annually in 1978, then tripled to $6 billion in 1985.

"These subsidies have done the cities a disservice," concluded a 1985 report by the Joint Center for Urban Mobility Research, affiliated with Rice University in Houston. The federal subsidies "masked the underlying structural weaknesses and encouraged city officials to expand services into low-density areas without regard to their economic soundness. The result was to compound an already precarious state of transit finances."

A 1983 analysis of federal mass-transit subsidies by Charles River Associates calculated that only 23% of operating subsidies benefited persons below the poverty level, or about a 12-cent subsidy per trip for poor riders, compared to a 20-cent subsidy for persons with incomes over $50,000 annually. The discrepancy occurs because upper-income persons inordinately benefit from subway and commuter rail systems reaching out into the suburbs and sustained by federal subsidies.

The more obvious impact of federal subsidies was to permit an escalating series of wage increases for local transit workers. Between 1970 and 1980, only about 27% of federal subsidies directly benefited transit riders in the form of fare reductions and enhanced service; the remainder went mostly for various forms of employee compensation, enabling transit wages to rise faster than labor costs in comparable occupations and faster even than other public-sector job categories. Newly hired stock clerks with the Washington, D.C., Metro system, for instance, can earn $30,000 a year, substantially more than first-year policemen and firemen who have more responsibility and training. Transit bus drivers in many cities earn $35,000 and more. Token sellers for the New York City subway were found to be making $21,888 a year back in 1978, while tellers in nearby banks, a role requiring much higher skills, made less than $12,000.

Even though the skills required for operating transit vehicles are commonly possessed by most American adults, of $6 billion in nationwide transit-operating costs in 1980, 73% went to salaries, wages, and fringe benefits for transit employees, observes Simon Rottenberg, a professor of economics at the University of Massachusetts. Successful performance of vehicle operation, Rottenberg wrote in the *Cato Journal*, requires only "motor vehicle operating skill, a common courteous manner, good moral character, and capacity to read and to tell time." These attributes are common enough in the population, yet those utilizing the traits in transit are paid at rates comparable to persons with advanced degrees. Not only are base hourly wages for transit workers higher than what would evolve under normal competition, earnings are further enlarged by overtime, spread time, shift premiums, and other arrangements based on status that bear no relationship to vehicle operation time.

Transit wages ballooned all out of proportion to realistic market value primarily because the public employees were given monoply control over their transit systems by Section 13c of the 1964 Urban Mass Transportation Act. That section protects local transit employees from any adverse effects of programs involving federal capital or operating subsidies, which has been transformed into a labor negotiating tool endowing transit unions with veto power over local transit decision-making. They have generally succeeded at preventing the contracting-out of service to cut costs, while advancing work rules to prohibit the employment of part-time drivers and the implementation of other labor-saving and cost-cutting steps. Such monopoly control over all jobs associated with transit operations gives the transit unions direct power to greatly influence, if not dictate, the course of wage negotiations.

Above-market wages for bus drivers forced transit systems to utilize larger vehicles, which in turn reduced ridership. "With drivers often making $35,000 or more per year, a transit agency's incentive is to get as much out of each driver as possible — by having them drive a 70-seat bus rather than a 20-seat minibus," Robert W. Poole, Jr. of the Local Government Center shrewdly noted. This move toward larger vehicles is wrong for passengers because the frequency of service declines with larger buses. Poole uses the example of 600 daily seats on a given bus route being parceled out in 20-seat minibuses, making 30 vehicles available. If those same 600 seats are provided by 60-seat buses, only 10 vehicles will be on the route and frequency of service will obviously be three times less. Like new subway lines which have failed to attract anticipated levels of ridership despite huge subsidies that hold down fares, long waits for buses can mean a drastic loss of potential ridership. A Census Bureau study in 1980 found 75% of all those interviewed commuting to work by car refused to use public transit, not because they preferred sitting in congested auto traffic but because the transit system did not conveniently serve their needs. Several other studies have found transit riders to be twice as responsive to service changes, such as more frequent scheduling of buses, than to lower fares.

The key to any change in the fortunes of the transit industry rests with the introduction of competition, offering a proven alternative to the unpalatable choice between increasing tax and fare revenues or cutting service. Public-transit institutions and their supporters argue that allowing competition, either through the bidding process for contract services, or more directly through an unrestricted free-market approach, will endanger the poor by raising fares too high, and endanger public-transit systems by enabling the private sector to "skim the cream" off transit revenues. If the poor are to be subsidized, it would be far less costly and far more equitable to use vouchers or another form of direct-user subsidy than to erect a low-fare structure that subsidizes all passengers, those able to pay and those not, regardless of need. Most public-transit agencies seem to view peak-period service, principally morning and evening rush-hour, as the "cream" of their revenues. But when the high operating costs of peak periods are taken into account — with more buses on the road, and restrictions on using cheaper, part-time drivers—shedding the load of peak periods to less costly providers would instead skim some of the deficits of public-transit systems.

Allowing the private sector to compete in operating mass transit should reduce costs, provide more variety in services, and introduce innovations to benefit both riders and taxpayers. A private operator's interest in retaining its contract, obtaining future contracts, and luring riders from the competition, creates powerful incentives to assure quality service. "A public agency, holding an exclusive monopoly on providing services and protected from competition, lacks that strong motivation," reports the Joint Center for Urban Mobility Research in a study for the U.S. Department of Transportation. "Incentive contracting, whereby a portion of the private contractor's compensation is contingent upon real and measurable performance, can be used as an added stimulus. A major advantage of contracting with private providers is the flexibility in reduced risk it affords the contracting public agency."

For those few areas of the nation that already contract with private firms for bus service, savings of 50% and more are commonplace. Westchester County, New York, outside New York City, operates one of the largest contract systems with 11 private companies running 323 buses a day. Though the county continues to set fares and schedules, operating costs in private hands are $3.26 a mile, compared to $4.27 a mile for neighboring Nassau County where the bus system is publicly owned. Employees in both systems belong to the same union and have similar salary and benefit levels, yet in 1984 Westchester got by with federal and local tax subsidies of $9.1 million annually compared to $17.8 million for Nassau, while carrying about the same number of riders. Westchester County also used a competitive bidding process to find a private company to finance, install, and maintain bus-passenger shelters throughout the county at 252 locations. By selling advertising space on two panels of each shelter the company made a profit while supplying the county with shelters free of charge.

In Phoenix the bus system is managed and operated by the American Transit Corporation. Even though the city of Phoenix determines the quality and frequency of service and sets bus routes, private operation of its system saves 62% over what it would cost the city to provide the service itself. Phoenix also estimates that it saves $700,000 a year by substituting contracted-out "demand responsive" transit, otherwise known as taxis, in place of its regular Sunday fixed-route services. The Tidewater Regional Transit Authority of Virginia plans, operates, and regulates public transportation services in a five-city area around Virginia Beach. The authority has encouraged the formation of private citizen-operated van-pool services carrying about 1,000 persons to and from work without tax subsidies. Had the authority provided this service, 25 buses would have needed to be purchased, and costs to taxpayers would have exceeded $3 million a year.

Overseas the same sort of pattern emerges among private firms that are allowed to offer frequent and unsubsidized service. In Buenos Aires, Argentina, private microbuses operate at a profit and account for 75% of all transit trips. In Calcutta, India, one of the most densely populated cities in the world, private buses were banned in 1960 and replaced by a government entity, but six years later, in response to strikes, public demand, and the need for quick cash, permits were sold enabling 300 private buses to go into business. As Gabriel Roth, a former transit economist for the World Bank, discovered, Calcutta experienced a boom in transit provision. By the late 1970s more than 1,500 full-size private buses were operating, providing two-thirds of all city bus trips, and doing so without tax subsidies. Meanwhile the government bus system, monopolizing the best routes at the same fare levels, continued to need a tax subsidy of $1 million a month. Roth attributes this private-public contrast to the private companies providing better vehicle maintenance and higher labor productivity. Other studies conducted in Australia and England of public versus private transit costs found private to be typically 50% to 60% cheaper.

To encourage more private involvement in American transit, the Urban Mass Transportation Administration issued regulations requiring local transit agencies seeking federal funds to allow private firms to bid for contracts for new or reorganized bus lines, giving priority to applicants for capital grants that "demonstrate their commitment to competitive bidding and private sector involvement." The Reagan administration's fiscal 1987 budget proposed combining mass-transit capital funds and a portion of federal aid to highways into one urban-mobility block grant. This would give local officials flexibility in determining whether to invest in bridges and highways or to address transit needs by buying buses and building rail lines. More importantly such a block grant might discourage duplication between highway construction and transit projects, forcing localities to make cost-effective infrastructure choices by ending their reliance on federal programs that have induced them to design transit projects more to obtain "cheap" federal money than to satisfy genuine local needs.

California already uses a block grant for its state transit-subsidy program. When eligible counties reach a certain level of transit service, any state funds left over can be used for streets and highways. This gives local governments an incentive to free more funding for street and highway repairs by cutting transit costs using private contractors to provide bus service. One result has been that California boasts more private-sector involvement in transit than any other state. A federal block grant, as a transitional step toward free-market delivery, would begin to shift primary responsibility for financing mass transit to the local level, where the services are planned and received and where all ultimate responsibility belongs.

A case can be made that the private transportation market has been suppressed for so long that few potential providers would be available if the nation began a wholesale shift away from public monopolies. Yet holders of that view overlook the remarkable resilience and resourcefulness of private providers and the American people. The city of Chicago once had 30 private mass-transit companies, ten railroads, and dozens of taxi and jitney companies, before the Chicago Transit Authority was formed and all these providers were consolidated into one rigid system. A four-day transit strike in December 1979, shutting down the public monopoly, rejuvenated the entrepreneurial instincts of Chicago commuters. In the downtown loop where 80% of peak-hour commuters arrive by public transit, an array of private buses, vans, taxis, and car pools materialized. By the third day of the transit-union strike, absenteeism for businesses in the loop area was only 12% above normal. Something similar occurred in 1981, when Chicago's commuter rail fares were nearly doubled. Groups of passengers rebelled against the increase in fares and decrease in service levels by forming commuter clubs with daily chartered bus service for more than 3,000 commuters. In the southern Chicago suburbs an average cost per passenger trip on subscription came to $1.15, a fare that covered all service-provision costs, compared to the commuter rail cost of $2.80 per passenger trip, which covered just 69% of the public operating expense.

Relatively recent trends that relieve the fiscal strains in transit appear encouraging. In 1985 directors of the Dallas Area Rapid Transit contracted with a consortium of three companies to operate 204 buses on local and crosstown routes in nine suburban cities north of Dallas.

The $103.5-million contract utilized the Trailways Corporation to provide drivers and management, Ryder Truck Systems for bus maintenance, and ATE Management and Service Company as general manager. A previous express-service contract between Trailways and the transit authority signed in 1984 saved the city about $9 million annually. Most cities still maintain laws prohibiting the operation of jitneys, but Indianapolis broke from tradition in 1982 to allow the operation of seven 14-passenger jitney vans, and San Diego in 1983 placed 36 jitneys in service. Homeowner associations have begun providing their own range of transportation services to supplement, or avoid entirely, the local public-transit systems. In Fairfax County, Virginia, the Rotunda and Montebello apartment complexes operate shuttle buses connecting with regional bus lines and shopping malls. More than 1,000 households are served, each contributing $20 extra a year in condominium association fees to cover operating costs. Montclair, a 1,600-unit single-family project in northern Virginia, 35 miles south of Washington, D.C., runs daily commuter bus services into the nation's capital financed by homeowners' association fees and an annual grant from the developer, the Chemical Bank of New York.

Still another emerging model of local-transit delivery is the Transportation Management Associations, voluntary organizations formed by corporate employers, developers, and merchants to provide transportation services in suburban areas. These TMAs generate revenues through voluntary assessments or membership fees, and by 1985, according to the Joint Center for Urban Mobility Research, at least 20 large associations could be found around the nation. Outside Houston, the Woodlands is a 10,000-resident development with a fleet of 45 vans and a budget of $475,000 annually. Fifty-four thousand dollars is contributed by the developer, a subsidiary of Mitchell Energy and Development Corporation that uses the program as a persuasive marketing tool to attract new residents. In Los Angeles, the El Segundo Employers Association, with 18 member companies representing 65,000 employees, was formed to relieve traffic congestion around the International Airport where the firms are located. Area-wide van pools serving local neighborhoods were established with voluntary assessments from the participating firms.

Imaginative service redesign, along with innovative use of private alternatives, offers the most realistic course away from the tired, conventional solutions of government that rely on raising fares or cutting service to meet fiscal challenges. Service redesign, as defined by Ted

Kolderie, director of the Hubert Humphrey Institute's Public Sector Redesign Project, simply means restructuring the way transit services are organized and managed, utilizing the forces of competition to increase efficiency, and adopting the marketing creativity of multiple providers, using local transit agencies as brokers and coordinators rather than as providers. Service delivery has now been separated from policymaking by the cities of Minneapolis–St. Paul, Dallas, and San Diego.

The simplest way to privatize American transit would be to let the municipal systems declare bankruptcy. This action would void all existing labor agreements and allow the assets to be sold off to private operators who could then start providing services in a fresh competitive environment.

Across the transit horizon other glimmers of hope can be seen for the long-term fiscal health of transit infrastructure. Numerous plans have been finalized for private-sector financing, and construction and operation of high-speed rail systems, an area monopolized by government for a half-century. A law passed by the Florida legislature in 1984 created a commission to oversee the award of a franchise to a private company for the construction and operation of high-speed rail system connecting Miami, Orlando, and Tampa. The franchise for the 120-mile-per-hour system would be competitively bid, with no government tax monies involved. In Orange County, Florida, expressions of interest were solicited in 1985 for private firms to design, construct, and operate a rail system that would connect the Orlando International Airport to hotels, tourist attractions like Disneyworld, and the Orlando business district. A high-speed passenger rail line with private backing has been proposed to link the Washington, D.C., subway system and Dulles Airport in northern Virginia, a plan endorsed by the U.S. Department of Transportation in late 1985 when it became clear that no federal funds would be required. The largest and most precedent-shattering private transit-construction project of the 20th century was formalized in early 1986 when Britain and France signed an agreement to build a 31-mile twin-tube rail tunnel connecting the island kingdom with the continent of Europe. A consortium of construction companies and banks from both sides of the English Channel agreed to undertake the $6.6-billion project without the use of tax monies from either country. What will become the biggest civil-engineering feat in this century should finally dispel the idea that only governments can summon the resources, the coordination, and the resolve to meet the large-scale public-works needs of society.

To get subway construction off the federal dole, a few enterprising public officials are turning to the private sector, offering access for development around subway stations in return for financing to help build those stations. Such a policy was adopted in early 1987 by the regional Metro board of directors for the Washington, D.C., system. Developers seeking approval for a $500-million hotel and apartment complex in nearby Alexandria immediately offered to pay $19.2 million for a new subway station to serve the area. In San Francisco, the Bay Area Rapid Transit board of directors approved a $150,000 study to determine the feasibility of attracting private-sector financing of a 94-mile, $3.5-billion subway extension. BART board members had been impressed by the completion of a privately financed rail system in Istanbul, Turkey.

What American transit desperately needs is a flexible, decentralized, and competitive package of services. The protective cocoon of regulation government has woven around mass transit has stifled innovation, encouraged waste and duplication, created massive boondoggles, and driven deficits up and ridership down. Public-transit agencies should end their monopoly on service provision, sever their role of policymaker from that of provider, and become agents or facilitators to insure the widest variety of transit services for riders at the lowest possible cost for taxpayers. By injecting choice and competition into urban transportation, we can revitalize a once-proud industry while tailoring its services to fit the diverse and changing needs of the American public.

Selling Off the Roads and Bridges   — Crazy!!

An old melancholy country song, "The Streets of Laredo," tells of dusty upaved streets and cowboys down on their luck. Though times may have changed down on the Texas border, those streets of Laredo, at least until 1982, remained dusty and mostly unpaved. In that year a modern version of the ballad might have been written, beginning with the words: "As I was out buying the streets of Laredo. . ."

Confronted by limited resources, explosive growth, and the need to pave or repave half of all city streets, officials in Laredo, population 100,000, took action some thought at the time was drastic, even for a pioneering state like Texas. They announced that all streets except major thoroughfares would go on sale. The idea was to unload unpaved or underutilized streets to eliminate them from the city maintenance inventory, in the process raising revenue to surface and repair other more heavily traveled thoroughfares. Within three years about 150 city blocks had been sold for prices ranging from $2,300 to $108,000, collecting money for a special fund devoted entirely to street paving. Streets were purchased by motel owners, lumber yards, the Missouri Pacific Railroad, and ordinary citizens. A supermarket bought an adjoining street and closed if off to create more parking spaces. One street went to a trailer-park owner to park additional trailers; another became transformed into a community swimming pool; a church took another on which to build a new meeting hall.

Texas has been in the forefront of innovative policies in road and street financing, construction, and maintenance. In 1984 the Texas Legislature passed the Road Utility District Act and the Texas Transportation Corporation Act, which offer attractive incentives for private participation in highway development. Road utility districts enabled property owners to finance road construction using tax-exempt bonds through a specially created district. San Antonio became the first city to take advantage of the new law, resurrecting a four-lane West Side Expressway project that had been dormant for 30 years because of inadequate financing. Landowners along the 10-mile route contributed land for rights of way and half the costs of frontage in return for enormous increases in the value of their mostly agricultural properties.

Transportation corporations are perhaps best used in tandem with road-utility districts for right-of-way donations of public roads, with the value claimed as a tax deduction by the donor. The first corporation organized under the act was the Grand Parkway Association, a group of Houston developers who donated 95 miles of land rights of way, initiated engineering studies, and set dates for contracts to be let in 1987 to build a 155-mile scenic parkway around Houston. By the summer of 1985, other transportation corporations had been formed in Austin, Dallas, and Fort Worth, with the value of donated rights of way estimated at $500 million. In the Dallas area, the Joint Center for Urban Mobility Research reported, "Private landowners' donations of rights of ways for highways and funds for ramp and bridge modifications have become commonplace. Almost every new facility built in the last five years has had some private-sector contribution."

In the western part of Houston and Harris County, a group of 113 corporations, developers, and businesses, known collectively as the West Houston Association, have been financing and building much of the area's roadway network. They found themselves initially forced to participate in road projects when a frenzy of unbridled growth beginning in 1978 overwhelmed the resources of state and local government. Developers and large landowners at the intersection of Mason and Peek roads, for instance, realized in 1981 that the two-lane highway overpasses then in place would stifle growth. They paid for engineering costs and went ahead with construction of two five-lane overpasses. To relieve congestion on the Katy Freeway, the association built a four-lane highway 10 miles long to parallel the freeway and feed traffic into offices and warehouses of association members. Dozens of other similar projects involving freeway interchanges and new roads, all privately designed, financed, and built, prompted a columnist for *The Houston Chronicle* to marvel: "Something particularly interesting is taking place on the city's far west side. Members of the West Houston Association are banding together to build roads. . .These are not simply roads within a subdivision—these are main thoroughfares which will eventually be major traffic arteries."

Why are private firms volunteering to play a role previously monopolized by government? "Private-sector participation is easy to get from these members," says Patricia Stofer, executive director of the association, "because they see it as self-enlightened interest to do such projects and pay for them in part or whole. It increases their property values, it helps in recruiting good employees or keeping good employees, and if you're a corporation, it protects the value of the facilities already built. Instead of developers first asking what government can do to help them, they ask what they can do for themselves and then see how government fits into the picture."

Local officials reap public benefits from the private-sector role because the West Houston Association wisely gives them credit for what its members accomplish. County commissioners can tell their constituents, "Look here, I got all these roads built for free and saved you taxpayers money." Such ego-stroking makes politicians less inclined to erect barriers and dictate private-sector priorities in construction.

To keep its state roadways clean, Texas initiated an "Adopt-a-Highway" program in 1986 using privately funded volunteers, and within a year had attracted support from 2,200 service clubs, Boy Scout troops, and other organizations, each agreeing to keep a two-mile section of highway free of litter. With more than 4,000 miles of highway under private maintenance, Texas became a model for similar programs under development in a half-dozen other states.

In other parts of the nation entrepreneurs initiated significant road and transportation improvements. A group of developers and landowners in Denver formed the Joint Southeast Public Improvement Authority to pursue a $20-million privately funded program of highway improvements to relieve traffic congestion in the Southeast corridor of the city. The Irvine Company in Orange County, California, agreed to provide $60 million in transportation construction to develop Irvine Center, a 480-acre complex in the triangle formed by the Santa Ana, San Diego, and Laguna freeways. The improvements involve three freeway off-ramps, two parkways, a new interchange, and 14 traffic-control projects. In northern San Diego County, Shapell Industries, developer of the 1,500-acre Rancho Carmel, bankrolled 33 separate capital infrastructure projects for $57.5 million, including arterial roads, freeway overpasses, and interchanges. Outside Washington, D.C., landowners and developers in Prince William County, Virginia, paid $300,000 for the design of a 12-mile highway bypass and agreed to donate rights of way where needed.

Stronger private-sector involvement in developing and maintaining our infrastructure is now a necessity because federal, state, and local governments concentrated on constructing new highways while deferring the financing of needed repairs of already existing roadways and bridges. The political process helped create our infrastructure problems by forcing interest groups to compete for the same common pool of tax resources. Politicians and interest groups tend to favor spending that provides immediate and easily identifiable benefits, a bias that shortchanges long-term spending needs for politically unattractive programs like preventive maintenance.

A consequence of such shortsightedness can be catastrophic. On 28 June 1983, three people plunged to their deaths and another three were critically injured when a 100-foot section of Connecticut's Mianus River Bridge on Interstate 95 collapsed. Much of the revenue intended for the rehabilitation and maintenance of bridges like this one had been siphoned off into other government accounts. An article about the disaster in Connecticut's *Business Times* concluded: "We charge our residents the fifth highest gasoline tax in the nation and rank near the bottom on the list in highway spending...Hundreds of millions of dollars per year were collected from all sources of highway related revenues, but the citizens of Connecticut did not get their money's worth."

The U.S. Department of Transportation issued two reports on bridge and highway conditions in 1987 that painted a graphic and grim picture with statistics. About 42% of the nation's 574,100 inventoried highway bridges were found to be deficient. Even as federal aid to highways was reduced in Congress, the Secretary of Transportation warned, "If the nation's highway bridges are to be maintained in a safe and serviceable condition, a significantly scaled-back bridge program will not be possible in the foreseeable future." Reduced federal aid will have dramatic impact on some states. Texas, for instance, with 25,152 bridges in its inventory, had 3,816 rated as functionally obsolete and another 1,049 classified as structurally deficient. The State of Kansas already had 168 bridges closed because of structural problems, nearly three times the number of the next highest state, Massachusetts. In 1983 Kansas ranked thirty-first among the states in the number of vehicle-miles traveled on its highways, yet Kansas was judged to have 83.1% of its urban interstate pavement in deficient condition, higher than any other state.

A possible solution to the maintenance crisis was proposed by science writer Jeanne McDermott in a 1982 issue of *Technology*. She asked the following question: "Given high interest rates and severe cutbacks in public spending, why not convert bridges to private ownership?" A long list of successful investor-owned bridges can be cited. The best-known private bridges are in Detroit, where two competing systems link that city with Windsor, Ontario. The Ambassador Bridge, a steel suspension structure built in 1929, and the Detroit-Windsor Tunnel each charge identical tolls, are well maintained, and turn a profit. The Florida Bridge Company of Venice, Florida, owns the two-mile-long Samuel Schuckman Bridge and Causeway connecting Boca Grande to the mainland. In Texas the B&P Bridge Company owns a quarter-mile span called the Progresso that crosses the Rio Grande River between Progresso, Texas, and Mexico—one of three private bridges over that river.

The United States has only 334 toll bridges, nearly all of them operated by semiautonomous government entities. What strikes one about these bridges is that all are well maintained. Bridges insulated from the political-interest-group competition for tax revenues remain safe and in good repair, whereas publicly owned and managed bridges using taxes for upkeep suffer from deferred maintenance. Science writer McDermott offered three possible scenarios of privatization to rehabilitate the nation's bridges: sell or give them to private firms that would be allowed to charge tolls for their upkeep; create toll-bridge authorities to contract-out bridge operation and maintenance; or erect incentives for the private sector to both build and refurbish bridges which would then be leased back to the government.

At least $48 billion is needed to replace or renovate deficient bridges, at which rate, given recent funding levels, it would take nearly 300 years to repair them all. Several possible private-sector approaches to alleviating the quandary could be implemented quickly. A county engineer in Pike County, Indiana, for instance, formulated a plan to replace or repair 50 bridges in his jurisdiction almost immediately and simultaneously, by contracting with private construction firms under lease-purchase agreements, using the county's bridge-construction budget to finance the leases. Clauses would be added to the contracts for the county to purchase the bridges, if it ever so decided, at some future date. An entrepreneur from Peoria, Illinois, Jerry Janssen of Build-A-Bridge, proposes that not-for-profit public corporations be formed to collect lease payments for new bridges from local or state governments; initial funding for construction would be provided by contractors in exchange for mortgages on the projects issued through the public corporations.

Bridge privatization in concept took a step closer to reality when, in September 1987, the Municipal Development Corporation (MDC) based in New York entered into a franchise agreement to finance, build, and operate a $1.6-million bridge across the Red River linking Fargo, North Dakota, with Moorhead, Minnesota. Under the agreement MDC will assume all liability and responsiblity for cost overruns, charging a 25-cent-per-vehicle toll over the 25-year life of the franchise, at which point the bridge will be turned over to Fargo and Moorhead for operation. Using this arrangement as a model, MDC intends to expand nationwide with proposals to rehabilitate existing bridges using tolls to repay the financing of improvements under lease agreements with states and localities. Mastermind of the scheme was Ralph Stanley, a senior vice president of MDC and the former head of the Urban Mass Transportation Administration in the Reagan administration.

As with toll bridges, America's 240 toll roads — 30 of them under private ownership — are better maintained than other highways. Toll roads and private ownership of roads and bridges are more common in Europe than in the United States. In 1977 the International Bridge, Tunnel, and Turnpike Association surveyed five European countries —

Britain, Spain, Italy, Belgium, and France—and found a total of 8,868 miles of toll roads, compared to 4,416 miles in the U.S. More than 5,000 miles of toll highways were built in France, Spain, and Italy by companies under long-term contracts with those governments to construct and then operate the highways as business enterprises. Under these toll systems, heavy trucks that impose the most damage and wear on roads must pay accordingly, whereas on U.S. highways, supported by gas and excise taxes, trucks pay proportionately less.

Roads have been described by some economists as a classic example of a "public good"—a service or asset from which it is impossible or impractical to exclude nonpaying consumers—seemingly rendering road provision as the sole province of government. Yet national defense is a nonexcludable good; the Air Force can't simply say it won't defend the skies over sleepy little Moscow, Texas, even if its citizens were to refuse to pay taxes for defense. Although government must provide defense, it does not own the factories and infrastructure that produce the material and services purchased for defense. In both theory and practice the same application could be made to highways. Government is expected to insure the provision of highways, but it doesn't necessarily have to own them.

Toll collection for road-use privileges extends to early Babylonian civilization, but the origins of our modern toll roads can be traced to 12th-century England, where "murags" were charged those passing through city walls to help maintain the structures and a tax called "pavages" was levied to improve roads. In early America, privately built, owned, and operated turnpikes were commonplace, and created the nation's first transportation infrastructure.

Private pay-as-you-go financing of turnpikes came about in early America because state governments were without adequate resources and already existing government roads were poorly maintained. In 1794 the first private turnpike was completed in Pennsylvania by the Philadelphia and Lancaster Turnpike Company. By 1800 at least 72 turnpike companies had been chartered, using stock subscriptions and tolls for construction financing. In New York, for example, 4,000 miles of roadway had been built by 278 companies by 1821, with these private firms having invested nearly $12 million in roads and bridges compared to only $622,000 spent by the state government. Colorado's first toll road sprang from a fur trapper who carved a short-cut through Raton Pass in the southeastern part of the state, charging a dollar a wagon—funerals and Indians could travel free. In northern

Virginia, a Quaker businessman named Phinneas Janney, president of the Little River Turnpike Company, charged commuters three cents to travel by horse or donkey along his road, which stretched from Alexandria into Loudoun County. He used the tolls for upkeep on the dirt highway and to return a profit to his many shareholders.

State governments avidly regulated these private roads by issuing specifications for road widths, surfacing, maintenance, and the use of guideposts and mileposts. New England states were especially severe in restricting toll charges and the placement of toll booths. Wholesale outright toll evasion was guaranteed by such regulations, which typically forced road owners to build toll gates 10 miles apart, enabling renegade roads to be cut bypassing the gates. Some companies lost half their revenues through this form of evasion. Private roads lowered transportation costs, stimulated commerce, and increased land values, reports transit historian Daniel Klein of New York University, but legally sanctioned toll evasion, and toll charges kept artificially low by legislative fiat, made the turnpikes unprofitable to operate. As canals and railroads became more common modes of transportation, state governments reclaimed control over road ownership and construction.

Road-financing mechanisms available to government expanded with vehicle registration fees in 1901, state gas taxes in 1919, and a federal gas tax in 1932. In 1916 the U.S. Congress adopted legislation prohibiting the use of tolls on any roads or bridges built in part or whole by federal taxes. When the 41,000-mile interstate highway network went into construction in the late 1950s, about 2,500 miles of already existing toll roads, bridges, and tunnels were incorporated into the federal system.

Our nation's Highway Trust Fund, established to collect gas taxes for the upkeep of federal roads, totters near bankruptcy. Oil embargoes in the 1970s depleted gas-tax revenues by slowing gas consumption at a time when road maintenance costs began to soar. Outlays from the Highway Trust started exceeding income in 1986. An article in *Financier* magazine estimated that this investment gap between needs and revenues from 1986 through the year 2000 will be at least $350 billion, most of it for repair and rebuilding.

As stated by the Transportation Infrastructure Advisory Group, a consortium of private firms in Washington, D.C., "In reality, what drivers have bought and paid for (with gas taxes) is the initial construction and 25-year design life of the interstate system. The gas tax *does not* pay for the considerable cost of ongoing maintenance and for extensive repairs as the end of the 25-year design life nears."

By properly harnessing the private sector, officials at all levels of government can summon relief for investment strains that otherwise would call for massive, probably unpalatable tax increases. A *Washington Post* article on private toll roads in 1986 concluded, "a new era of governmental austerity could mean that a relic of the past will become the wave of the future." Here and there across the infrastructure landscape are signs of such change. Two developers in suburban Washington, D.C., have proposed building and operating a 10-mile toll road from Dulles International Airport through Loudoun County, with the entire $35-million construction cost to be recovered in tolls. Private completion would be within four years, whereas under Virginia state construction schedules it could not be finished until the year 2000. "As private businessmen we think this is an economically viable project and we can make money from doing it," says John D. Miller, president of the Municipal Development Corporation, a specialist in financing roads and public improvements. A group of businessmen in Colorado announced plans in 1986 to build a 200-mile, four-lane private expressway linking the cities of Fort Collins and Pueblo.

Several studies by the Urban Institute found that congestion on our nation's main highways could be reduced using a demand-sensitive pricing system, toll roads being one example. The principle at work is known in economic theory as the tragedy of the commons. Those using communal property, be it natural resources or the highways, attempt to maximize its value by using as much of the resource as often as possible. Such exploitation results in waste, overuse, and disincentives for preservation. In the case of "free" highways, traffic congestion results in large measure from the absence of use-pricing.

"We constantly see private services faced with congestion problems; for instance, movie theaters have a rush hour during the evening showings while their afternoon showings are sparsely attended. To solve this problem, they charge lower fees during the matinee showings," observed Douglas Conway and Jim Peron, in a special report on highways they prepared for The Connecticut Institute. Demand-sensitive pricing would entail varying the price of highway usage according to the time of day, level of demand, and type of vehicle. When the city of Singapore, one of the fastest-growing areas in the world, experienced severe traffic overcrowding, a pricing system was instituted that prohibited access to the downtown area between 7:30 A.M. and 10:15 A.M. except to vehicles displaying a sticker purchased for $1.67

a day. A study by the World Bank later found that traffic during morning rush hour dropped 65% under this pricing scheme.

Toll roads utilizing toll booths may be the least desirable type of road pricing. Toll barriers slow driving time, create congestion bottlenecks, and may increase traffic accidents. A better method of road pricing is the automatic vehicle-identification system. "AVI is similar to an electronic license plate because it can electronically identify uniquely and automatically any vehicle driving at normal highway speeds," report Conway and Peron. "And since AVI has the potential for identifying any vehicle, it can also charge different prices according to time, location, and type of vehicle — making it superior to any other pricing technology."

An AVI system has three components: A transponder, which can be the size of a thick credit card, is mounted somewhere on the vehicle; the transponder's code number is intercepted by an interrogator, placed along the highway on a road sign; and in turn the interrogator transmits to a central computer system that identifies the vehicle and makes a record of the time of day. Billing could occur when the driver reaches a toll collection point, or it could be sent each month in the mail, itemized according to trip length, time, and cost. Most technology today centers on using microwave infrared systems or radio-frequency induction.

The Port Authority of New York and New Jersey made the first road test of radio-frequency AVIs for the Federal Highway Administration in 1972. The authority fitted 4,000 buses with transponders, using four different manufacturers of AVIs, and tested them for accuracy of vehicle identification at normal driving speeds. All four systems were found to operate at 99% efficiency. Oregon installed transponders at several state weigh stations in 1984 to expedite truck identification and clearance. Other similar systems are in operation in private California parking lots.

From 1983 to 1985, Hong Kong conducted an extensive electronic road-pricing experiment by fitting more than 2,500 vehicles — half of them government cars and buses — with tamper-proof electronic number plates the size of a cassette tape. Eighteen on-street sites identified the vehicles and sent the information to a central computer that recorded the tolls and billed vehicle owners each month. The technology was proven reliable, and demonstrated potential for monitoring traffic conditions, traffic accidents, and even tracing stolen vehicles. Only politically did the experiment fail. Motorists felt that the identification fees would not be offset by lower taxes that they would be charged for road usage, and others raised a privacy issue—they objected to having computers monitor their whereabouts. The first argument seems borne of suspicion, perhaps warranted, that government officials would use the prospect of electronic pricing and privatization as a way of introducing a double tax on road usage. Of the latter objection it can be pointed out that few people complain about private telephone companies knowing where and to whom they speak, so presumably this fear concerning vehicle monitoring would dissipate if private concerns were the monitors. AVI technology can be a useful tool in restraining traffic, raising revenues, and privatizing roadways.

A first step in America toward practical introduction of AVI came in late 1987, when a British firm—Castle Rock Consultants—contracted with the Virginia Department of Transportation to produce such a system for the Dulles Toll Road, a highway linking suburban Washington, D.C., with Dulles International Airport. Vehicle identification will occur at the main toll plaza and at entry points for drivers who have voluntarily fitted their vehicles with electronic plates, enabling them to avoid payment lines at the toll plazas. Once the system is operational in 1989, "it may become the passport for large-scale entry by the private sector into road provision," predicts Gabriel Roth, a transportation economist.

A sensible way to depoliticize the construction of highways and insure proper road and bridge upkeep might be to privatize either the entire system or those roads and bridges in most urgent need of rehabilitation. As Conway and Peron propose, "the state would simply sell their ailing highways and bridges to private investors to be operated as businesses paid for entirely by users' fees collected from AVI systems and other incidental sources of revenue. Such enterprises offer two major attractions to investors: large, dependable cash flow and attractive depreciation write-offs." Liability laws and covenants would force the road owners to maintain them in a safe condition, while relieving government and taxpayers of any further funding burdens. For the poor and those unable to pay directly for road usage, government could issue vouchers similar to food stamps.

Privatized roadways offer revenue-generating potential beyond just fares from road users, according to John Semmens, senior policy analyst for the Arizona Department of Transportation. Renting space to advertisers along the road would bring in substantial sums, especially in urban areas. Air space over the roadway could be of value for construction overhangs in congested urban environments, and access charges might be levied on businesses seeking enhanced convenience to their premises. Highway privatization would provide for new road-way construction and raise revenues on old roadways without increas-ing taxes; it would improve highway-usage efficiency, improve maintenance of new and existing roadways, and expand the quality of roadside services.

Our roads are economic assets desperately in need of financing mechanisms that depoliticize investment decisions. Whatever ap-proach to privatization is taken, in the words of Semmens, "we in the public sector must satisfy ourselves with cultivating the conditions that are conducive to private solutions to human needs. The aim is to unleash private-sector market forces and its abundant creating capabilities to transform our highways into more efficient mechanisms for benefiting the general welfare."

Financing Clean Water

When the U.S. Congress passed the Federal Water Pollution Control Act in 1956 it overrode a veto by President Dwight Eisenhower—who wanted those directly responsible for pollution to pay cleanup costs—and appropriated a modest $50 million annually to build wastewater-treatment plants for municipalities. That program expanded dram-atically until by 1972, $4.5 billion a year was being spent on plant con-struction, making it, after interstate highways, the second-largest public-works program ever undertaken in this country. It turned into a pork-barrel diner's dream, larding out federal tax money, often regardless of need, while shifting the accountability for pollution prob-lems from local jurisdictions to the federal level.

Federal funding encouraged communities to build larger sewer capacity plants than they had water in supply, creating frequent water shortage crises. Routine maintenance suffered neglect because the federal grants emphasized only capital-investment construction. One result was that on any given day 40% of the water going into the na-tion's sewage plants was groundwater that leaked through the under-ground pipes, raising the costs of treatment even as municipal engineers pleaded for building ever-larger-capacity plants to handle the surge. An investigation by *The Washington Post* in 1981 found that up to 90% of the wastewater plants built with federal funds failed to perform up to anti-pollution standards. The *Post* series of articles concluded: "what little information exists suggests that there has been little or no change in basic water quality since 1972...Certainly there is no evidence that the $30-billion grants program has helped measurably." The two primary explanations for failure seemed to be federal money and federal control.

As an anti-pollution lobbyist for consumer advocate Ralph Nader, Larry Silverman gradually came to realize that corporations are often more responsive to environmental laws and issues than are the federal, state, and local governments that write those laws and set our social-policy agendas. One set of statistics in particular kept gnawing at him. Within the industrial sector, compliance with pollution laws averaged about 90%, while among municipal governments it is just 60%. The only reason governments score that high is that the Environmental Protection Agency keeps extending the deadlines for municipalities to comply with wastewater-treatment standards. From these statistics and his own experience lobbying for passage of the 1977 Clean Water Act, Silverman concluded that the entry of private firms into the waste-water-treatment business would be the most promising if not the only remaining viable route to affordable, clean, and safe water.

In rural areas the use of the urban technologies prescribed under the federal grants program had proven ruinous, Silverman discovered, as residents of some communities were being slapped with sewer bills of $400 and more a month. "You frequently find people who have perfectly adequate septic tanks who are forced to destroy their tanks and tie in to a sewer line and pay a very large tie-in fee, maybe a couple of thousand dollars, and pay high bills for a treatment plant that may not work."

When the Reagan administration had cut the sewage-construction-grants program budget from $4.5 billion down to $2.4 billion annually in 1981, Silverman and an environmental organization he founded, the American Clean Water Association, lobbied on behalf of the funding reduction. He viewed the cuts as a method of accelerating privatization and cost efficiency. "We're not against growth, but let it pay for itself, and if it pays for itself, it will probably be more ecologically sound, as well as economically sound. In this respect it seemed that David Stockman [then Office of Management and Budget director who supported the cuts] was to the left of the Sierra Club which opposed them. When you've got EPA involved paying for everything it's stultifying, all the uniformity, the special interest and bureaucracy. We wanted to loosen it up to allow for innovation."

By giving the private sector responsibility for what Silverman describes as "the gastro-intestinal system of cities," consumers benefit with lower costs, cleaner water, and more accountability. "How do you force a municipality to comply with a pollution control law? Do you put the mayor in jail; do you fine him? This is one reason I like privatization, because you can muster an attack on a corporation much easier than you can on a city. It's so much easier to affect them where it hurts — in their profits if they have to pay a big fine. It's not the same when a public entity is causing the pollution. Taxpayers can't sue their local public utility for bad service because they'd be suing themselves. Privatization allows you to pinpoint responsibility and establish standards of performance."

Private firms can build a wastewater-treatment plant 20% to 40% less expensively than government because they do not have to be concerned with procurement regulations, federal intervention, or the red tape ensnaring municipal construction. Private firms can spread development costs over many plants in different localities, a luxury that municipal operators cannot enjoy, and adopt technological innovations more rapidly, with more flexible designs closely approximating needs. Large private firms utilize economies of scale more effectively than government, and provide profit-sharing and stock-ownership incentives to employees that municipalities cannot duplicate. Private operators relieve local governments of the burden of maintaining liability protection, effluent-fine coverage, and responsibility for negligence. With state limits often imposed on bonded indebtedness and on property taxes, allowing private firms to assume all the financial risks of a project protects a city's bonding capability and credit rating.

Impetus for a large-scale introduction of privatization in wastewater treatment came no less from federal grants reductions than from the 1981 Reagan administration tax bill, which awakened the private sector to financial rewards. That legislation provided investment-tax credits for capital investments, allowing companies to subtract the credit from taxes owed; it provided for accelerated depreciation, a rapid write-off of assets; and industrial development bonds, the interest on which was tax exempt, with the debtor a private company that has received the sanction of a municipality.

A contract for the nation's first privately financed, owned, and operated wastewater-treatment plant was signed in 1983 between the city of Chandler, Arizona, 25 miles southwest of Phoenix, and The

Parsons Corporation of California. Chandler was in the midst of an explosive cycle of growth, doubling in size from 29,000 in 1980 to 58,000 residents a few years later, severely straining city services. The city also rated low on the priority-grant list for federal funding of a wastewater plant. Chandler was no stranger to privatization, having already contracted-out its refuse collection, groundskeeping, and other city services. City Manager Hal Schilling explained his city's philosophy: "We are a city with no reservations on the issue of private ownership of public services. As long as the service offered is equal to or better than that which could be provided by a public agency, and as long as the cost is right, we will go to the private sector." Parsons financed the $22-million project by issuing industrial-development bonds backed by the Bank of America. Chandler figures to save $1.1 million a year over the 25-year life of the contract, with savings passed on to users. Instead of sewage bills averaging $18.50 a month under city ownership and operation, customers should pay only about $8.85 a month.

Within a year of the Chandler contract, at least 15 other local governments decided to privatize their wastewater-treatment facilities. Typical was the university town of Auburn, Alabama, 50 miles east of Montgomery, which signed a $26.7-million deal for two new plants and 25 miles of new intercepting sewers with the Massachusetts firm of Metcalf & Eddy, Inc. Savings to the city from privatization are estimated at up to $40 million over the 25-year life of the contract. Under terms of the agreement, no city sanitation employees lost their jobs; all were either offered employment with the private operator or transferred to other duties within city departments.

Downingtown, Pennsylvania, a suburb of Philadelphia, became the first city in the nation where an already existing federally funded treatment plant was privatized. Under federal regulations a treatment plant built with federal funds cannot be handed over to a private entity unless the money used to build it is paid back to the federal treasury. The accounting and consulting firm of Touche-Ross designed a service contract that allowed The Parsons Corporation to finance, design, construct, and operate new additions to upgrade the existing parts of the facility, and gave Parsons a management contract to operate and maintain the federally funded portion. As in Auburn, city employees were given retention rights to work for the private operator. Touche-Ross later arranged a similar privatization model for Kerrville, Texas.

Professor John Heilman of Auburn University contrasted three

Alabama wastewater-treatment plants—two funded through government with bonds or grants, the third a privatized facility—and found the private plant to have been built in two years, versus seven and 11 years for the government projects. His data led him to the conclusion that unifying the functions of plant designer, owner, and operator in privatization produced the incentives for efficient choices throughout the entire process, resulting in time savings and reduced economic costs. Political savings for city officials came about under privatization because they no longer had to invest so much time in project management or with regulatory agency requirements.

Of all essential public services worldwide, providing piped water for drinking is the one with which the private sector is the least involved, observes Gabriel Roth, formerly an international economist with the World Bank. "It may not be a coincidence that water is also the sector that, in many countries, seems to have the greatest problems." One result has been a boom in the bottled-water business and home water filtration, particularly in the United States, which would seem to indicate that people no longer trust the quality of water or their dependence on the big government systems that provide it.

During the entire history of piped water, nongovernment provision turns up rarely, although some remarkable exceptions can be found. The brothers Perrier in France founded a company in 1782 that received a license to supply piped water in the Paris area. The brothers set up two steam pumps, four tanks, and a wooden supply system, and as the venture became a quick success they expanded their operations. "The Parisian system has evolved into one of the world's largest, most sophisticated, cost-effective waterworks systems," writes Steven H. Hanke, a former senior economist for the Council of Economic Advisers, who has made a study of private water systems. "The success of the Parisian system can be laid squarely at the feet of private ownership and regulation through competition, rather than public regulatory bodies."

Two economists writing in a 1978 issue of the *Journal of Law and Economics* compared 24 private and 88 public water enterprises in the United States, using an econometric cost model, and found private operating costs to be 25% less than municipal costs. Despite this cost-effectiveness, at most one-fourth of the nation's water is supplied by private, investor-owned companies. Hawaii is the one state where water has been traditionally a privately owned and provided resource. The nation's largest single private water system is in San Jose, California, where the San Jose Water Company, founded in 1866, provides about 90% of city water using 200,000 hookups. Many municipalities actually try to take over privately operated water utilities in order to capture the income and divert it to other government programs. "They seem to forget that the facility will fall apart some day, and then they'll have to recapitalize it," comments Franklin J. Agardy, president of URS Engineers.

Treating underground water as a free commodity or as an under-priced resource produces reflexive depletion and shortage problems, much as what happens with overuse of public grazing lands, over-fishing on the "communal" lakes and oceans, and other realms where resources are not priced or underpriced and lack clearly delineated ownership rights. Among the desert tribes of Arab countries Islamic law recognizes the right to own and sell water, that most precious and scarce of resources, from an oasis, with the sole proviso that the thirsty will never be denied the right to drink, even if they are penniless.

Gabriel Roth identifies one of the worst features of government monopoly of the water supply as the use of uniform water charges over given areas. This forces customers who use little water to help subsidize those who use a lot, especially the corporate and wealthy users. The recognition that undercharging for water creates inequities and scarcities has dawned on many leaders of the environmental movement. Marion Clawson of Resources for the Future calls federal water-development projects the catalyst for exacerbating the nationwide water crisis by pricing water at absurdly low levels—backed by tax subsidies—and tying it to particular tracts of farmland. "Low prices for water encourage waste," Clawson declares. "The resulting scarcity and crisis are strictly man-made, institutional rather than hydrologic or engineering in character." Clawson, Larry Silverman, and other environmentalists now see the market allocation of water, utilizing private firms, as the most effective means to insure conservation.

An equally serious problem resulting from underpricing is the inability of urban water systems to raise sufficient capital to expand or even properly maintain the systems. "Price controls have caused the industry's capital shortage," Steven H. Hanke concluded in a 1981 article for *The Wall Street Journal*. "Whether imposed by state public service commissions or local political bodies, these curbs have forced water purveyors to keep their prices far below their costs." The Russian economist Yakov Usherenko once bragged that the Soviets were able to eliminate the private sector in the 1920s solely through the use of price controls without ever having to resort to force. In this country it has been an illusory conservation, not communism, that has been the banner under which municipalities have invoked price controls to squeeze out private providers. Continued stringent price regulation of private water suppliers by local governments, coupled with municipal takeovers of private water companies, reduced the number of private suppliers in the industry between 1984 and 1985, dropping the number of customers receiving water from the private sector from 4.9 million to 4.6 million.

Privatization of water supplies has taken a few steps forward. When the Washington Suburban Sanitary Commission, a water and sewer utility in two Maryland counties outside Washington, D.C., decided to try privatization, a water-storage facility was selected as a cautious step. Commission general manager John Brusnighan settled on a private water-storage project under $5 million as the initial experiment simply to overcome "the fear of the unknown and loss of control" he says has created reluctance among the water and sewer fraternity of public officials to utilize private financing and operation. The project now produces 20% annual savings for the commission without any federal grant entanglements.

A subsidiary of the Triton Energy Corporation—the Whalen Corporation—launched a water-privatization project in 1972 by drilling a well for the city of Irving, Texas. Whalen drilled a second well in 1979, arranging the financing, operations, and continued management, and sells the water to Irving under a ten-year contract at a fixed fee. This arrangement saved Irving from using its bond money for the project, relieved it of dependence on water purchases from neighboring Dallas, and lowered overall water rates for the city.

Water-utility officials can no longer assure themselves of complacency about avoiding privatization. Under 1986 amendments to the Safe Drinking Water Act, more than 60,000 drinking-water utilities must install new treatment technologies or build more sophisticated water-treatment plants just to comply. Coincident with these requirements is the even more pressing concern of adequately maintaining old and neglected distribution systems. To meet the immense capital needs of our water systems, either a federal subsidy and tax bailout must be initiated—which seems unlikely—or the industry must be further deregulated and privatized to attract sufficient investment capital. With users paying the real cost of their water, prices would fluctuate according to supply, and conservation as well as cost-effectiveness would emerge to help assure the long-term supply and maintenance needs of our most vital resource.

Under tax-reform legislation passed by Congress in 1986, many of the incentives luring the private sector to invest in wastewater-treatment and water-supply infrastructure were diluted or eliminated. Issuance of tax-exempt industrial-development bonds for "private activities" was tightened, and the legislation abolished investment-tax credits for privately owned projects while extending depreciation schedules. This should drive many investors seeking tax shelters out of the infrastructure market and may produce more transactions based on real economic merit.

"The future of privatization will not have to depend on staying within the tax laws," predicts Philip D. Giantris, a senior vice-president at Metcalf & Eddy, Inc. He expects an increase in the number of lease-purchase agreements between municipalities and private firms in which ownership might revert to the government at the end of a contract's initial life. Private-sector participation must continue, no matter what incentives remain in the tax law, because "we can no longer afford to ignore the role of maintenance in improving performance and lessening the chance of major breakdowns. Long-term operation and maintenance is just as important as the construction, and that is where contract operations and privatization serve a growing need."

6
Unleashing Our Hoarded Assets

Selling Surplus Properties

At the intersection of Wilshire Boulevard and the San Diego Freeway in Los Angeles, on the doorstep of exclusive Beverly Hills, our federal government owns 442 acres of property occupied by the Veterans Administration Medical Center. On any given day the site resembles a ghost town. Few people wander among the 142 buildings, many of them World War II-vintage frame structures, or around the 42 parking lots, a nine-hole golf course, three baseball diamonds, basketball courts, tennis courts, or the acres more of barren, unused land. More doctors and staff than patients can usually be found taking advantage of the recreational facilities. Three-fourths of the parking spaces stay empty, and one large parking lot is reserved for the use of students and faculty at UCLA, located nearly a mile away.

"There is absolutely no reason why the federal government needs to hold all that property," insists Joshua Muss, former director of the now-defunct White House Property Review Board, which valued the land at $2 billion. In 1982 the Property Review Board wanted to sell part of this land and hundreds of other unused, underutilized, or unneeded federal properties to raise a minimum of $17 billion to help offset the budget deficit, while streamlining government's management of its assets.

This was only a small fraction of Uncle Sam's vast landholdings, 27,688 separate properties covering 727 million acres, about one-third of the nation's entire land area. Even excluding all national parks, wilderness areas, and historical sites, the American Society of Appraisers in 1982 estimated that 5,000 federal properties could be categorized as surplus. If put on the market, they could raise over $100 billion in revenue.

When the Property Review Board attempted to enact even its modest program of surplus sales, federal agencies like the Veterans Administration resisted giving up anything, and members of Congress, wanting to retain or give the properties away for political gain, interceded with legislation protecting the targeted sites. As the Property Review Board persisted in pressuring federal agencies to help reduce the deficit, Congress voted to eliminate budgetary authority for funding salaries and expenses of the board, effectively abolishing it.

When the board had been created by the Reagan administration in February 1982, hopes were raised that its composition—the president's five most senior policy advisers—would give it a high enough profile and level of influence to overwhelm the natural lethargy of federal agencies to give up anything. No one in the administration doubted that government's management of its own property was nothing short of scandalous. An eight-month, nationwide investigation of federal property management by the *Philadelphia Inquirer*, published in May 1982, endorsed that conclusion: " The U.S. government has cost the taxpayers billions of dollars by acquiring land it does not need, by holding on to property it does not use, by delaying for years the disposal of land when it finally decides to let go, and by giving away thousands of valuable properties it could sell."

Federal landholdings are so vast and its management so poor that abandoned facilities often slide off into a sort of bureaucratic Twilight Zone. One caretaker couple at a closed Navy facility in Kingston, Washington, waited for a decade for the federal government to return and claim the property. Only the curiosity of a Navy real-estate appraiser, who accidentally stumbled onto the site, rescued the elderly couple from living out their lives anonymously tending a forgotten piece of history and wondering why Uncle Sam had forsaken them.

Statutory responsibility for the surplus property disposal program rests with the General Services Administration. Yet in many ways GSA has no real authority because Congress has layered the disposal process with a veritable maze of senseless laws and regulations. Under the Federal Property Act of 1949, GSA must first offer surplus properties to all other federal agencies. If all decline it, then the property is offered free to state and local governments or nonprofit groups. Only after all have passed up this gift can GSA finally put the property up for sale. Even at this point the revenue raised must go into a special

Interior Department fund for the purchase of still more privately held properties by federal agencies.

No one in government knows how much the total inventory of federal properties is worth. Outdated accounting methods still value this property at the original cost to the government. So the White House grounds, for instance, are valued at $1,000, the price one would have paid more than a century ago. In Fairfax County, Virginia, outside the city of Washington, Uncle Sam holds onto 109 acres that were declared surplus back in 1975. Appraisers value the tract of land in excess of $20 million, yet on the government's books it is carried at only $14,465 — what the land brought in 1917.

The White House Property Review Board encountered little difficulty in targeting a lengthy list of worthy properties for surplussing. There was the federal building in Laguna Niguel, 50 miles south of Los Angeles, worth $20 million and designed for 7,500 office workers, yet only 500 persons had ever worked there since it opened in 1974. In Hawaii the board found a deserted Air Force station called Bellows, sprawling over 1,500 acres of beach-front property on the island of Oahu, 15 miles from Waikiki Beach. It had been closed since 1958 and become a hangout for military families wanting to avoid crowded beaches closer to Honolulu. "Bellows is a piece of land that's being completely wasted by the federal government," Honolulu mayor Frank Fasi told the *Philadelphia Inquirer.* "When they try to tell an old Marine like me they need the whole thing, I say baloney."

In San Antonio old Camp Bullis contines to encompass 26,000 acres worth more than $200 million, though the facility was long ago rendered useless to the government because it sits in the approach of a nearby airport. Twelve miles of ocean frontage at Camp Pendleton, California, used only once every few years for training, seemed an obvious candidate for surplussing because only one division was stationed at the camp and even it never engaged in division-sized exercises. At the entrance of the Golden Gate Bridge in San Francisco is the largest military installation within a U.S. city's limits — The Presidio, 1,774 hilly acres owned and managed by the U.S. Army. This largely underutilized facility remains a favorite posting for military personnel, with its housing commanding a breathtaking panoramic view of the Golden Gate Bridge, San Francisco Bay, and the city below. Nearly 149 acres is devoted to a golf course used since the turn of the century by a private, civilian golf club. The U.S. Sixth Army stationed at The Presidio has seen its mission over the years reduced to nothing more than providing civilian relief in time of natural disaster.

Most federal agencies, using stalling and evasion tactics, refused to cooperate with the White House Property Board in identifying surplus properties, nor could the board acquire from them figures to estimate the total cost to taxpayers of maintaining surplus and un-needed real estate. Federal agencies have stalled GSA for years over giving up property, anticipating that GSA would eventually lose its institutional memory and the asset would be forgotten. In 1973 GSA recommended disposal of 27 acres of unneeded Navy property in northern California's Contra Costa County; the Office of Management and Budget concurred with the decision. Over the years, each time a GSA official inquired about the status of the land, Defense Department memo writers responded that "ongoing studies" were being prepared to determine the proper method of disposal. Twelve years later those studies were still "ongoing."

"The agencies know 11 ways to hide a piece of property," says Joshua Muss, who was a real-estate lawyer in Dallas before assuming directorship of the board. "Asset hoarding is the rule because they are no-cost assets to the agencies, with no taxes, no capital costs, and no incentives to give the land up. The administration of government real estate is simply a disaster."

GSA first began surveying the various federal agencies for surplus properties in 1970, but is able to conduct only about 100 surveys a year because of inadequate staffing. At this rate, with more than 27,000 properties to evaluate, it will take GSA at least until the year 2240 to finish the process.

Congress gave GSA and the Property Review Board precious little support in their debt-reducing mission. "Every congressman says there is a lot of surplus property out there, but not in my district, not in my constituency," complains Earl E. Jones, acting commissioner of GSA's Property Resources Service. Rep. Ken Kramer (R-Colorado) did propose legislation in 1983 to streamline the property-disposal process and insure that proceeds go to debt reduction. But the House Government Operations Committee, chaired by Rep. Jack Brooks (D-Texas), refused to act on the reforms. Later, when Rep. Kramer was running for reelection in 1984, his opponent accused him of "wanting to sell off our national treasures." Although he won reelection, Kramer abandoned the surplus-property issue to avoid any future controversy. Other attempts by GSA to reform the process, such as giving federal agencies financial incentives to declare property surplus, have similarly been suffocated by the House Government Operations Committee.

As GSA and the board continued tenaciously to promote surplus sales in 1983, a flurry of legislation was introduced in Congress to protect targeted properties while sabotaging the entire sales program. Residents of Queens, New York, sent 20,000 letters protesting the proposed sale of 32 of 150 acres of old Fort Totten, which would have brought the U.S. Treasury at least $22 million. Residents wanted the land for recreation. Rep. James Scheuer and Sen. Daniel Moynihan, New York Democrats, introduced a law to force GSA to give up the land to the city of New York at no cost. Sen. Charles Mathias (R-Maryland) advanced a prohibition on any change in the status of 228 vacant acres of the Beltsville Agricultural Research Center in Maryland, and Sen. Paul Laxalt (R-Nevada) interceded to force the U.S. Army to give away 237 acres to Mineral County, Nevada.

What finally prompted Congress not only to cripple the surplus-sales program, but also to abolish the board itself, was an attempt to declare surplus 35 acres adjoining a hotel on Hawaii's Waikiki Beach. On this tract of land, part of the larger 72-acre Fort DeRussy, are a 416-room luxury hotel and 17 acres of beachfront used by military personnel and their families. Fort DeRussy itself is a misnomer—there is no real fort on the site, just a luxury resort valued at $13 million an acre, or about $221 million for just the beachfront. The Board and GSA argued that the hotel and beach property should be owned and operated by the private sector, which would still enable the resort to cater to military families and retirees by offering comparably reduced rates, as most other Hawaiian hotels do.

Senator Daniel Inouye (D-Hawaii) got quick approval for legislation preventing the sale of any portion of the resort. To insure that the Property Review Board never again threatened this property or any other, Rep. Daniel Akaka (D-Hawaii) tacked a provision onto an appropriations bill eliminating the entire $400,000 budget for the board for fiscal 1985. With no funding for salaries or office expenses, and lacking firm support from the White House, which recoiled from the sales controversy in an election year, the board effectively ceased to exist.

The impact on the surplus-sales program was dramatic. During the 1982 sales push, GSA produced $191 million in revenues, more than twice that of the previous year, with only 3% of that property inventory given away free. For fiscal 1984, with the board and its cajoling powers gone, GSA sales dropped to just $91 million, with 40% of the total inventory value donated to local governments. Petty local power-grabbing had once again triumphed over the national interest.

Of the Defense Department's 3,800 military installations in the continental United States, many were established long before modern communications, interstate highways, and jet aircraft rendered them uneconomic and obsolete. Only about 300 have been designated as essential to our national defense. If the military-base structure was realigned, taking into consideration strategic needs and cost factors, at least 50 major installations would be closed. Former Senate Armed Services Chairman Barry Goldwater of Arizona estimates that closure of just ten of these bases would result in savings of $1 billion a year. The Office of Management and Budget in 1982, and the Grace Commission in 1983, both calculated potential taxpayer savings at $2 billion or more annually.

Although the Defense Department, unlike other federal agencies, traditionally pursued property surplussing, if only to streamline defense-support needs, no military-base closure and realignment package has been sent by DOD to Congress since 1979. The reason is that every state and almost 60% of all congressional districts contain or border military installations, and all recent attempts by the Pentagon to close unnecessary facilities have been met by widespread, united opposition in Congress. Lawmakers argue that base closures would mean a loss of jobs and economic vitality for affected communities. To the extent that that argument has prevailed, our military-base structure has been transformed into a massive employment agency, or just another jobs program, rendering national defense and cost considerations secondary to selfish parochial concerns.

For more than a decade the Pentagon has wanted to close Fort Sheridan, which sits sandwiched between residential neighborhoods on the shore of Lake Michigan, 28 miles north of downtown Chicago. Established in 1887, this antiquated facility is staffed mostly by recruiting and administrative personnel. Only 62 of its 695 acres is devoted to training or operations, while more than 150 acres — including two lovely beaches and a superb 18-hole golf course — are used for recreation. Closure would save American taxpayers perhaps $10 million annually, with another $50 million or more coming from sale of the property. An Army study of the fort's usefulness is blunt: "No strategic or mobilization mission has been identified for Fort Sheridan."

When the Pentagon announced in 1978 that it would study

terminating Fort Sheridan, 23 members of the Illinois congressional delegation wrote to the Secretary of Defense demanding that he "terminate these studies." As DOD's closure study neared completion several years later, other letters making cases for retention began to arrive. The commander of the Chicago-area Army Reserve Command warned that Fort Sheridan must remain open because "cutbacks in the various social/welfare programs" by the Reagan administration might result in riots in Chicago requiring an armed response by Fort Sheridan's administrative and recruiting personnel. The adjutant general of neighboring Wisconsin wrote, voicing what was on the minds of many Sheridan apologists: "Many retired personnel make use of Fort Sheridan facilities like the commissary, post exchange, beaches, and golf course."

Finally, in July 1981, the Secretary of the Army announced that the U.S. Army Forces Command study supported closure because the functions of Sheridan could be more cost-effectively performed at other installations. Closure was set for 30 September 1985. This decision only spurred Illinois congressmen to a new level of lobbying frenzy. Rep. Robert McClory (R-Illinois) began addressing direct appeals to the White House, and 24 members of the state's delegation wrote the Pentagon demanding that "rather than studying the closure of Fort Sheridan, the Army should expand its activities." Faced with such fierce congressional opposition, as well as irritation from President Reagan, who was personally tired of hearing emotional pleas on behalf of a fort he had never heard of, the Army relented and allowed Sheridan to remain an active installation.

Until 1977, the Executive Branch enjoyed a relatively free hand in fashioning the nation's base structure. But in that year Congress passed, and President Jimmy Carter signed, legislation requiring DOD to notify Congress when it is even considering a base closing. The Pentagon must then prepare economic, environmental, and strategic impact studies that can take up to a year and $1 million each to complete. Finally, Congress must give its specific approval to any closure—something which it has not subsequently been willing to do. According to *Policy Review,* the secretary of defense has authority to close about 90% of the bases in this country—thanks to Congress having made it easier for him to close installations with fewer than 300 civilian employees—but Secretary Casper Weinberger never used that authority. Therefore, "the blame for the foot dragging does not all belong to Congress."

An argument can be made that keeping obsolete bases open not only endangers the Pentagon's budgetary priorities, it can imperil the security of the nation. In 1979 an Air Force study concluded that Loring Air Force Base, located in far northeastern Maine, was vulnerable to surprise missile attack by enemy submarines, and its poor weather hampered flying and training exercises. "It doesn't do you any good to have a strategic base if you can't fly out of it half the time," former Defense Secretary Melvin Laird has said of Loring. The Air Force proposed that Loring be reduced from a major Strategic Air Command base to a Forward Operating Base and that its B-52 and KC-125 refueling aircraft be reassigned elsewhere. Such an action would have saved American taxpayers $26.7 million annually.

Maine's two senators, Republican William Cohen and Democrat Edmund Muskie, now retired, rejected the strategic considerations and inserted language into a military-construction bill prohibiting any change in the status of Loring. Since then Sen. Cohen has used his seat on the Armed Services Committee to spend more than $155 million on the base for new dormitories, a dining hall, a hospital, and a sewage plant, all with the intention of making the base too expensive for the Air Force to ever consider closing. None of these improvements could hide the base's obsolescence when, in December 1984, a B-52 bomber suffered an abortive takeoff, effectively closing the base's single 12,000-foot runway and forcing other Strategic Air Command bases to fly Loring's missions for several weeks. "Let other bases fly Loring's missions long enough," warned a columnist for the *Bangor* (Maine) *Daily News* "and you only arm the critics who say Loring isn't needed in the first place, and that its presence is all a game of politics."

The list of military bases being kept open by Congress for alleged "economic" impact reasons reads like a page from the nation's history books. Fort Monroe on the southern Virginia coast is a relic from the War of 1812, probably the only remaining active military installation in the world with an eight-foot-deep medieval moat around it. The Army had wanted to turn the fort into a museum, transferring its personnel elsewhere for savings of $10 million a year, but Sen. Paul S. Trible, Jr. (R-Virginia) has used his legislative clout to keep the relic open and avoid "socioeceonomic" dislocation in the surrounding community. Likewise, Fort Douglas outside Salt Lake City, built in 1862 to guard the overland stage route and keep watch on the Mormons, remains open thanks largely to Sen. Jake Garn (R-Utah). The U.S. Army Forces Command had found the fort to be "nonessential" and recommended that it be turned into a museum, since it had already been designated a National Historical Landmark. To keep the base and its post exchange, swimming pool and two night clubs open, Sen. Garn and Rep. Gunn McKay, the local Democratic Congressman, used their positions on the Senate and House Appropriations Committees to deny the Pentagon any funds to close the fort or transfer personnel.

Economic dislocation as an automatically valid reason to thwart base closures and property surplussing falls into disrepute if one examines the fate of properties privatized before Congress constipated the disposal process. A Pentagon-commissioned study of 12 converted military installations found that in most cases the closure turned out to be a boon to the local economy. "Not only have the local economies not suffered the severe setbacks anticipated," reported Booz Allen & Hamilton, Inc., which conducted the study, "but civilian acquisition and operation have had unexpected benefits. In almost every case, the civilian jobs which were lost due to the base closure have been offset with an equal or greater number of new jobs." Pentagon investigators examined the job-generation and base-reuse experience of 100 communities in 1986, and found that 138,138 civilian jobs now located on the former Defense facilities were more than replacing the 93,424 civilian jobs lost when the bases were closed.

When the Pentagon announced in 1961 that the 100-year-old arsenal at Benicia, California, would be closed, it seemed at the time that a killing economic blow had been dealt the surrounding community. With a payroll of 2,100, Benicia's arsenal was one of Solano County's largest employers. Some civic leaders possessed the foresight to realize that the abandoned facility offered a golden industrial-development opportunity. With a port, airstrip, roads, and buildings already in place on more than 2,000 acres of rolling hills, potential development was limited only by the initiative and imagination of the area's residents. Today, the Benicia Industrial Park is home to dozens of businesses, from small speciality manufacturers to major warehouses and a refinery, employing more than 4,500 persons.

In Michigan's cold Upper Peninsula, Kinchelow Air Force Base was closed in 1977, depriving the largely rural community of 700 jobs and $36 million in annual revenues. Rather than accept catastrophe, the Chippewa County Board of Commissioners established a local Economic Development Corporation to offer low-interest loans to businesses willing to relocate or expand on the base property. "The key to success or failure is local initiative," William Laubernds, president of the Development Corporation, told *Forbes* magazine. "The military was actually still constructing buildings after they left the place." Nearly 50 companies settled at the former base, creating an industrial park employing over 1,000 local residents. "In the long run the community is probably better off" with the base closed, admits Laubernds.

Other privatization success stories abound. After Walker Air Force Base at Roswell, New Mexico, closed with a loss of 379 jobs, the Greyhound Corporation moved in and uses the base hangars for manufacturing buses, employing more than 1,000 local residents. The site of the Air Force's former Mitchell Field on New York's Long Island now hosts a 16,000-seat arena, a convention center, a 1,651-room hotel, and numerous office buildings. "The late Mitchell Field is becoming the downtown hub of the entire county," reports the Nassau County commissioner of commerce. "Thus will be added thousands of jobs and millions of dollars in additional tax revenue."

Politicians and bureaucrats use an economic-protection rationale to justify hoarding federal assets either because they are too myopic to see the potential economic advantages of privatization, or because their real motives and hidden agenda must be cloaked in the guise of a public good. For the politician, pleasing his constituents and voters—in this case those government employees who may wish to remain stationed in pleasant surroundings without fear of dislocation—is more important than insuring that those surroundings serve the needs and interests of the nation's taxpayers. For the bureaucrat, whose incentives revolve around the retention if not expansion of agency powers and turf, holding onto assets to fulfill some unspecific "future need" simply assures that his or her job will be perpetuated no less than the jobs of the other fellow "civil servants" vested with direct responsibility for "managing" those assets.

Releasing the federal government's surplus properties to the private sector would help reduce the national debt burden on U.S. taxpayers, place on local tax rolls property that the government cannot afford to maintain, while improving government management of its resources. That so much property is surplus to the legitimate needs of government raises other more fundamental questions about the size, value, and stewardship of all nationalized holdings. Together, our federal, state, and local governments own 42% of the nation's entire land area. Are taxpayers well served by having government play so dominant a role in the management of our assets? Have we abdicated the economic principles of private property on which this nation was founded? As an alternative, can the private sector simultaneously manage, conserve, and develop these resources, advancing the public good through private gain?

Denationalizing the Public Lands

Down on Vermilion Bay, about 100 miles west of New Orleans, can be found a 27,000-acre wildlife preserve bequeathed to the Audubon Society in 1924 by big-game hunter Paul J. Rainey, who wanted the brackish marsh set aside for migrating snow geese. Around 1940 oil and natural gas were discovered within the preserve, prompting the society to strike a deal with the Rainey heirs splitting the proceeds from development at 60–40, with the larger percentage going to the society. A lease was drawn up to cover production, enabling the society to impose restrictions on the oil companies, including the requirement that companies winning the oil or gas lease must build protective levees to provide new, dry nesting areas to attract other species of birds and animals. Over the years one oil and three gas wells went into operation providing the society with an income of about $1 million annually, enabling the group to increase its yearly budget to $27 million and help fund the purchase of other environmentally sensitive properties.

In its literature the Audubon Society describes the Rainey preserve this way: "There are oil wells in Rainey, which are potential sources of pollution; yet Audubon's experience during the past few decades indicated that oil can be extracted without measurable damage to the marsh. Extra precautions to prevent pollution have proven effective." With the dry areas provided by levees, alligators, deer, rabbits and heron, along with the snow geese and ducks, have made the preserve their home. The oil companies have "improved by tenfold the capacity of certain areas of the marsh to sustain wildlife," says John M. Anderson, Audubon's vice president in charge of the sanctuary. "There has never been an accident on the refuge." In Texas an oil and gas field has been operating on the Welder Wildlife Foundation Refuge since the 1930s, helping to finance wildlife research and preservation of the refuge without appreciable disturbance to indigenous wildlife or their habitat.

What Audubon permits on its own ecologically fragile property—exploration and development—it strenuously opposes on federal public lands. When the suggestion was made by the Reagan administration that oil be explored in Montana's Bob Marshall Wilderness, for instance, Audubon officials joined other environmentalists to label the idea a "desecration" and lobby against it. Audubon's dual standard illustrates that behavior changes according to the incentives vested by ownership. That a respected environmental group can find a compromise between preservation and resource exploitation—a private use for public good—underscores the potential benefits and applications for the federal government's own vast holdings.

Two centuries ago the economist Adam Smith noticed that the productivity of public lands in Europe was at best one-quarter that of comparable private properties. He concluded that privatizing the public commons would create incentives for owners to eliminate waste and make the assets more productive. Institutional incentives influence behavior in even more pronounced ways today, given the sheer size and scope of government and its "public commons" holdings. Because government administrators experience no personal gain or loss from the resources they manage, they are effectively divorced from any consequences of their decisions, and thus wholly responsive to political rather than economic pressures and considerations. "It is not that bureaucrats are bad people; they simply face bad incentives," explained a specialist with the California Senate's Agriculture and Water Resources Committee, in an interview with *The National Journal.* "Because government agencies are not subjected to the cost-benefit calculations that any private company that wishes to remain in business is, they engage in some of the most wasteful and destructive practices imaginable."

If one proceeds from the assumption that a resource whose rights are unassigned is likely to be abused, something economists call the "tragedy of the commons," then by contrast private ownership allows owners to capture the full value of their resource and provides the right incentive to maintain its long-term value. The owner of a fishery, a forest, or a mine wants production from it today, tomorrow, and into the foreseeable future. But with a resource owned in common by everyone, its value can be captured only if it is exploited quickly before others do. Economists R. J. Agnello and L. P. Donnelley studied the oyster industry in the Chesapeake Bay by contrasting the Maryland side, where oyster beds are publicly owned, with the Virginia side, where oyster resources are in mostly private hands. Without a property-rights incentive to wisely harvest and maintain the resource, Maryland's "public commons" oyster beds were depleted, its fishermen harvesting as fast as possible. On the Virginia side harvests did not suffer disastrous declines. These fishermen had incentives through property rights to insure they left something to harvest the next year, properly managing the resources so that one day these beds could be passed on to relatives, or to prospective buyers, with their value preserved.

Communally owned resources actually promote ecologically damaging behavior, argue economist Richard Stroup and political scientist John Baden, two "free-market environmentalists" who co-founded the Political Economy Research Center (PERC) at Montana State University. *The San Francisco Chronicle* economics editor summarized the Center this way: they "represent the leading edge of a new wave of 'resource economics' environmentalists who believe markets solve environmental problems far better then governments do." PERC postulates that environmental problems evolve largely from unclear or unenforceable property rights to natural resources. Lack of accountability leads to pollution. Baden says federal agencies, "pork barrel" politicians of both parties, and the timber and livestock industries together form an "iron triangle" of special interests he believes is "causing Americans to subsidize the destruction of their environment." Solutions to environmental problems that meet the test of a market economy have now been adopted by most of the major environmental groups. "Market incentives are a key part of the way we look at environmental issues," conceded Thomas Graff, an attorney for the Environmental Defense Fund.

To carry foward their argument about the ecological damage caused by communally owned resources, Baden and Stroup point to the experience of the Plains Indians and speculate that if weaponry had been introduced into their culture sooner and if the numbers of these nomadic people had been greater, then the buffalo would almost certainly have been nearly extinct two centuries earlier. As white men introduced horses, firearms, and other technological advances, the price of buffalo was lowered for the Indians and many of the animals were killed simply for the tongue and two strips of the back hide, rather than to utilize the entire carcass as had been the case when killing them in large numbers was more difficult. UCLA economist Harold Demsetz uses the example of the Montagnais Indians of the Labrador Peninsula, tribes of hunters who subsisted on caribou and beaver and who established private hunting grounds when the Europeans appeared and began treating the resources in common. A system of private ownership developed among these Indians as the fur trade expanded, and they farmed their beaver houses under recognized territorial boundaries, managing the beaver harvest as a sustained yield with adequate attention to conservation. Meanwhile, for Europeans exploiting the public commons their beaver rapidly disappeared.

Under the Audubon Society's private ownership a Rainey Wildlife Preserve can flourish, protecting its wildlife and conserving the environment, and yet simultaneously be self-supporting, yielding up its riches to underwrite the costs of human concern. Everyone benefits—Audubon funds its educational activities and buys more land for preserves, taxpayers are relieved of additional government conservation expenditures, consumers use the oil and gas, and the oil companies make a profit.

Within its own bailiwick the Audubon Society understands that wilderness is not a value against which every human activity must be judged harshly. Ecological museums, a term journalist William Tucker coined to describe what the wilderness concept creates, can coexist with the economic needs of civilization, though not necessarily as creatures of government. Were the Rainey preserve under federal management, it would be the taxpayers rather than oil companies paying for ecological enhancements, if any improvements to enhance wildlife were made at all; mineral exploration and production would, in all probability, be banned, denying consumers another source of energy and driving up prices; less environmental education would occur, and political pressures from interest groups would randomly dictate how the preserve was managed and to whom access would be permitted or denied.

Most of the nation's remaining valuable resources exist on federal lands. By one government calculation, our "public commons" contain 85% of our estimated oil reserves, 72% of the oil shale, 37% of the natural gas, and more than 50% or our remaining mineral deposits. Clearly, at some point in this nation's future, we will need to use a portion if not all of those resources. The question becomes one of whether we can trust politicians and bureaucrats, given the incentive structures that constrain them, to conserve, manage, and plan for the use of these natural resources in a manner that serves the needs of consumers and taxpayers no less than the cause of preserving these "trust" lands from ecological harm.

Less than one-fourth of federally owned land has been explored for oil and gas, and more than half of all federal lands are legislatively exempted from oil and gas leasing. "Environmental quality and the development of oil and natural gas on federal lands can coexist, but not under the matrix of existing institutions," warns John Baden, now head of the Maguire Oil and Gas Institute at Southern Methodist University. He advocates creation of "wilderness endowment boards" to foster environmental values while retaining the authority to manage, buy, and sell wilderness lands, protecting those of low commercial value, but generating revenues from other properties to finance wildlife management and preservation. He points to the highly encouraging record of oil exploration and production in the Arctic as a model. As The National Wildlife Federation has stated, "The oil industry spent the last 15 years profitably developing Prudhoe Bay and did a commendable job in protecting its wildlife resource."

Markets and profits have been stereotyped as the enemy of wildlife and the environment, yet environmental groups are discovering private ownership to be the most certain way of protecting wilderness areas. The Nature Conservancy of Arlington, Virginia, a group with more than 200,000 members, has saved 2.4 million ecologically significant acres since 1951 by purchasing the properties with membership monies and donations. Clifford Messenger, a member of the Nature Conservancy board, confessed to *Industry Week* magazine that he had switched his membership from another environmental group, the Wilderness Society, several years earlier after "I began to realize that you can win a victory today in Congress but lose it eight years later. But if you own the land, it will stay protected."

Why do 95% of Americans, according to a Gallup Poll, believe that the National Park Service, the federal agency that operates our federal parks, is the one arm of the government they can trust? That myth was destroyed in a variety of ways in a disturbing article for *The Atlantic Monthly* by Alston Chase, who in 1987 pointed out that within the national parks, animals and their habitats are disappearing, while the same animals and habitats thrive just outside the park boundaries. He gives numerous examples: Yellowstone National Park lost its mountain lions, wolves, and white-tailed deer, and is losing bears and beaver, yet most of these species multiply outside the park. "A growing consensus among park professionals holds that a major reason for our parks' decline is the National Park Service itself," he writes.

Part of the problem revolves around the agency having two different constituencies—environmentalists and the recreation industry—and two contradictory missions: preserving the parks, and enabling the general public to experience park surroundings. Two competing ideas of what our parks should be have emerged: a landscaping philosophy that treats the areas as large city parks, and the wilderness philosophy of keeping parks undisturbed by keeping people out. Park Service policy has vacillated between use and preservation according to changes in the political lobbying power of the various interest groups. Research studies of park needs and ecology tend to be politically directed, and research results that reflect badly on the government bureaucracy tend to remain within the system. A century of strict fire control and the elimination of predators, combined with other faulty policies and institutional inadequacies, have thrown all of our parks, even the wildest, into an ecological disequilibrium that has destroyed the ecosystem's capacity to restore itself.

Management and operation of some federal park facilities have been proposed for takeover by the private sector by several high-ranking officials of the Department of Interior. Inspector General James Richards, in a February 1986 report to the secretary, wrote: "there is a probability that these organizations [in the private sector] could operate the National Park Service activities as well as NPS and possibly at lower cost."

Demand for campgrounds and outdoor recreation can be met to a larger extent by the private sector. In Maine an association of private landowners has pooled 2.8 million acres of forest for camping, hunting, fishing, and other recreation. North Maine Woods, Inc., a non-profit group, charges its visitors lower fees than a nearby state park. Private business will build and operate a new base lodge at the foot of a skiing area in New Hampshire's Mount Sunapee State Park, turning over part of the profits to the state to help maintain park-operating costs. State parks nationwide occupy nearly 11 million acres, just one-seventh of the acreage of federal parks, yet host nearly twice the number of visitors.

To understand why we cannot depend on government in the long term to behave in an ecologically efficient, sensitive, or rational manner, one need only examine its record of managing our timber-land and grazing-land resources. The national forests contain 142 million acres located in 40 states, with up to 90 million of these acres holding enough timber to qualify as commercial forest lands. These forests have been so mishandled by government that, in the words of a former Council of Economic Advisers economist, Steve Hanke, "from an economic standpoint, the federal commercial lands in the portfolio are not assets, they are liabilities."

An erroneous perception at the turn of the century stampeded the U.S. Congress into halting sales of most remaining forest lands. Because lumber was so cheap and forests so plentiful, the timber business in this country began as a "mining" rather than a "farming" industry, resulting in a large-scale deforesting of the Great Lakes area. This development alarmed conservation-minded lawmakers who feared that rapacious timber barons would never have an incentive for replanting, since it might take 50 years for a mature forest to give them a return on their investment. That was before the age of the corporation, where long-term investments that outlive the investors are routinely made. Nor did lawmakers take into account speculation that would transfer benefits to future generations. "Why produce Napoleon brandy today when it can't be drunk for 125 years?" asks Dr. Richard Stroup, by way of analogy. "Because if you produce it today, you can sell it in ten years to a speculator, who can sell it to a speculator who will then sell it to the drinker."

A Bureau of Forestry was established around the turn of the century to manage the nationalized timberlands, with its primary purpose the provision of housing for American families. Something called the "even-flow concept"—the quantity of public timber entering the marketplace as determined by timber inventory volume and growth rates—became enshrined as the harvesting method with the stated objective of promoting the stability of communities reliant on the timber industry. It was felt that timber production should be used to keep employment and economic conditions in logging towns constant.

This policy has produced numerous side effects. As the timber, wood-processing, and housing industries developed a dependence on government lumber, economic disruptions occurred in the marketplace because the even-flow concept restricted timber supplies in the face of demand. Even flow assumes that an arbitrary inventory level of timber must be preserved indefinitely. Government currently owns 63% of the nation's softwood, saw-timber inventory, the raw-material base for the plywood and lumber that are essential to housing. Bureaucratic timber-marketing policies keep these timber supplies constant, a condition which props up the price of wood products at a level higher than it should be under free-market conditions. Softwood-lumber prices escalated more than 60% between 1967 and 1979, sharply raising the costs of wood products for consumers, and housing for home buyers, a phenomenon attributable in large measure to federal unwillingness to increase harvests in government forests. Another resultant phenomenon, identified by economists Steve Hanke and Barney Dowdle, has been a private-sector shift in production from the Pacific region to the South because, although the Pacific has a timber inventory three times greater than the southern United States, most of it is in public ownership while most in the South is privately held. "By restricting supplies, the Forest Service and the Bureau of Land Management are creating and apparently will continue to create, an artificial timber shortage," the economists write. "Private ownership in the South provides a more secure timber supply."

The U.S. Forest Service currently runs a negative cash flow of about $1 billion a year. With commercial timberland in the federal inventory valued in excess of $100 billion, and assuming an interest rate of 10%, Professor Dowdle, a forestry expert at the University of Washington, estimates the capital costs of these timber resources at about $10.4 billion per year, which are costs not counted or reported by the federal government. Nevertheless, Dowdle calls them legitimate costs, against which any benefits produced by the national forests must be weighed. He calculates the cost to the average American at $50 per person per year for maintaining the U.S Forest Service in the business of timber production, meaning that if the Forest Service were a corporation, it would be assessing stockholders their share of corporate deficits.

"Why is government in the business of producing timber in the United States? Government doesn't produce corn or wheat. Why should it produce timber?" asks Professor Dowdle. These questions are being raised by both economists and environmentalists now that it appears that private companies have surpassed the Forest Serivce in applying scientific methods to enhance forestry growth and timber yields, and because the federal government actually spends more on the timber-sale process than it retrieves in timber revenues.

Environmental folly is almost always economic folly, contends Gaylord Nelson, the former U.S. Senator from Wisconsin and a founder of Earth Day. He cites the Tongass National Forest in southeastern Alaska, where the U.S. Forest Service loses more than $50 million a year selling trees and, in the process, "an irreplaceable and priceless old-growth rain forest is being destroyed." At over 16 million acres, Tongass remains the only largely intact rain forest left in the temperate zones of the planet. In the 1950s the Forest Service undertook a job-creating venture in the area, persuading two pulp companies to locate within the forest with an inducement of 50-year contracts and absurdly low timber prices. Just to reach trees targeted for cutting, the Service had to build roads costing $150,000 for each mile. Congressional legislation in 1980 pursued by Sen. Ted Stevens (R-Alaska) provided for a minimum annual appropriation of $40 million on a permanent basis to provide roads and other subsidies to timber companies harvesting the forest. For each job the Tongass program supports, American taxpayers fork up $36,000 a year. Though timber jobs in Alaska have declined by 40% since 1980, mostly due to technological substitutes for pulp in product production, Forest Service officials contine to defend the jobs program as important to the American economy. For taxpayers, who pay more for the timber program than timber companies pay for the wood, it is less a jobs program for timber towns than corporate welfare for large timber harvesters.

The federal government's pricing system, failing to take into account the costs of growing and selling the timber, produces environmental damage and perpetuates a subsidy to favored timber buyers which can flood the timber market, depress prices, and unfairly hurt small, private timber growers. Federal-government harvests in Wyoming's Bighorn National Park returned just 21 cents on the dollar. Even when lumber companies don't want the timber, government bureaucrats have pursued policies to spend tax money to attract buyers for the already subsidized wood. In Montana's Bitterroot National Forest, about 9,400 acres of virgin timber on a mountainside was offered for sale in 1976, without a single bid from lumber companies. So the Forest Service built a 10-mile road into the area costing $312,000 to convince the lumber companies to harvest the site.

For many independent timber growers, below-cost timber sales and tax-subsidized lumber severely restrict their ability to compete in the marketplace. "All we ask for as small woodland owners is a chance to compete fairly," Keith Argow, president of the National Woodland Owners Association, a group of small growers, explained to *The Wall Street Journal.* "We can't compete fairly when you've got this timber being subsidized one way or another."

On the federal government's nationalized rangelands—more than 170 million semiarid acres covering 11 western states—taxpayer subsidies to a favored group of sheep and cattle ranchers long ago became a way of life. These federal rangelands are larger in area than New England and are suited only for grazing large livestock herds. The $100-million annual negative cash flow from federal ownership means that about $5 is spent on management for every $1 the lands yield in grazing fees. Taxpayers are in effect paying simply for the privilege of allowing the 31,000 ranchers who possess grazing permits to use the land at below-market rents.

Back in the 18th century, Thomas Jefferson warned the federal government to avoid ownership of the means of production by selling these vast tracts to insure they would "never again...revert to the United States." Land disposal was federal policy until 1934, when passage of the Taylor Grazing Act changed the emphasis to bureaucratic administration and continued federal ownership. Most ranchers then, as today, preferred holding licenses to actually owning the land because grazing fees are minimal — one-third to one-seventh of rents charged on private lands — and grazing permits allow them to avoid paying property taxes, which in some localities can be high.

With grazing lands, as with our forest lands, environmentalists are beginning to grasp the connection between bad economics and poor ecology. The Wilderness Society studied public ownership of grazing lands as administered by the Bureau of Land Management and concluded that users of these rangelands have no economic incentives to conserve the resources. "As a result," wrote Gaylord Nelson the former U.S. senator and counselor to the society, "overgrazing of public rangelands in the West has become a serious problem, damaging these lands' other resource values. Wildlife populations have declined, cultural and historical artifacts have been destroyed, watersheds have been degraded, and opportunities for hunting, fishing, and other forms of outdoor recreation have been greatly diminished."

Ranchers using public lands have an inherent short-term bias in their cattle-stocking decisions, argues economist Gary Libecap, and that prompts them to overgraze the lands to increase current returns, while neglecting conservation. The federally imposed lack of well-defined property rights on these lands creates insecure tenure which "encourages overstocking and discourages investments in improvements such as fences and wells."

As far back as 1925, a study of 111 ranches in the Southwest by the Department of Agriculture demonstrated the obvious impact of ownership on production. The study contrasted 28 ranches in far west Texas, where 73% of the acreage was owned and the rest leased, and 83 ranches in southern New Mexico and Arizona, where 8% of the land was privately held and the rest held as open range. Ranch sizes, cattle per ranch, and climate were all comparable. Study data found the calf crop 47% greater for ranches with secure property rights, the death loss 50% lower, the average cow weight 15% greater, and the average value per cow 43% greater than for the ranches that relied on the open range. The researchers concluded that an absence of incentives for ranchers not holding land rights reduced the quality of their herds and the land. Texas ranchers with secure land rights, for instance, invested $7.30 per head of cattle in water wells, compared to only $2.85 invested by New Mexico ranchers grazing on public lands.

Professor Libecap argues that secure property rights to the western range are necessary for the efficient use of rangeland, and to insure that long-term decisions can be made regarding investment in improvements and stocking practices. Secure land rights through outright privatization would help end overgrazing and the depletion of land quality. One possible formula is for each rancher currently holding a grazing permit to be offered, on first refusal, the right to purchase his grazing license and the property that goes with it.

A first step toward ending the dependence of permit holders on subsidized grazing land would be to raise the fee charged to extract a fair market value, much as the law—which has been waived year after year—requires. Such a proposal was made by the Office of Management and Budget when the $1.35-per-animal-per-month fee came up for renewal in early 1986. (Grazing rights on private lands generally cost from $6.65 to $7 per animal per month.) But under political pressure from 28 U.S. senators representing western states, President Reagan issued an order continuing indefinitely the same low grazing fee, even though his own 1987 budget message stated the administration's conviction that "those who benefit directly from a specific federal service should pay the cost of providing that service."

Many of the senators pressuring President Reagan had been proponents or leaders of the Sagebrush Rebellion, a protest against federal land-use policies that reached its peak in 1979, when the Nevada state legislature passed a bill declaring that the state was rightful owner of all federal lands—about 86% of the state—within Nevada boundaries. Sagebrush leaders simply wanted to substitute one form of government ownership, in this case by the state, for the other more centralized form of public ownership. Once the Reagan administration took office the "rebellion" lost its momentum, making it appear, so *The Wall Street Journal* suggested, "to have been more a protest against overbearing federal bureaucrats than against federal land ownership." Not even that favorite bogeyman of environmentalists, former Interior Secretary James Watt, favored privatizing federal lands. He simply wanted control vested in state rather than federal authorities.

Nor do those special corporate interests, which environmentalists often claim are eager to despoil the environment, evidence much enthusiasm for actually owning the federal resources they now exploit. "Industry is generally not interested in free enterprise. They're interested in subsidized wood," says forestry professor Barney Dowdle, who has spent more than 20 years trying to organize industry support to sell off the federal timberlands. Nevada State Senator Dean Rhoades, a Sagebrush Rebellion founder, agrees that ranchers do not want to own more rangeland on which they would have to pay taxes any more than energy companies are interested in owning vast tracts of taxable property. "As long as the resources of the West are publicly owned, the cost of managing and exploring them will be taken from another common resource—the public treasury," environmental consultant Robert J. Smith told a Manhattan Institute policy forum. "Why should mining companies bear all costs of purchasing public lands and of then exploring for resources if the U.S. Geological Survey will do it for them, after which they may file a mining claim for a few dollars? Many corporations are as much opposed to privatization as environmentalists are."

Europeans are generally greatly astonished by the amount of land the U.S. government owns. Less than 5% of Alaska land, for instance, is in private ownership, a figure that is smaller than the percentage of land devoted to private property in the Soviet Union. Since most land in Western Europe remains in private hands, they can honestly wonder which nation is more socialistic—one that periodically nationalizes industry, as most European countries do, or one with almost half its land mass already nationalized, as we have. The answer should give pause to any self-respecting corporate entity or management board that feeds off federal subsidies while professing a belief in the economic principles on which this nation was founded.

To change both attitudes and the focus of debate over public lands, a convergency of interests must be found and stimulated between environmental organizations and taxpayer groups, each of which is already beginning to perceive the connections between economics and ecology. Such coalitions have worked legislative wonders in the recent past. Environmentalists and the National Taxpayer's Union teamed up to kill in Congress further federal funding of the Clinch River breeder reactor in Tennessee, as well as subsidies to numerous federal water projects, using potent arguments that combined concern for environmental protection with concern for the pocketbooks of taxpayers.

A hopeful sign can be seen in the position of Dr. Marion Clawson, a senior fellow at Resources for the Future, who has offered several possible solutions to the problems of government management of public lands. He suggests that substantial amounts of federal land can be transferred to private individuals or corporations. "If the Nature Conservancy can be the recipient of a gift of private land, why not let it be the recipient of the gift of federal land?" he asks. Mixed public-private corporations could be created to manage selected areas of public lands. Long-term leasing of other federal lands could be extended indefinitely into the future, with terms of such leases written to make them attractive to wilderness, recreation, wildlife, and other nature groups, no less than for the commercial companies seeking to extract the resources. "Privatization is clearly a step in the direction of establishing more efficient resource allocation through improved incentives," Professor M. Bruce Johnson has written. "Whether the government-held land is auctioned off, or simply given away, is of far less consequence in the long run than the improved efficiencies that will surely result."

Public-lands privatization could also be used to help solve other social and budgetary problems. Richard Stroup and John Baden propose that commercial timberlands in the national forests gradually be sold to raise revenue that would compensate the generation whose Social Security contributions have already been spent and who are about to retire. As a transition was made from Social Security to a private insurance system, timberland and mineral rights sales could eliminate the mismanagement of the resources while helping relieve the structural deficit that haunts our Social Security program. One potential big buyer of federal timberland, according to business writer Bruce Ramsey, might be pension funds that possess money traditionally invested in long-term assets such as 30-year government bonds. Since government bonds are vulnerable to inflation, investing in hard assets like trees would more efficiently protect the long-term value of the pension monies.

A privately administered wilderness system could be managed under a series of binding covenants that would free the public lands from competing political pressures. Writing in a Cato Institute journal, Vernon L. Smith, professor of economics at the University of Arizona, recommends writing restrictive covenants permanently into the deeds for public lands once they are handed over to environmental or other groups. For instance, the surface rights to the Grand Canyon might be permanently restricted to use for wilderness and recreational purposes. Professor Smith goes so far as to suggest that the federal government sell its military bases and lease them back at market rates. Such leases would insure that the true cost of such facilities would be included in budgets, and such a rental policy would help discipline the decisions relating to the location of facilities, forcing an overriding economic rationale for the nation's base structure on legislators who keep obsolete bases open. As a model for the ownership and management of our nationalized lands, he holds up the National Audubon Society and the Nature Conservancy, which together have preserved more than 2 million acres and created more than 800 private sanctuaries and wildlife preserves. "It can be expected," writes Professor Smith, "that environmental organizations, by diverting funds now being spent for political action, and by launching new fund raising efforts for direct land acquisition, would be able to bid successfully for many of these public lands."

As a hypothetical question for privatization skeptics, John Baden asks, "If national security considerations mandated the development of a cobalt mine in a wilderness area, who would an environmentalist prefer to manage that development—James Watt, secretary of the interior, or Russell Peterson, president of the Audubon Society?" On contrasting the federal government's record of management on public lands with the Audubon Society's experience protecting and developing the Rainey Wildlife preserve, only the most dogmatic among us could fail to acknowledge the obvious answer.

Changing the public-lands ownership role of government poses several value-laden questions about the compatibility of our free-enterprise system with the need, be it real or imaginary, of preserving huge swaths of territory for the total preservation of nature in the raw. Must we completely exclude the human race from nature in order to save the wilderness? If not, what economic activities can we afford to allow without irreparably damaging nature's bequest to future generations? Suppose we rephrase the question. Would you favor oil and mineral exploitation if these resources could be taken from public lands without any harm to the environment? Most people might be inclined to agree, unless they simply wanted to protect these resources with the ulterior motive of forcing America into eventual shortages and scarcity. The fundamental question then becomes whether the Audubon experience can be translated into a broader environmental policy with success equal to its promise. Only through experiment, concerted trial and error, can we formulate a scientific answer, and that means the federal government must begin endowing selected environmental groups with authority to take a few calculated chances.

Journalist William Tucker, author of *Progress and Privilege,* offered this assessment in *Reason* magazine: "In the hard-pressed 1980s, protecting the environment is going to mean getting resources out of government hands and into the private sector. Only then can the spontaneous corrections of the marketplace spur ownership to maintain the value of resources far into the future."

Preventing Environmental Destruction

Probably the most important resource produced by our public lands is water. Throughout the western United States the federal government has maintained a policy of channeling floods of grossly underpriced water from federal lands to agribusiness, so these corporate interests can profitably farm soils some of which produce toxins. This policy has yielded a witches' brew of environmental dangers and problems that threaten to eventually soak taxpayers.

By damming hundreds of rivers to control their flow, the U.S. Bureau of Reclamation essentially nationalized the West's most precious natural resource. By building huge water-distribution systems costing taxpayers tens of billions of dollars, then selling the water to large growers for one-tenth or less of its true worth and cost, Congress and its agent, the Bureau, have promoted a form of corporate welfare that institutionalizes the "tragedy of the commons." No better illustration exists of the folly of these federal water subsidies than the catastrophe that befell the Kesterson Wildlife Refuge.

As part of the bureau's massive Central Valley Project in northern and central California, Friant Dam was built to trap the waters of the San Joaquin River, which traditionally irrigated the San Joaquin Valley between Fresno and Sacramento. A distribution system was erected to direct the waters through aqueducts to the west side of the valley around Fresno, where several hundred large corporate farms comprising the Westlands Water District were located. Membership in

Westlands was dominated by Southern Pacific Railroad (with more than 100,000 acres), the Standard Oil Company, and the J. G. Boswell Co., California's biggest grower.

Because the Westlands area is a semiarid climate with an annual rainfall average of just 6 inches, only by adding floods of cheap irrigation water could the soils be made productive and profitable. A 40-year contract signed between Westlands and the Bureau of Reclamation in 1968 called for water deliveries at $7.50 an acre-foot—enough water to flood an acre one foot deep—even though the true cost of delivering the water to Westlands would be nearly $100 an acre-foot.

This taxpayer subsidy amounted to a value of about $217 per acre per year to the owners of Westlands property that would eventually produce crop revenue of less than $300 an acre. With taxpayer-subsidized water, land values in the Westlands skyrocketed from $100 an acre to more than $3,000. Cheap water would transform the Westlands Water District into America's largest irrigation district, and the largest single recipient of federal water and agricultural crop subsidies. More than half of the Westlands acreage is devoted to cotton; J. G. Boswell alone received $10 million in cotton subsidies from the U.S. Agriculture Department in 1986.

Corporate farmers reaping subsidized water to grow subsidized crops that are in surplus translates into farming operations that farm the U.S. government. But the "Alice in Wonderland" dimension of this story has an even stranger twist. An impermeable clay layer underlies most of the Westlands' 603,000 acres, creating serious drainage problems. If unflushed, high salinity levels combined with numerous toxins in the area, including concentrations of selenium, mercury, and arsenic, would poison plants and the soil.

Selenium is a trace element often found in ancient seabeds, as the San Joaquin Valley had once been; it is water soluble and can biomagnify its way up the food chain, increasing in toxicity as small organisms are consumed by larger ones, until it eventually accumulates in animal or human tissues. Since 1939 the U.S. Geological Survey, the Bureau of Reclamation's sister agency in the Interior Department, had known that dangerous levels of selenium laced the Westlands soils. At least 325 separate medical and scientific studies documenting the dangers of selenium in agriculture were ignored by the bureau when it erected its huge irrigation project on the arid, selenium-laden soils of the Westlands.

To remove the wastewater containing the selenium and other

toxins, farmers hooked up subsurface tile drains — underground perforated pipes — that collected the waste after use in irrigation and fed it into a concrete master drain built by the bureau. The bureau charged Westlands only $.50 an acre-foot for drainage costs, at which rate it would take 270 years for the farmers to repay the cost of building the 82-mile-long drain.

Eighty-two miles to the north, near the little town of Los Banos, Janette and Frank Freitas had been introduced to the Bureau of Reclamation in 1967, when two Bureau of Reclamation employees showed up at their ranch wanting to buy 800 acres on which to build "temporary evaporation" ponds for agricultural wastewater. Because this land was their best high ground, and had belonged to the family for four generations, they refused to sell. The bureau condemned their property and took it anyway, adding it to 4,000 acres that had formerly been the Kesterson ranch. When construction commenced Mrs. Freitas watched from her kitchen window each day as bulldozers carved out 12 huge evaporation ponds, scooping out the clay layer underneath the soil which would have prevented seepage. A 1966 feasibility study of the Kesterson area had warned the bureau to keep the topsoil and clays intact or significant seepage would occur; apparently the bureau wanted the ponds to leak to provide more storage capacity for the Westlands. A 1973 bureau memo even describes them as "evaporation/seepage ponds."

Kesterson became both a wastewater-disposal site and a wildlife refuge for migratory birds along the Pacific flyway, a concept the U.S. Fish and Wildlife Service modeled after the Stillwater Wildlife Refuge in Nevada which had evolved from a marsh created by the dumping of agricultural wastes. Creating such a dual purpose for the project — disposing of wastewater, maintaining a habitat for birds — also helped assure continued congressional funding, but no rigorous studies had been undertaken to determine what effects wastewater would have on wildlife.

Agricultural wastewater mixed with fresh water began flowing into Kesterson from the Westlands in 1978, and by 1981 the entire flow along the 82-mile concrete drain was toxic tile water. In that year, early one summer morning, 15 registered cattle belonging to Jim and Karen Claus drank from an irrigation ditch next door to the Kesterson refuge, and one by one the cows lay down and died. Soon calves on the Claus property adjoining Kesterson were aborting with abnormal frequency, and a foul odor began to permeate the air. As months passed, bass and catfish disappeared from streams in the area, and rabbits from fields; birds fell dead by the dozens, and irrigation ditches which had been thick with croaking frogs fell silent. One afternoon the Claus retriever dog walked in with a live swan in its mouth and set it down; the bird simply stared at the dog in drunken apathy. Family confusion turned to alarm — they could literally see the environment degenerating around them.

Within months other landowners adjoining Kesterson began experiencing their own problems. On the 5,000-acre Freitas ranch, sheep and cattle gulped water seeping out from the ground, apparently from Kesterson, until they slobbered and staggered about half-blind before dropping dead. Once-productive gardens on their property now refused to grow. A third landowner, brothers Frank and Charles Schwab, dug a ditch between their property and the Kesterson refuge; within a day the ditch had filled with foul-smelling water from Kesterson.

To explore the potential for expanding the use of this wastewater elsewhere, a Fish and Wildlife Service environmental-assessment specialist, Felix Smith, was sent to the Kesterson refuge in June 1983, accompanied by two scientists. As they walked he was struck by the quietness of the marsh. No bullfrogs or the normal quacking of birds could be heard, and the entire area stank. Finding a nest of mud hens he reached down and picked it up — inside were badly deformed chicks without eyes or legs. Nests everywhere contained horrible deformities. The entire marsh had degenerated into a veritable genetic nightmare.

Bureau testing of drain water between March 1981, when the entire flow became tile wastes, and February 1982 had found arsenic, boron, and selenium in concentrations known to be harmful to freshwater life. Analyses of mosquito fish taken from Kesterson ponds revealed arsenic, mercury, and the highest concentration of selenium ever found in living fish. Additional samplings in 1983 found selenium concentrations twice as high as in the previous year. Yet the Bureau of Reclamation would not publicly admit to any of these findings for another 14 months!

Examinations of the ponds in 1982 had also revealed that 60% of the wastewater flowing into Kesterson was seeping out, apparently onto adjoining private property. This information, too, remained under wraps. A possible explanation for the bureau keeping both the contamination data and seepage information secret would emerge years later from Donald Swain, chief of Environmental Resources in the bureau's planning division. He would testify in a court affidavit that the bureau found "significant" seepage in 1982 but "determined not to take any corrective action" because the bureau was "sensitive to the increasing need for disposal of subsurface agricultural drainage" and corrective action might limit Kesterson's holding capacity. To appease Westlands the bureau decided to ignore environmental dangers. In July 1983, U.S. Geological Survey scientists tested water samples from Kesterson ponds and found selenium, originating in the Westlands, to be responsible for the genetic deformities.

When Smith presented his findings and the Geological Survey data to Bureau of Reclamation officials in Sacramento, they refused to listen. They told Smith he did not know what he was talking about, his controls were inadequate, his scientists inadequate, his information wrong. Smith came away angry but philosophical: "The bureau has a vested interest here of maintaining their empire. Through the movement of water, who gets a water contract, and who gets massaged, they've got the natural resource in their hands, and they control land use. The bureau is considered untouchable in this valley because it made the desert bloom. But the bureau never takes seriously their other role—cleaning up their damn mess after they make it."

A survey of wildlife-refuge contamination carried out by the Fish and Wildlife Service in 1986 found 85 western refuges suffering from confirmed or suspected contaminant problems, most caused by agricultural irrigation drainage from bureau projects. Thirteen refuges in eight states—California, Arizona, Montana, Nevada, Texas, Colorado, New Mexico, and Utah—were contaminated from selenium carried by agricultural drainage. At Stillwater's Wildlife Management Area in Nevada, the model used to establish Kesterson, monitoring by the Bureau of Reclamation turned up selenium levels comparable to Kesterson's and even higher levels of arsenic and mercury. Early in 1987 literally millions of fish and birds including pelicans, herons, and geese died at Stillwater. Like Kesterson, Stillwater is part of the Pacific flyway for migratory birds and sits beside the nation's oldest agricultural irrigation project. The eventual cost to taxpayers for cleaning up contaminated areas could reach into the tens of billions of dollars. For Kesterson and Westlands alone, solving the drainage and contamination problems might cost $13 billion, conceded the bureau's western regional director.

American taxpayers subsidized problems in the Westlands in at least five ways: The Bureau of Reclamation sells water and power for a fraction of what it costs taxpayers to develop it; taxpayers pay again to support the prices of surplus crops produced by the subsidized water; and still again to support the bureau in draining the resulting wastewater. The other two ways have been described by William Sweeney, former California area manager for the Fish and Wildlife Service: "We pay again in the loss of our fish and wildlife resources, and again for living in, and trying to clean up, a fouled environment."

Taxpayer subsidies of underpriced water to Westlands brought about the crisis at Kesterson because the area would not be economic to farm in the absence of large subsidies. Donald Anthrop, professor of environmental studies at San Jose University, calls Kesterson "an ecological disaster brought about by the application of publicly subsidized irrigation water to marginal land that never should have been irrigated in the first place." Subsidized water producing surplus crops like cotton depresses crop prices nationwide—perhaps even driving out of business unsubsidized cotton farmers in states like Mississippi— while creating monumental environmental problems. The issue has been framed by the Natural Resources Defense Council: "Does the continued profitability of a relatively small number of farmers justify continued water subsidies when those subsidies are being used largely to grow surplus crops and are creating what may prove to be an insoluble threat to human health and the environment?"

Nationwide, the U.S. Bureau of Reclamation recovers only 17% of the costs of its irrigation projects, amounting to a taxpayer subsidy exceeding $1 billion annually. The World Resources Institute, in a study of public irrigation systems, was prompted to declare that subsidies are "inefficient, inequitable, fiscally disastrous, wasteful of increasingly scarce water and environmentally harmful."

If environmental groups controlled the public lands producing this water, they could sell it at market rates to agricultural water districts, municipal water systems, and other users, utilizing the proceeds to fund a constant program of environmental conservation on preservation status lands. At the very least, ending the practice of subsidizing water, especially for toxin-producing soils, would help prevent our nation's wildlife refuges from becoming toxic dumps. Unleashing water as a hoarded government asset would end this form of corporate welfare, and avoid the creation of new, more tragic Kestersons.

7
Privatizing Federal Spending

Turning Down the Spending Spigots

For advocates of public-spending restraint and the "Small is beautiful" philosophy of government, the Reagan administration's assumption of executive power in 1981 seemed to signal a fundamental alteration in the nation's economic balance of power, or at least a shift in the pattern of federal spending trends that had dominated the previous half-century. Never before had budget cutters, budget balancers, and tax cutters had access to a politician occupying the White House who shared their rhetoric and seemed committed to championing their agenda. Somewhere along the way each group would, with the possible exception of "supply-side" tax cutters, eventually find in this administration's approach to politics the seeds for their own disappointment and alienation.

We have now witnessed an administration twice elected on promises of a balanced budget and reductions in the growth and size of the federal government preside over the largest budget deficits and the highest levels of spending and government employment in our nation's history. Despite rhetoric by the admininstration about halting the growth of government, Americans employed by government at all levels reached an unprecedented 16.6 million in 1985, of whom 4.4 million were employed by school districts, 5.2 million by local governments, 3.9 million by state governments, and 3 million in federal civilian jobs (5.2 million federal employees if one includes military personnel). As his first official act of Inauguration Day 1981, President Reagan signed a hiring freeze on federal employment, declaring such an action would "eventually lead to a significant reduction in the size of the federal work force." Within a few months the hiring freeze quietly was lifted, at a time when civilian and military federal employment stood at 4.9 million. Five years later, at the start of fiscal 1986, a federal civilian hiring binge—mostly by the U.S. Postal Service and the Defense Department—had pushed the employment total beyond 5.2 million.

Sen. Daniel P. Moynihan (D-New York) has called this governmental growth a natural, inevitable product of our political bargaining process among special-interest groups to secure government outlays that directly benefit them. A less charitable view might describe the growth as further evidence of government spending out of control, America living beyond its means, and the stranglehold certain special-interest groups and public-employee unions seem to have over the selection of the delivery mechanisms government uses for public services.

Cutting government from the top is a strategy that has largely failed. The Reagan administration's gamble that the stimulative effect of its tax cuts on the economy would bring in sufficient new tax revenues to avoid politically dangerous spending cuts obviously has not paid off in time to avoid huge deficits. It may also be that administration officials wanted to force Congress to reduce spending by pushing through tax cuts that would starve the federal government of revenue. But Congress responded with only minor cuts in the growth of spending, and the strategy boomeranged with unconscionable deficits approaching $200 billion annually. Unable to abolish as promised the Departments of Energy and Education, the Small Business Administration, or any major agency or spending program of consequence the Reagan administration next trumpeted a campaign to reduce spending and balance the budget by identifying and removing waste, fraud, and abuse from federal agencies.

About 2,000 specialists from private industry were brought in to evaluate the management efficiency of executive-agency operations, and in 47 reports they made 2,478 recommendations for reform estimated to save $141 billion a year. The Grace Commission, as it came to be known, found most of its major recommendations ignored on Capitol Hill, where there was suspicion if not open resentment at having corporate America lecture government about efficiency. Within the dozens of federal agencies, where the typical economy or efficiency reform had been to limit the number of officials entitled to limousine privileges, or to require wall calendars to conform to a modest size, many of the commission's sweeping recommendations were swept into a bureaucratic "Bermuda Triangle." Few efficiency reforms of enduring value ever seem to outlast the tenure of their implementers or advocates. Some proponents of tax increases, like George F. Will, the syndicated columnist, ridiculed the commission for "not facing facts...the odious principle that the public must pay its bills." Others associated with Ralph Nader protested the entire commission's war on waste as a thinly disguised "attack on social-welfare programs."

A central reason why many of the Grace Commission recommendations failed, or were destined to fail even if implemented, is that government cannot be expected to operate like a business. Applying business-management principles to the operations of government, much as the Grace Commission attempted to do, may yield a few short-term benefits, but ultimately political rather than business considerations will dictate the way government functions. The commission failed at trying to "use private-sector methods that promote public-sector efficiency," argues Steven H. Hanke, an economist for the Council of Economic Advisors when the commission was at work, because "public ownership without public waste is a myth." Without ownership there is no effective accountability. Government-owned or managed enterprises and activities do not adhere to the economic laws of supply and demand, or to incentives and competition, and as a result waste and spiraling costs are endemic. By the very nature of its bureaucratic decision-making, government is unsuited to play the role of landlord, banker, or insurer.

Equally important, several studies contrasting behavioral differences in motivation between public- and private-sector employees have found "public employees are more risk averse than those in the private sector, with risk aversion measured as an index of insurance owned, use of seat belts, and smoking and drinking habits," observes Walter F. Baber of the University of Nevada, Reno. Likewise, study results indicate that government employees value job stability much more highly than workers in the business sector, and because within government weaker relationships exist between performance levels and rewards, public employees can be expected to resist reforms affecting organizational structures and job stability.

Asset sales and related forms of privatization became enshrined as a deficit-reduction manuever beginning in 1983, when the Reagan administration proposed selling the government's four weather satellites to the private sector, and initiated its program to auction off surplus federal real estate. By 1986 the Office of Management and Budget director, James Miller, replacing David Stockman, was proposing elimination of the entire federal deficit by selling off an array of assets headed by the major federal dams and power systems, and privatizing the post office, the Federal Housing Administration, and other functions performed by numerous federal agencies.

Critics pounced gleefully on the proposals. An economics writer for *The Washington Post*, Hobart Rowen, ridiculed privatization as "innovative gimmickry" and "mischievous nonsense." Rowen, a tax-increase adovocate, took his own survey of the public pulse using mail he received "in response to an earlier column challenging the assumption that private industry can always out perform the public sector," and not surprisingly he discovered among his federal employee-dominated readership "outrage at the effort to transfer public wealth" into private hands. He predicted that any lawmaker who supported privatization "had better run scared in the next election." The House Budget Committee chairman, Rep. William Gray (D-Pennsylvania), characterized asset sales as tantamount to a homeowner selling his garage to pay this month's mortgage and then his car to pay next month's.

On one level the garage-sale metaphor fits. "After all," quipped Miller, "what does almost any American family do when it finds its living space crammed with objects it no longer needs or wants? The common-sense solution is to hold a garage sale and barter those useless items for cash." To take that comparison further, any analogy between federal asset sales and home garage sales must take into consideration the homeowners' relative financial worth and credit standing. Would the average homeowner regularly spend more than he earns, live in a home so large he cannot afford to maintain it, drive a car that costs him more in repairs than he derives in driving benefits, or tolerate the upkeep on a car garage big as a B-52 airplane hangar? Obviously a rational homeowner would perform only those tasks for which he is competent and contract-out or sell the rest. Why should government be any different? Selling federal assets would be desirable even if there were no budget deficit because most of these assets require subsidies that are a drain on taxpayers, nor should government be in the business of competing with its own citizenry by providing subsi-dized competition on the production of goods or services.

House Speaker James Wright (D-Texas) protested that privatiza-tion means we will "sell off the public's legacy." To the extent that "legacy" entails inefficiency, exorbitant costs, and unfair competition, we would be better off shedding the burdens of public ownership. But few, if any, assets sales or other privatization proposals have received a fair hearing on the floor of the U.S. Congress, where fiscal judgments are too often rendered on reaction rather than merit.

Consider the treatment given in Congress to the idea of privatizing federal oil fields. Federal oil resources, called the Naval Petroleum Reserves, reside in two government-owned and operated fields—Elk Hills in California and Teapot Dome in Wyoming—producing oil too thick and heavy to be used by Navy vessels. It is sold to private buyers in the market, often for $7 and less per barrel, half the real market price, bearing out the Reagan administration contention that the government should not be in the oil business because bureaucracies are ill-equipped to play the market. In its fiscal 1987 budget the administration proposed selling the reserves, whose production is dwindling, to private buyers for between $3 billion and $5 billion. In the event of a national emergency, be it war or another foreign oil embargo, enough oil has been stored in the Gulf Coast salt domes of our Strategic Petroleum Reserve to serve both military and civilian needs. Newspapers like *The Washington Post* endorsed getting the government out of a business "best left to private companies." Yet members of Congress were marching to the beat of a naysayer drummer. Led by Rep. Philip Sharp (D-Indiana), Congress blocked the sale, accepting Sharp's rhetoric that "if oil prices rebounded" the government would have sold the fields for less than true worth. Objections that the federal government is selling too soon, or selling at too low a price, when stripped of subterfuge, really amount to arguments "for continuing subsidies, for more federal involvement in the private sector, and for higher taxes," cautioned James Miller of OMB.

A second case in point of Congress rejecting before looking concerns the four federal weather satellites. In October 1983, the U.S. Senate adopted an amendment by Sen. Larry Pressler (R-South Dakota) prohibiting the Commerce Department from spending any money to solicit bids or to even study the sale of the weather satellites and their ground stations. This privatization idea had originated in the Carter administration and was inherited by Reagan's OMB, but few in Congress had bothered to understand the rationale for selling these assets.

Provision of weather data is deemed an integral function of

government by the National Oceanic and Atmospheric Administration (NOAA), a part of the Commerce Department and the federal government's primary weather agency. Each year it spends about $1 billion to gather, analyze, and disseminate raw weather information acting as a wholesaler, giving it essentially free to retailing "customers" such as television and radio stations, newspapers, and private specialized weather forecasters. In turn these retailers sell this information in packaged form to their clients — us the general public, and sectors of the economy in need of specialized data, like airlines and the shipping industry. Communications Satellite Corp. (COMSAT), a federally chartered, stockholder-owned company which had taken over government communciations satellites in the 1960s, offered to purchase the four federal weather satellites, along with the Landsat remote-sensing satellites that produce photos of crop and geological formations. In return for a 15-year contract under which the government would buy data under prearranged prices, Comsat promised to design and launch replacement satellites as necessary, and in the process save taxpayers large sums in three ways: consolidating ground-sensing and weather stations and developing dual-purpose satellites; eliminating the $150-million-a-year government cost of operating the weather satellites; and avoiding much of an estimated $1 billion in technological improvements that were needed.

Objections were raised that the Pentagon needed access to the satellites for security reasons; but any sale would have provided for priority use by the Defense Department, and the U.S. Navy was already using Comsat satellites for its maritime UHF radio communications. Lastly the argument arose that weather-data collection constitutes a "natural monopoly" because it is too costly for competing firms to operate separate satellite and ground-station systems. That scenario has already been proven false in the provision of satellite communications and will soon be so proven in the space-launch field with entry by numerous competing companies. The government weather monopoly exists for reasons other than practicality. The real beneficiaries of a taxpayer-subsidized government monopoly over weather-data collections are not the general public but primarily the broadcast media which, in the words of Patrick Cox, a policy analyst for the Pacific Research Institute, present their weather forecasts "not as a public service" but because "it generates advertising revenue."

Private weather-forecasting firms do utilize data from the federal government's National Weather Service (NWS), at minmal costs, and often to the embarrassment of the federal agency. An incident involving predictions of a New York City snowstorm in 1978 illustrates the potential benefits of private competition to produce accurate forecasts and calls into question the need for any government role. Accu-Weather Inc. of State College, Pennyslvania, predicted four days in advance the timing and size of a snowstorm that struck New York—a prediction the National Weather Service had scoffed at—although the private firm relied on data identical to that used by NWS. One of Accu-Weather's 300 clients was New York City's Sanitation Department, which paid $2,000 a year for information that would save tens of thousands of dollars. "When you're depending on the U.S. Weather Service," a department spokesman admitted to *The New York Times,* "they put it out on their time, at their convenience, on their schedule—they're not working for us. With Accu-Weather, we're the boss."

In his fiscal 1988 budget message, President Reagan said the federal government "has no business providing services to individuals that private markets...can provide just as well or better." His budget proposed selling off government loans, Amtrak's Northeast rail-corridor service, the Naval Petroleum Reserves, five Power Marketing Administrations, and phasing out subsidy programs in agriculture, mass transit, and urban development. Asset and loan sales were predicted to provide about $10 billion in revenues.

Contrasted to this budget message the administration's record on its rhetoric, especially during its first term, has resembled selective hypocrisy. It has been an administration with schizophrenic treatment of privatization in general and subsidies in particular, decrying some, yet previously supportive of subsidized electric power and grazing fees, subsidized crop programs and water projects, and every other kind of subsidy benefiting western Republican interest groups. By turning a blind eye to, or even promoting, subsidies for political supporters during the period 1981–85 and repeatedly retreating on privatization proposals, the administration sacrificed much of its influence and credibility.

When the Reagan administration proposed selling the five major Power Marketing Administrations in 1986, its own Energy Department sabotaged the idea by refusing to lobby for it, encouraging the U.S. Senate to vote 73–25 against even studying the prospect. Thomas Gale Moore, the member of the President's Council of Economic Advisors placed in charge of coordinating privatization, similarly had trouble getting the Energy Department to study the feasibility of contracting for naval petroleum shipping needs. Cooperation was equally lacking from the Defense Department and the Veterans Administration. In late 1986 the Congress voted to lease the federal government's two suburban Washington airports—National and Dulles—to a regional authority formed by the State of Virginia, which agreed to pay $47 million over 50 years. Although the airports had been valued in excess of $2 billion, and several private consortiums had indicated a willingness to purchase the facilities, Congress elected to simply transfer responsibility from federal taxpayers to Virginia taxpayers when it could have saved both groups millions of dollars in taxes and $700 million in necessary improvements. Transportation Secretary Elizabeth Dole lobbied vigorously against privatization and for intergovernmental transfer, personally convincing a Texas congressman to withdraw his legislation to privatize, and even winning over one Senate opponent of her plan, Ernest Hollings (D–South Carolina), by promising him more funding for roads and bridges.

When the National Technical Information Service—an arm of the Commerce Department which collects government-funded technical research and then leases out its data base—was considered for privatization in late 1986, several national associations of librarians objected, and the administration quickly withdrew the proposal. A similar fate awaited a proposal to privatize the Federal Housing Administration (FHA), which insures home loans by reimbursing the lender for losses if a homeowner defaults. Citizens for a Sound Economy president Richard Fink had accused FHA of "stifling the development of competing, private mortgage-insurance plans for low and middle-income families," while it helps the wealthy obtain second homes. Some segments of the housing industry, particularly the Mortgage Bankers Association, denounced privatization of FHA if only because the federal government has been willing to take insurer risks the private sector might avoid. In September 1986, the administration retreated from the idea of selling the FHA on the private market, despite evidence of widespread fraud by investors and use of the program by homeowners with incomes sufficient for them to qualify for privately insured mortgages.

Federal loan programs would have been an ideal issue on which the Reagan administration could have advanced its privatization arguments. As of April 1987, outstanding federal credit totaled $701 billion, with the guaranteed-loan portion of the portfolio ($450 billion) never included in the federal budget, making it appear as if the loans were free, would never default, and contained no government subsidy. With more than 350 federal loan programs benefiting exporters, foreign governments, utilities, farmers, and students, that adds up to a colossal "silent" part of the budget. Take the guaranteed student-loan program, which had accumulated nearly $5 billion in delinquent debt by 1986. More than 30% of the face value of every student loan constitutes a taxpayer subsidy because the federal government must pay the interest while the student is in school, stretch out repayment periods far beyond normal banking practice, and keep interest payments below market rates.

In early 1985, Sen. Daniel P. Moynihan (D–New York), proposed that the federal government sell off its loan portfolio to help reduce the principal of the national debt. He estimated that the sale would save taxpayers at least $200 billion—including future debt service avoided—over a period of seven years. Sales would help reduce the scope of the government's gigantic lending programs, bring greater efficiency to the poorly managed credit process, and help remove government from competition with the private sector while revealing the extent to which taxpayer subsidies are hidden in the loan program. Corporate welfare was a key consideration, since many of the loans directly benefit international corporations, such as the Export-Import Bank loan of $2 billion to the Korean Power Company so it could purchase nuclear power plants from Westinghouse. Moynihan called the size of the subsidies given as federal loans "quite extraordinary."

When Sen. Moynihan offered his privatization scheme to the Republican-controlled Senate Budget Committee, it was voted down, 18–4. He was voted down again on the floor of the Republican Senate, 71–26. "I asked one of our most sincere budget balancers why he had voted against us," recalled Sen. Moynihan. "The reply came that this would only postpone the day of final reckoning. That happens precisely to be my idea of what you try to do in politics." Then OMB director David Stockman had opposed the loan sales fearing that Congress would use them to postpone more permanent forms of deficit reduction. Stockman would leave OMB to work for Salomon Brothers, an investment-banking firm lobbying for federal-loan sales.

Pressure from deficit-reduction targets set by the Gramm–Rudman–Hollings law prompted Congress to partially reverse itself on loan sales. In the closing days of the session in late 1986, as spending cuts were being rejected one after another and lawmakers were desperate for bailouts, Congress adopted legislation to increase the administration's proposed pilot loan sale program from $2 billion in revenues to $5.5 billion. That represents only a tiny fraction of the nearly $1-trillion loan portfolio, but it at least demonstrated that Congress and the administration could be pressured into giving up a few politically valuable subsidies.

When one considers the immense fiscal problems we face as a nation, selling off unneeded assets and the federal loan portfolio would seem a painless, if only partial, remedy. Just the interest on our $2- trillion federal debt came to $147 billion in the 1987 budget, a figure that works out to $2,400 every family of four will owe as their share of the financing; the principal on that debt amounts to $8,500 for each and every American. Once before in our history America faced a debt crisis of similar dimensions. When the accumulated deficits from the Revolutionary War and the War of 1812 began to dwarf the federal government's then $10-million-a-year budget, still a considerable sum in those days, Treasury Secretary Albert Gallatin devised a plan to retire the debt through land and other asset sales. A sinking fund was started for that purpose in 1817, and by 1835 the entire federal debt had been paid off.

Without understanding among our public officials of the underlying commonsense philosophy of privatization, without their willingness to transcend parochial concerns and reactionary fiscal prejudices, we are left mired in a dilemma without resolution. In a fit of frustration and hyperbole, John Baden, a "free-market environmentalist," described the administration's approach to market incentives for environmental protection: "The Reagan administration didn't understand the issue. Those people are really brain-damaged. All they can see when you mention environment is Jane Fonda chaining herself to a tree."

Exceptions to Baden's characterization did emerge within several agencies: OMB Director James Miller; Ralph Stanley, administrator of the Urban Mass Transportation Administration; James K. Stewart, director of the National Institute of Justice within the Department of Justice; and certain officials within the Office of Territorial and International Affairs in the Department of the Interior, and the private-sector office of the Agency for International Development. In September 1987, a Commission on Privatization was named by President Reagan to review all federal activities and recommend, within six months, ways to eliminate unfair government competition with the private sector using asset sales and the privatization of government services. University of Chicago Economics Professor David Linowes, a Democrat, chaired the bipartisan presidential commission.

Other glimmers of understanding came from an unexpected quarter. "America does not have to spend more to do more," remarked Sen. Edward Kennedy (D–Massachusetts), on assuming chairmanship of the Senate Labor and Human Resources Committee in 1987. Democrats, observed a *Washington Post* reporter, are "turning increasingly to marketplace solutions," as evidenced by Kennedy who abandoned his pet idea of comprehensive national health insurance financed by the federal government. Doing more with less when spoken by Democrats has been described as the pursuit of liberal ends by conservative means, or low-cost social justice.

Whatever the motivation for initiating it, once set in motion privatization signals a sorting-out process, redefining the proper roles and responsibilities of individuals, of neighborhoods, of cities, of states, and of central government.

Contracting-Out Federal Functions

As the sun rises over the flatlands of northern Oklahoma, just a few miles from the hometown of folk singer Woody ("This land is your land") Guthrie, cars stream through the gates of Vance Air Force Base bringing in the private contractor work force. About 1,000 employees of Northrop Aircraft Service perform jobs here for which other comparable Air Force bases utilize twice the number of military and government workers. In the aircraft-maintenance hangars at Vance, where T-37 and T-38 trainer jets are overhauled, four-man crews are cross-utilized to play three and more roles which other bases typically perform with separate teams of hydraulic, engine, and electrical specialists, often 12 people in all. Vance regularly has a lower percentage of its planes grounded for maintenance compared to these other bases, meaning that a higher quality of service is being provided at less cost. In the supply, transportation, and procurement building, a 22-year retired veteran of the Air Force directs a single department other bases operate as three. Under him, about 100 employees operate base-supply and fuels functions that bases elsewhere perform with 225 people. Over at the office-supply sales section one woman alternately stocks shelves and assists customers, roles that other bases delegate to three or more employees. All over the base Northrop uses working supervisors and multiskilled workers. At the warehouse, employees who mop the floor also stock shelves and deliver supplies; the pavements and heavy-equipment-operations sections have been combined into a single shop, its employees cross-trained to operate each type of equipment; and two general-purpose maintenance mechanics perform carpentry, painting, electrical, and mechanical work on the 230 units of base family housing, work which elsewhere would be delegated to teams of "specialists."

Nearly $9 million annually is saved—22% below costs at comparable bases—by using a private contractor at Vance, performing 17 services ranging from fire safety and food preparation to operating the instrument flight simulators. A Pentagon study of the base glowingly concluded: "Vance has the most innovative reorganization...and has vastly streamlined its work flow and response times." Officials of the Office of Management and Budget unreservedly describe Vance as "the most cost-effective base in the U.S. Air Force."

While everyone acknowledges the contracting-out experience at Vance, begun in 1960 as an "experiment," and consistently demonstrates its value, little progress has been made in adapting its savings and efficiencies approach to the rest of the military, or to the federal government as a whole. Of the Pentagon's 1,300 or so military bases, Vance is one of only three (one each in the Army, Navy, and Air Force) to have contracted-out most base maintenance. Yet the potential for savings within the Defense Department is vast. Since 1979 about 50,000 commercial positions in the military were studied for contracting-out and then subjected to a competitive-bid process in which in-house performance costs are evaluated against contractor bids. Savings just from these competitions are estimated by the Pentagon at $500 million annually. When one considers that 350,000 positions remain to be studied by the Pentagon, future savings could exceed $3 billion a year from the military side of government alone.

"The role of government should not include performing services and activities that can effectively be carried out by the private sector," said President Reagan in 1983. He urged renewed emphasis on contracting-out federal commercial activities such as custodial and maintenance work in federal buildings, printing government publications, data processing, and dozens of other services. Begun by the Eisenhower administration in 1955, this contracting-out program, which came to be known as A-76, directs federal agencies to contract all products and services "that can be procured more economically from a commercial source." Exceptions to this rule were made only for inherently governmental functions like criminal investigations, tax collection, regulation of industry, and military combat roles.

Although this policy of reliance on the private sector has been in effect for 30 years, more than 600,000 federal employees, most of them in the Defense Department, still perform 11,000 different types of commercial activities, from cutting lawns and washing clothes to processing public information. For instance, more than 10,000 government employees are painters and paperhangers, more than 20,000 prepare and serve food, more than 10,000 are librarians, and more than 30,000 are supply clerks. A Small Business Administration study estimated that if all these functions were contracted-out, savings in excess of $3 billion annually would result, with millions of dollars in new tax revenues being generated by the contractors. But less than one-quarter of the 600,000 federal commercial positions have even been studied by government agencies for contracting under A-76 guidelines. Currently about 40% of federal goods and services are procured from the private sector, a precipitous decline from 1967, when an estimated 60% came from private providers.

"A-76 competitions save 33% of the original cost of doing business without harming, yet often enhancing our ability to execute our mission," Assistant Secretary of Defense Lawrence Korb testified before Congress. Despite this endorsement of contracting from the Pentagon hierarchy, progress toward saving taxpayers money through the A-76 process remains excruciatingly slow. Bureaucratic obstructionism plagues the entire A-76 program. A 1984 Pentagon study of contracting by the four armed services grimly concluded: "The services have exempted more activities from competition than [the Office of the Secretary of Defense] would like, and we observed a very prevalent tendency. . .to postpone preparing for competition as if hoping the threat would pass." Military commanders and their civilian counterparts often throw up elaborate roadblocks, sometimes with congressional help, to subvert the contracting process. They simply do not have incentives to cooperate, says Hugh Witt, a former acting assistant secretary of the Navy. He tells of an unsuccessful attempt to contract-out the Navy weapons-test facility at Point Mugu, California, where he had hoped to cut 40% from operating costs. He met with the leader of Navy employees who had helped block the contracting move. "I asked him if it was not true that savings at Mugu would come from fewer employees and more effective use of employees," remembers Witt. "He agreed, then bluntly said that if he had fewer employees it would lower his civil-service rating from GS-13 to a GS-12, resulting in less take-home pay. Why should he cut his own throat?"

Across the federal government, compliance with A-76 has been "inconsistent and relatively ineffective," reports the General Accounting Office, Congress's investigative agency. Over at the Health and Human Services Department, an agency with the largest federal budget, only three cost studies were performed in all of 1986. Much of the blame for this intransigence and lost opportunities for savings must rest with the U.S. Congress. Pressured by public-employee unions to resist contracting, lawmakers usually retreat rather than stand firm on behalf of taxpayers and efficiency. Congress refuses even to endorse the principle of a national policy of reliance on the private sector for the government's goods and services. In 1978 members of Congress began imposing the first in a series of 20 legislative prohibitions on contracting, singling out the Defense Department. Rep. Abraham Kazen (D–Texas), won passage of restrictions preventing the Pentagon from contracting most major functions for three years. Another Texan, Rep. Marvin Leath, also a Democrat, placed a permanent ban on the Veterans Administration contracting positions incidental to patient care.

A 1981 GAO study concluded that it costs the General Services Administration "over 50% more to clean offices with its own custodians than with contractors and almost twice as much as its landlords pay to clean federal leased space." One year later, when the GSA attempted to contract-out some of its custodians, guards, elevator operators, and messengers, Rep. Robert Edgar (D–Pennsylvania) slapped restrictions on all such contracting, prohibiting the agency from even studying cost savings. Despite excellent contracted firefighting service at Vance Air Force Base, and exemplary security-guard contracting at the Navy submarine base in Bangor, Washington, Rep. Sam Gejdenson (D–Connecticut) won prohibitions on the Pentagon contracting any new firefighting or security functions through fiscal 1985. To exempt the National Park Service, the Fish and Wildlife Service, and the Bureau of Land Management from contracting-out maintenance and other operations, Sen. Dale Bumpers (D–Arkansas) and Rep. John Seiberling (D–Ohio) pushed through a ban on any cost-comparison studies through fiscal 1988.

Faced with these and other legislative hurdles, and hearing no clear endorsement of contracting-out from Capitol Hill, agency bureaucrats have only the Office of Management and Budget to fear when they undermine Circular A-76. Yet OMB has insufficient resources to fully monitor agency compliance, and agencies have become so skilled at manipulating A-76 guidelines that they could befuddle even the shrewdest of investigators. In hearings before the U.S. Senate Governmental Affairs Committee, dozens of examples came to light where agencies, primarily at Defense, had rigged cost comparisons or altered competition after bids were opened to avoid contracting-out. At Fort Sheridan, Illinois, competition for audiovisual services resulted in a $3.5-million in-house bid and $1.8 million from a private contractor. The government then began adding new costs, such as excessive severance pay, to the private bid, while underestimating in-house costs of supplies until Fort Sheridan was able to declare itself the winner. "The procurement process is being manipulated to frustrate the intent of Circular A-76," maintains William D. Russell, the official in the Ford and Carter administrations in charge of implementing A-76. "The present cost-comparison procedures for review of a government commercial activity are heavily weighted against contract performance."

Agencies use three methods most frequently to undermine the contracting-out program: A contractor must allocate full overhead costs in a bid, while agency estimates usually include minimal overhead costs; a contractor must include the full cost of Social Security, retirement, and unemployment in bids, while agencies routinely, in Russell's words, "grossly understate" civil-service retirement costs; and most importantly, under current A-76 regulations, private contractors must demonstrate that they can do a job a minimum of 10% cheaper than the agency would in-house before a contract can be awarded. That means all potential savings of less than 10% are lost. "The whole A-76 program has been turned backwards," complains Frank Sellers, director of the Business Alliance on Government Competition, a coalition of 47 trade associations and business federations. "Government is still competing against the private sector and that violates the intent of the A-76 program. It is the agencies, not the private sector, that should have to prove they can do these commercial jobs 10% cheaper!" Despite significant obstacles, private-sector firms were able to win more than 60% of agency cost-comparison competitions through 1983. But, beginning in 1984, thanks to new undermining techniques, federal agencies retained half of all functions put out in bid competition.

"Cost comparisons have no significance. They are a fraud on their agency, they are a fraud on the Congress, and they are a fraud on the American people," charges Senator Warren Rudman (R–New Hampshire), the only member of Congress to vigorously seek the contract conversion of all federal commercial activities. "Procurement from the private sector represents the least possible distortion of the economy, stimulates private investment, creates jobs, and generates tax revenue."

Since 1972 more than 90 General Accounting Office reports have condemned instances of unwarranted government competition with the private sector. Take the case of the Marine Corps Base at Camp Pendleton, California, north of San Diego. In 1982 the Special Services component at the base began selling on-base scuba and skin-diving instruction, whale-watching cruises, and charter sportfishing trips using a surplus Army boat refurbished with $80,000 in military funds. Customers include active and retired military personnel, their families, and civilians responding to ads for the services placed in local newspapers. The U.S. Small Business Administration filed a complaint with the Pentagon charging that private companies that had been offering similar services to the area have, without the benefit of taxpayer-supplied facilities, lost about 40% of their revenues since the military went into competition with them. For businessmen near the base like Fred Talasco, with $100,000 invested in his sailboat-chartering company, when the military rents out its sailboats at subsidized rates of $30 a day there is no way he can compete when he must charge $200 a day for the off-season. Five sportfishing boats in nearby Oceanside saw business slide from 90 chartered Marine Corps trips in 1983 to just one in 1985.

On a larger scale the U.S. Forest Service operates 13 nurseries around the country producing 150 million tree seedlings annually for reforestation. There are also nurseries operated by state, local, and regional government soil-conservation districts, all started with federal help. Together, government nurseries produce more than 300 million seedlings a year. This activity clearly falls under the designation of commercial as defined by A-76 guidelines, yet the American Association of Nurserymen has been objecting to this taxpayer-subsidized government competition—to no avail—since federal involvement in the nursery business began in 1908.

Our federal government also finds itself in the grocery-store business competing with private supermarkets for customers. Each of the four military services operates its own grocery chain—in all, 247 domestic stores and another 100 or so overseas—relying on annual taxpayer subsidies of nearly $1 billion in direct, indirect, and hidden appropriations and costs, and employing about 25,000 commissary personnel. Commissary shoppers receive taxpayer-subsidized discounts of 15% to 30% and more, and pay no sales taxes. Originally the commissaries were intended to service frontier and other outposts far from convenient shopping, but over the years a standard evolved that commissaries should be built if commercial food stores were located more than 15 miles from the center of base housing. That standard and other eligibility criteria have regularly been ignored. In the Washington, D.C., area, where six commissaries can be found, nearly 100 major grocery outlets exist within a three-mile radius of the military stores.

The General Accounting Office estimates that there would be millions of dollars in savings if only the four military services would consolidate their commissary management systems. Yet the services resist, pleading that cooperation could lead to an "identity crisis" within each service that would harm morale. In 1976, after finding that most domestic commissaries operate in urban areas in violation of regulations, the Ford administration proposed a phase-out of the taxpayer subsidy so that commissaries would be self-supporting, much like the military post-exchange system. No commissary would have been closed and studies indicated that shoppers could still expect a 15% savings without the subsidy. This phaseout passed the Senate but suffocated in the House Armed Services Committee, long a pressure point for military-employee lobbying, which decreed that the system should be immune to cost tampering.

When the President's Private Sector Survey on Cost Control, known as the Grace Commission, recommended that commissaries be contracted-out to the private sector to eliminate the taxpayer subsidy, military-lobby groups led by the Retired Officers Association responded with the scare argument that to touch the system is to destroy it, and generated thousands of protest letters to the White House. Similarly when the Mobil Corporation used commissaries as one of a series of national ads promoting Grace Commission recommendations, reaction was so antagonistic that the company paid for another ad reprinting a Fleet Reserve Association letter defending the commissary status quo. Predictably this ad focused on the impact a "loss of the commissary benefits could have on military retention," once again resurrecting the canard that cost cutting through contracting would somehow automatically close down the entire system. For those who worked on the issue for the Grace Commission, nothing smacks harder than the insinuation that contracting-out would somehow jeopardize national defense. "No Grace recommendation has been treated more unfairly," complains Keith Kendrick, an Ohio chemical executive who served on the commission's privatization task force. "We don't need four separate grocery chains run with taxpayer funds. But this outmoded delivery system is protected by the best organized lobby in Washington."

In 1984, Senator Ted Stevens (R–Alaska) tacked on a provision to a defense bill authorizing the contracting-out of three commissary operations on a two-year trial basis to test the savings potential. That provision was later deleted at the insistence of the House, led by Rep. Joseph Addabbo (D–New York), who urged his colleagues "not to send a wrong signal" that would upset military personnel. What was that wrong signal? That government should not compete with the private sector? That the private sector might operate the commissary system more efficiently and at less cost than the military?

Contracting-out the domestic commissaries could simply involve turning them into warehouse food stores, which in the private realm already provide savings of 20% and more over regular supermarket prices. Such a move could expand the number of products available to shoppers — presently with access to just half the number of items carried in normal supermarkets — and extend the hours of operations, since private operators have more incentives to please customers.

If one divides up the annual taxpayer subsidy to commissaries among the number of commissary shoppers, each patron receives about $244 a year in benefits. Simply raising salaries for active-duty military personnel by $244 a year to replace the subsidy would still save taxpayers considerable sums if the system were contracted-out, replacing taxpayer-supported military employees with privately-funded civilians. Although commissary benefits may have been promised enlistees, no one decreed, nor should anyone expect, that the stores be operated by military employees.

Neither current military personnel being serviced by the commissary system, nor the system's 25,000 employees, can entirely account for the system's resistance to change. By the Pentagon's own estimate, about 60% of the 10 million eligible commissary shoppers are military retirees living near base facilities. In Los Angeles the El Segundo commissary was not even designed to service military personnel or a military base—it exists for the benefit of retirees. Furthermore, findings from a GAO study challenge the service contention that commissary benefits are essential to recruitment. After polling military personnel for each service nationwide, GAO found only 13% who cited commissaries as a factor in their enlistment. What keeps taxpayer funds flowing and immunizes the system from reform is an "Iron Triangle" of employees, beneficiaries, and legislators in whose districts commissaries reside, which together raise a special-interest chorus louder than any collective whisper from those of us forced to pay the bills.

Congress sometimes more readily adopts privatization in its own operations than in the federal domain as a whole. With unhappy employees, and a nearly $1-million deficit in operating its two House cafeterias and members' dining room, the House Administration Committee turned the facilities and the House's 245 restaurant employees over to a private contractor, Service America Corp. Under special legislation the former House employees remained in the federal pension system. Similarly, after the USSR withdrew Russian employees of the American embassy in Moscow and the consulate in Leningrad during 1986, Congress went along with the State Department's decision to award a contract to the Los Angeles firm of Pacific Architects and Engineers—specializing in maintenance, operations, and support staff—to provide replacements for the Russian personnel.

For years Congress went along with public-employee-union assertions that the conducting of nautical surveys is an inherently governmental function that cannot be contracted-out, until a Commerce Department official casually pointed out that the Defense Mapping Agency had been contracting-out similar work for over a decade. Other public-employee-union representatives appeared before congressional committees claiming that contracting-out the National Oceanic and Atmospheric Administration weather observers at airports "would result in numerous air crashes." The union conveniently failed to mention that 21 airports, including Miami, New Orleans, and St. Louis, had been using contract weather observers for more than five years without one accident due to incompetence. In similar fashion the American Federation of Government Employees issued a paper claiming that federal contracting costs under Circular A-76 had "substantially increased, thereby wiping out any purported savings and increasing the federal deficit." Several examples were cited as evidence. For instance, "A GAO report on Selfridge Air National Guard Base and the Tank Automotive Command in Michigan showed a cost increase of 60% over three years, from $7 million to $11 million." The GAO report in question, issued in 1984 as a response to queries from Michigan's two senators, actually found that the cost increase was due to a decision by the Army to have the contractor provide materials and equipment originally to be supplied by the government. Even despite this additional expense, the decision to contract-out still saved $3.6 million from the cost had the services been performed in-house by government employees. The union distributed a chart purporting to show that the Defense Department had experienced cost overruns of $89 million on its A-76 contracts. A follow-up investigation by the Office of Management and Budget found just the opposite: "Costs would have increased by $89 million *if the functions had remained in-house*...the American Federation of Government Employees took the result totally out of context and presented a skewed version of what was reported."

Obfuscation of contracting-out issues by the unions, agency resistance to any loss of turf or personnel, and congressional ambivalence if not hostility all combined to emasculate the A-76 program. Office of Personnel Management director Constance Horner acknowledged as much in 1986 when she declared that the federal government's attempts to implement a contracting-out policy had failed, with only 30,000 jobs contracted over six years of the Reagan presidency. She unveiled a new initiative late that year, nicknamed Fed Co-Op, to defuse opposition among public employees by privatizing entire activities in government agencies and giving federal workers an ownership role. Federal Employee Direct Corporation Ownership Plan would move government services like agency cafeterias, car maintenance, and data processing into the private sector under joint-venture arrangements with private firms. Groups of federal employees would retain their present jobs and a percentage of ownership in companies that would perform the services under exclusive contracts for three years; after that, the firms would compete with others in the private sector for the contracts.

Fed Co-Op could unlock the "golden handcuffs," that entire package of generous federal retirement benefits which keep many people clinging to government jobs. Since privatization often comes wrapped up in the question of what degree of labor protection society will afford, such a transferral of rights and benefits might defuse the opposition to federal privatization while still rejecting the notion that federal employment somehow constitutes a sort of entitlement program. There is life after federal employment for government employees, and under Fed Co-Op, if properly administered, there could be improved productivity, taxpayer savings, and new opportunities for business and enterprise.

At the very least, to insure fairness in the A-76 process, an auditing office to conduct A-76 cost studies should be created within the Office of Management and Budget. Having federal agencies themselves make the in-house cost estimate and the determination whether contracting-out is more efficient resembles, in the words of Heritage Foundation policy analyst Stephen Moore, "asking the PLO to arbitrate a border dispute between Israel and Syria." Moore further proposes that OMB's role as auditor be contracted-out to a private auditing firm that would calculate cost estimates, award contracts, and monitor performance in return for payments based on a percentage of any resulting taxpayer savings and according to levels of performance reached by the contractors being monitored.

Reforming Defense Procurement

Public perceptions of defense contracting tend to fixate on revelations of $600 toilet seats, $436 hammers, and others in a collection of waste and fraud allegations and outrages. For the average person such stories might tempt one to conclude that the entire contracting-out concept amounts to a feast for the corporate greedy. Largely overlooked in the aftermath of these tawdry, titillating tales is the extent to which the Defense Department and its overseer, the U.S. Congress, share the blame for creating and at times encouraging abuses and waste in military procurement.

Congressional involvement in the procurement process, each individual member seeking to assure that defense spending reaches his or her district or state, cripples the system. Overcharges by contractors sometimes result from accounting methods mandated by Congress requiring the pricing of overhead charges on spare parts, or other centralized purchasing procedures devised to prevent the very waste that is spawned. Those overpriced toilet seats and hammers, for instance, did not occur because the Pentagon bought too much too quickly, a study by the Center for Strategic and International Studies concluded, but rather because it bought "too few and too slowly in strict accordance with regulations." Those procurement regulations are issued by 79 different government offices and total more than 30,000 pages, monitored by 29 committees and 55 subcommittees of Congress.

Meddling in the procurement process by members of Congress usually insures higher prices to taxpayers. Even though the U.S. Air Force said it did not want or need the T-46 aircraft, New York's two senators fought to keep the plane in production because its manufacturer was located on Long Island. When the Army attempted to inject competition into its procurement of engines for the M1 tank, congressmen representing the state where M1 tank engines were then being produced as a monopoly interceded, led by Rep. William R. Ratchford (D–Connecticut), and persuaded the House to vote 241–187 against competition in order to save jobs at the monopoly contractor.

Competition too often deprives members of Congress of the crass political rewards that flow from dictating which favored contractors will receive taxpayer money. The big winners in such an environment "are often the companies that flunk the test in the competitive marketplace," observes Richard Stubbing, a former deputy of the National Security Division of the Office of Management and Budget. He illustrates his point with the case of Lockheed Aircraft, which used its political friends in Congress to obtain a contract for the C5B transport aircraft "over the contractor recommended by the military services when Lockheed was not even a finalist in the competition."

Other problems have emerged from the historic reluctance of the military services to engage in competitive bidding for contracts and the Pentagon's self-exemption from the free-market process. Eleven Pentagon and congressional studies over the past decade found that competitive bidding saves 50% and more over sole-source procurement, while improving product quality. U.S. Air Force procurement officials cut the cost of fuel-tank brackets for fighter planes from $185 apiece to $6.90 simply by seeking competitive alternatives to the original manufacturer. When a wing component for the F-4 fighter was competitively bid, its price fell from the $2,066 under a monopoly supplier to $194 under dual-sourcing of the contract. Yet, despite all the evidence supporting competition, in 1984 only 5.5% of military procurement contracts were formal advertised sealed bids—all the others were sole-source or negotiated contracts.

Increasingly the defense-contracting industry seems to be viewed as an extension of government. Pentagon and congressional officials warn that allowing a major contractor, or sometimes even a minor contractor, to go bankrupt will cost jobs while undermining our defense industrial base, and so, they argue, sole-source contracting must continue. "This is nonsense," concluded Gregg Easterbrook in a thoughtful article for *The Washington Monthly.* "When companies go bankrupt their assets do not disappear...the valuable parts of the company's capital base...would have been sold off, for operation by new and, one hopes, better management. Only the inefficient parts of the company, and the managers responsible for the mess, would have suffered. This is how the market disciplines slackers, and it's an extremely effective sanction."

Subjecting major defense contractors to market mechanisms, allowing those that don't compete to fail, will provide a more reliable check on contractor abuses than any army of auditors. When the Pentagon pays contractors a negotiated price based on manufacturing costs plus overhead expenses, the system is automatically structured "to reward foot-dragging, whereas the market is structured to reward results." Why not just sell weapons for a price, argues Easterbrook, with no billing of anything but the bottom line, much as happens in the marketplace when IBM or Xerox "shepherd complex technology into the market without subsidies."

Bidding could also be changed on defense-related contracts to eliminate reimbursement of contractors on the conventional "cost-plus" basis, which defines "plus" as government paying the contractor an additional percentage of actual expenditures on the contract. Simply by changing the "plus" to a percentage of the bid, rather than a percentage of expenditures, profit margins would become a more fixed and less variable amount, helping to restrain contractors from submitting unrealistically low bids while lowering their expectations of benefiting from chronic cost overruns.

Other problems associated with contracting can be dealt with only through internal management reform of government. For instance, Hill Air Force Base in Utah paid $2,000 each for certain missile parts that a few months earlier cost $677—the disparity due to the contractor costs of restarting the assembly line—without having checked its excess-parts inventory where Hill would have found a 32-year supply of the same parts provided free when the contractor had first shut down its assembly line.

New Pentagon regulations in late 1986 reduced average industry profit rates on negotiated contracts from 12.3% to 11.3%, by forcing contractors to invest more of their earnings on plant and equipment modernization. These regulations also eliminated profits on general and administrative overhead, which in previous years had produced such sensational unallowables as a bill submitted by a General Dynamics Corp. official for dog-kennel fees. And, beginning in fiscal 1986, greater use of the Pentagon's ultimate penalty—suspending or permanently banning contractors from new contracts—resulted in 417 bans or suspensions.

Tinkering with regulations is no substitute for the beneficial effects of competition to break up the weapons production monopolies, nor will tinkering replace the need for procurement officials in government dedicated to the competitive process. "The system of defense contracting has been corrupted by weak and willful individuals," contends Senator William Proxmire (D–Wisconsin), a frequent critic of Pentagon waste. Contract abuses will never be entirely cleaned up until the Washington bureaucracy is reformed, and "that means putting individuals into positions of authority who are committed to making the system work."

A presidential commission headed by David Packard, a former Pentagon official and chairman of Hewlett-Packard Corp., recommended streamlining the procurement system in 1985 partly through the creation of an "acquisitions czar" with sweeping authority to reform Pentagon purchasing procedures. Congress endorsed the reforms and created the position of undersecretary of defense for acquisition, filled in 1986 by Richard P. Godwin, a former president of Bechtel. After a year on the job Godwin resigned in frustration, complaining that his suggestions for improvements were routinely ignored or rejected by a Pentagon command structure resistant to any change in the "iron-triangle" working relationship between the armed services' weapons-buying bureaucracies, defense contractors, and the Congress. It is an iron triangle that thrives on the lack of competition. New regulations, more auditors, and acquisitions czars alone will not break this chain in the absence of a commitment within Congress to legislating reforms mandating a competitive procurement environment. "The noncompetitive defense industry has long been a model of socialist planning and inefficiency," editorialized *The New York Times*. "To break the iron triangle requires introducing the grubby coterie of defense contractors to the rigors of a free market, reducing the services' bloated procurement bureaucracies, and slamming the revolving door between the Pentagon and contractors."

Getting Out of the Railroad Business

At Union Station in Washington, D.C., two blocks from the U.S. Capitol, an unmarried mother of three steps up into a city bus for the trip to her $10,000-a-year clerical job, just as a young unmarried businessman earning $40,000 annually boards an Amtrak train nearby bound for New York to attend a luncheon. Neither probably realizes that one is helping subsidize the other's trip. The financially struggling mother pays through her federal taxes to support the prosperous businessman's ride on the federal government's passenger train, which requires a 26-cent-per-passenger-mile tax subsidy compared to intercity bus subsidies costing less than one cent per passenger mile. Since the average Amtrak rider has a higher income than most taxpayers, operating the train service in effect amounts to a reverse Robin Hood scheme that redistributes income from those who cannot afford a train ticket to those who can already afford to pay.

In 1987, for the third year in a row, the Reagan administration budget proposed selling Amtrak's Northeast Corridor, the rail passenger line serving Boston, New York, Philadelphia, and Washington, D.C., with a sale price of up to $2 billion estimated for the corridor and the four rail stations Amtrak owns. Amtrak operates in 43 states, carrying nearly 21 million passengers annually, but half of those passengers travel the Northeast Corridor. Other revenues come from real estate, leases to telecommunications firms that lay fiber-optic cable along Amtrak's right-of-way, and payments for carrying mail.

"It would be better to make a one-time adjustment in the nation's transportation system than to continue to subsidize indefinitely," said John Riley, administrator of the Federal Railroad Administration, pointing to Amtrak's high costs, its narrow segment of the population served, and its competition with private airline and bus-travel alternatives. Amtrak revenues barely cover daily operating costs, but provide nothing to fund huge capital outlays to maintain tracks, signals, switches, and trains. The result is that it requires taxpayer subsidies of $800 million a year. Since 1972, when it began operation, taxpayers have sunk about $16 billion into a railroad that was intended to be self-sufficient. When the interest-free, 99-year, renewable loans Amtrak has received from Congress are factored in, this hemorrhage could be almost twice the reported loss figure.

Money-losing routes are routinely retained at the whim of

Congress. A classic example is the thrice-weekly Amtrak service from Washington, D.C., to Chicago, a train known as The Cardinal, which Amtrak officials have tried repeatedly to derail because it regularly operates with half its seats empty. West Virginia Sen. Robert Byrd, majority leader of the Senate, through whose state the train runs, legislated continuance of the train to serve his constituents, or those few that use it, even though the route fails to meet minimum-ridership requirements Congress itself mandated.

Each time attempts have been made to reduce the taxpayer subsidy, Amtrak management and employees, its middle and high-income passengers, and select members of Congress like Sen. Byrd have combined to force continuation of the subsidies at the same or higher levels. "The stridency of their demand that others be forced to pick up the tab is clear demonstration that Amtrak's cost exceeds value," wrote John Semmens, senior policy analyst with the Arizona Department of Transportation, in *Reason* magazine. "For its part, Amtrak management corroborates this view when it assures us that without forced extractions from unwilling taxpayers, no train service will be provided."

Though the Northeast Corridor may produce half of the Amtrak system's riders, it contributes less than 30% of system revenues. Long-distance Amtrak lines, mostly in the West, despite their artificially and arbitrarily imposed limits on capacity, carry only 20% of riders yet produce nearly 60% of Amtrak-system revenues. The line from Chicago to Seattle, for instance, often outgrosses all the Northeast Corridor Metroliner trains, while any three of the primary western long-haul routes bring in more revenues than the entire Northeast Corridor. "In the high-density corridors in the Northeast, unit costs exceed unit revenues so that true financial break-even is essentially unattainable at any level of output," contends Andrew C. Selden, a Minneapolis attorney and president of the Minnesota Association of Railroad Passengers. He makes the case that the economics of operation make folly of Amtrak's attempts to compete with the airlines in the Northeast because adding train service carries with it unit costs "so high that more volume simply widens the losses."

Privatization of Amtrak in areas outside the Northeast, which Selden sees as possible by 1991, would end this inefficient deployment of federal resources by forcing Amtrak to use honest accounting in trying to justify the social utility of continued high taxpayer subsidies that mainly benefit a narrow northeastern segment of the population.

Ending the taxpayer subsidy by privatizing Amtrak, selling off its profitable routes, or creating a corporation to run it with stock turned over to its employees, would probably raise train fares in the Northeast and make some routes automatically uneconomical to operate. That is a small price to pay for ending a system that subtly exploits the poor, who contribute through taxes even though most cannot afford to ride, to favor an economic class with the means to pay the real cost and value of the service.

A possible model for Amtrak's privatization was provided by the sale of Conrail—the Consolidated Rail Corp., the northeastern rail-freight system which the federal government nationalized after the 1973 bankruptcy of the Penn Central system. Taxpayers had pumped more than $7 billion into Conrail to save it from the fate of Penn Central and other private railroads, which had been shoved into bankruptcy by Interstate Commerce Commission regulations that prevented the companies from abandoning service on unprofitable routes, and by labor regulations that encouraged excessive costs and feather-bedding of employment. An attempt by the U.S. Transportation Department to sell Conrail to Norfolk Southern Corp. for $1.9 billion had foundered in 1986 due to opposition by Rep. John Dingell (D–Michigan), chairman of the House Energy and Commerce Committee, who insisted on a public offering of stock. On 26 March 1987, an initial public offering in Conrail sold more than 58 million shares at $28 a share, with the total offering to yield at least $1.6 billion. Uncle Sam sold its 85% stake in the railroad, with the remaining 15% ownership retained by 35,000 current and former Conrail employees. Privatization put Conrail back on corporate tax rolls to generate millions of dollars in new revenues, turning a taxpayer-loser into a gainer.

Allowing Competitive Mail Delivery

For 14-year-old Kenny Maguire of Charleston, South Carolina, opportunity in our free-enterprise system meant earning $10 pedaling his bicycle around town delivering wedding invitations, until one day he learned that his entrepreneurship was a threat to the U.S. government. The Postal Service forced him out of business for "interfering with their legal monopoly" over letter delivery. A similar fate befell 25-year-old Patricia Brennan after she started a citywide delivery service in Rochester, New York. Before the Postal Service shut her down, she had attracted 357 regular customers, mostly lawyers and law firms, by guaranteeing same-day delivery of checks and documents and charging five cents a letter less than the government. "I think there's a question of an individual's right to use a service like ours," Mrs. Brennan argued after being served with a court injunction. "It angers me that a system that is inefficient is allowed to stay in business, while one that's efficient, and pays taxes, isn't." Such a sentiment occurred to Harold O'Brien when, in November 1985, the Postal Service filed suit against his House and Senate Delivery Service in Washington, D.C., which delivers messages to members of Congress at one-fourth the Postal Service cost and at twice the speed. The government suit sought to close down O'Brien's firm, prevent it from serving the government, and require it to reimburse the Post Office for lost postage business. "I intend to go on until they throw me in jail," an angry O'Brien vowed. His crime, and that of a 14-year-old boy and a 25-year-old woman, threatening them with $500 in fines and six months in prison, was for having been more competent than government at serving the needs of the public.

We borrowed our postal-monopoly model from England, whose system developed from a period of 16th-century coercion when a Tudor monarch banned private post deliveries in an attempt to suppress the spread of rebellious sentiment. In 1845 the U.S. Congress passed private express statutes to prohibit persons or businesses from carrying letters for hire. With the success of the Pony Express and other private delivery alternatives that emerged through loopholes in the Postal Act, Congress extended the monopoly in 1860 by tightening the law, increasing legal penalties, and expanding enforcement.

During the first half of the 19th century, increases in the size of our federal government were almost solely due to growth in the Postal Service. From 1816 to 1861 nearly 90% of the expansion in federal employment came from hiring by the postal monopoly, a trend that continued until by 1894 the City of New York alone had 3,000 postal employees, as many federal workers as staffed the entire federal government when the century began.

Despite its private express statutes—that body of law giving the government a monopoly over delivery of most addressed mail and sole use of residential mailboxes—the Postal Service still feels compelled to contend with other forms of competition. After losing 50% of its parcel-package volume to the private United Parcel Service (UPS), the post office decided in 1974 to spend $1 billion for 21 centralized bulk-mail centers around the country, a program that degenerated into a mismanaged disaster. As postal critic James Bovard quipped, in a study for the Cato Institute: "A billion dollars in taxpayers' money was spent so that a government corporation could try to take away business from a private company." Today, the United Parcel Service handles twice as many parcels as the U.S. Postal Service, generally charges lower rates, makes faster deliveries, and has a lower damage rate, all the while making a profit while the government service continues to stagger under huge losses.

UPS now controls 70% of the parcel market once monopolized by the Postal Service, and the reason, concluded an investigation by the General Accounting Office, is quite simply that "UPS provides faster, more consistent and more highly predictable parcel delivery than the Postal Service does."

The Postal Service lost $251 million in the 1986 fiscal year at a time when first-class postage went from 20 to 22 cents and its work force grew from 702,000 to 746,000, representing one-quarter of all nonmilitary federal workers. First-class stamps must rise another five cents to 27 cents, the Postal Service announced in 1987, just to fund a new federal retirement program for postal workers costing $1 billion a year. With median salaries of $29,000 annually, wages already claim 84% of the Postal Service's yearly $26-billion budget. Postal Rate Commissioner John Crutcher has called postal employees the aristocracy of labor for being "the highest paid semi-skilled workers in the world."

During the period 1981–85, when postal workers won more than $3 billion in new wage concessions, stamp prices were raised at a rate all out of proportion to inflation—rising 12% versus 4% annually for the economy—just to underwrite the labor demands. On average, Postal Service compensation is 33% higher than for comparable jobs in the private sector. Even Postal Service janitors make $10.89 an hour compared to $4.44 an hour for the privately contracted janitors who clean some other federal-agency offices. A study of wage comparability conducted for postal commissioners concluded: "the Postal Service pays a wage that is higher than the wage paid in every major industrial sector of the American economy, with the exception of mining."

The Postal Service's monopoly position insures that labor costs will remain out of control so long as the unions hold the threat of national paralysis from work stoppages over the heads of postal commissioners. Professor Douglas K. Adie did a study for the American

Enterprise Institute that identified the institutional deficiency that helps insulate this monopoly from competitive wage rates. "Managers make decisions in a way to reduce their psychic rather than dollar costs. One important psychic cost is friction of employee relations in dealing with the postal unions. Employee unrest can result in breakdowns or slowdowns that would harm the postal managers' status and prestige. It is therefore 'cheaper' for management to be generous with wages than to stand firmly for efficiency."

Defenders of the postal status quo claim that privatizing any segment of the service to allow competition would result in worse service and higher prices. They call free entry, or the competitive process, tantamount to "cream-skimming," giving private firms the most profitable routes and services. To such charges James Miller, director of the Office of Management and Budget and onetime head of the Federal Trade Commission, responds that "cream-skimming" opportunities occur only "when prices exceed costs. The existence of such opportunities is therefore evidence that current pricing misallocates resources." Fears of significant reductions in rural service after postal deregulation are likewise overstated, Miller believes, as demonstrated by how well rural areas have been served by new providers that emerged in the wake of airline and trucking deregulation. Telephone service, and truck and bus lines, before deregulation, were all cartelized for reasons now given in defense of the postal monopoly—preserving uniform service and cross-subsidization of rural areas. Keeping entry into mail delivery restricted simply preserves an inefficient and inequitable rate structure in which first class subsidizes other mail classes.

Technological changes will inevitably weaken the Postal Service's hold over its market. As the electronic-mail industry represented by such firms as ZapMail and MCI Mail expand their electronic-mail services, either the Postal Service must begin to monopolize or outlaw private use of the new technologies, or go into direct competition. The market research firm of International Research Development in Connecticut studied this emergent industry and predicted the effect within a decade would be that "the U.S. Postal Service may be restructured along the lines of the post-divertiture AT&T and privatized à la British Telecom."

The Adam Smith Institute recommends repeal of the postal monopoly and the granting of licenses for mail delivery to those private companies that agree to maintain uniform first-class-mail-rate delivery throughout the nation. This would help calm the fears of rural residents that the price of stamps would rise uncontrollably and that service would be poor in the absence of a government monopoly. Postal Commissioner John Crutcher, one of the mavericks on the commission, proposes bidding-out rural carrier routes—the entire rural delivery system—to companies or individuals over a period of years as a first step toward privatization. Then he would privatize "the processing, delivery, and retail functions in each city and award them periodically as franchises to the lowest bidder." The savings from privatizing rural delivery alone could reach $6 billion annually. Congressional attempts to decriminalize private mail delivery, led by Rep. Philip Crane (R–Illinois), traditionally die in the House Post Office and Civil Service Committee, where postal unions exercise firm control.

Citizens for a Sound Economy, based in Washington, D.C., advocate contracting-out retail-service functions such as stamp sales and window services; allowing nonprofit groups to deliver their own mail; giving utility companies the authority to use mail boxes for on-the-spot billing, which would save money on utility bills; contracting-out both rural and urban delivery routes; and turning over the processing and pre-sorting of mail to private contractors for savings the group calculates at $1 billion a year. Stuart Butler of the Heritage Foundation proposes breaking up the entire Postal Service into private companies, perhaps on a regional basis, to be quoted on the stock exchange, and providing intercity and interregional mail distribution in a manner similar to the new regional telephone companies. Britain has already laid the groundwork for postal privatization by splitting its service into four separate divisions—letter delivery, parcel delivery, counter services, and the National Girobank. Each unit will either be sold, with substantial allocation of shares to employees, or given away to the work force as separate companies, abolishing its monopoly status.

"The way to privatize the Post Office is to transfer it to the people," says Milton Friedman, the Nobel Prize-winning economist. "Convert it into a private corporation and give each citizen one or more shares of stock in the new corporation."

Whatever approach finally becomes the American experience, it is important for economic no less than philosophical reasons that the pervasive restraint of trade practiced by this government monopoly be diminished. As postal critic James Bovard has written, "It should not be a federal crime to provide better service than the government."

Ending Subsidized Federal Electricity

Whether they know it or not, taxpayers in such cities as Baltimore and Philadelphia pay two electric bills—the one that comes through the mail with their name on it, and a second bill hidden in federal taxes that subsidizes more than half of someone else's electric rates in states like Idaho and Washington. Imagine the response if you were to ask the average citizen of Baltimore or Philadelphia if he or she would be willing to directly pay up to 70% of the monthly electric bill for some other average citizen or company in Boise or Spokane. Yet 75% of the American population unknowingly subsidizes cheap power for the other 25%, mostly in northwestern states, not because they are poor, or in need, or even because they asked for it. The blessing was bestowed simply as an accident of geography.

Early in this century the Department of Interior began irrigation projects in the West, building dams that could also be used to generate power. As a secondary consideration Congress authorized the marketing of power produced by the federal dams, with preference given to providing electricity for municipal governments. Revenues from the sale of this power were to be earmarked to defray the costs of building the dam facilities. At the height of the New Deal programs in the 1930s, with the emphasis on job creation, two massive power-producing authorities were created—the Tennessee Valley Authority along the Tennessee River and the Bonneville Power Administration encompassing the Columbia River Valley in the Pacific Northwest. The TVA obtained authority to build and operate dams, power plants, and transmission lines; Bonneville could build its lines and market the power, but constructing and operating the power-producing dams was vested in the Bureau of Reclamation and the U.S. Army Corps of Engineers. From 1944 to 1977, four more Power Marketing Administrations (PMAs) similar to Bonneville were established, all but one in the far western states. Today, those six power entities operate 174 hydroelectric plants located at dams impeding the flows of dozens of rivers, and together account for about 10% of the nation's electricity generation.

No federal mandate ever existed for the government to enter, much less remain, in the business of providing some consumers with cheap, subsidized energy. As the Heritage Foundation's senior policy analyst Milton Copulos puts it, "At no point did Congress ever intend to create a vast federally controlled electric utility. Congress's primary concerns have been irrigation projects for the west, munitions production during the First World War, job creation during the Great Depression, or flood control along the Mississippi River."

Power generated by the PMAs is priced, on the average, one-third less than what private-power companies must charge. For Bonneville power, largest producer of the five PMAs, customers pay just 30% of what other Americans do for electricity. "The underpricing of power increases demand for electricity, undercuts conservation efforts, and generates political pressures for new dams," concludes a study by the National Wildlife Federation, one of several environmental groups critical of the federal power system.

Western senators like James McClure (R–Idaho) defend subsidized power as essential to the aluminum industry, ten of whose plants were built near Bonneville simply to take advantage of the available cheap power. Sen. McClure cosponsored an amendment that specifically forbade the Executive Branch of government from even *studying* any change in the PMA pricing structure. When criticized for this in *Reader's Digest,* Sen. McClure wrote back claiming that any price increase in electricity "would seriously endanger our national security" by forcing the aluminum industry to close or move, making us "dangerously dependent upon foreign sources of aluminum," such as that produced by Canada and Australia. He did not explain how buying aluminum from our allies, Canada and Australia, would endanger our own security, nor did he make a case why aluminum companies should be any more deserving of taxpayer subsidies than any one of hundreds of other industries.

PMA supporters who use the aluminum argument also conveniently forget to mention that many of the smelters benefiting from PMA subsidies are owned or partly owned by foreign companies, primarily Canadian, Australian, and Japanese. For example, Comalco Limited of Australia has owned aluminum plants in PMA-served areas of Kentucky, Washington, and Oregon. Alcan Aluminum Ltd. of Canada runs a smelter in Kentucky with PMA power, and its costs with the utility are based in large measure on the price of aluminum. At its Canadian smelters the company produces relatively low-cost, unsubsidized power from its own hydroelectric generating plants.

Montana State University Professors Richard Stroup and John Baden have identified conservation as well as economic reasons for ending the aluminum subsidy. "The aluminum plants could be modified to use new processes to consume at least one-third less electricity per ingot of aluminum than is currently used. But since neither [Bonneville] nor their aluminum customers own the electricity and cannot benefit from conserving it at a cost in order to sell it, the conservation and the socially efficient transfer never occur."

By law the PMAs are to repay the cost of their facilities and investments to the U.S. Treasury within 50 years of being established. But they have routinely postponed, ignored, or manipulated schedules to the point that together the five PMAs have repaid less than 20% of the $16 billion the federal goernment has lent them. Bonneville was created in 1936, more than 50 years ago, yet has repaid American taxpayers only 8% of what it owes. During the 1981-to-1984 period, Bonneville was supposed to repay $1 billion to the government, but coughed up only $2 million, and then in 1985 borrowed another $394 million from federal taxpayers. Members of Congress from the affected regions look the other way when repayment fails to occur and tacitly encourage the practice by continuing to appropriate taxpayer money to renovate facilities to insure continuance of the subsidy. In 1984, for instance, Congress approved $5 billion for repairs and expansion to the Hoover Dam, assuring its customers of long-term cheap power bills.

Like any government bureaucracy the PMAs have acquired a gift for survival. Frequently, a bureaucracy will redefine its legislated mission, going beyond its mandate to encompass new areas of authority that will accumulate special-interest support, which helps insulate the agency from budget-cutting or obsolescence. Both Bonneville and TVA have developed programs for the coordination of economic planning and development in the regions they serve, covering everything from job creation to education and waste control. Economists Craig Bolton and Roger Meiners have described this phenomenon in connection with the TVA: "The TVA has an administrative structure staffed mostly by lifetime employees; at the upper levels, these managers devote considerable energy to developing new programs to justify the continued expansion of an agency that met its original purpose years ago."

Privatizing the PMAs, selling off each as a separate entity, could bring the U.S. Treasury more than $70 billion, perhaps more than $100 billion if the TVA were included. The Citizens for a Sound Economy recommends that each PMA be incorporated, with shares of each sold in the stock market, giving preference to current residential and small-business customers by offering below-market rates. That might help create a constituency for the sale among those interests most liable for rate increases with the end of subsidies. Besides getting the federal government out of the electricity-producing business where it never belonged, and raising immediate revenue to offset the budget deficit, privatization would produce new, large corporations subject to taxation. And as Milton Copulos of Heritage reminds us, "Because each of the newly created utilities, moreover, would be debt free, they would be in far better financial position than most private electric power companies. Thus, they likely would be able to finance any needed expansion through internally generated funds and keep customers' rates low."

From an environmentalist perspective, privatization would end a ridiculous situation where one arm of the federal government persistently violates pollution standards set by other federal agencies. One study found the TVA in compliance with Environmental Protection Agency pollution standards at only 16% of its facilities, compared to about 74% compliance among privately owned electric utilities. The National Wildlife Federation, which endorses PMA privatization, sums up its case this way: "In the long run selling PMAs will result in more efficient resource allocation, cessation of taxpayer subsidies to favored power customers, additional transfers to the Federal Treasury, and the damming of fewer rivers."

A series of nationwide newspaper ads in 1987 by the National Rural Electric Cooperative Association, featuring its vice-president, former U.S. Secretary of Agriculture Bob Bergland, branded privatization as "scuttling programs of proven worth" when it is applied to the federal power program and rural electrification. Loan programs of the Rural Electrification Administration (REA), said the ad, are "an essential constructive force in revitalizing a devastated rural economy." Since these electric cooperatives, along with municipal utilities, are given preferential rate and power allocation by PMAs, perhaps the history of the REA program and its actual fiscal needs and health should be scrutinized.

Rural-electrification programs began as unemployment relief in the Depression, when less than 12% of farms had electricity. That mission expanded in 1949 with federal loans for telephone service, then possessed by only 36% of American farms. Within 30 years 99% of American farms had electricity and 95% had telephones. With the program's original goal of financing electric service to farms and rural areas accomplished, REA bureaucracy had to cultivate new goals in order to perpetuate itself. Loans for new generating-plant construction became one agreed-upon mission.

Most REA loans are made at a 5% interest rate, though some borrowers remain eligible for loans at 2%. The subsidy on direct loans evolved most rapidly between 1973 and 1982, as market interest rates rose to 12% while REA rates remained at 5% and less. During this period REA lending rose by 760%, but the number of its customers increased by only 32%, a reflection of intense borrowing for new generating-plant construction. In that same 10-year period, REA loaned out $9.9 billion in tax money yet collected in return only $5.2 billion in principal and interest.

Many REA cooperatives are in better financial shape to receive unsubsidized private-sector loans than neighboring municipal or privately owned utilities. A Department of Agriculture auditor examined the books of 50 REA cooperatives and found 44 to be in a better financial position than nearby public and private electric services. Since cooperatives generally have rates lower than either private or municipal utilities, a federal financing subsidy would seem even more unnecessary.

Numerous cooperatives continue to receive taxpayer funding even though they no longer qualify under law as rural areas. At least 38 major cooperatives around the nation serve city suburbs. Parts of suburban Atlanta are served with subsidized power where the median household income exceeds $22,000, parts of outlying Minneapolis-St. Paul with median incomes beyond $23,000, and parts of suburban Washington, D.C., particularly Fairfax County, Virginia, where the 1985 median income was $30,000.

Federal borrowing, like that pursued successfully at subsidized rates by the REA, tends to crowd private borrowers out of the funding market. As two economists concluded in a Cato Institute study, "Publicly backed financing substitutes political resource allocation for the market allocation of resources, and the results are neither efficient nor equitable. . .the benefits accrue to well-organized interest groups, whereas the costs are widely dispersed among the general public."

Making the Skies Safe to Fly

Our nation's air-traffic control (ATC) system faces formidable problems that continue to frustrate and alarm air passengers. Flight delays are commonplace, safety seems in jeopardy, controllers are in short supply, and those controllers on the job suffer from overwork and low morale. Some airline passengers voice sentiment for renewed government regulation of the airline industry, as if that were some kind of panacea. But all of the problems passengers bear witness to are only symptoms of an underlying structural weakness in the system, identified by a National Academy of Public Administration study in 1986 as the "political and policy environment" forced upon the Federal Aviation Administration (FAA).

To begin with, Congress shares the blame for the perilous condition of the air-traffic-control system. Airline deregulation in 1978 increased air traffic significantly, but statistically has had no detrimental effect on safety, and yields $6 billion annually in consumer savings, according to a study by the Brookings Institution. From 1982 to 1986 the number of air-traffic controllers decreased by 14%, and the number of control-tower maintenance personnel fell to half what it was before deregulation, all at a time when air traffic was steadily increasing. Congress sets aviation user taxes, giving the FAA no control over pricing, and it is Congress that oversees the aviation trust fund, the government account financed by taxes on fuel and tickets that is supposed to maintain the air-traffic-control system. In late 1986 this trust fund had a $4.3-billion surplus, money that Congress refused to spend on needed aviation improvements so it could use the fund as part of general revenues to make the federal deficit appear smaller.

Too many layers of government bureaucracy are involved in FAA oversight, resulting in a loss of control and accountability, much of it emanating from congressional micromanagement. By its nature as a bureaucracy of government, the FAA cannot adequately allocate staffing or handle workload demand for air controllers because of civil-service rules. Former administrator of the FAA Langhorne Bond made this revealing statement: "I don't see how, if an agency remains within the executive branch and subject to civil service, budget constraints, cost-benefit analyses, and congressional opposition, that it can do much better than it is now."

At least two structural weaknesses inherent in the FAA are readily apparent. Fuel and ticket taxes — user charges set by Congress — represent severe pricing inequities that encourage air-traffic congestion. "Guiding a Learjet carrying two or three people between Newark and O'Hare costs just as much in the way of air controller manpower and equipment as guiding a huge DC-10 airliner," points out Robert W. Poole, Jr. "Yet the Learjet pays a tiny fraction of what the DC-10 must pay...Unless users face the true cost of this service, they will tend to demand more of it than is available or can be provided." Because the

FAA is prevented by Congress from pricing landing slots, it must rely instead on charges calculated by aircraft weight. Pricing landing slots based on time of day would give airport users an incentive to economize, persuading airlines in particular to operate only high-priority flights into major airports at peak times of use. Such market pricing should significantly reduce airline landing and departure delays.

Second, the FAA is engaged in an inherent conflict of interest. It must promote civil aviation while regulating aviation safety, making it the only federal safety-regulatory agency which is also responsible for promoting the economic interests of the industry it regulates. Separating the FAA's regulatory functions from its other roles, specifically divesting it of responsibility for the air-traffic-control-system operations, would enable the agency to focus its attention on insuring safer air travel.

After 14 years as an air-traffic controller, Larry Phillips, national secretary of the U.S. Air Traffic Controllers Organization, concluded that radical surgery was needed—turning the entire air-traffic-control system over to the private sector. "There is no single more important reason for putting air traffic control in private hands," Phillips declared, "then that the FAA has consistently proved itself to be unworthy of public trust and incapable of effectively managing its work force."

America's first air-traffic-control system, established in 1935 in the cities of Newark, Chicago, and Cleveland, was operated by a private firm, sharing costs among participating airlines in proportion to airport use. Within a year the federal government stepped in and asserted its control over the system and substituted taxpayer financing to replace airline-company user fees. Over the years suggestions for a return to the original system have periodically been made. In 1969, an aviation consulting firm, Glen A. Gilbert and Asssociates, proposed privatization of the air-traffic-control system based on the success of a private firm in providing FAA-qualified controllers to the military in Vietnam. That same year the air-traffic-controllers' union even endorsed the idea of resigning en masse to set up a corporation and then contract with the government to operate its system. In 1981, just after the controllers' union went on strike, AFL-CIO president Lane Kirkland conceded: "there's no reason why [the ATC system] could not be a service maintained collectively by these private, profit-making companies [airlines] and carried out in that way." And in 1985, the Air Transport Association, representing most major U.S. airlines, endorsed creation of a corporation to run the ATC because the current system "does not permit effective, businesslike decision-making and innovative planning."

Models for such a privately operated system already exist overseas. Switzerland uses a private nonprofit corporation, called Radio Suisse, to operate its air-traffic-control system, funding it entirely by user fees. Saudi Arabia contracts out its ATC needs to private firms under five-year agreements.

As a result of the 1981 controllers' strike, when 11,500 were fired—about 80% of the work force—privatization became a necessity for some communities. At least 66 small towers were closed because of the strike, inspiring a group of nonstriking FAA controllers to form their own company—Air Traffic Control Services, Inc.—to reopen, under contract, the tower at the Davis County Airport in Kentucky. Other small tower contracts were won by Midwest ATC Services of Kansas, which began operating the tower in Farmington New Mexico, for $99,000 a year, contrasted with a cost of $287,000 annually under FAA operation. Altogether, 15 towers reopened nationwide under private management, and costs dropped by one-third.

For privatization of the entire ATC system, Robert Poole recommends a two-level structure: System and design coordination could be handled by a not-for-profit corporation with user organizations as stockholders; this corporation in turn could contract-out control centers to profit-making firms. Such a structure would "provide competition among suppliers to maximize cost-effective innovations...yet maintain the safety advantage of a single, nationwide ATC system."

Under privatization, an ATC corporation could raise the revenue necessary to automate and modernize the system, and could recruit immediately from the 11,500 experienced controllers now banned from federal employment for participating in the 1981 strike. With a quick infusion of sorely needed capital to improve equipment, and a large pool of already trained controllers to draw upon, air safety would be enhanced immeasurably.

Carrying Free Enterprise into Space

With the 28 January 1986 explosion of the Challenger space shuttle, NASA came to an inescapable conclusion: Only with private-launch-company help could it ever hope to meet its contractual obligations to loft satellites into orbit. That conclusion could have, and should have, been reached decades ago, before catastrophe finally awakened the NASA bureaucracy and its protectors in Congress from their monopolistic complacency.

"The shift to private launch operations ought to be based on cost, not on a politically enforced scarcity of shuttle flights," argues David Gump, former associate publisher of *Space Business News*. Prices for government space launches are actually going up, not down, he calculates, with the shuttle costing $6,000 per pound of cargo compared to earlier Saturn rocket launches that could boost cargo into orbit for only $3,800 a pound. "It is astounding—costs went up on a vehicle NASA expressly designed for cheap flights . . . the Administration must change the shuttle's pricing structure. If it does not, NASA will be free to reenter the commerical launch market and crush private competitors" with its taxpayer-subsidized rates.

For years NASA's space-transportation bureaucracy tried to maintain its monopoly over the field by continuing, and where possible increasing, the taxpayer subsidy of commerical satellite launchings so the private sector could not afford to compete. Taxpayers pay half or more of the costs each time NASA sends an RCA, AT&T, or other corporate or foreign-government satellite into orbit. Each shuttle launch costs at least $200 million, not including the $20-billion taxpayer costs in development and construction. With that price tag included, the Congressional Budget Office has estimated that the shuttle costs $360 million per launch based on its 1985 flight rate. Until 1985 NASA charged only $35 million to launch a full-cargo-bay load into orbit; in that year the price was raised to $74 million, still less than half of true cost.

In 1983 the Reagan administration established an Office of Commercial Space Transportation in the U.S. Department of Transportation to facilitate the private sector's move into space and to license launch sites and launches. One of the office's first acts was to approve plans for a group to launch Cremains, ashes of cremated humans that will circle the planet for 62 million years in tiny metal "burial" tubes. During 1983, shortly after the administration directed NASA and the military to make their expendable launch vehicles available to private companies, NASA officials privately warned executives at General Dynamics and Martin Marietta—both planning commercial space launches—that each would be locked out of future agency contracts if they pursued plans for competition with NASA in the launch field. It was not the first, nor would it be the last, attempt at monopoly coercion by the NASA bureau

The long-term objective of U.S. space policy should have lower costs as quickly as possible because, in the words of J. Bennett and Phillip Salin, "the more it costs to get to space, the le we can afford to do there." Many American space programs, particularly Apollo and Skylab, were mostly exercises in building up national prestige, with massive investments made only to have NASA discard the operational systems to pursue new ones. The fundamental error in space-transportation policy "from which all other difficulties have followed," argue Bennett and Salin in a Reason Foundation study, is that since 1958, the emphasis of space policy has been on government development, ownership, and operation of space-transport vehicles rather than on utilizing the strengths of direct private-enterprise participation. The authors recommend complete denationalization of launch services, divesting NASA of all commercial uses of the Shuttle—leaving the orbiter to specialized military missions—and returning the agency to its original role as a research organization in planetary and space exploration.

A similar conclusion was reached by Dr. Eugene Covert, head of MIT's astronautics department and a member of the presidential commission that investigated the Challenger disaster. NASA should turn its fleet of space shuttles over to private companies for operation, said Dr. Covert. "In terms of its original charter, NASA might well be better served if the 'operational' aspect of the shuttle were transferred away from the agency . . . the cost of the shuttle is having an adverse effect on NASA's ability to conduct both astronautical and aeronautical research and space exploration," wrote Dr. Covert in the July 1986 *Aerospace America*.

General Space Corp. of Pittsburgh offered to replace the Challenger shuttle with a new orbiter, its entire $2-billion cost coming from private financing, to be leased back to NASA over 15 years. As with two previous similar proposals for private-sector participation, NASA rejected this one too, preferring instead to rely on continued taxpayer funding. A member of the House science committee with NASA oversight responsibility, Rep. Robert Torricelli (D-New Jersey), belittled privatization in this instance as a "tax scheme" designed, so he curiously contended, to "take advantage of the Challenger tragedy through a fire-sale arrangement." How saving taxpayers $2 billion in construction costs amounted to a "fire sale" seems unclear, though Rep. Torricelli apparently thought the mere questioning of motives

...he privatization concept to preserve the

...administration's cabinet-level Economic ...rring NASA from launching satellites us-...s the private sector was otherwise unable ...ities. More than 40 commercial satellites ...ch on shuttle missions that were scrapped. ...l of NASA reopening the production lines of Expendable Launch Vehicles—unmanned rockets—U.S. taxpayers would save up to $400 million from production start-up costs alone.

On 4 September 1986, Martin Marietta Corp. signed an agreement to launch a communications satellite for Federal Express Corp. in 1989 on a Titan-class rocket the firm manufactures for the Air Force. The contract came almost four years to the day since the private commercial space industry first actually arose, 9 September 1982, when a millionaire Houston real-estate developer, David Hannah, Jr., launched his Conestoga I rocket on a suborbital flight from Matagorda Island off the coast of Texas, ushering in the new age of space flight. *The New York Times* had headlined the story on its front page: "Texas Rocket Built on 'Shoestring' Carries Free Enterprise Into Space."

Commercial space-launch privatization promises to yield numerous benefits to the nation. No longer will we be solely dependent on the high-cost shuttle system, nor will space activities be solely dependent on taxpayer financing or subsidies. By encouraging the creative and entrepreneurial abilities of the private sector, we will obtain a wider range of space-transport systems, more technological options and innovations, and the prospect of ever-lower costs from the impact of choice and competition.

Redefining Government's Health Care Role

Medicare spent more than $80 billion in tax money during 1987, accounting for 40% of the revenues of a typical hospital. It has two components: Hospital Insurance, financed through a 2.9% payroll tax; and Supplemental Medical Insurance, a voluntary program with a subsidized premium to provide certain physician and outpatient services. Many analysts of the system predict the Hospital Insurance part of Medicare will go bankrupt between now and 1995, when the cumulative deficit in the program reaches $400 billion. When Americans now entering the work force retire, Peter Ferrara estimates in a Cato Institute study, their payroll taxes to cover Medicare will have risen from the current 2.9% to 15% or beyond. Coming on top of greatly increased Social Security taxes, this burden will be unmanageable.

Medicare as it is constituted also discriminates against blacks and Hispanics, according to Michael Becker, a research fellow at the Center for the Study of Market Processes at George Mason University. Life expectancy for blacks is 64.8 years, and 66.6 years for Hispanics. Because Medicare will not pay medical bills until age 65, most members of these ethnic groups will never receive the benefits they have paid for over their entire lives. Whites by contrast live on the average 74 years and can expect at least a partial payback, but a black male today at age 20 should prepare to pay up to $14,000 more in taxes for Medicare than he will ever receive in benefits.

To relieve some of the strain on the system, a plan initiated in 1985 by federal regulation, known as the Private Health Plan Option, allows beneficiaries to enroll voluntarily in private health plans to which the federal government makes lump-sum monthly payments to provide all medically necessary services. Nearly one million Medicare recipients have enrolled. "Under this initiative," says Dr. William Roper, administrator of the Health Care Financing Administration, "government polices the market, channeling competition to achieve socially desirable ends." He identifies those ends as ensuring access to quality care, increasing incentives for efficiency, expanding the range of choices available to beneficiaries and providers, and reducing government's role in deciding medical practices and service payments.

Rather than pay for hospital and doctor services on a fee basis, as the federal government had for 20 years, these fixed monthly payments to private health maintenance organizations (HMOs) and similar plans, more than 150 in all, stimulate competition enabling HMOs to negotiate discounts with hospitals and doctors. While offering a more comprehensive treatment of the health-care needs of the elderly, it helps restrain Medicare costs by reducing unnecessary procedures and surgery. Ultimately, to defuse the Medicare funding timebomb, the Reagan administration wanted to provide a voucher to each Medicare beneficiary to purchase coverage by a private plan, but Congress rejected that approach in favor of voluntary enrollment in private plans.

Legislation creating Health Care Saving Accounts, allowing

individuals to take 60% federal income-tax credits on amounts equal to hospital-insurance payroll taxes paid, was introduced in the 1986 Congress, cosponsored by 38 members. It provides a formula for extricating ourselves from a future Medicare-funding dilemma. This voluntary program would be operated similar to IRAs, with contributions accumulating over a person's working life to be drawn on retirement. Calculations by the Citizens for a Sound Economy indicate that a person earning $17,000 a year over a 45-year work career—assuming a 3% growth in wages, a 7% real rate of return, and the maximum allowable contribution—would find $227,000 in his Health Care Savings Account on retirement. That sum would be sufficient to give the person either self-insurance or the prospect of purchasing the full range of private insurance, posing a solution to the problem of funding chronic long-term needs for catastrophic illness and nursing-home care. If death occurs before retirement, accumulated benefits would go to heirs. As more persons become responsible for providing their own care, Medicare spending would decline, our nation's individual savings would increase, and government would no longer face the dilemma of how to lower program costs without affecting the quality of care.

Along with Medicare for the aged and Medicaid for the poor, our federal government maintains still a third massive health care system—the $12 billion annually spent by the Pentagon for military medical care, including more than $400 million for construction projects related to 168 military hospitals and 500 military clinics. Free military health care goes to active-duty personnel and their dependents, and to retirees and their dependents, but the quality of care varies widely.

"The military provides a haven for doctors who would rather not—or are unable to—stand up to the rigors of civilian medicine," charges Dr. Lawrence H. Fink, a neurosurgeon who served ten years in the Navy Medical Corps as a captain. Military clinics and pharmacies suffer hopeless overcrowding, questions constantly arise about the professional qualifications of many attending physicians and staff, and quality care has no safeguard of incentives—pay raises and promotions are based on time of service rather than on initiative or excellence. It is the poorest of enlistees and retirees, those unable to seek private health care, who must endure this dangerous and ineffective military health-care system.

One solution, made by Dr. Fink and others would be to dismantle the military medical system, selling off or closing all military hospitals, to underwrite a health-care delivery system using private insurers that will provide better-quality care to military personnel at less cost to taxpayers. To satisfy any military need for a standing body of physicians in the event of war, a reserve corps of doctors and nurses could easily be created. Selling military medical facilities nationwide, such as the Walter Reed Hospital in Washington, D.C., while terminating military medical salaries, operating costs, and equipment maintenance, would create a more than adequate fund for military care in the private sector while annually saving the federal government hundreds of millions of dollars. In the process, shifting military care to the private sector would, in the words of Dr. Fink, "add a large number of young, healthy individuals (active duty personnel) to the population base, reducing the per-patient cost of insurance across the board."

A few steps have been made in this direction. Rather than spend $34 million to restore the 78-bed Philadelphia Naval Hospital, Navy officials unveiled a pilot project, in March 1987, to award contracts to health-care organizations in Philadelphia to minister to the needs of 70,000 area residents eligible for treatment at the hospital, which the Navy ordered closed. Congress in late 1986 voted to allow the Pentagon to privatize its $1.8-billion insurance program for military dependents and retirees called CHAMPUS—Civilian Health and Medical Program of the Uniformed Services—which provided 6 million beneficiaries care at civilian health facilities under a fee-for-service plan. The network of military hospitals and clinics providing care for active-duty soldiers also accommodates their families and retirees when space is available; when not, CHAMPUS pays their health bills in the private sector. Dissatisfaction with the military facilities, for reasons of inefficiency and quality of care, had caused a mass exodus to private providers, increasing the costs of CHAMPUS by 15% annually and threatening its fiscal viability. Under the privatization scheme voted by Congress, management of CHAMPUS was turned over to private companies that, for a set fee, provide all the health care to enrollees in a specified region of the country.

Averting Inter-Generational Conflict

President Jimmy Carter predicted in 1978 that Social Security legislation he had signed would "guarantee the soundness of the system through 2030." Five years later impending bankruptcy forced

Congress to launch the most massive rescue effort of the system in its history, raising both Social Security payroll taxes and the maximum annual tax payment. This time lawmakers guaranteed the system's solvency only through the year 2026. As for whether young people believe the system will have its promised benefits available when they retire, three-fourths of those polled in the 25-to-34 age group in 1985 replied negatively. Young people suspect, with good reason, that Social Security has become nothing more than a mechanism to redistribute income from one generation to another. It is a government-operated chain letter—some would say Ponzi scheme—that works only because government has the power to levy taxes. But as with any chain letter, a point comes when people are no longer willing or able to pay.

When President Franklin Roosevelt received the original proposal for a Social Security system from a subcabinet committee in 1935, he asked that it be modified from a partially unfunded pay-as-you-go system into one that would force each generation to pay for its own retirement benefits. "It is almost dishonest to build up an accumulated deficit for the Congress of United States to meet in 1980," Roosevelt reportedly told his secretary of labor. On reaching the U.S. Senate, this revised legislation faced an unexpected obstacle. Senate conservatives raised objections to a fully funded system, fearing that a large accumulation of reserves, once invested by federal officials in the private sector, would give government too much power over the national economy. As a shift occurred back to a pay-as-you-go system in 1938, Roosevelt greatly increased program coverage with higher benefits and by including wives, widows, and dependent survivors.

"The system set sail on a current that would unerringly erode its fundamental premise of not encumbering future taxpayers," writes Herman B. Leonard, a Harvard political scientist. The program that came out of Congress "adopted a funding orientation that started an intergenerational transfer on a grand scale . . . ." Over the years even more benefits were added—earlier retirement, cost-of-living escalators, disability coverage, and health insurance for the elderly. "Its mixed heritage—part insurance and part welfare—is the root of both the program's political strength and its accountability weakness," Professor Leonard observes.

Persons who retired in the early years of the program reaped bonanzas. The first recorded Social Security retiree, a woman in Brattleboro, Vermont, named Ida Fuller, paid only about $23 in Social Security taxes after the system's creation, yet she reportedly received more than $200,000 in benefits over her lifetime. But the economics of changing demographics cannot long support such inequities without collapse of the system. In the late 1930s ten taxpayers for every one beneficiary were in the system; by the 1980s that ratio had fallen to three taxpayers supporting with their taxes each beneficiary. Designers of the Social Security system had forecast 10 million recipients in 1980—the actual figure turned out to be more than 30 million.

What had been a low tax burden for Social Security increased over the years, from $189 as the maximum annual tax on an individual in 1958, up to $348 in 1965. That FICA tax today has a maximum of more than $3,500, and will continue escalating over the next decade. At 14.3% of income, the FICA tax now costs most working-class people more than their income taxes. Already the baby-boom generation pays an unprecedented share of its income—more than $1 out of every $7 earned—to support current retirees. And that 14.3% tax jumped to 15.02% in 1988, and will jump again to 15.3% in 1990. By contrast, current Social Security recipients get back about $3 for every dollar that each person and his or her employer paid into the system. A *Fortune* magazine article calculated how future retirees will get less money back than what they paid in: A working couple born in 1945, together making $50,000 a year, will end up losing $124,000 during their lifetime, the difference between what they will have paid in and what they can expect to receive, not even including any future benefit reduction. The former chief actuary for the Social Security Administration, A. Haeworth Robertson, estimates that in 50 years workers will be forced to pay 41% of their income in Social Security taxes alone if they expect to receive the current level of retirement benefits.

Any attempt to restrain the growth of spending and the size of government will fail unless Social Security and Medicare—which account for over 50% of federal domestic spending—receive scrutiny for reform. Social Security pension payments will total $217 billion in 1988, nearly double the amount paid in 1980 thanks to automatic cost-of-living adjustments and growth in the elderly population. Social Security benefits have been increasing faster than inflation—from 1970 to 1983, inflation was 156%, while benefits escalated by 273%.

Questions of fairness and intergenerational equity are now being raised. Paul Taylor, a national reporter for *The Washington Post*, summarized the problem in a thoughtful commentary for that newspaper headlined, "The Coming Conflict as We Soak the Youth to Enrich the

Old." "In the new America, the old are being enriched at the expense of the young, the present is being financed with tax money expropriated from the future and one of the legacies children appear to be inheriting from their parents is a diminished standard of living." Declaring that Social Security had become "anti-social," *The New York Times* in a February 1987 editorial called for drastic reform, but cautioned: "Congress is far from eager to stand up to a well-organized lobby representing one voter in six. If the large and growing Social Security elephant remains free to graze where it pleases, however, other public interests will be unjustly trampled."

Demographic patterns similar to our own threaten the pension systems of most industrialized nations and raise the same troubling questions of intergenerational transfers and equity. Within two decades, the number of pensioners as a proportion of the working population will rise from the current 18% to 40% in Japan, and from 29% to 41% in West Germany. These huge increases in the number of pensioners come as the active work force—which must pay the pension bills—stagnates or even declines in each country, essentially placing each worker in the position of having to support through taxes all the basic needs of one pensioner.

Affected by these same factors, Britain and Chile have taken steps to forestall the bankruptcy of their state pension systems and avoid ugly generational conflict. Both countries have adopted the principle that any promised benefits must and will be paid to intended beneficiaries, but each has set in motion a partial dismantling of the state pension system and replacement by private programs. After 1 December 1982 all new workers entering the Chilean labor force automatically become participants in private social-insurance programs, using competing IRA accounts into which they place a regular percentage of their paychecks. Chilean workers already covered by the government system were encouraged to switch to private plans, and within five months about 60% of the nations's work force complied. In Britain, one layer of its two-layer social-security system was privatized. Everyone pays into the lower or basic layer and at retirement draws the same pension benefit, about $54 a week for a single person. The upper layer is related to earnings—the more one earns, the more one pays and then receives in retirement. It is at this second layer that workers are being encouraged to opt out for private pension plans. This shift to private provision has several long-term implications, points out Peter Young, executive director of the Adam Smith

Institute. "The financial crisis in the next century would be averted. Personal wealth would be increased, since a worker's pension would become one of his largest assets. The buildup of private pension funds would create a pool of capital that, invested in private industry, could contribute to economic expansion."

America needs more than the promise that some future U.S. Congress will force future taxpayers of the baby-bust generation to pay for the baby-boom generation's retirement. If those persons now entering the labor force were allowed to invest their Social Security taxes, along with their employer's share, in IRAs to earn historical rates of return, "most would receive 3 to 6 times the retirement benefits promised under Social Security," estimates Peter Ferrara, a former White House aide who has written two books on Social Security reform.

Under Ferrara's privatization program, Social Security would gradually be phased out, though those workers retiring under the old system would still be entitled to receive full benefits. Workers would be allowed to direct their employers to contribute an amount up to 20% of the employer's share of the tax to their individual retirement accounts, with each employer receiving full income-tax credits for this amount. This reform would offer workers a better deal in the private sector without cutting the program's benefits or increasing the program's taxes. "Through the private IRA investments, each worker would be developing a substantial ownership stake in America's business and industry. This would revolutionize political attitudes. Instead of retirees developing a psychology of dependence on big government, as with Social Security, they would instead tend to support private enterprise and free markets, as would average workers watching their stake in the private economy grow." When each worker died, a tangible asset would be left to the family, in contrast to the present system where only more promises of support are made.

Retirement really depends on a three-legged stool of security: personal savings, employer-sponsored pension plans, and Social Security. An IRA system could strengthen those first two legs of the stool. At first glance, a Super-IRA like what Ferrara proposes seems too good for truth, writes William Hoffer in *The Nation's Business*. "How would you like to—at no cost—amass a fortune for your own retirement, help your employees do likewise, see the government grant all promised and deserved Social Security benefits and increases to current retirees and to anyone who chooses to receive them in the future, strengthen the national economy, and reduce federal spending?"

Former Delaware Governor Pierre du Pont IV proposed a long-term restructuring of the system, permitting young workers to fund their retirement through an IRA mechanism, while preserving benefits of current retirees. "One of the things the baby boomers know," du Pont declared, "is that you can't wait until the year 2000 to solve the problem of their retirement. You've got to start now." Rep. Newt Gingrich (R-Georgia) offered a more binding version that would abolish current FICA payroll taxes, force all workers under age 40 to establish IRAs, and utilize a national sales tax to pay the benefits of current retirees. Beyond these two public figures, few public officials have had the courage to speak out on the Social Security issue for fear of jeopardizing their political careers.

Baby-boomers must reform the Social Security program not so much to benefit themselves, but to save their children and grandchildren from becoming wage slaves to the system. Reform cannot long be postponed or the severity of the impending collapse may sweep away rational solutions in the panic of chaos. As a University of Minnesota philosopher, Loren Lomasky, has written in *Reason* magazine, "If Social Security were finally to expire early in the next century, those who are now young would lose a lifetime of taxes pumped into the floundering system. By then, Claude Pepper and his cronies will be in that happy realm in which fiscal mismanagement is unfelt. Better an opportunity for the young to buy out now than suffer truly disastrous consequences later."

8
Spreading the Global Revolution

Privatization is a quiet revolution sweeping the world. More than 50 countries have engaged in some form of the process, either selling off state enterprises, deregulating agricultural or industrial sectors, or contracting-out government services, at a speed and breadth of global transformation that have been almost breathtaking. Since 1981 the trend has accelerated until it now embraces governments of all ideologies, from capitalist to socialist and even communist, and nations at all states of development from the most highly industrialized to the poorest of the poor. For nations as diverse as Turkey, Britain, and Bangladesh, privatization is an idea whose time has already come.

"Privatization has become one of the important trends of the 1980s; it is happening in the developing as well as the developed world," reported *The Financial Times*. "The selling of state assets — from airlines to jute mills — is captivating politicians everywhere, even in socialist Spain and communist China," wrote *The Economist*. "Privatization of public enterprise is gripping Asia like a fever," concluded the *Far Eastern Economic Review*.

A principal motivation for the spread of privatization, especially in the less-developed countries, has been an awareness born of budgetary crises that state-run enterprises are usually white elephants. Spain's nationalized companies lost $1.1 billion in 1983; Thailand's 70 state enterprises ran a deficit of $1.7 billion in 1985, the same year the Philippines' 248 government corporations lost about $1.5 billion. "Instead of accumulating surpluses or supplying services efficiently, these enterprises have become a drain on the national treasuries," confessed Babacar N'Diaye, president of the African Development Bank. "From our reappraisal, a view has emerged—the need for enhancement of the role of the private sector."

Over the years, most state-owned monopolies became nothing more than employment agencies, providing job havens for political cronies, defeated politicians, and retired military officers. These government enterprises exact both direct and indirect costs from the citizens of every country in which they are found. Tax subsidies must continually prop them up, and further subsidies, siphoned as loans from foreign and domestic banks, crowd the private sector out of capital markets. On top of inefficiency and exorbitant costs, the very presence of these resource-draining state firms infects economies with a malaise that stifles entrepreneurship and innovation. "Political considerations have a major impact on the employment and pricing policies of public enterprises," observes Gary S. Becker, a University of Chicago economist. "They cannot easily lay off workers. They also tend to yield to union demands of generous wage settlements and to consumer pressure for low prices. No wonder that unions and subsidized consumers are strong opponents of privatization."

As governments ran out of money and their citizens became disenchanted with the performance of public enterprises, pragmatism began to replace ideology. A realization dawned that the social safety net of the welfare state too often became a hammock. In 1984 the state's share of the economy in 19 West European countries began declining for the first time since before World War II. Privatization spread so quickly in Europe, speculates Lester C. Thurow, an MIT economist, because "government ownership of the means of production did not bring about what it was supposed to—less hierarchy and more involvement on the part of the labor force." And it spread because our interdependent world economy demands competitiveness, and a capital-base for companies to expand on an international scale with few inefficiencies.

Britain took the lead in the privatization revolution by transferring about one-third of its nationalized work force—600,000 jobs—to the private sector through the sale of state-owned companies. These liquidations combined with the proceeds from the sale of public housing to tenants brought the British treasury more than $26 billion and reduced the state's share of total domestic output from 10% to 6%. With the aim of making Britain a nation of homeowners and shareholders, Prime Minister Margaret Thatcher's government introduced a form of privatization known as "popular" or "worker capitalism," offering sales of stock in some state enterprises and selling or giving away others to their employees.

For decades the Jaguar Car Company had symbolized British manufacturing quality. After Jaguar was nationalized in 1975 and made a bureaucracy of government, employee morale plummeted, managerial initiative disappeared, and production slumped from more than 30,000 cars in 1974—before nationalization—to only 14,000 in 1979. Profits turned into losses until the government was losing £3,000, or about $6,000, for every car sold. In 1983 Jaguar was sold to private investors, with almost immediate dramatic effect. Before privatization, only 20% of Jaguar's American customers expressed satisfaction with their cars 30 days after purchase; by 1985 the figure was 90% satisfaction, as car sales jumped from 3,000 to 18,000 over the same period. Since privatization, Jaguar has added 3,000 new jobs and seen its annual profits climb to $178 million. "Privatization, by freeing management and workers from the burdens of state control, is allowing businesses to concentrate on what should be their main aim —providing what the customer wants," says the Right Honorable John Moore, a member of Parliament and transport secretary under Thatcher.

In 1982 employees of Britain's largest trucking company, the inefficient and unprofitable National Freight Consortium, purchased 83% of company stock, contributing about $500 each. Since the buyout, employee productivity has increased 30%, and the company is so profitable that the stock is now worth more than 40 times the price they paid for it. Next to be sold was British Telecom, the world's sixth-largest telephone company, which needed capital to modernize its technology. In the largest stock offering in history up until then, Thatcher's government sold a 51% share to the public. British Telecom employees were given first preference, and 96% of the work force bought shares. After privatization, British Telecom posted a profit increase of 25%.

When Thatcher came into office in 1979, one home in three was government-owned and rented at subsidized rates. Over the next six years, nearly one million homes—about 17% of the nation's public housing—were sold to tenants at discounts of up to 60%, depending on the number of years they had been renting. These sales represented the largest transfer of property in Britain since the 16th century, when King Henry VIII dissolved the monasteries.

In late 1986 an $8-billion public offering of British Gas Corp.—

the nation's gas-supply monopoly—became one of the world's biggest stock flotations and the Thatcher government's single-largest sale of a state enterprise. Advocates of competition criticized the sale for passing over opportunities to break up the monopoly and introduce competition into gas provision by separating local supply lines from the national network. Competition was sacrificed to enable the government to raise quick revenue, since the funds generated by such asset sales were enabling the government to avoid raising taxes, borrowing, or printing more money, to maintain desired levels of state spending in support of social programs.

Similar questions surfaced in connection with Telecom's privatization, after the Thatcher government permitted only one company—Mercury—to compete with Telecom to provide phone service. Mercury chose to pursue business rather than residential customers, leaving Telecom with its technologically backward equipment—the result of decades of underinvestment in government hands—to satisfy customer needs. By late 1987, even with profits of more than $3 billion annually, Telecom still had not introduced a modern nationwide electronic telephone exchange, and consumer complaints of slow repairs and installations, broken telephone booths, and rate increases threatened to sour the public on Telecom's new private-sector role. Simply replacing a public monopoly with a private one obviously did not serve the immediate needs of consumers. "The interests of shareholders (and the British Treasury's interest in raising cash from the sale) took precedence over creating a competitive environment," observed a media analyst for the London *Sunday Telegraph*.

At the end of 1987 the state sector of industry in Britain was 40% smaller than when Thatcher took office. In 1979 only 5% of the British public owned stock; by the end of 1986 the figure had reached 16%. An American syndicated economics columnist, Warren T. Brookes, attributes much of the Thatcher government's success in reducing Britain's inflation rate from 24% to 4% to its sell-off of nearly half of the nation's state-owned industries. Even in that diminished public sector, Brookes calculated that government cost inflation was running more than 7% in 1986 compared to only 3% in Britain's private sector. For the United States Brookes contrasted costs for two largely government-subsidized services—health care and public education—to the rise in consumer prices for such largely private services as housing and transportation. He found consumer prices for the two government services escalating at about 8% a year, versus less than 3%

for the private-sector services, supporting his argument that government ownership or control embodies fewer incentives to hold down costs and restrain inflation.

Since Britain's privatization program began, delegations from 20 or more countries have sought advice from the British treasury on how to go about privatizing their economies. At least 22 different methods of transferring government entities and functions partially or wholly into the private sector have been identified. These techniques range from selling or giving away state enterprises, to contracting-out services, establishing user charges, selling public housing to its occupants, and repealing state monopolies to enable competition to spread. "People like having their services provided more cheaply. They like having choices," says Madsen Pirie, president of the Adam Smith Institute in London and one of Britain's privatization architects. "They like paying lower taxes because state services no longer consume massive subsidies. They like owning a piece of industry. They like being capitalists."

France's National Assembly and Senate, over the socialist opposition of President François Mitterrand, approved a law in August 1986 permitting the denationalization of 65 state-owned companies and banking groups over a five-year period to raise $50 billion. Foreign ownership was limited in the sales to 20% in deference to national pride. By June 1987, ten companies had been sold, increasing the number of French people owning stock from 2 million to 5 million. Many of the stocks were intentionally underpriced to broaden stock ownership among a population that had traditionally stayed away from the stock exchange, viewing it as a speculators' playpen. The government also came to regard its version of "popular capitalism" as a way of giving French companies more freedom to compete in international markets. Among the state-owned enterprises sold were three banks, an advertising company, and a telecommunications firm. "In terms of attracting shareholders, the privatization program is an indisputable success," conceded Jean Loyrette, an adviser to the Socialist Party.

Austria's ruling socialists decided to rescue the state holding company—comprising 198 enterprises that together had lost $1.4 billion in the three-year period through 1985—by selling off chunks to private investors. "It's not a question of theology or of selling out [principles] but of practicality," argued Rudolf Streicher, the minister of state-owned industries and transport. Spain's socialist government of Prime Minister Felipe Gonzalez sold off more than 200 corporations from its holding company, including majority ownership of the ailing state car-maker SEAT. "The days of socializing business losses are numbered," Gonzalez declared, telling a group of businessmen why state enterprises should be sold off. "I am not interested in ideology but in policies that work." Other Spanish socialists seem to agree. "We're no longer for nationalizations," Celedonio Martinez, general secretary of the socialist chemical workers' association, told the London *Sunday Times*. "I don't think they solve anything."

Privatization momentum in Italy has been fueled in part by frequent scandals involving the misuse of public monies by local and national officials, and well-publicized horror stories about the inefficiencies of government bureaucracy, which employs 4 million in a nation of just 57 million people. But in West Germany, ruling Christian Democratic Party attempts to sell all government shares in the car manufacturer Volkswagen, and in Lufthansa, the national airline, fell victim to opposition by Franz Josef Strauss, prime minister of Bavaria, normally thought of as a free-market proponent who, in this case, apparently allowed patronage considerations to take precedence over principle.

Sale of the national phone company, Nippon Telegraph and Telephone, a 100% government-owned monopoly, brought the Japanese government more than $13 billion in 1986 on an initial sale of only one-eighth of NTT stock, making it the world's largest privatization of a government enterprise. By law proceeds from the sale went into a special budget account for retiring Japan's national debt. Japan also began the process of placing its deficit-plagued national railways—which lost $11.5 billion in 1985—in private hands by splitting the passenger and freight lines among seven companies.

A survey of 13 Latin American countries found the ratio of government spending to gross domestic product had risen from 15.5% in 1970 to 20.6% in 1980, creating economic havoc. Costa Rica began borrowing heavily in the 1970s to finance the expansion of its government, but was forced to stop in 1981 when the government suspended interest and principal payments on its foreign debt of more than $4 billion. The government then began divesting itself of many state enterprises, and liberalized its economy, until the gross domestic product—which fell 9.2% in 1980-82—began to grow again, by over 10% in 1983-85.

Horror stories about mismanaged government monopolies are legion. Residents of Argentina had to wait up to 20 years and pay up to

$2,000 for phone installation by the state communications monopoly. To begin turning around the economy, Argentina's government announced plans in 1986 to sell government-owned steel and petrochemical companies and its state oil fields.

Brazil's new government, reeling under a $100-billion foreign debt and burdened by state enterprises that account for 60% of the nation's economic output, sold off a dozen state firms in 1985 and drew up a list of 77 other enterprises for privatization to reduce the cost of subsidies and raise much-needed capital. President José Sarney vowed in June 1987 to further deregulate Brazil's economy, allowing the conversion of 20% or more of the nation's commercial debt into foreign-equity investment. Such a debt-equity swap, Sarney predicted, would unlock capital frozen in unproductive government investments for use throughout the economy.

Mexico, suffering from similar debt pains, put 236 state-owned companies up for sale in 1985 and offered to sell 80 more, including the national airline, Mexicana. Under the socialist Allende government, Chile in 1973 had 377 state enterprises which accounted for 39% of the nation's gross domestic product. Under its version of "popular capitalism," Chile's military rulers distributed among many investors the shares in state-run companies, mostly banks, insurance firms, and utilities, until only a few dozen of the state enterprises remained intact.

Turkish Prime Minister Turgot Ozal was elected in 1983 as a result of promising to sell most of his nation's more than 200 state-owned enterprises. A year later, the Bosphorus toll suspension bridge linking Europe to Asia was sold to the public, offering investors an 18% return over three years. Revenue-sharing certificates in the Keban dam on the Euphrates, a hydropower station that is Turkey's principal source of electricity, were sold to the public in early 1985 and are predicted to yield an average net interest of 50% a year. Turkey also plans to finance future power plants with private investor groups which have already pledged more than $1 billion, with the only government support being long-term contracts to purchase the electricity produced. Under a master privatization plan developed in 1986 by a U.S. bank, Morgan Guaranty Trust, Turkey began a two-step process of privatizing 40 state economic enterprises that accounted for one-third of the nation's industrial production. Each required heavy government subsidies to compensate for overstaffing and management inefficiencies. Step one involved selling the government's minority interest in 22 enterprises, including a chain of tourist hotels and a steel plant on the Black Sea.

In the second stage, larger wholly-state-owned enterprises were targeted, employing hundreds of thousands of workers who were expected to be resistant to a change in public ownership.

A U.S. Agency for International Development study describes Bangladesh as "one of the developing world's more spectacular examples of denationalization," its "essentially socialist economy" being rapidly transformed into one with far greater reliance on the private sector. Since 1975, Bangladesh denationalized more than 600 state companies, many in the chemical, textile, and jute (burlap and twine) industries, and privatized the distribution of fertilizer, an act that substantially increased retail fertilizer sales. Within two years of privatization the new textile-mill owners were making substantial profits compared to heavy losses suffered by the same mills under government ownership.

Entire economic sectors worldwide are undergoing a privatization transformation. Brazil, Malaysia, and South Korea now encourage private-sector generation of electricity, having previously prohibited the sale of privately produced power. In North Yemen, south of Saudi Arabia, privatization of electricity came about when Yemeni workers returned from jobs in Saudi Arabia with television sets and other appliances, only to find their villages still without power. Workers in villages across that nation pooled their resources and purchased generators to electrify their communities.

In transportation as in agriculture and other fields, especially in less-developed countries, private systems already existed, but they operated unofficially as part of the underground economy. "Every city has its illegal taxicabs," points out Gabriel Roth, a longtime transport specialist for the World Bank. "Now governments are encouraging the underground economies to rise to the surface. In Malaysia minibuses have been allowed to run. In Bangkok, Thailand, and in Singapore, the illegal taxis have been recognized and licensed. What was illegal in many economies is simply being made legal." In India the city of Calcutta had banned private buses when a state transport corporation was formed. With the state firm losing both money and riders, Calcutta sold permits for private buses, quickly spawning a fleet of 3,400 vehicles that now operate at a profit without government subsidies. Meanwhile, the government bus fleet must be subsidized at $1 million a month even though it uses similar routes at the same fares as the private buses.

Africa presents a particularly challenging environment for privatization. After independence nearly all African leaders renounced the forms of state capitalism imposed on them by colonial powers and embraced socialism. Private companies were nationalized and replaced by state enterprises, controls were raised over the entire range of economic activities—import, export, rents, prices—and collective agriculture or state farms squeezed out most private tillers. "Many African leaders," writes Dr. George B. N. Ayittey, a Ghanaian economist, "mistook the communalism of African tribal life—strong kinship ties and participation in local affairs in village meetings—as evidence that Black Africa was ready for socialism. Africans are communalistic but they are not communists." It was the wrong ideology, in the wrong place, at the wrong time. Village markets in Africa had historically been free, open bazaars, and Africa's traditional village chiefs had never imposed price controls, free-trade restrictions, or other market restraints on their subjects. Much of the funding that allowed the less-developed countries to expand state ownership over industry and agriculture, then continuously prop up the inefficient enterprises with subsidies, came from Western governments and lending institutions.

At a meeting of the Organization of African Unity in Addis Ababa, Ethiopia, in July 1985, the assembled heads of state conceded publicly for the first time that "the primacy accorded to the state has hindered rather than furthered economic development." World Bank and International Monetary Fund (IMF) lending policies were beginning to pressure numerous recipient nations to enact austerity programs, forcing them to privatize state-owned enterprises. In West Africa, Togo embarked on its privatization splurge in 1983 after "consultations" with the World Bank and IMF, resulting in the sale or lease of five state industries ranging from a dairy-processing plant to a marble quarry. Two dormant textile mills, both of which had been drains on the government treasury, were sold to an American-financed firm for $30 million, providing employment for 5,000 Togolese. Tax concessions were granted along with duty-free imports of materials. "We will make it as easy as possible for entrepreneurs," declared Togo's ambassador to the United States, Ellom-Kodjo Schuppius. "If you don't help yourself, no one else will. We're not relying on aid, because while it may offer temporary relief, it provides no long-term solutions."

At independence in 1957, the former British colony of Ghana was the world's largest producer of cocoa, mined 10% of the world's gold, and had a per-capita income at least twice that of South Korea. With the introduction of nationalization and African socialism, everything began to fall apart. As the Ghanaian publication *Christian Messenger* editorialized, "Our once-rich and prosperous nation, which boasted of substantial revenues from exports of our abundant natural resources which in the past earned us the name Gold Coast, has now been reduced to beggar status, subsisting almost exclusively on foreign loans and aid." One of the aid-givers was South Korea. Ghana has more than 100 state-owned enterprises (SOEs), all of them on the brink of bankruptcy despite huge annual subsidies. The IMF, World Bank, and Western lenders pressured Ghana to undertake wholesale privatization, but Ghana's Provisional National Defense Council ignored the advice. As one official explained to *AfricAsia* magazine in mid-1987: "we still feel that with appropriate reforms, adequate back-up and competent management, the SOEs could excel in their functions." His comments came after confessing that favoritism and nepotism traditionally ensured "that most of the SOEs management positions came to be occupied by incompetent and questionable functionaries." Ghana did take a few positive steps after 26 years of socialism. It devalued its currency, liquidated a few state enterprises, and cut its civil service—which had grown four times faster than the population during the 1970s.

Tanzania's version of African socialism, orchestrated by its president, Julius Nyerere, with collective farming and state ownership of business, turned what had been a productive, resource-rich land into a pot-holed ruin. When Nyerere retired as president in 1985, he conceded that his policies had maimed the economy. A new president took over and established free-enterprise incentives for farmers—within a year, for the first time in a decade, Tanzania's economy grew faster than its population, enabling its farmers to begin exporting some crops. But bureaucratic resistance still thwarts many privatization attempts. For six years middle-level bureaucrats in Tanzania have prevented the sale of the state cereal-marketing firm, National Milling Corp. In socialist or welfare-state societies, diluting the concentration of power that resides in the hands of those few officials wielding economic control will be resisted precisely because privatization redistributes influence and authority.

Nigeria ended government price-fixing controls over cocoa and dozens of other crops in 1986 on realizing that the decline in production, which saw cocoa slide from 300,000 metric tons in 1965 to only 100,000 in 1985, would not otherwise be reversed unless the private sector took over. Until 1969 Somalia's grain market was privately held;

then a socialist government came to power and created state monopolies over all aspects of the grain trade. Production rapidly declined. In the face of a deteriorating economy, Somalia in 1984 abolished all grain-price controls and eliminated the government monopoly over grain transport and storage. Farmers responded to these incentives by increasing major grain-crop production 119,000 metric tons, or 27%, in just one year.

Privatization's winds of change have swept much of the communist world as well. China's four "special economic zones," with tax rates lower than even nearby Hong Kong's, attracted more than $3 billion in foreign investment in the five years after 1979, prompting China to extend similar free-market incentives to 14 coastal cities. Within these zones China privatized the provision of roads and other infrastructure, relying on private foreign firms for planning and construction. Free zones like China's designated areas offering a combination of low tax, tariff, and deregulation incentives, have been adopted worldwide by governments seeking to stimulate private development. Since 1978 the number of free zones worldwide has exploded from 220 to more than 800, employing more than 4.2 million people. Hungary and Yugoslavia have also established such zones to lure foreign companies and investment.

Modernization is a term used by China and the Soviet Union to describe an expansion in the role of free-market forces in their economies, an attempt to make Communism work by redefining it. China's Economic Reconstruction Committee's plans, such as removing 70% of production from direct state control by the year 2000, have encountered spirited resistance from Communist Party mid-level cadres afraid of losing authority and privileges with the decentralization of economic power. To stimulate grain production, China did open its markets to private trade. In 1985 it allowed farmers to sell livestock products in relatively free markets. Similarly, the marketing and trade in vegetables was opened to private traders with prices determined by supply and demand.

An "individual labor" law that went into effect in the Soviet Union on 1 May 1987, May Day, legalized 40 categories of private services, from plumbers and hairdressers to café managers. By issuing licenses and taxing earnings, the law brought into the open a huge underground economy in which the USSR had become a nation of moonlighters, selling their services directly to consumers illegally to supplement the low fixed pay of government employment. Although the new law restricts the size of these private enterprises and prohibits the hiring of outside labor, its very existence concedes the government's inability to stifle or control the entrepreneurial instincts of the people. Within a week of the new law's implementation, 2,000 persons in Moscow had applied to become entrepreneurs, which is remarkable for a country brainwashed for 70 years to believe that private enterprise constituted a criminal form of parasitism. Another series of laws in effect since October 1986 allows groups of up to three people to open cooperative businesses to manufacture for local distribution items like furniture and clothes, with profits split among members of the cooperative. Officials in the city of Riga even proposed a shopping mall with government stores along one side facing cooperative businesses on the other, forcing competition on the government outlets for the first time. These officials, reported *The New York Times,* "express little doubt about which side would flourish."

Cuba's dictator, Fidel Castro, recoiled from timid steps toward privatization when in 1986 he discovered numerous farmers and truckers had become near-millionaires from supplying meat and produce to private farmers' markets that he created in 1980 to reduce food shortages. One farmer was found to be making $150,000 a year—more than 30 times what Cuba paid its skilled workers—by hauling fruit and vegetables to the private markets. Similar discoveries in the housing field, which Castro had liberalized by allowing private home ownership and construction in mid-1985, prompted him to end that experiment as well as abolish the private markets. Doctrinaire disapproval of any accumulated individual wealth made him willing to sacrifice his nation's hopes for reviving its economy.

For capitalist, welfare-state, socialist, and even communist economies, privatization holds out the prospect for reinvigoration. But limiting privatization to the lifting of price controls or the sale of a few state assets misses the opportunity to revitalize the entire economy, especially in less-developed countries, by turning a range of services like utilities over to private competition. "If privatization in the developing world is to succeed," argues Peter Young of the Adam Smith Institute, "then its vision will need to be broadened. Privatization must be understood as a creative process, a process designed to shift whole areas of economic activity from the politicized, noncommercial state sector to the consumer-responsive profit-making private sector."

Relieving Dependence on Foreign Aid

When you walk along the dusty, palm-shaded streets of Palau, one of the lush island chains of Micronesia in the Pacific, you will find stores selling tuna in cans—fish which had been caught by Koreans in the world's richest fishing grounds just offshore and then shipped to Japan where it is canned and transported at great expense back to Palau. Lettuce, tomatoes, and rice once grew plentifully on these islands. Now they, too, come from overseas. Nearly two-thirds of all wage earners in Micronesia are employed by island governments financed by American taxpayers. Most Micronesians have actually come to regard government jobs as a form of welfare, an entitlement program if not a natural right from birth. The people of Palau, like their fellow Micronesians, abandoned fishing and farming and the cultural vestiges of self-sufficiency because three decades of U.S. federal programs corroded their spirit of enterprise, addicted them to easy government money, and insulated them from responsibility for their own destiny.

"We have no technicians, no plumbers, no electricians," complains Haruo Willter, Palau's minister of administration. "We have no economic base to be self-sufficient because the U.S. Government just handed us everything and didn't ask us to do anything for ourselves."

Governments have a habit of exporting mirror images of their own inefficient, monopolistic structures, bureaucratic methods and attitudes. Within Micronesia, as has been true, to varying degrees, throughout the "aid-recipient" world, these prescriptions induced more dependency than development. As Lazarus Salii, president of Palau, put it, "America is the land of free enterprise, but it only gave us big government."

In many respects Micronesia was a giant laboratory for the American experiment in government. Given that the 2,100 islands are dispersed over 3 million square miles of Pacific Ocean, populated by 140,000 persons who are separated by geography, diverse cultural traditions, and nine mutually unintelligible languages, any uniform overlay of systems and attitudes by a more dominant culture should in theory be expected to produce mixed results. One island society might seemingly prosper using government as a catalyst, while another might flounder in failure. One culture might enjoy a limited renaissance of enterprise, while others might lose any appetite for initiative and risk-taking.

What should confound sociologists but vindicate free-market enthusiasts is that nothing of the sort occurred. The uniform application of government in Micronesia, placing it at the center of economic life, produced in every culture and among every island group a uniform result—stagnation, dependence, disaster, and despair.

The result is a fiscal timebomb ticking in the Pacific. Half the Micronesian population is below age 16—the islands have one of the highest birthrates in the world—yet the only available jobs are on the already bloated government payrolls. Washington has endowed Micronesia with a large infrastructure of roads, airports, and utilities, but left the people with an economy that cannot generate enough revenue to operate it and doesn't possess enough skilled personnel to maintain it. Privatization is a word whispered in Micronesia, but it is a concept now so foreign, so alien to the people's experience, that they might just as well be fantasizing about life on a polar ice cap.

How we hamstrung these proud people with kindness in the name of government "doing good" serves as a reminder, albeit an extreme one, of what can and does happen when we allow government at any level to dominate and direct our economic priorities. The legacy of dependence that we brought Micronesia, and the disastrous consequences for the islanders, can be traced back to American policy at the end of World War II. By 1945 the United States had wrested control of the Marianas, the Palauan, Caroline, and Marshall island chains from the Japanese. Under an agreement between the United States and the United Nations, imposed upon the Micronesian people, the entire area was designated a "strategic trust" territory of the United States to be administered as a security zone. U.S. military authorities then made three decisions that sealed the area's economic future. All foreign civilians (mostly Japanese, Koreans, and Taiwanese) were repatriated, depriving the islands of a skilled work force. A quarantine was extended over the islands—which covered an area comparable to the continental United States—preventing any unauthorized entry without a security clearance and written permission from the U.S. High Commissioner's office. And, most important, outside investment in the area was actively discouraged. When the Peter Paul Candy Company proposed building a coconut-processing plant in the islands, U.S. Navy officials said no because, in the words of one, such commercial enterprises would "reduce the people to cheap labor." The Navy then undertook a policy of giving the islanders free clothes, food, and "surplus" military supplies.

Throughout the 1950s under Navy and Interior Department administration, an annual budget ceiling of $7 million was kept in place, although the actual figure was much higher due to the Navy's unbudgeted giveaway program. Restricting entry and investment in Micronesia was justified by federal officials as adherence to a "zoo theory"—a belief that native cultures should develop at their own pace without foreign interference or influences. In 1962 a group of Micronesians complained to a visiting United Nations delegation that the United States had failed in its pledge to promote the health, education, and well-being of the islands. The resulting U.N. criticism of U.S. policy as "benign neglect" prompted President John Kennedy to double funding for Micronesia, unify the entire territory under civilian control, and lift the quarantine to allow entry by American citizens. A presidential commission headed by economist Anthony Solomon issued a three-volume report urging the United States to bring Mirconesia into the 20th century as quickly as possible with a crash program of political, educational, and social-welfare development.

English was installed as the language of instruction in schools throughout Micronesia. Employment of Micronesians by the U.S. government more than doubled within a year, from 1,893 persons in 1962, before President Kennedy's action, to more than 4,000 by 1963. The first group of 445 Peace Corps volunteers arrived in Micronesia in 1966. Most were teachers and few possessed any skills that would prove beneficial to economic development. Within two years more Peace Corps volunteers would be stationed in Micronesia, relative to population, than anywhere else in the world. Their most enduring impact, many Micronesian officials now concede, had been to encourage the people to expect and demand more social-welfare programs and government involvement in the economy.

A United Nations report in 1967 sharply criticized U.S. policy in Micronesia for emphasizing government employment and government programs to the exclusion of private economic development. "Further increasing government employment while neglecting the needs of private enterprise," wrote the U.N. report authors, "will create an economy supported mainly by the government and increasingly dependent on imported goods of all kinds." Outside investment was needed to foster development; specialized personnel from the private sector, rather than government bureaucrats, would need to be recruited to teach the islanders useful entrepreneurial skills.

Two years later, instead of private-sector experts on self-help, U.S. officials sent in military Civic Action Teams, nine groups altogether, with bulldozers and other construction equipment. Over the next three years these teams built 75 medical and 32 recreational facilities, 37 public buildings, 37 sanitation and 9 electrification systems, and more than 200 miles of roads. Micronesia now had an infrastructure, but still no source of independent revenue or skilled personnel to keep the systems operational.

For a culture that had never known hunger, perhaps the most devastating blow to self-sufficiency and development came in 1970, when the U.S. Congress extended Agriculture Department feeding programs to Micronesia. Since practically everyone in the islands fell below the U.S. poverty line, all were eligible for free commodities under the Needy Family Assistance Program, along with free school lunches and breakfasts, child-care and nutrition benefits, and meals for the elderly. A Trust Territory Administration official later reported that these programs had allowed "an expansion of social occasions such as fiestas and wedding parties, so that it is hard for a non-USDA recipient to reciprocate and entertain at the same level." Those who were self-reliant, grew or caught their food, now needed free commodities to entertain their neighbors. Some of this free food, such as macaroni, cheese, and corn syrup, was discarded or fed to the pigs because the Agriculture Department had failed to take into account Micronesian taste preferences. When Trust Territory employee Linda Parkinson moved into a house on Saipan in 1975 she was shocked to discover a shed in her backyard "simply filled with discarded USDA commodities."

When the feeding program came to the Truk Islands, enough food began arriving for 41,000 adults even though the entire population of Truk was only 36,000, half of whom were children. In one four-month period the USDA flooded the island of Moen with 4.8 million pounds of rice, 8,701 cases of corned beef, 3,460 cases of chicken, 13,939 cases of orange juice. Some local grocery stores were bankrupted by the influx of free food, while most other stores lost at least 20% of revenues, further weakening the local tax base. An investigation by Trust Territory officials in 1979 came up with a predictable result: "families now no longer put much effort in farming and fishing." Interviews found that those receiving the free food also vowed to vote for any local politician wanting to keep and expand the feeding programs, and against any politician who advocated a return to self-reliance.

Statistics paint the grim picture of how U.S. tax dollars undermined Micronesia. From 1963, when the Kennedy policy went into effect, through 1973, imports of food that could have been produced locally increased by five times, while exports—mostly coconut and fish products—declined by nearly half. Based on acreage planted, every category of agriculture nosedived—from 157,522 acres of coconuts planted in 1963 to only 74,978 a decade later, from 2,179 acres of vegetables to just 627 acres, and from 1,149 acres of citrus fruit to less than 500 acres.

Another United Nations study in 1973 found new, more alarming trends. People in most Micronesian communities were "now expecting to be paid like any other government employee" for community and charitable work that had once been a fixture of cultural life. This drift toward dependence on subsidies and government wages had sabotaged most aspects of comunity self-sufficiency. Furthermore, "a potentially dangerous situation" had been created by U.S. education policies that produce "a large number of highly trained and well-qualified Micronesians for whom jobs will not be available." The unrestricted extension by the U.S. Congress of the Pell Grant Program, providing free tuition and board to Micronesian college students, placed 871 of them in American universities in 1973. Of that number only a few dozen majored in agricultural or vocational skills useful in the islands, while the rest pursued degrees in education and the social sciences intending to become teachers and government bureaucrats.

A 1963 U.S. State Department report on the Trust Territory, issued before Kennedy's crash program, had described Micronesia this way: "In the territory, family, clan, and community social organization and relationships provided social welfare for their members. As a result there has been no need for organized social welfare programs." Why such an abrupt change in how the U.S. government viewed the Micronesian capability to care for themselves? "I kept asking my friends in Washington: Why don't you give us some kind of productive program which will make the people produce instead of just handing us everything?" remembers Haruo Willter, a Micronesian in charge of the territorial budget during the early 1970s. The answer he got back was a classic: The business of government is to provide services, not to interfere with the private sector.

The U.S. Congress continued extending federal programs to Micronesia until by 1976 more than 480 were available. Father Francis

Hezel, a Jesuit and teacher in Micronesia for several decades, got an insight into the real motivation: "A High Commissioner of the Trust Territory once told me these federal programs were begun not so much for the services they provided as for the government employment opportunities they afforded."

Some voices among Micronesian leaders were raised in protest. In the Congress of Micronesia, a territory-wide legislature estabished to give the islanders limited self-government, a proposed $5-million low-cost housing program was defeated after being branded as "giving the U.S. additional strings to pull in Micronesian affairs." An outspoken critic of U.S. policy, Petrus Tun, a senator from the Yap Islands, warned that Micronesia had embraced federal services which the islands could no longer afford. "Where a real need does not exist, an artificial one should not be created," Tun told his colleagues.

These Micronesian politicians who spoke out against dependence were walking a tightrope. While they understood that federal dollars had created a false economy, giving them a standard of living they could not afford to maintain, they also had to contend with constituents now dependent on feeding programs and government jobs. Those campaigning by extolling self-reliance—up against political opponents promising more government services—began to be defeated at the polls, until by 1980 few voices of principle were left.

Development continued to stagnate in the absence of a strategy or policy with emphasis on private-sector solutions. When U.S. government experts in fisheries or agriculture were sent to the islands they were without comprehensive development plans. So when a project was completed, like raising chickens, and the experts left, indifferent islanders usually abandoned the enterprise because they had few incentives to raise what they already received free. Several large fishing boats were built at U.S. expense and transported to Yap, where a group of islanders were trained to operate them. After the U.S. government experts left, these boats remained at anchor unused because by tradition the Yapese fished only in lagoons, never in the open sea for which the boats had been designed. Other bureaucratic comedies ensued, such as U.S. government teachers training Micronesians to be refrigeration repairmen and sending them home to remote islands where there was no electricity—or when the United States gave the natives farming and construction equipment which, when it broke down, was pushed off into the bushes in the expectation that Washington, as it always had before, would provide new equipment on request.

"The administrators who were sent here were government people who were trained that it was not the business of government to interfere with the private sector," says Lazarus Salii, a senator in the Congress of Micronesia during this period. "The big mistake was not bringing in developers from the U.S., inviting private companies to come and see the potential here. But the U.S. Congress took the easy way out—they just threw the money at us."

Still another United Nations study critical of U.S. policies in Micronesia appeared in 1976. In retrospect it seems ironic, if not remarkable, that the U.N. Development Programme—representing a collection of nations committed to government economic controls—would condemn U.S. suppression of private enterprise not once, but in three separate reports over a decade. This particular study recommended a healthy dose of privatization to help cure the economic malaise in Micronesia. It pointed out that 67% of taxable wages in Micronesia come from government employment and the huge cost of "this large cadre of highly paid government workers...is far beyond the ability of the economy to support" and must be cut deeply. U.S. funding should be shifted from investment in social infrastructure toward private-sector development; social services provided free by government should be either abandoned or financed by user fees. Daily wages in the agricultural sector of Micronesia were found to be six times that of the neighboring Philippines, where labor output was also higher. The reason for inflation in Micronesian wage rates could be directly connected to "the high salaries paid by the government which are distributed throughout the agricultural community through the extended family system."

Like its predecessors, this study never found an audience within the U.S. Congress. The director of the Interior Department's Office of Territorial Affairs, Fred Zeder, did establish an economic development council composed of American businessmen interested in Micronesian investment. But when Zeder requested a modest $100,000 from Congress to implement the plan, then House Interior Committee Chairman Rep. Philip Burton rejected the proposal out of hand, directing that the money be used instead toward a college Burton wanted to see established on an island in Ponape.

Micronesia's only growth industry is government and politics, with public education—employing nearly 3,000 teachers and administrators—one principal source of jobs. In 1982 about 2,100 Micronesians were enrolled in colleges; of that number only 56 were studying agriculture, fisheries, or vocational training, while more than 1,200 were pursuing degrees in education. Clearly, at some point, if not already, there will be as many teachers as students in Micronesia. An entire generation of young people have grown up without the skills necessary to survive in the islands. An overeducated elite, nurturing Stateside expectations about the quality of life, can be expected to exert continuing pressure for an expansion in government employment. "Secondary education not only failed to train the younger generation in appropriate skills," concluded a 1984 environmental impact statement prepared for the U.S. State Department, "but it has created structural unemployment" and has "been a major element in the growth of the Trust bureaucracy and payroll."

This State Department report goes on gloomily: "Despite massive infusions of funds, the development of the local fisheries sector in each of the Micronesian states is virtually no further developed than when the Japanese left the islands in 1945...imports of canned fish have increased in nearly every year of the Trusteeship." The report predicts that "current prospects are that the operations and maintenance/ energy crisis," caused by the United States giving Micronesia over-designed, energy-intensive water and sewage systems they can't afford to maintain, "will worsen due to rapid population growth, expectation of modern living standards, government-subsidized water, sewer and electric rates, and the completion of new capital improvements." These conditions began a steady deterioration in 1980 when Palau found itself owing $3 million for diesel fuel, yet its entire public-works budget amounted to only $2.8 million. Palau and the other Micronesian governments have been running sizable public-works deficits ever since.

The sole enduring U.S. accomplishment in Micronesia would seem to be the creation of four democratic constitutional governments—in Palau, the Marshall Islands, the Carolines, and Northern Marianas. After a series of plebiscites, the Marianas opted for commonwealth status with the United States, while the other three endorsed a looser arrangement known as a Compact of Free Association. Under this relationship the islands retain political autonomy while American taxpayers continue to pay their bills. About $2.7 billion in Compact funding will be provided the islands over the next 15 years, in return for which Micronesia grants the United States the right to defend it. By contrast, during the previous 38 years of American rule, only about $2.4 billion was spent to bring Micronesia to its current level of dependence.

Even our legacy of democratic government may prove of dubious long-term benefit. Micronesians treat their politics and the patronage jobs created with a seriousness that borders on the ludicrous. Palau has more elected officials per capita than any other nation on earth. The island republic has only 8,000 voters, but it has created 16 state governments, some with bicameral legislatures and each with its own constitution. In the Palau congress members receive a $13,500 salary, four times that of a parliament member in the Philippines, 600 miles to the west. To cure unemployment it appears that Palau, like much of Micronesia, has decided to make practically every citizen an officeholder, a nation of kings, with their subjects—those who pay the bills—being their rich relatives far to the east, somewhere beyond Hawaii.

Creation of a vast public work force has locked Micronesia firmly in the grip of a vocal, activist interest group opposed to any reductions in the size of government employment or the scope of government services. Public employees are virtually the only organized political force in the islands, and they have flexed that power at will. In 1982 Palau's president, Hauro Remeliik, proposed that user fees be imposed for government-subsidized power. He also resisted public-employee wage demands. The Palau Association of Government Employees went on strike, and President Remeliik's office was bombed and gutted by fire. As a result, the minimum wage in Palau was doubled, creating a deficit of $2.5 million in 1983, which went even higher in subsequent years. Despite Reagan administration opposition, these deficits were covered by appropriations from the Senate Committee on Energy and Natural Resources, chaired by Senator James McClure (R—Idaho). On 30 June 1985, President Remeliik was shot and killed outside his home by an unknown assassin.

"Over the years since Palau became a republic in 1980, I've seen more and more dependency on the United States," concedes Don Shuster, dean of instruction at the Micronesia Occupational College and a resident of the islands for 20 years. "The major mistake the U.S. made in Micronesia was being too generous. The best way to bring about social change here is the shock effect—cut off all U.S. money and say: Okay, you want to be independent; pull yourself up by your own bootstraps."

To avoid condemning these proud island peoples to living with our mistakes for generations to come, and to create incentives for the emergence of a private sector that might offer hope for long-term self-sufficiency, privatization must be aggressively introduced into the islands. A few Micronesian officials recognize this necessity. Lazarus Salii, a travel agency owner who succeeded Remeliik as president of Palau, would like to see the island's power plant turned over to private operation. "The whole public-works area, running food services, everything, there is no reason why they cannot be run by private businessmen," says Salii. "And personally I would rather see the private sector run things. As a businessman, I know it works."

The legacy our federal government left Palau and Micronesia it duplicates elsewhere through our foreign-aid program. Since World War II Americans have provided "needy" countries with more than $330 billion in aid, making this nation the world's most generous donor. Each year through foreign aid, U.S. taxpayers give away on average $14 billion, almost evenly divided between economic and military assistance, to more than 100 countries. Nearly half of all aid—$6 billion annually—goes to just two countries, Egypt and Israel.

American foreign assistance is distributed through the Agency for International Development (AID), an economic development arm of the State Department. AID defines its role as promoting economic self-sufficiency in recipient countries, encouraging them to adopt policies to increase food production and give "full play to free-market forces" by privatizing costly and unproductive state-owned enterprises. "U.S. foreign aid is targeted to those developing countries whose governments are committed to building progressive, market-oriented economies," claims an AID position paper.

Even a casual perusal of AID's annual recipient list reveals an altogether different picture. Dedicated Marxist and socialist governments frequently receive American tax dollars. Between 1984 and 1987, for example, Marxist Zimbabwe got $109 million and Marxist-ruled Mozambique $63 million. But the problem of honesty and accountability in the dispersal of aid dollars goes far deeper, raising questions about the effectiveness of assistance and whether it reinforces the power of ruling elites and expands the economic role of the public sector in recipient countries.

Instances abound of the misuse of direct-aid dollars and those assistance payments made in the form of loans by American banks, backed and encouraged by the U.S. government. Government officials in the Congo sold that nation's U.S. food assistance to finance a weapons factory; aid money helped construct 11 presidential palaces in Zaire for its ruler; and U.S. aid built 50 crop-storage depots in

Senegal that stand empty because they were placed in locations never frequented by native farmers. Venezuela under a socialist president used much of the money loaned it by foreign, mostly American, banks to triple the number of government employees between 1974 and 1984, hiring operators for every public elevator and attendants for every public bathroom in the nation.

Development aid seems predicated on the assumption that insufficient financial resources alone, rather than cultural, social, political, and economic factors, account for backwardness in the Third World. Yet that view of aid does nothing to explain why, for eight West African nations stretching from Chad to Senegal, despite $13 billion in economic assistance over a decade—$1.1 billion from the United States—per-capita food production has actually declined, making those nations even more dependent on outside help.

Too often foreign aid does nothing more than subsidize government policies and bureaucracies that are the source of economic problems. A study of AID assistance practices by the Cato Institute, a free-market think tank in Washington, D.C., accused AID of encouraging political irresponsibility among its recipients, leaving a legacy in the Third World characterized by such "white-elephant" projects as idle cement plants, abandoned roads, "and a growing phalanx of corrupt, meddling, and overpaid bureaucrats." As an official of the International Monetary Fund explained to *The Washington Post,* commenting on how foreign aid allowed Zambia to expand its payroll for government employees until it consumes 20% of the nation's gross domestic product: "What we have done is to allow Zambia to maintain a standard of living for its civil servants which is totally out of synch with the rest of the eocnomy."

Early in 1987 an investigation by the General Accounting Office (GAO) found that "AID operates in an environment which makes the funds it administers vulnerable to misuse without detection." Under a program called Economic Support Funds (ESF), AID distributes assistance in three forms—for specific development projects, for commodity imports, and as cash transfers for general-budget or balance-of-payments support. Greatest potential for abuse occurs in the cash transfers, where GAO found the fewest controls over expenditures in Egypt, Israel, and Turkey. "In all three cases," reported the GAO, "the U.S. agreed to provide the assistance without requiring an accounting for its use."

Direct cash transfers of American tax money to Israel under the

ESF program, averaging $1.2 billion a year, were described by the Cato Institute study as financing "wage and price controls, subsidies for scores of inefficient government companies, and a make-work full-employment program." In the period 1984–86 Israel received more than $14 billion in combined economic and military assistance from the United States. With a population of only 4.2 million, that translates into over $3,400 in aid for each Israeli citizen. U.S. assistance to Egypt is so massive—$2.4 billion in 1986—that AID officials confessed to the GAO that Egypt cannot effectively absorb the economic portion of it. Concluded a GAO investigation: "the consensus of the development experts with whom we spoke was that U.S. economic assistance to Egypt would range from $100 million to $200 million if it was based solely on relative economic need." Increasingly, with Israel and Egypt receiving nearly half of all our foreign aid, the question becomes, how much longer must we continue bribing these two nations to remain on friendly terms with each other?

Problems of overgenerosity confront recipients of American aid throughout Africa. GAO repeatedly warned, beginning in 1978, that large amounts of assistance should not be provided eight nations of West Africa comprising the Sahel region until those governments took steps to insure that the money was used effectively. AID's African Bureau admitted in 1985 that Sahel governments "are saturated with development assistance. . .and are themselves in danger of becoming obstacles to development." But high levels of aid continued flowing despite the inability of these recipients to effectively utilize it. The sheer number of donors to the region—15 countries and 14 multilateral organizations, like the World Bank—and their lack of coordination results in needless waste and duplication of efforts. Sahel governments, charges the GAO, have become "more preoccupied with fund raising than structuring effective development plans," and must create large expensive bureaucracies just to administer the maze of differing, sometimes conflicting rules and conditions imposed by the diverse donors.

For our economic assistance to be effective, AID concedes that recipients must undertake internal reforms eliminating government subsidies, price and wage controls, inefficient state-owned enterprises, and, in the words of former AID Administrator Peter McPherson, "other similar forms of interference with market solutions." Without economic reforms, American assistance becomes nothing more than a bandage over a wound in need of surgery. As a study by the U.S.

Treasury Department warned in 1985, "We believe that postponing the date when recipient countries must confront the need for policy reform is not a responsible approach...underlying economic imbalances deteriorate further, increasing dependence on external support and the likelihood of more severe crises in the near future."

Attempts by AID to place conditions on U.S. assistance to bring about necessary reforms have largely been ignored, improperly enforced, or undercut by actions of the U.S. Congress. In the Dominican Republic, which got $73.8 million in fiscal year 1987, few AID conditions on assistance have been set. Reports GAO, "The government has demonstrated little interest in implementing key reform in areas such as divestiture of public enterprises." In Jamaica, recipient of $86.6 million in 1987, most major policy reforms recommended by AID were ignored. GAO attributed this resistance to "the government's belief in a managed economy," to pressures from the political opposition, and to the Jamaican prime minister, Edward Seaga, who "believed he could by-pass AID and go directly to the U.S. president when he objected to U.S. conditions." Since 1984 AID weakened or removed many of the conditions it had placed on assistance. El Salvador and Honduras, which together received $771 million in 1987, have both been reluctant to implement economic-policy reforms to make U.S. aid effective, and AID has not pressured either government to comply. Warns GAO: Failure to make reforms means "the economic situation in both countries will remain unstable," requiring uninterrupted infusions of American taxpayer assistance.

Because of the political nature of the assistance program to Egypt—demonstrating U.S. support for peace in the Middle East—achieving long-term economic development with U.S. tax monies has been rendered difficult if not impossible. AID reports that it is under pressure from Congress to find projects "which can absorb large amounts of annual funding," and AID is prevented from using the withholding of funds to encourage changes in Egypt's economic policies. More than $100 million a year of Egyptian assistance is in the form of direct cash transfers which AID cannot monitor because Congress decreed that the funds be unrestricted in use.

In the case of Israel, one-third of U.S. assistance—$1.2 billion—goes in the form of an annual cash transfer that Congress refuses to allow AID to monitor. Nor will Congress allow AID to set conditions on how the money is spent. "Our ability to persuade Israel to do anything insofar as economic reform is really zero, to put it bluntly," says Richard Bissell, AID's assistant administrator for Program and Policy.

U.S. assistance should be used to ease the pain of austerity measures designed to stimulate long-term economic growth, not to avoid making those necessary reforms. One way to influence reform is to withhold assistance until changes are made. But Congress had mandated that all appropriated funds for each recipient country must be spent by the end of the fiscal year, apparently out of fear that any disruption in aid dispersals would cause political problems within recipient countries. An analysis by the Office of Management and Budget in 1985 disputes that argument: "The consequences of postponing economic reform can be as politically destabilizing as withholding aid disbursements. Aid without strings may serve only to 'bail out' a country temporarily."

U.S. aid programs on the whole may simply do more harm than good. Assistance usually obstructs development rather than promotes it, contends Professor P. T. Bauer of the London School of Economics, because "aid enables governments to pursue policies which patently retard growth and exacerbate poverty," such as restricting foreign investment, propping up state enterprises, and maintaining price controls and subsidies.

One visible example occurs in AID's Food for Peace program, giving poor but not necessarily starving countries more than $2 billion a year in surplus U.S. agricultural commodities. While food assistance helps deplete embarrassingly large crop surpluses created by federal agricultural subsidies, it often retards agricultural production in recipient countries by undercutting native farmers, and provides a cushion enabling Third World regimes to pursue price controls, forced collectivization, and other policies detrimental to growth. Such food aid for many years disguised, if it did not exacerbate, the eventual disastrous consequences of farm collectivization in Tanzania, where President Nyerere's socialist policies destroyed local agricultural markets and produced massive relocations of subsistence farmers. An AID inspector-general investigation in Egypt concluded that U.S. food aid undermined domestic wheat production in that country and forced farmers out of business. By holding down farm prices in recipient countries and discouraging local farm production, food assistance usually makes the nations that receive it even more dependent on handouts.

A report written by the head of the Swedish Red Cross in 1984 concluded that most drought aid in the less-developed world ends up reinforcing political and social systems responsible for creating the disaster, and in the process blocks changes needed to avert future suffering. Africa's famine, reports Bernard Nossiter, former United Nations bureau chief for *The New York Times,* was "largely man-made, not just a caprice of nature but the predictable result of policies pursued by Africa's new governments and reinforced by Western programs labeled 'development aid.'" Africa now produces less food per person than it did in 1960. A report by the Organization for Economic Cooperation and Development also found the region to have made no progress in per-capita income during the same period, despite tens of billions of dollars in aid from the United States and other donors.

In 1984, The President's Task Force on International Private Enterprise issued a report condemning U.S. aid programs for not sufficiently encouraging private-sector growth in countries receiving foreign assistance. This panel recommended that the United States channel its foreign aid through the private sector rather than through governments, that it coordinate conditions and policies with the IMF and World Bank to bring about economic reform in developing countries, and that AID's policies should reflect greater private-sector emphasis and reward countries adopting strategies for private development, including the use of food assistance as an incentive.

Few of these recommendations have since been considered seriously, much less implemented. For example, support for policies of the IMF and the World Bank, which routinely require reforms to reduce the size of the public sector and deregulate the economies of recipient nations, might help accelerate economic reforms. Closer coordination could also help alleviate the problem of recipient governments being unable to manage multiple donors. But since 1984, Congress has restricted any linkage between U.S. assistance and recipient-country compliance with the economic-reform policies of multilateral-aid instructions. Private-sector projects, even when implemented with funding, have often fallen prey to host-country ambivalence. An AID report in 1984 found that after five years and $33 million, an AID-sponsored "Private Investment Encouragement Fund" in Egypt had not made a single loan to private business, yet maintained a payroll of four employees including a chauffeur.

Without a willingness to impose sanctions on countries refusing to use American tax dollars wisely or effectively, much meaningful reform will remain elusive. "Aid in its present form defeats its intended goals, both strategic and economic," writes Bernard Nossiter, in an essay for The Twentieth Century Fund. "It is unlikely that the promise of aid will convert a socialist third world economy to an open system. . .There is little evidence that aid promotes the 'social health' of recipients; to the contrary, it reinforces the status quo of third world regimes."

Foreign investment, not foreign aid, offers the greatest assurance of success for policies to encourage self-sufficiency, sustained economic growth, and political responsibility. Debt-for-equity swaps in which bank loans are exchanged for ownership in developing countries provides one such vehicle. In 1986 these swaps, where banks sold their foreign loans at a discount to companies wanting to invest in the Third World, reduced the debt of less-developed countries by about $5 billion. This unconventional method of reducing debt was made necessary by the inability of most debtor nations to make payments on interest, let alone the principal. With the decision by Citicorp Bank in 1987 to begin selling its Latin loans, these swaps became institutionalized as a debt-reduction tactic. In Mexico during 1985–86, 23 debt-for-equity swaps reduced that nation's international obligations by $350 million, prompting Mexican officials to propose debt swaps involving partial ownership in the nation's state-owned companies to reduce its World Bank loan obligations.

Creation of free ports and free-trade zones can be facilitated by using debt conversions to attract investment capital, a concept developed and put into practice by The Services Group, an international consultancy based in Washington, D.C., specializing in free zones and privatization reforms in developing countries. Costa Rica became the first to approve a debt conversion for free-zone development by establishing a private zone near San José; other similar initiatives inspired by The Service Group were undertaken in Jamaica and the Dominican Republic. By reducing tax burdens, permitting the duty-free movement of goods, and deregulating foreign-exchange controls, free zones can create islands of prosperity within countries unable to adopt a nationwide policy liberalization because of entrenched institutions that resist any significant dilutions of government economic control. Within these zones privatization of airports, roads, and telecommunications services is commonplace, providing a role model for host countries. In Freeport, Bahamas, private investors financed and built an international airport and harbor, roads, and water and sewer systems. "Combining privatization with debt conversions," writes Mark Frazier, founder of The Services Group, "can help revive capital inflows while alleviating debt burdens and enhancing the value of a country's assets."

To undertake these new strategies for development, governments must first recognize and understand the damage of past mistakes. "Aid policies have seriously impaired the ability of many countries to achieve viable economies," says Paul Craig Roberts, professor of political economy at Georgetown University. "The moral obligation may be not to give more, but to stop giving." At the very least the United States should refrain from subsidizing governments pursuing policies that neutralize the intended benefits of our assistance. What aid we do give, if any at all, should go to encourage and reward market-oriented programs directly helping the people of recipient nations, perhaps by requiring their governments to devote an increasing percentage of U.S. assistance to private-sector and privatization endeavors. AID's motto is that it wants "to work itself out of its job" by enabling poorer nations to become self-reliant. Congress should give the agency enough tools and policy cooperation to do just that, so foreign aid becomes something more than a handout for aid-addicted beggars.

Encouraging Worker Ownership

A town of 28,000 people in the foothills of the Allegheny Mountains almost suffocated and died in 1982. In that year the National Steel Corporation of Pittsburgh initiated closure of the Weirton Steel mill, the principal employer in Weirton, West Virginia, laying off all 12,500 employees. An economic rot quickly took hold of the small community. Banks began foreclosing on mortgages, retail stores faced bankruptcy, parking lots filled with the repossessed cars of unemployed steelworkers, and in the bars around town, divorce, dislocation, and even suicide became the topics of drunken conversation and despair.

Other than massive federal relief, only one option remained to save the community and its way of life. Under an Employee Stock Ownership Plan (ESOP), workers could take pay cuts of 20% and more in return for stock in the company. The wages and benefits from this cut formed a pool of money to guarantee the repayment of bank loans to cover the $66-million sale price. Representatives of the Independent Steel Workers Union, company officials, and community leaders endorsed the idea, and soon signs and bumper stickers saying

WEIRTON WE CAN DO IT! and WEIRTON PRIDE could be seen around town. Weirton's employees voted overwhelmingly for the ESOP plan in 1983, and they became the proprietors of the largest employee-owned company in the United States.

By reducing labor costs significantly, and imbued with a new spirit of cooperation that improved productivity and reduced waste, Weirton Steel returned to profitability. Despite severe depression in the steel industry, Weirton posted profits of $60 million in 1984, $61 million in 1985, and $45 million in 1986, after having invested $136 million in modernization. On 14 March 1986, employees began receiving checks averaging $2,000 each for their share of the profits, injecting new economic vitality into the once-threatened community and insuring that this one-industry town will not die.

Only within the last decade has employee ownership become something more than a curiosity in the world of American business. The U.S. Congress beginning in 1974 enacted a series of laws using tax incentives to encourage the formation of ownership-sharing arrangements within companies. At least 8,000 firms in America, according to the National Center for Employee Ownership, now have ownership plans involving about 10 million employees. In 1,000 or so of these companies the employees are majority stockholders. Only a small percentage of ESOPs, perhaps 2% in all, came about to save bankrupt or financially troubled firms like Weirton Steel. Profitable firms established most of the existing ESOPs for one of three reasons, says Corey Rosen, executive director of the National Center: "as a means for a tax-favored and company-financed transfer of ownership from a departing owner to the firms' employees; a way of borrowing money relatively inexpensively; or to fulfill a philosophical belief in employee ownership and as an additional employee benefit."

Giving workers a financial investment in their jobs results in their reciprocating with a psychological investment. Pride of ownership affords them a stake in the nation's economy no less than in their own destiny, helping to preserve their jobs, their community, their way of life. As a preventive medicine, employee ownership can help keep government out of the subsidy business, by providing welfare and unemployment for employees or by injections of tax support for ailing firms. As a pragmatic matter, ESOPs should be immune to ideological considerations or rivalries. "Political personalities as different as Sen. Russell Long and Ronald Reagan," reports *The Washington Post*, "have praised the worker-ownership concept as an appropriate way to spread the benefits of the nation's economy around within the framework of the free-enterprise system."

To facilitate acceptance of privatization within state-owned firms, defusing opposition from labor, Britain has made frequent use of employee buyouts. The first worker takeover occurred with the privatization of the nation's largest trucking company, the National Freight Consortium. In 1982 its employees purchased 83% of company stock; since the buyout, employee productivity increased by 30%, and within five years company stock was worth *40 times* the price employees paid for it. Next to be sold was British Telecom, the world's fourth-largest telephone company, which needed a large infusion of capital to modernize its technology. Rejecting raises in either telephone rates or taxes, Thatcher's government chose instead to sell a 51% share of its ownership to the public. British Telecom employees were given first preference. When the stock went public in December 1984, nearly $4.6 billion was raised, more than doubling overnight the total number of Britons owning stock from 1 million to about 2.8 million. After privatization, British Telecom posted a profit increase of 25%. When Telecom had gone on sale, union leaders ordered their membership to refuse the offering and fight for continued government ownership, yet 96% of Telecom workers ignored the union and bought stock in the new private company anyway. Privatization of British Gas resulted in each of its 90,000 employees being given free shares based on years of service and two more shares free for every one share they purchased.

These workers' buyouts have become extremely popular with many employees. "I bought British Telecom and made 300 pounds' profit," crows Bill Latham, a 65-year-old socialist and former chairman of the draftsman's union at the Vickers and Cammell Laird shipyards. "I have certainly invested in my own company, and my missus has too." Vickers and Cammell Laird, in the northwest of England, was sold for $150 million to a consortium of its 14,000 employees, to be paid out through 1993. The Thatcher government rejected a higher bid from a private firm to keep the yards in the hands of its employees.

Besides the capital raised, other benefits of state-owned-enterprise sales include the expansion of capital ownership by giving employees stock, and by giving fair treatment to government workers who took those jobs in the expectation of benefits and job security, if not employment for life. To the extent that government jobs can be interpreted to have de facto property rights attached, worker buyouts transfer those rights for a corresponding market price to employee-owners.

Ownership can reshape the work standards and expectations of employees previously inclined to a narrow labor point of view. A subsidiary of the worker-owned National Freight Consortium—Waste Management—obtained a five-year refuse-collection contract from the Somerset local council of Taunton Deane. It replaced the council's 43 government employees with only 22 of its own workers, yet raised productivity while paying wages identical to government. Said Waste Management officials, "We can keep our costs down by making better use of vehicles and changing working practices. We insist, for example, on a full 40-hour working week with no early finishing!" The powerful incentive for productivity its employees have is owning shares in the company that employs them, creating concern for efficiency that motivates everyone.

For nations with a collectivist tradition or outlook, or which lack experience with free enterprise, worker ownership of state industries offers a convenient compromise between ideology and economic circumstance. In Somalia the fishing industry's entire fleet of 700 boats had been owned by the government. A World Bank consultant on Africa, Elliot Berg, found that a "lack of incentives for proper maintenance, low official prices and other unsuitable policies" kept most of the fleet idle. The consultant recommended that the boats be sold to the fishermen, and in 1982 about 110 of the fishing boats were sold to their crews. "Results are remarkable," reported Berg after his return trip. Within two years, 85% of the privatized boats were operating efficiently and with much greater productivity than the boats that remained in government hands.

Since 1981 at least 30 companies in Guatemala have turned ownership over to their employees under ESOPs modeled after a program in Costa Rica, where more than 700 companies and 120,000 employees are ESOP participants. Transforming government workers into owners can, in similar fashion, advance the common good on several levels: economically by divesting the state of resource-draining holdings, giving the working class an opportunity to profit, while relieving the enterprise of many problems of absenteeism, theft, and labor relations that plague other forms of ownership; and politically, even spiritually, by endowing the powerless with incentives to defend and expand the free-enterprise system.

If the British public-sector-ownership experience were applied to privatization at the federal level in America, using our own Weirton Steel as a model, worker takeovers would be feasible across a broad spectrum of government activities. Candidates for ESOPs include Amtrak, the Postal Service, military commissaries, the U.S. Government Printing Office, air-traffic control operations, the Power Marketing Administrations, General Services Administration functions like vehicle-fleet management and maintenance. The considerable assets of each could be sold or given away to the work force, breaking up the services under separate companies based on function or geography. At the state and local levels, worker takeovers could help resuscitate our municipal transit systems and revitalize an entire range of public-service roles from garbage collection to hospital care. In some areas worker ownership is already commonplace. Employees own the Parson Corp., an engineering and construction firm heavily involved in U.S. privatization of wastewater-treatment plants and other public facilities. In the mass-transit field, nearly two-thirds of private bus companies operating under contract with local governments have employee-owned or union work forces. In 1986 the South Lake Tahoe City Council, forced to eliminate subsidies for its bus system, turned over operations to a new firm comprised of bus line employees—the Area Transit Management Corporation. Nine of the original 19 city bus-service employees purchased stock, and the firm quickly became profitable by expanding bus contracts to include a nearby resort and a neighboring city.

Opposition to privatization usually comes from the public-employee labor movement, which often sees it as a threat to jobs in overstaffed state enterprises, from government bureaucrats whose power of control would be diminished, and from ex-politicians and military officers who serve on the boards of many state industries. Constituencies must be created for reform in order for privatization to succeed, which means workers and management must profit from the public-to-private transformation.

If a country lacks sufficient private-capital markets to finance the buyout of state-owned firms, the firms could simply be given away to the management and employees, giving workers a stake in the company's future and eliminating any further subsidy burdens on taxpayers. Providing employees with stock makes them responsible for managing costs and improving service—incentives that ultimately benefit both the company and the public—while allowing them to participate directly, often for the first time, in the dynamism and opportunity of a competitive economy. Declares the Adam Smith Institute, "Although it was Karl Marx who advocated handing over the means of production to the workers, it is free-market privateering governments who are making his dream a reality."

Privatization grants the average citizen more direct control over the services of former state enterprises through the power of consumer choice—whether to buy or not—that forces business to be responsive. Under state ownership, a citizen can rarely, if ever, influence service behavior except through the political process, which all too often is dominated by special interests and bureaucratic inertia.

Privatization can mean the freedom to produce, to choose, to innovate and prosper. It provides an environment for healthy competition that can unleash the creative and productive potential in any society. "What began in Britain as Margaret Thatcher's doctrinaire privatization will come to seem pragmatic and routine throughout Western Europe and many other countries as well," editorialized *The Economist* magazine. 'It will be done not to 'destroy the state' but to give the bulk of it that remains a chance to serve the people."

Accepting Choice and Competition

An Englishwoman living with friends in Washington, D.C., complained that she dislikes shopping in America because the stores "have too many products, too many options to choose among. It makes me dizzy." That peculiar notion often infects immigrants from Eastern Europe and the Soviet Union who, after a lifetime of limited choices and coddling by government, suddenly find themselves in America facing a dizzying array of options and duties affecting the quality of their lives—from specialty stores and specialized services to separate billings for rent, electricity, gas, and telephones. A vast number of human beings would simply be content to invest government with the latitude to make most of the relevant decisions about their everyday lives, and that very passivity may expose one Achilles' heel of privatization.

Expanding the range of our choices in the delivery of those services traditionally provided by government will require a new awareness, if not an exercise, of personal accountability and responsibility. Choosing from among a half-dozen private firms for trash collection, rather than relying on a municipal sanitation department, means investigating prices and comparing services. Privatization can be a whole new layer of decision-making that some people would rather not bother shouldering. The fear of choice and responsibility may produce an even greater clinging to government among that part of the citizenry, especially in the older urban areas, long accustomed to the seemingly secure environment of monopoly providers.

Public-employee unions already routinely exploit public fears and insecurities over the prospect of privatization. To thwart the emergence of private fire services, the International Association of Firefighters sends its members door to door telling rural people that private firms will not find it profitable to service remote locations, or warning nursing-home residents that profit means the elderly become expendable. Other government unions at the federal and state level now commonly resort to court suits, the threat of work stoppages, and bureaucratic subterfuge to delay or undermine government reliance on the private sector. While in the short term, public-employee unions may succeed at stalling some moves to implement contracting-out, other labor unions in the private sector will not prove faithful or valuable allies in helping public employees resist privatization.

Organized labor as a whole harbors few if any incentives, other than the appearance of solidarity, to endorse the continuance of a public-employee monopoly over government functions and services. Too many private-sector firms under contract to government are already unionized. The prevalence of employee stock-ownership and company profit-sharing plans also defuses much of the sentiment for public-employee union membership. Rural-Metro, for instance, the nation's largest private fire company, is owned by its employees under an ESOP and pays the same or higher wages than comparable municipal departments. We may someday see an unusual struggle develop pitting public-employee unions against their private-sector counterparts for control over government-related jobs.

Partial privatization through contracting-out poses certain dangers that could undermine public support. If politicians and bureaucrats resort to the exclusive use of franchising or sole-source contracting, or fail to rebid contracts over a long period of time, private monopolies might evolve replacing the government monopolies, eliminating the benefits to consumers and taxpayers from competition. Political temptations may also prompt officials to rewrite bid specification so that only one favored firm qualifies, or to allow favored firms to buy into contracts and later raise prices. The only sure antidote to these abuses of the contracting process is open, fair competitive bidding.

Critics of privatization, when practical arguments fail, generally elevate their criticisms to a loftier plane. Editors of *The Nation* magazine have described privatization as a social project of the far right that orders private values over communal ones, sanctifies greed, and sacrifices civic virtue in the pursuit of self-interest. In perhaps the strangest and least relevant criticism of all, *The Progressive* magazine in 1986 editorialized that the "cult" of privatization was "a scandal and a disgrace. . .what is happening now reflects a shameful decline in humane values. . .It is in the name of privatization that old people are paying more for medical services, that farmers are losing their land, that children are being shortchanged of education, and that scholars are learning that the world's mightiest nation can no longer afford to keep evening hours at the world's greatest library."

Privatization diminishes neither the concept of community for society nor the sense of public purpose of a program, argues Ted Kolderie of the Hubert Humphrey Institute, because the use of nongovernmental producers in no way lessens the social commitment to a program — only government can reduce that commitment as a matter of policy. Pursuing rational self-interest is not synonymous with greed. It is precisely those most obvious yet subtle forms of self-interest that often advance the greatest civic virtues, as evidenced by the ego rewards most philanthropists receive when their names and dollars promote worthy causes.

Social institutions must be devised to synchronize private incentives and social returns in an efficient, cost-effective manner that simultaneously promotes moral imperatives. But public-spiritedness as a motivation for behavior in the governing process need never be diminished by privatization and that emphasis on self-interest that this term implies; to the extent that policymakers and the public understand that privatization is a tool, no less than a program, public spirit can still be harnessed to make the delivery of services connected to policy goals more effective, and thus increasingly the servant of public virtue. Using private-delivery mechanisms to replace government-delivery bureaucracies may actually reinforce norms of public-spiritedness — the view that discourages selfishness in political behavior — by offering policymakers wider and wiser choices in how to implement decisions designed to advance the common good. Privatization broadens rather than limits the role of government as a forum to actualize our concern for others. A government able to delegate the implementation of its policy goals finds itself with fewer administrative chores, and more time and resources to devote to its primary task—making sound and just laws in response to the popular will.

The global nature of privatization is tacit acknowledgment that statism and socialism have led to stagnation. Privatization offers the promise of raising standards of living by introducing competition that will bring about efficiency, lower costs, and better service. Selling assets affords governments potentially large one-time capital gains, which may be the sole impetus for some debt-ravaged nations to experiment with denationalization. For that reason those who defend government's role as central to human economic existence will portray privatization as nothing more than a fad, a momentary swing of the pendulum until people once again regain their senses and seek salvation in the strong arms of government. If indeed we are in the midst of such a pendulum swing, it may last far longer—perhaps even centuries—than any statist in his worst nightmares could envisage. History records only one other similar wholesale retreat or global retrenchment of state power—during the 9th and 10th centuries, when the Frankish and other kingdoms, finding they had severely overtaxed their resources, began a massive farming-out of responsibilities to the private sector for water and road systems and other infrastructure elements that had been centralized.

Privatization upholds the fundamental economic principles on which America was founded, even as it redefines the nature of political debate in this country and abroad. The quiet revolution going on in the world around us may be evidence of a rebirth of faith in the efficacy of a free market, or it could simply be symptomatic of expediency prompted by disillusionment with the failings, in concept and practice, of all statist ideologies. Whatever the motivation, we are witnessing another swing in the pendulum of history. Necessity may be a mother of the privatization revolution, but its ultimate inspiration will always remain the human pursuit of economic freedom with dignity.

Bibliography

INTRODUCTION

Becker, Gary S. "Why Public Enterprises Belong in Private Hands." *Business Week,* February 24, 1986, p. 20.

Blinder, Alan S. "We Need More Government—in the Right Places." *Washington Post,* August 19, 1986, editorial page.

Broder, David S. "The Great American Garage Sale." *Washington Post,* February 16, 1986, p. C7.

Butler, Stuart M. *Privatizing Federal Spending: A Strategy to Eliminate the Deficit.* New York: Universe Books, 1985.

"Deficit Worries Bolster New Push for Privatization." *Washington Post,* January 13, 1986, p. A11.

Drucker, Peter F. "Can The Businessman Meet Our Social Needs?" *Saturday Review,* March 1973, pp. 41–53.

Drucker, Peter F. *Innovation and Entrepreneurship.* New York: Harper and Row, 1985.

Fixler, Philip E., and Robert W. Poole, Jr. "The Privatization Revolution." *Policy Review,* Summer 1986, pp. 68–72.

"Getting Ready for a Federal Fire Sale." *Newsweek,* February 10, 1986, pp. 44–45.

Goodman, John C. ed. *Privatization.* Proceedings of a conference sponsored by the National Center for Policy Analysis and the Adam Smith Institute, Dallas, Texas, 1985.

Holmes, Peter A. "Taking Public Services Private." *Nation's Business,* August 1985.

Main, Jeremy. "Why Government Works Dumb." *Fortune,* August 10, 1981, pp. 144–68.

"Private Everything." *New York Times,* October 20, 1980, p. A18.

"Privatization in the U.S.: Cities and Counties." Dallas Texas: National Center for Policy Analysis, No. 116, June 1985.

"Privatizing the Public Sector: An Initiative for Service and Savings." *The State Factor.* Washington: American Legislative Exchange Council, January 1986.

"The Rush to Privatize." *New York Times,* January 13, 1986, p. A14.

Savas, E. S. "Tax Plan's Boost to Privatizing Services." *Wall Street Journal,* July 10, 1985.

Tolchin, Martin. "New Momentum in the Selling of Government." *New York Times,* December 18, 1985.

CHAPTER 1

"Associations to Be Reimbursed for Road Services." *CAI News* (Alexandria, Va.: Community Associations Institute), October 1985.

Bjornseth, Dick. "No-Code Comfort." *Reason,* July 1983, pp. 43–47.

"Boston Housing Authority is Placed in Receivership." *New York Times,* July 26, 1979.

Butler, Stuart M. "Public Housing: From Tenants to Homeowners." *Heritage Foundation Backgrounder,* No. 359 (June 12, 1984).

"Cities Turn to Private Groups to Administer Local Services." *New York Times,* May 23, 1983, p. 1.

Conference on Urban Revitalization. Washington: National Center for Neighborhood Enterprise, August 1985.

Coulson, Crocker. "The $37,000 Slum." *New Republic,* January 19, 1987, pp. 15–16.

Durst, Seymour B. "Zoning in New York Has Hurt Manufacturing and Housing." *New York Times,* letter, November 22, 1986; and advertisement, January 9, 1987.

"End Rent Control." *New York Times,* May 12, 1987, p. A30.

Fixler, Philip E., Jr. "Applying Privatization to Public Housing." *Fiscal Watchdog,* No. 115 (May 1986).

"Founders vs. Rent Control." *Wall Street Journal,* March 9, 1987, p. 20.

Gage, Theodore J. "Getting Street-Wise in St. Louis," *Reason,* August 1981, pp. 18–26.

Garreau, Joel. "The Shadow Governments." *Washington Post,* June 14, 1987, p. A1.

Gilliam, Dorothy. "Brooklyn's Housing Miracle Needed Here." *Washington Post,* October 17, 1985, p. C3.

"Homes, Hope Rising from N.Y. Rubble." *Washington Post,* July 12, 1985, p. 1.

International City Management Association. *Neighborhood-Based Service Delivery.* Management Information Services Report, Vol. 15, No. 10 (Washington, October 1983).

Johnson, M. Bruce, ed. *Resolving the Housing Crisis.* San Francisco: Pacific Institute, 1982.

Jordan, Mary. "Help from Closer to Home." *Washington Post,* March 30, 1987, p. A1.

Longman, Phillip. "The Mortgaged Generation: Why the Young Can't Afford a House." *Washington Monthly,* April, 1986, pp. 11–19.

Marshall, Sue A. "Public Housing and Mediating Structures: The Case for Tenant Control." Paper for the Neighborhood Revitalization Project of the American Enterprise Institute, Washington, D.C., May 1984.

Marti, Eric. "Self-Help Housing." *Reason,* December 1982, pp. 23–30.

"Neighborhood Revitalization: Building the Future." *NAN Bulletin* (Washington: National Association of Neighborhoods), Fall 1985.

"New Neighborhood Partnerships Forming as Business Steps In." *Memphis Daily News,* October 29, 1985.

Newman, Oscar. *Community of Interest,* Chapter 6, "The Private Streets of St. Louis." New York: Doubleday, 1980.

"Pennsbury Village 2 Years Later: It's Working." *CAI News,* November 1979.

Phillips, J. Brian. "Houston's Laissez-Faire Housing Policy." *Freeman,* June 1987, pp. 215–17.

Postrel, Virginia I. "Tapping the Shadow Housing Market." *Wall Street Journal,* March 13, 1987, editorial page.

Raspberry, William. "Cargo Cult." *Washington Post,* January 3, 1986, p. A19.

Raspberry, William. "In Topsy-Turvey Land." *Washington Post,* January 29, 1986, editorial page.

"Rebuilding of an Inner-City Neighborhood." *St. Louis Post-Dispatch,* November 15, 1976, p. 8C.

Riggenbach, Jeff. "Berkeley's Radical Slumlords." *Reason,* October 1986, pp. 22–29.

"Salvaging City Streets." *Fiscal Watchdog,* No. 48 (October 1980).

"Stimulating Self-Help." *Fiscal Watchdog,* No. 63 (January 1982).

"12 Apartments for Homeless Cost City $3,078 a Month Each." *Washington Post,* January 25, 1987, p. A1.

U.S. Department of Housing and Urban Development. "Neighborhood Revival." Prepared by Sabre Foundation, Washington, D.C., November 1983.

U.S. Joint Economic Committee of Congress. "Stimulating Community Enterprise: A Response to Fiscal Strains in the Public Sector." Prepared by Sabre Foundation, Washington, D.C., December 31, 1984.

Vigilante, Richard. "A Successful Test of the Agenda in D.C." *Washington Times,* January 1, 1985, Commentary section.

Williams, Walter E. "Paternalism Has Its Price." Heritage Features Syndicate, Heritage Foundation, February 16, 1983.

Woodson, Robert L. "Helping the Poor Help Themselves." *Policy Review,* Summer 1982, ppl. 73–86.

Woodson, Robert L. "Self-Help, Not Big Daddy, Must Rescue the Black Underclass." *Washington Post,* May 12, 1985, Outlook section.

Wooster, Martin, and John Fund. "Up from Public Housing." *Reader's Digest,* July 1987, pp. 139–43.

"Young Professionals Join the Needy as S.R.O. Tenants." *New York Times,* January 22, 1986, p. B1.

CHAPTER 2

"Alternatives to Traditional Public Safety Delivery Systems." Berkeley, Calif.: Institute for Local Self Government, September 1977.

Armington, R. Q., and William D. Ellis, eds. *This Way Up: The Local Officials Handbook for Privatization and Contracting Out.* (American Society of Local Officials.) Chicago: Regnery Gateway, 1984.

Bennett, James T., and Manuel H. Johnson. *Better Government at Half the Price.* Ottawa, Ill.: Caroline House, 1981.

Bennett, James T., and Thomas J. DiLorenzo. "Public Employee Unions and the Privatization of 'Public' Services." *Journal of Labor Research,* Vol. 4, No. 1 (Winter 1983), pp. 33–43.

Benson, Bruce L. *Crime, Police, and the Courts: Privatization and the Failure of Government.* San Francisco: Pacific Research Institute for Public Policy, forthcoming.

Blundell, John. "Privatisation—by Political Process or Consumer Preference?" *Economic Affairs* (London), October–November 1986, pp. 59–62.

Blundell, John. "Privatisation Is Not Enough."*Economic Affairs* (London), April 1983, pp. 184–87.

Breuer, Daniel D., and Daniel W. Fitzpatrick. "An Experience in Contracting Out for Services." *Government Finance,* March 1980, pp. 11–13.

"Cities, Towns Facing Money Crunch." *Washington Post,* June 30, 1987, p. A5.

"City Contract for a Full Range of Sanitation Services." *Privatization,* Vol. 2, No. 11 (June 7, 1986).

"Contracting Out Professional Services." *Fiscal Watchdog,* No. 108 (October 1985).

"Dolphins Reel in Funds on Their Own." *Washington Post,* March 23, 1987, p. A7.

Dorffi, Christine. "San Francisco's Hired Guns." *Reason,* August 1979, pp. 26–29.

"Entrepreneurs Can Do Everything Government Can Do, Only Better. Or Can They?" *Inc,* December 1984, pp. 169–76.

Fitzgerald, Randy. "We Can Lower Taxes." *Reader's Digest,* September 1985, pp. 39–44.

Fixler, Philip E., Jr. "Can Privatization Resuscitate Emergency Medical Service?" *Fiscal Watchdog,* No. 98 (December 1984).

Fixler, Philip E., Jr. "Contracting Out Management/Administration." *Fiscal Watchdog,* No. 89 (March 1984).

Frazier, Mark. "Privatizing the City." *Policy Review,* Spring 1980.

Gage, Theodore. "Cops, Inc." *Reason,* November 1982, pp. 23–28.

"Georgia Officials Face Possible Ouster for Job Cuts." *New York Times,* February 9, 1979, p. A18.

Hanrahan, John. *Passing the Bucks: The Contracting Out of Public Services.* Washington: American Federation of State, County, and Municipal Employees, 1983.

Hatry, Harry P. *A Review of Private Approaches for Delivery of Public Services.* Washington: Urban Institute, 1983.

Heins, John. "Government Is on the Defensive." *Forbes,* December 15, 1986, p. 128.

"La Mirada: A City with a Different View." *Government Executive,* May 1981, pp. 47–48.

Marlin, John Tepper. *Contracting Municipal Services: A Guide for Purchase from the Private Sector.* New York: Wiley, 1984.

Marlin, John Tepper, and Karyn Feiden. "To Avoid Private Firms' Public Scandals." *New York Times,* February 15, 1986, Op-Ed page.

Mercer, James L. "Growing Opportunities in Public Service Contracting." *Harvard Business Review,* March/April 1983, pp. 173–87.

"More Cities Playing Industry to Provide Public Services." *New York Times,* May 28, 1985, p. 1.

Morgan, Tracy A. "Toward a State Policy on Privatization," *Privatization Review,* Summer 1986, pp. 38–45.

"The Newark Experience: Public Work Service Contracting." Newark, N.J.: Newark Department of Engineering, 1986.

Peron, Jim. "Blazing Battles." *Reason,* November, 1983, pp. 39–43.

Poole, Robert W., Jr. *Cutting Back City Hall.* New York: Universe Books, 1980.

Poole, Robert W., Jr. "Helping Neighborhoods Help Themselves." *Fiscal Watchdog,* No. 85 (November 1983).

Poole, Robert W., Jr. "Private Fire Service Heats Up." *Fiscal Watchdog,* No. 86 (December 1983).

Privatization Council. *Privatization Review* (New York), Fall 1985.

"Privatization Links Municipal Golf Courses to Savings." *Privatization,* Vol. 2, No. 6 (March 21, 1986).

Public Services Redesign Project of Hubert H. Humphrey Institute of Public Affairs. "An Equitable and Competitive Public Sector." Proceedings of a Conference, St. Paul, Minnesota, November 25–27, 1984.

Public Services Redesign Project. "The Declining Need for the Fire Department." Humphrey Institute, University of Minnesota, Minneapolis (undated).

Rethinking Local Services: Examining Alternative Delivery Approaches. Washington: International City Management Association, March 1984.

Savas, E. S. *Privatizing the Public Sector: How to Shrink the Government.* Chatham, N.J.: Chatham House, 1982.

Savas, E. S. "Municipal Monopoly." *Harper's,* December 1971, pp. 55–60.

Savas, E. S. "Private Firms Can Do Public Work Honestly." *Newsday,* June 25, 1986, editorial page.

Smith, R. Gaines. "Feet to the Fire." *Reason,* March 1983, pp. 23–29.

Spann, Robert M. "Public versus Private Provision of Governmental Services." *Budgets and Bureaucrats: The Sources of Government Growth.* Durham, N.C.: Duke University Press, 1977.

Starr, Paul. "The Limits of Privatization." *Prospects for Privatization,* edited by Steve H. Hanke. New York: Academy of Political Science, 1987.

Stewart, Jon A. "The Falck Organization: A New Model for Delivering Social Services?" *Transatlantic Perspectives,* February 1982, pp. 10–13.

Sundquist, James L. "Privatization: No Panacea for What Ails Government." *Public-Private Partnership: New Opportunities for Meeting Social Needs.* New York: American Academy of Arts and Sciences, 1984.

"Trump Reports Large Profit from Wollman Rink." *New York Times,* April 1, 1987, p. B3.

Tullock, Gordon. "The National Domain and the National Debt." Fairfax, Va.: Center for the Study of Public Choice, George Mason University. (Unpublished.)

"Unique S.F. Private Corps and How They Operate." *San Francisco Chronicle,* July 30, 1984.

U.S. Department of Housing and Urban Development. "Comparative Study of Municipal Service Delivery," by Ecodata Inc., New York City, February 1984.

"Which Police Services Can Be Privatized?" *Fiscal Watchdog,* No. 111 (January 1986).

"Why Not Contract Policing?" *Fiscal Watchdog,* No. 72 (October 1982).
Will, George F. "As Government, Naturally, Gets Bigger." *Washington Post,* November 20, 1986, p. A27.

CHAPTER 3

"The Age of Privatization." *World* (Peat-Marwick), May-June 1986, pp. 24-37.
"California's Swift, Costly Private Judicial System." *New York Times,* February 24, 1986.
"Corporate-Run Jail Locking Out Doubts." *Tampa Tribune,* March 12, 1987.
"Corporate-Run Prisons a Growth Industry." *Los Angeles Times,* March 29, 1985, p. 27.
"D.C. Jail Crisis Heightens Debate over Role of Private Prisons." *Washington Post,* March 18, 1986, p. A1.
"D.C. Legal Disputes Become a Mediator Event." *Washington Post,* May 7, 1987, p. D1.
"Financing Alternatives for Prison and Jail Construction." *Government Finance Review,* August 1985, pp. 7-13.
Fitzgerald, Randy. "Free-Enterprise Jails: Key to Our Prison Dilemma?" *Reader's Digest,* March 1986, pp. 85-88.
Fixler, Philip E., Jr. "Can Privatization Solve the Prison Crisis?" *Fiscal Watchdog,* No. 90 (April 1984).
Fixler, Philip E., Jr. "The Appeal of Private Courts." *Fiscal Watchdog,* No. 99 (January 1985).
"Free Enterprise: Private Concerns Begin Delivering Public Services." *Philadelphia Inquirer,* August 12, 1984, p. 10C.
Gordon, Paul. "Justice Goes Private." *Reason,* September 1985, pp. 22-30.
"Justice Without Law." Current Affairs Department, KQED, Channel 9, San Francisco, December 19, 1984.
Krajick, Kevin. "Prisons for Profit: The Private Alternative." *State Legislatures,* April 1984, pp. 9-14.
Kravitz, Lee. "Tough Times for Private Prisons," *Venture,* May 1986, pp. 56-60.
"More Firms Turn to Private Courts to Avoid Long, Costly Legal Fights." *Wall Street Journal,* January 4, 1984, Section 2.
"New Alternatives to Litigation." *New York Times,* November 1, 1982.
"New Private Court Gets Justice Done Quickly." *Phoenix Business Journal,* April 8, 1985, p. 3.
Perin, Monica Wilch. "Prisons Might Prove Worth of Privatization." *Houston Post,* April 5, 1987.
Poole, Robert W., Jr. "Can Justice Be Privatized." *Fiscal Watchdog,* No. 49 (November 1980).
"Prisons for Profit." *TWA Ambassador,* November 1985, pp. 26-30.
"Prisons for Profit: A Growing Business." *U.S. News and World Report,* July 2, 1984, pp. 45-46.
"Prisons for Profit—Public Boon or 'Burglar King?'" *Fort Worth Star-Telegram,* June 12, 1987.
"Private Business Goes to Jail." *Dun's Business Month,* June 1984, pp. 64-67.

"Private Company Asks for Control of Tennessee Prisons." *Washington Post,* September 22, 1985, p. F1.

"Private Courts with Binding Rulings Draw Interest and Some Challenges." *New York Times,* May 12, 1985, p. 38.

"The Privatization of Corrections." Washington: U.S. Department of Justice, National Institute of Justice, February 1985.

"The Profit in Providing Public Services." *Money,* May 1986, pp. 27–38.

Pruitt, Gary. "California's Rent-a-Judge Justice." *Journal of Contemporary Studies,* Spring 1982, pp. 49–57.

"Public Services in Private Hands." *Venture,* July 1984, pp. 34–44.

Raspberry, William. "How Lawyers Can Help the Poor." *Washington Post,* December 16, 1985, p. A15.

"Rehabilitating the Correctional System." *Fiscal Watchdog,* No. 81 (July 1983).

Ring, Charles R. "Private Prisons Need a Fair Trial. *Wall Street Journal,* May 8, 1987.

"Should Prisons Be Privately Run?" *ABA Journal,* April 1, 1987.

"Should Private Firms Build, Run Prisons?" *Washington Post,* May 7, 1985, p. A15.

"Silverdale: A Prison Run Like a Business." *Winston-Salem Journal,* August 11, 1985, p. A1.

Smith, George H. "Justice Entrepreneurship in a Free Market." *Journal of Libertarian Studies,* Winter 1979, pp. 405–26.

Tolchin, Martin. "When the Justice System is Put Under Contract." *New York Times,* August 4, 1985.

"Tough Times for Private Prisons." *Venture,* May 1986, pp. 56–60.

"250 Million Offered by CCA for Prisons." *Nashville Banner,* September 12, 1985, p. 1.

"With New Private Court System, You Can Shop Around for a Judge." *Philadelphia Inquirer,* November 11, 1983, p. C1.

CHAPTER 4

"As Companies Buy Hospitals, Treatment of Poor is Debated." *New York Times,* January 25, 1985, p. 1.

Berger, Peter L., and Richard Neuhaus. *To Empower People: The Role of Mediating Structures in Public Policy.* Washington: American Enterprise Institute, 1977.

Biderman, Daniel A., and Richard I. Morris. "How to Give Away Money Intelligently." *Harvard Business Review,* November-December 1985, pp. 151–59.

Boschee, J. Arthur. "The Privatization of Human Services." Remarks at the Public/Private Sector Networking Conference, Lake Buena Vista, Florida, January 31, 1986.

Butler, Stuart M. "Power to the People." *Policy Review,* Spring 1987, pp. 3–8.

"Can Your Employees Read This?" *Nation's Business,* June 1984.

Coleman, James, and Thomas Hoffer. *Public and Private High Schools.* New York: Basic Books, 1987.

Cowden, Dick. "States Are Taking the Initiative on Enterprise Zones."

Barron's, September 23, 1985, pp. 24–26.

"Developing Public/Private Approaches to Community Problem Solving." International City Management Association *Management Information Services Review,* Vol. 14, No. 7 (July 1982).

Drucker, Peter F. "Doing Good Makes Cents." *Reason,* November 1985, pp. 39–43.

Everhart, Robert B., ed. *The Public School Monopoly.* (Pacific Institute, San Francisco.) Philadelphia: Ballinger, 1985.

"Everything's Up-to-Date in Minnesota." *Nation,* May 25,1985, pp. 645–51.

"Ex-Nun Helps 3,000 Single Mothers out of Welfare Habit." *Washington Times,* September 25, 1985, p. A4.

"Faring Well Without Welfare." *Washington Post,* June 5, 1983, p. B1.

Fixler, Philip E., Jr. "Contracting Out Social Services." *Fiscal Watchdog,* No. 96 (October 1984).

Frazier, Mark, and Dick Cowden. "Strong Medicine for Sick Cities." *Reader's Digest,* June 1983, pp. 158–60.

Goodman, John C. "Privatizing the Welfare State." *Prospects for Privatization,* edited by Steve H. Hanke. New York: Academy of Political Science, 1987.

Goodman, John C. *The Regulation of Medical Care: Is the Price Too High?* Washington: Cato Institute, 1980.

"Governors Opt for Choice of Schools." *Wall Street Journal,* August 28, 1986.

"Growth of Franchised Education Outlets Reflects Concerns About Public Schools." *Wall Street Journal,* October 15, 1985.

Hamill, Pete. "Doing Good." *New York,* October 13, 1986, pp. 35–79.

"Hospitals for Profit: What Price Care?" *Los Angeles Times,* March 31, 1985, p. 1.

"Investor-Owned Hospitals: Rx for Success." *Reader's Digest,* April 1983, pp. 82–85.

Kelman, Steven. "Public Choice and Public Spirit." *Public Interest,* Spring 1987, pp. 80–94.

Kolderie, Ted. "Business Opportunities in the Changing Conceptions of the Public Sector Role." *Public-Private Partnership: New Opportunities for Meeting Social Needs.* New York: American Academy of Arts and Sciences, 1984.

Lieberman, Myron. "Privatization and Public Education." *Phi Delta Kappa,* June 1986, pp. 731–34.

"Louisville Leads Way in Health Care for Indigent." *Orlando Sun-Sentinel,* November 14, 1985.

McClaughry, John. "Who Says Vouchers Wouldn't Work." *Reason,* January 1984, pp. 24–32.

"Merging Profit Motives with Moral Imperatives." *Human Service Entrepreneur* (Alpha Center for Public/Private Initiatives, Minneapolis), Summer 1987.

Norris, William C. "A New Role for Corporations." *Public-Private Partnership: New Opportunities for Meeting Social Needs.* New York: American Academy of Arts and Sciences, 1984.

Peirce, Neal R. "Denver's Charitable Happening." *Los Angeles Times,*

April 6, 1987.

"Privatization: Rx for Sick Hospitals." *Fiscal Watchdog,* No. 77 (March 1983).

Ratteray, Joan Davis. "Alternative Educational Options for Minorities and the Poor." Washington: National Center for Neighborhood Enterprise, September 1983.

"Seeking to Aid Society, Control Data Takes on Many Novel Ventures." *Wall Street Journal,* December 22, 1982, p. 1.

"A Sharp Debate on Hospitals." *New York Times,* April 2, 1987, p. D1.

Sloan, Frank A. "Property Rights in the Hospital Industry." *Health Care Policy,* edited by H. E. Frech. San Francisco: Pacific Institute, 1986.

Staaf, Robert J. "The Public School System in Transition: Consolidation and Parental Choice." *Budgets and Bureaucrats: The Sources of Government Growth.* Durham, N.C.: Duke University Press, 1977.

Thomas, Cal. "A New 'Trickle Up' Welfare Theory." *Washington Times,* December 18, 1986, p. 3D

U.S. Department of Housing and Urban Development. *Enterprise Zone Notes,* January 1986.

"A University Hospital in Louisville Thrives in Its For-Profit Status." *Wall Street Journal,* January 21, 1986, p. 1.

West, Edwin G. "Are American Schools Working? Disturbing Cost and Quality Trends." *Cato Institute Policy Analysis,* August 9, 1983.

"When Public Services Go Private." *Fortune,* May 27, 1985, pp. 92–102.

Whitehead, John C. Remarks at the Graduation Ceremonies of the Graduate School of Business of New York University, June 1, 1983.

Wineman, Steven. *The Politics of Human Services: A Radical Alternative to the Welfare State.* Boston: Southend Press, 1984.

CHAPTER 5

"BART Directors to Consider Private Financing for System." *San Francisco Business Journal,* September 29, 1986, p. 3.

Chapman, Stephen. "Clean Water Act's Failures." *Washington Times,* November 18, 1986, p. 2D

Clean Water Finance. Washington: American Clean Water Association, 1984.

"Contracting Shelters Westchester's Riders." *Privatization,* April 21, 1987.

Conway, Douglas E., and Jim Peron. "The Road Not Taken: Resolving Connecticut's Highway Crisis." Hartford: Connecticut Institute, 1984.

"Dallas Negotiates Its Way out of the Commuter Business." *New York Times,* February 2, 1985.

"Developers Want to Build, Run Loudoun Toll Road." *Washington Post,* November 4, 1986, p. B1.

Dorschner, John. "Metrofail?" *Miami Herald Tropic Magazine,* September 15, 1985.

Fitzgerald, Randy. "Mass Transit vs. the Taxpayer." *Reader's Digest,* June 1986, pp. 121–24.

Fixler, Philip E., Jr. "Wastewater Crisis—The Privatization Treatment." *Fiscal Watchdog,* No. 92 (June 1984).

Giantris, Philip D. "The Marketing Strategy for Profitable Privatization."

Privatization Review, Summer 1986, pp. 29–36.

Gunderson, Gerald. "The Private Road to Improvement." *Wall Street Journal,* June 5, 1987.

Hanke, Steve H. "A Case for Privatization." *Baltimore Sun,* May 10, 1983, editorial page.

Hanke, Steve H. "The Private Provision of Public Services and Infrastructure." Report submitted to the Agency for International Development, Washington, D.C., May 31, 1984.

Hazlett, Thomas. "They Built Their Own Highway." *Reason,* November 1983, pp. 22–30.

"How a Subway Project in New York Has Led to Doubt and Dismay." *Wall Street Journal,* October 25, 1985, p. 1.

"The Infrastructure Crisis." Touche-Ross, MIT, Prudential-Bache Securities Roundtable, 1983.

"Infrastructure Privatization After Tax Reform." *Fiscal Watchdog,* No. 120 (October 1986).

Joint Center Exchange. Houston: Rice University, Joint Center for Urban Mobility Research, July 1985.

Kristof, Dawn C. "Privatization and the Environment: Taxing the Future." *Privatization Review,* Summer 1986, pp. 24–28.

Lave, Charles A., ed. *Urban Transit: A Private Challenge to Public Transportation.* San Francisco: Pacific Institute, 1985.

Leonard, Herman B. *Checks Unbalanced: The Quiet Side of Public Spending.* New York: Basic Books, 1986.

"Making Bridges Self-Supporting." *Fiscal Watchdog,* No. 65 (March 1982).

Marshall, Jonathon. "How To Break Up Traffic Jams." *Wall Street Journal,* September 15, 1986.

Poole, Robert W., Jr. "Privatizing Transportation Infrastructure." *The State Factor* (American Legislative Exchange Council), Vol. 10, No. 6, pp. 1–10.

"Private Cash in Public Pipes." *Engineering News Record,* January 19, 1984.

"Privatization of Wastewater Treatment: Auburn, Alabama." *Privatization Review,* Fall 1985, pp. 38–47.

"Privatized Treatment Plants Are Built Faster." *Privatization,* June 21, 1987.

Rainie, Harrison. "Tunnels to Nowhere." *Washington Monthly,* March 1986, pp. 43–48.

Rottenberg, Simon. "Job Protection in Urban Mass Transit." *Cato Journal,* Spring/Summer 1985, pp. 239–58.

"San Antonio Partnership Paves New Highway." *Privatization Report* (New York: Council on Municipal Performance), April 1986.

Semmens, John, and Gabriel Roth. "The Privatization of Highway Facilities." Paper for Transportation Research Forum, Washington, D.C., November 1983.

Silverman, Larry. "Buckling Pipes." *New York Times,* November 14, 1983, editorial page.

Teal, Roger F. "Transit Service Contracting: Experience and Issues." Institute of Transportation Studies, University of California at Irvine, January 1985.

"$30,000 for Stock Clerks Stirs Call for 2-Tier Metro Salaries." *Washington*

Times, February 24, 1986, p. B1.

Tolchin, Martin. "Transit Aid Called No Help for Poor." *New York Times,* March 9, 1987, p. A1.

"Towns Near Boston See Incinerator As Solution." *New York Times,* June 29, 1987, p. B8.

Transportation Research Board Conference on Roles of Private Enterprise and Market Processes in the Financing and Provision of Roads, Baltimore, Maryland, July 7-10, 1986. Papers.

> Barker, William G., and Larry C. Cooper. "Private Sector Roadway Funding in Texas."
>
> Catling, Ian, and Gabriel Roth. "Electronic Road Pricing in Hong Kong: An Opportunity for Road Privatization."
>
> Doland, Joseph F. "Public/Private Involvement in the Development of Roadways and Interchanges in Colorado."
>
> Geltner, David, and Fred Moavenzadeh. "The Economic Argument for Highway Ownership Privatization."
>
> Klein, Daniel. "Private Turnpike Companies of Early America."
>
> Larsen, Odd I. "The Toll Ring in Bergen, Norway." Norway Institute of Transport Economics.
>
> Transportation Infrastructure Advisory Group. "Toll Road Financing in the Past and the Prospects for the Future."

"Two Successful Texas Water Projects." *Privatization,* February 7, 1987.

U.S. Department of Transportation. "New Directions in Urban Transportation: Private/Public Partnerships." Prepared by Joint Center for Urban Mobility Research, June 1984.

U.S. Urban Mass Transportation Administration. "Private Sector Involvement in Urban Transportation." Prepared by Joint Center for Urban Mobility, December 1985.

CHAPTER 6

Agnello, R. J., and L. P. Donnelley. "Property Rights and Efficiency in the Oyster Industry." *Journal of Law and Economics,* October 1975.

Anderson, Terry L. "Camped Out in Another Era." *Wall Street Journal,* January 14, 1987.

Baden, John. "Oil and Ecology Do Mix." *Wall Street Journal,* February 24, 1987.

Beach, Bennett H. "Time to Ax This Timber Boondoggle." *Reader's Digest,* October 1986, pp. 103-5.

Chase, Alston. "How to Save Our National Parks." *Atlantic Monthly,* July 1987, pp. 33-44.

Deacon, Robert T., and M. Bruce Johnson, eds. *Forest Lands Public and Private.* San Francisco: Pacific Institute, 1985.

Dennis, William C. "Wilderness Cathedrals and the Public Good." *Freeman,* May 1987, pp. 168-74.

Emerson, Peter. "All of Our Timberland Is Not Created Equal." *Washington Times,* October 15, 1985.

Fineman, Mark, and Jane P. Shoemaker. "Wasted Acres: U.S. Government

A Lessor at a Loss." *Philadelphia Inquirer,* May 9–14, 1982.

Fitzgerald, Randy. "Holding Pentagon Savings Hostage." *Wall Street Journal,* April 4, 1985, p. 30.

Fitzgerald, Randy. "Military Base Boondoggle." *Reader's Digest,* April 1985, pp. 11–16.

Fitzgerald, Randy. "Uncle Sam's Surplus Land Scandal." *Reader's Digest,* January 1986, pp. 33–36.

"A Florida Utility Wins Naturalists' Praise for Guarding Wildlife." *Wall Street Journal,* May 7, 1987, p. A1.

"Forest Service's Sales of Timber Below Cost Stir Increasing Debate." *Wall Street Journal,* April 18, 1986, p. 1.

Hanke, Steve H. "The Privatization Debate: An Insider's View." *Cato Journal,* Winter 1982.

Libecap, Gary D. *Locking up the Range: Federal Land Controls and Grazing.* San Francisco: Pacific Institute, 1981.

"Libertarian Group's Fervent Approach to Selling Off U.S. Land Gets Notice." *Wall Street Journal,* October 16, 1985, p. 64.

Nelson, Gaylord. "Timber Folly in Alaska." *Washington Times.* May 28, 1986, p. 3D.

Popovich, Luke. "Free Enterprise Zones in the Sticks?" *Journal of Forestry,* February 1984, pp. 92–96.

"Privatizing Public Lands: The Ecological and Economic Case for Private Ownership of Federal Lands." *Manhattan Report* (Manhattan Institute for Policy Research, New York City), Vol. 2, No. 3 (May 1982).

"A Push to Privatize Parkland." *San Francisco Chronicle,* December 15, 1986, p. A1.

Ramsey, Bruce. "Forest Socialism." *Reason,* December 1983, pp. 33–37.

Smith, Vernon L. "On Divestiture and the Creation of Property Rights in Public Lands." *Cato Journal,* Winter 1982.

Stroup, Richard L., and John A. Baden. *Natural Resources: Bureaucratic Myths and Environmental Management.* San Francisco: Pacific Institute, 1983.

Truluck, Phillip N., ed. *Private Rights and Public Lands.* Washington: Heritage Foundation, 1983.

Tucker, William. "Conservation in Deed." *Reason,* May 1983, pp. 34–39.

U.S. Department of Defense. "Summary of Completed Military Base Economic Adjustment Projects." May 1986.

U.S. Department of Defense, Office of Economic Adjustment. "Summary of Completed Military Base Economic Adjustment Projects, 1961–1986." President's Economic Adjustment Committee, April 1986.

CHAPTER 7

"Another Failure to Fix the Pentagon." *New York Times,* September 21, 1987, p. A16.

Baber, Walter F. "Privatizing Public Management." *Prospects for Privatization,* edited by Steve H. Hanke. New York: Academy of Political Science, 1987.

Becker, Michael. "Health Care Savings Accounts: A Cure for Medicare's Ills." Washington: Citizens for a Sound Economy, July 25, 1986.

Bennett, James, and Philip Salin. "Privatizing Space Transportation." Santa Monica, Calif.: Federal Privatization Project, Reason Foundation, March 6, 1987.

Bolton, Craig J., and Roger E. Meiners. "The Politicization of the Electric Utility Industry." *Electric Power: Deregulation and the Public Interest.* San Francisco: Pacific Institute, 1986.

Bovard, James. "The Last Dinosaur: The U.S. Postal Service." *Cato Institute Policy Analysis,* No. 47 (February 12, 1985).

Butler, Stuart M. "Privatizing Federal Services: A Primer." *Heritage Foundation Backgrounder,* No. 488 (February 20, 1986).

Cooper, Peter D. "Bonneville Power Administration: The Worst Mess by a Dam Site." *Cato Institute Policy Analysis,* No. 86 (February 6, 1986).

Copulos, Milton R. "Cutting the Deficit by Selling Federal Power Marketing Administrations." *Heritage Foundation Backgrounder,* No. 485 (February 13, 1986).

Copulos, Milton R. "The Perils of a NASA Space Monopoly." *Heritage Foundation Issue Bulletin,* No. 109 (June 20, 1984).

Cox, Patrick. "Fair Weather." *Reason,* June 1983, pp. 23–30.

Crutcher, John. "The Privatization of the Postal Service." *Washington Times,* June 2, 1983.

Davidson, James Dale. "Social Security Rip-Off." *New Republic,* November 22, 1985, pp. 12–14.

Doherty, John. "Towering Entrepreneurs." *Reason,* May 1983, pp. 21–39.

Easterbrook, Gregg. "Sack Weinberger, Bankrupt General Dynamics, and Other Procurement Reforms." *Washington Monthly,* January 1987, pp. 33–52.

Ferrara, Peter J. "A Winning Way to Trim Social Security." *Fortune,* January 6, 1986.

Ferrara, Peter J. *Social Security: The Inherent Contradiction.* Washington: Cato Institute, 1984.

Fink, Lawrence H. "Military Medicine Is a Terminal Case: It's Time to Pull the Plug." *Washington Post,* November 24, 1985, p. C1.

Fitzgerald, Randy. "A Painless Way to Slash the Deficit." *Reader's Digest,* March 1987, pp. 79–81.

Fitzgerald, Randy. "Feeding off the Taxpayers, Literally." *Wall Street Journal,* May 13, 1985, p. 22.

Fixler, Philip E., and Robert W. Poole, Jr. "The Privatization Revolution." *Policy Review,* Summer 1986, pp. 68–72.

Fossedal, Gregory A. " The Military-Congressional Complex." *Wall Street Journal,* August 8, 1985, p. 22.

Gump, David. "Space-Shuttle Subsidies Keep Private Launch Firms Grounded." *Wall Street Journal,* August 5, 1986, p. 30.

Hoffer, William. "Taking Social Security Private." *Nation's Business,* July 1986, pp. 30–34.

Lomasky, Loren E. "Buying Out of Social Security." *Reason,* January 1984, pp. 33–36.

Melloan, George. "Even Generals Get the Arms-Procurement Blues." *Wall Street Journal,* June 23, 1987, p. 31.

Methvin, Eugene H. "Our New Defense Weapon: Competition." *Reader's Digest,* September 1986, pp. 99–103.

Miller, James C. III. "End the Postal Monopoly." *Cato Journal,* Vol. 5, No. 1 (Spring/Summer 1985).

Moynihan, Daniel Patrick. "How to Defer the Day of Reckoning." *Wall Street Journal,* July 22, 1985.

Moore, Stephen. "Contracting Out: A Painless Alternative to the Budget Cutter's Knife." *Prospects for Privatization,* edited by Steve H. Hanke. New York: Academy of Political Science, 1987.

Pejovich, Steve. "The Grace Commission Report and the Military Commissary System." *Issue Analysis* (Citizens for a Sound Economy, Washington, D.C.), July 8, 1985.

Phillips, Larry. "Time to Change Our Stalling Air Traffic Control System." *Wall Street Journal,* July 5, 1984.

Poole, Robert W., Jr. "Air Traffic Control: The Private Sector Option." *Heritage Foundation Backgrounder,* No. 216 (October 5, 1982).

Poole, Robert W., Jr. "Privatizing the Air Traffic Control System." Santa Monica, Calif.: Federal Privatization Project, Reason Foundation, November 14, 1986.

Poole, Robert W., Jr. "User-Friendly Air Traffic Control, Now." *Wall Street Journal,* July 1, 1987, editorial page.

Proxmire, William. "Why Military Contracting Is Corrupt." *New York Times,* December 15, 1985.

"Public vs. Private Weathermen." *New York Times,* February 15, 1978.

Rasor, Dina. "If We're Serious About Weapons Waste." *Reason,* January 1986, p. 58.

"Reagan's Themes, Deficits Alter Course of Democratic Mainstream." *Washington Post,* March 9, 1987, p. A3.

Roper, William L. "Medicare's Private Option." *Wall Street Journal,* April 3, 1987.

Selden, Andrew C. "Sidetracked in the Northeast Corridor," *Wall Street Journal,* October 24, 1986.

Semmens, John. "Don't Let Amtrak Con You." *Reason,* May 1985, pp. 36–38.

Stubbing, Richard. "Uncompetitive Bidders." *Washington Post,* August 31, 1986, p. D5.

"Taking Social Security Private." *Nation's Business,* July 1986, pp. 30–34.

Taylor, Paul. "The Coming Conflict As We Soak the Young to Enrich the Old." *Washington Post,* January 5, 1986, p. D1.

"Teapot Dome for Sale." *Washington Post,* February 27, 1986, editorial page.

U.S. General Accounting Office. "Military Commissaries: Justification as Fringe Benefit Needed." Comptroller General of the U.S., January 9, 1980.

U.S. Joint Economic Committee of Congress. "Privatization of the Federal Government." Hearings, May 1, 2, 30, 1984.

"U.S. Postal Service: The Last Monopoly." *Christian Science Monitor,* July 31, August 1–2, 1985.

U.S. Senate Committee on Small Business. "The Impact of Government Competition on Small Business." Hearings, June 6, 1984.

"War on Military Waste May Turn on Battles of Small vs. Big Firms." *Wall Street Journal,* March 6, 1986, p. 1.

"When Social Security's Anti-Social." *New York Times,* February 9, 1987, p. E22.

"Why the Federal Power Marketing Administrations Should Be Sold." *Issue Alert* (Citizens for a Sound Economy, Washington, D.C.), No. 6 (April 9, 1986).

Wilson, James Q. "The Rise of the Bureaucratic State." *Public Interest,* Fall 1975, pp. 77–103.

Young, Peter. "Follow Britain's Lead on Social Security." *New York Times,* January 26, 1986.

Young, Peter. "A Wrong-Way Transportation Department." *Wall Street Journal,* October 15, 1986, editorial page.

CHAPTER 8

"Amid Pacific Coral Reefs, Assassination Mystery." *New York Times,* November 11, 1985, p. A2.

Ayittey, George B. N. "Africa's Agricultural Disaster: Govermnments and Elites Are to Blame." *Journal of Economic Growth,* Vol. 1, No. 3 (Third Quarter 1986), pp. 3–15.

Bauer, P. D. *Reality and Rhetoric: Studies in the Economics of Development.* Cambridge, Mass.: Harvard University Press, 1984.

Bendick, Marc. "Privatizing the Delivery of Social Welfare Service." National Conference on Special Welfare, Project on the Federal Social Role. *Working Paper* 6 (Washington, 1985).

Berg, Elliot. "Private Sector Potential in Africa." *Journal of Economic Growth,* Vol. 1, No. 3 (Third Quarter, 1986), pp. 17–23.

"The Big Sellout." *Nation,* January 4, 1986, pp. 3–4.

Blundell, John. "Privatisation Is Not Enough." *Journal of Economic Affairs,* Vol. 3, No. 3 (April 1983), pp. 184–87.

Blundell, John. "Ciskei's Independent Way." *Reason,* April 1985, pp. 22–33.

Bovard, James. "The Continuing Failure of Foreign Aid." *Cato Institute Policy Analysis,* January 31, 1986.

Bridges, Tyler. "Down the Toilet: Where Did Venezuela's Loan Money Go?" *Washington Monthly,* December 1986, pp. 21–27.

Butler, Stuart M. "Privatization: A Strategy to Cut the Budget." *Cato Journal,* Spring–Summer 1985.

Cowan, L. Gray. "Divestment and Privatization of the Public Sector—Case Studies of Five Countries." U.S. Agency for International Development, Economic Development Division, December 1983.

Dudek, Donna. "Priatization Is Samoa's Answer to U.S. Budget Constraints." *Wall Street Journal,* July 7, 1986, p. 13.

"Environmental Impact Statement." Washington: Office for Micronesian Status Negotiations, March 1984.

Fitzgerald, Randy. "Micronesia's Macro Welfarism." *Wall Street Journal,*

July 12, 1985, editorial page.

Frazier, Mark. "Zones Vie to Offer Freest Markets." *Competition,* Vol. 6, No. 1 (Fall 1985), pp. 6–7.

Frazier, Mark, and Govindan Nair. "Stimulating Growth in Developing Countries." *Cato Policy Report,* May–June 1987.

"Free-Market Policies Gain Across Europe, Even in Socialist Lands." *Wall Street Journal,* June 11, 1986, p. 1.

"Ghana to Reform State Enterprises." *AfricAsia,* May 1987, p. 22.

Glade, William P., ed. *State Shrinking: A Comparative Inquiry into Privatization.* Austin: University of Texas, Institute of Latin American Studies, 1987.

Greenhouse, Steven. "The Global March to Free Markets." *New York Times,* July 19, 1987, Business section, p. 1.

Hanke, Steven H. "The User Fee Illusion." *Reason,* August 1983, pp. 33–34.

"The Improbable Welfare State." *New York Times,* November 27, 1977.

"In Micronesia, A Gnawing Doubt amid the Palms." *New York Times,* November 4, 1985, p. A2.

"Liberalization of Agricultural Marketing." A study by The Services Group, Inc., for the World Bank. October 10, 1986.

"Looking Out for Number One." *Progressive,* May 1986, p. 10.

Marlin, John Tepper. "Privatization of Local Government Activities—Lessons from Japan." New York: Council for Municipal Performance, 1982.

Meltzer, Allan H., and Scott F. Richard. "Why Government Grows in a Democracy." *Public Interest,* Summer 1978, pp. 111–16.

Micronesian Reporter. (Trust Territory of the Pacific, Public Information Office, Saipan, Northern Marianas), Fourth Quarter 1969 through Second Quarter 1979.

"Modern Ailments Beset Pacific Island Paradise." *Washington Post,* September 1, 1985, p. A29.

Moore, John. "Privatisation in the United Kingdom." *Aims of Industry* (London), 1986.

"A New Age of Capitalism." *Time,* July 28, 1986, pp. 28–39.

Nossiter, Bernard D. *The Global Struggle for More.* New York: Harper and Row, 1987.

Pirie, Madsen. *Dismantling the State: The Theory and Practice of Privatization.* Dallas: National Center for Policy Analysis, 1985.

"Privatisation—Everybody's Doing It, Differently." *Economist* (London), December 21, 1985, pp. 69–84.

"Privatisation in Britain—Making the Modern Dinosaur Extinct." *Economist* (London), February 23, 1985, pp. 72–77.

"Privatisation in Britain: The Threat Turns into a Promise of Higher Efficiency." *Urban Innovation Abroad* (Council for International Urban Liaison), May 1984.

Rauth, Robert K., Jr. "An ESOP Fable." *Reason,* August–September 1986, pp. 26–27.

Roberts, Paul Craig. "Does Third World Aid Do More Harm Than Good?" *Business Week,* April 8, 1985, p. 22.

Rosen, Corey, Katherine J. Klein, and Karen M. Young. "When Employees

Share the Profits." *Psychology Today,* January 1986, pp. 30–36.

Roth, Gabriel. 'Free-Lance Transit." *Reason,* October 1982, pp. 35–39.

Roth, Gabriel. "Private Provision of Public Services in LDCs." Paper for the Conference of the Association of Priate Enterprise Education. Lincolnshire, Ill., April 21–23, 1985.

Starr, Paul. "The Meaning of Privatization." National Conference on Social Welfare, Project on the Federal Social Role. Washington, D.C. Working Paper 6, 1985.

Subasinghe, Devinda R. "Sri Lanka: A Success in Democratic Capitalism." *Journal of Economic Growth,* Vol. 1, No. 3 (Third Quarter 1986), pp. 31–36.

"Too Much U.S. Welfare Overwhelms Micronesia." *Washington Post,* July 24, 1978.

United Nations Development Programme. *Five Year Development Plan.* Saipan, Northern Marianas: Congress of Micronesia, July 1976.

U.S. Agency for International Development. "Privatization Gaining Global Momentum." *Front Lines,* February 1986.

U.S. State Department. *Report on Trust Territory of the Pacific.* Washington: Government Printing Office, 1963.

U.S. State Department. *Report to the United Nations on Trust Territory.* Washington: Government Printing Office, 1983.

Young, Peter. "Privatization Around the Globe: Lessons for the Reagan Administration." Dallas: National Center for Policy Analysis, Working Report #120, January 1986.

Young, Peter. "Privatization in LDCs: A Solution That Works." *Journal of Economic Growth,* Vol. 1, No. 3 (Third Quarter 1986), pp. 24–30.

Young, Peter, and John C. Goodman. "U.S. Lags Behind in Going Private." *Wall Street Journal,* February 20, 1986, editorial page.

Index

Pgs 151; 157 — Cntraro it?!.

Pg 163

Pg 80 * —